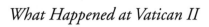

What Happened at Vatican II

What Happened at
VATICAN II

John W. O'Malley

THE BELKNAP PRESS OF
HARVARD UNIVERSITY PRESS

Cambridge, Massachusetts
London, England

First Harvard University Press paperback edition, 2010

A Caravan book. For more information, visit www.caravanbooks.org.

Library of Congress Cataloging-in-Publication Data
O'Malley, John W.
    What happened at Vatican II / John W. O'Malley
        p.   cm.
    Includes bibliographical references (p.   ) and index.
    ISBN: 978-0-674-03169-2 (cloth : alk. paper)
    ISBN: 978-0-674-04749-5 (pbk.)
    1. Vatican Council (2nd : 1962–1965)   I. Title.
    II. Title: What happened at Vatican 2.

    BX8301962. 046   2008
    262'.52—dc22   2008016924

For two friends, who are themselves friends, with gratitude,
Jill Ker Conway and John J. DeGioia

Contents

Preface

Wحile working on my dissertation in history at Harvard University, I was awarded a fellowship to the American Academy in Rome to complete my research on the sixteenth-century religious reformer Giles of Viterbo (Egidio da Viterbo). During my years at the Academy, 1963–1965, the Second Vatican Council was in session not more than a mile away. Through the Academy I obtained tickets to two of the great Public Sessions of the council, and through clerical contacts I managed to slip into a number of the press briefings that took place every afternoon. I was keenly interested in the council because I was a priest and knew that the decisions of Vatican II would certainly influence that side of my life.

But I also had a more specific, professional interest in the council. My work on Giles focused on his writings and activities as a reformer of the Augustinian order when he was prior general, 1506–1518. The council had taken *aggiornamento,* updating, as one of its themes, and I understood the term as a euphemism for reform. The council provided me with a good foil for understanding aspects of the sixteenth century, and the sixteenth century provided me with a foil for interpreting some things happening in Vatican II.

This experience was exciting and helped me formulate the arguments of my dissertation, but I did not dream at the time that within a few years I would begin writing about the council on a professional basis. In 1971, however, I published my first article on Vatican II, and I have continued to publish on it in academic and more popular journals ever since. During my many years at the Weston Jesuit School of Theology in Cambridge, Massachusetts, I taught a standard course, "Two Great Councils: Trent and Vatican II," which was symptomatic of how my academic interests oscillated back and forth between the sixteenth and the twentieth centuries. Meanwhile, my interest in styles of discourse helped me understand the two councils in a new way, to the point that my book *Four Cultures of the West* was for me a vestibule leading into *What Happened at Vatican II*.

This book has thus had a long gestation period and is indebted to the insights that conversations with colleagues and students have sparked over the course of many decades. It is more immediately indebted to the generosity of colleagues who have read parts of it as I produced them and offered me their criticism: John Baldovin, John Borelli, Heidi Byrnes, Mark Henninger, Richard McBrien, and Robert Taft. I am especially grateful to those intrepid and generous persons who read the entire manuscript: Paul Bradford, David Collins, Howard Gray, Otto Hentz, Ladislas Orsy, Francis A. Sullivan, and James Walsh. Their comments have much improved the text and saved me from many errors, some of which were elementary and embarrassing in the extreme. I want to thank Aaron Johnson for producing the chart found on page 168 and Doris Donnelly and Khaled Anatolios for supplying several photographs. To no one am I more indebted than to Jared Wicks, former dean of the theological faculty of the Gregorian University in Rome and friend for more than fifty years. He read the text with meticulous care, offered me detailed comments, and shared with me the fruits of his own research on the council. For the errors that remain in the text I alone am responsible.

This book would have been utterly impossible without the splendid edition of the official *acta* of the council published by the Vatican Press. Not counting indexes and similar instruments, the edition consists of fifty-one volumes, many of which run to more than eight hundred pages. The series was completed only in 1999. To the editors of those volumes over the past forty years I am deeply grateful. I am of course much indebted to the five-volume history of Vatican II edited by Giuseppe Alberigo and Joseph A. Komonchak. As with my three other books with Harvard University Press, I owe much to Lindsay Waters, Executive Editor for the Humanities, who has never lost faith in the viability of this project. I am delighted that for this fourth book of mine with Harvard, Christine Thorsteinsson was for the fourth time my congenial and sharp-eyed copyeditor. My debt is great to J. Leon Hooper, director of the Woodstock

Theological Library at Georgetown University, and to his able and generous staff.

For the sixteen final documents of the council, I have used, with some slight adjustments, the translations in Austin Flannery, ed., *Vatican Council II: Constitutions, Decrees, Declarations,* rev. ed. (Northport, NY: Costello Publishing Company, 1996); for papal encyclicals the translations in Claudia Carlen, ed., *The Papal Encyclicals,* 5 vols. (Wilmington, NC: McGrath Publishing Company, 1981); and for the documents of councils other than Vatican II, the translations in Norman P. Tanner, ed., *Decrees of the Ecumenical Councils,* 2 vols. (Washington: Georgetown University Press, 1990). All other translations are mine unless I specify otherwise.

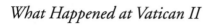

What Happened at Vatican II

It was only a little later on that it began to dawn on me . . . that I did not say quite the same things and was not the same person in Italian as in English.

—Iris Origo, *Images and Shadows: Part of a Life*

Introduction

Library shelves are filled to overflowing with books about Vatican Council II. The outpouring began almost as soon as the council was announced and has continued up to the present in a variety of genres—personal memoirs, theological analyses and polemics, popular accounts, two multivolume commentaries, and a five-volume, multiauthored history of the council.[1] The reason is obvious. Before the council opened it sparked hopes and fears, curiosity and speculation. During the four years it was in session, it held television audiences rapt with its elegant, elaborate, colorful, and magnificently choreographed public ceremonies, while the unexpected drama of its debates generated front-page news on an almost weekly basis. Although commentators assess the council's ultimate importance differently, many would agree that it was the most important religious event of the twentieth century.

Yet missing from the crowd of volumes on the library shelves is a basic book about the council. By basic I mean a brief, readable account that does three things: first, provide the essential story line from the moment Pope John XXIII announced the council on January 25, 1959, until it concluded on December 8, 1965; second, set the issues that emerge in that narrative into their contexts, large and small, historical and theological; third, thereby provide some keys for grasping what the council hoped to accomplish. That is the space on the shelves that I hope to fill with this book.

As my title indicates, I am trying to answer the simple question, "What happened at the council?" To that simple question there is no simple answer. I think, nonetheless, that by pursuing my three aims I provide the basics for addressing it. I am certainly not alone in believing, moreover, that the best—indeed, the indispensable—approach to understanding Roman Catholicism today is through Vatican II. Study of the council is at the same time study of the much larger phenomenon.

The council met in four distinct periods in the fall of every year from 1962 through 1965. Each of these periods, which lasted roughly ten weeks, had its own character. The first met under the pontificate of Pope John XXIII and the last three under his successor, Paul VI. Almost as important as the actual meetings of some 2,200 bishops in the basilica of St. Peter in Rome during these periods was the work done both before the council, 1959–1962, and during the so-called intersessions, that is, the nine or so months that intervened between each period. That work by bishops and the theological *periti* (Latin for experts) determined the course of the council almost as much as did the actual debate on the floor of St. Peter's.

By the time the council concluded, Pope Paul VI had promulgated sixteen documents in his name and in the name of the council.[2] They cover an extraordinarily wide range of subjects and do so at considerable length. They are the council's most authoritative and accessible legacy, and it is around them that study of Vatican II must turn. The air of serenity these documents breathe obscures the fact that some of them were hotly, often bitterly, contested in the council and survived only by the skin of their teeth. Moreover, although these documents are often lumped together without distinction of rank, theoretically they were not equal in dignity or in the authority to be attributed to them.

The highest in rank were the "constitutions," of which there were only four: On the Sacred Liturgy *(Sacrosanctum Concilium)*; On the Church *(Lumen Gentium)*; On Divine Revelation *(Dei Verbum)*; and On the Church in the Modern World *(Gaudium et Spes)*. Twenty years after the council, in 1985, the Synod of Bishops meeting in the Vatican to assess the council singled out these four as providing the orientations according to which the remaining documents were to be interpreted.[3] The special character of a constitution was clearly recognized during the council itself and hence generated discussion as to which of the documents deserved that designation.

Next in rank came nine "decrees": On the Mass Media *(Inter Mirifica);* On the Catholic Eastern Churches *(Orientalium Ecclesiarum);* On Ecumenism *(Unitatis Redintegratio);* On Bishops *(Christus Dominus);* On the Renewal of Religious Life *(Perfectae Caritatis);* On the Training of Priests *(Optatum Totius);* On the Apostolate of the Laity *(Apostolicam Actuositatem);* On Missionary Activity *(Ad Gentes Divinitus);* and On the Ministry and Life of Priests *(Presbyterorum Ordinis).* Finally, there were three "declarations": On Christian Education *(Gravissimum Educationis);* On Non-Christian Religions *(Nostra Aetate);* and On Religious Liberty *(Dignitatis Humanae).*

These sixteen documents differ not only in rank but also, more palpably, in impact and importance. The constitutions have managed to consolidate their theoretical importance by the attention, scrutiny, and, for the most part, positive appreciation they have consistently received from scholars. But the distinction between decrees and declarations, no matter what it originally meant, has become meaningless, with the decrees On the Mass Media, for instance, and On the Catholic Eastern Churches virtually forgotten, whereas the declarations On Religious Liberty and On Non-Christian Religions are just as important as they were during the council. Even granted this difference in authority and impact, all sixteen documents are interconnected in many ways. They form a coherent corpus, and they must be interpreted accordingly.

In this book I will analyze these documents, but I will not provide a detailed theological commentary on them. That has been done many times and by scholars more competent for the task than I.[4] What I will do, rather, is put the documents into their contexts to provide a sense of before and after. Unless such a task is undertaken and accomplished, the points the documents make run the danger of seeming like platitudes, a danger their literary style might seem to encourage. My approach, I hope, allows the high drama of the council and the profound, almost intractable, problems implicit in it to surface. Only by tracing the documents' genesis and, even more important, locating them in their contexts can their deeper significance be made clear.

Their contexts? We need a grasp of at least three, which in the limited space of this book I can only sketch. The first context pays homage to *la longue durée,* to the ongoing impact of events that happened centuries ago. It here consists in a few themes in the long and broad history of the Western church, such as the deep roots of the church-state issue. In that regard, for instance, scholars after the council described it as "the end of the Constantinian era," an allusion to the official recognition and privileged status granted to the church by the Roman emperor Constantine in the early fourth century. The decree On Ecumenism and the constitution On Divine Revelation make sense only against the backdrop of the Protestant Reformation and the Catholic reaction to it in the sixteenth century. Thus scholars sometimes described Vatican II as "the end of the Counter Reformation." This means that at Vatican II the Council of Trent (1545–1563) made more than cameo appearances.[5] More generally, Vatican II, recognized by the Catholic Church as the twenty-first ecumenical (church-wide, not local) council in its history, needs to be compared with all those that preceded it, beginning with the first ecumenical council, Nicaea, in 325, if we are to understand what, if anything, is special about Vatican II.

The more immediate context is "modernity" or, more concretely, "the long nineteenth century," which for the Catholic Church stretches from the French Revolution until the end of the pontificate of Pius XII in 1958. The French Revolution and the philosophy that undergirded it traumatized Catholic officialdom through much of that long century. The council was an attempt at healing certain aspects of the church's history in that period and at slipping out from under its vestigial weight. Vatican II was heir, however, to other aspects of the long nineteenth century, such as the developments in biblical, liturgical, patristic, and philosophical scholarship, the competition with Protestants in foreign missions, and the rise of Socialism and Communism. For the inner workings of the church no aspect of the nineteenth century was more important than the new prominence of the papacy in every area of Catholic life. Of all the previous councils, therefore, perhaps none entered more directly into the debates at Vatican II than Vatican I (1869–1870) because of its definitions of papal primacy and infallibility.

The third and most specific context is the period beginning with World War II and continuing up to the opening of the council.[6] Although this context overlaps with the long nineteenth century when viewed with an ecclesiastical lens, when viewed through a political and cultural lens it marks such significant changes worldwide that it needs to be considered a distinctive period. This was the era of the Cold War, which reached a perilous intensity in the Cuban Missile Crisis just a few days after the council opened. For almost two weeks the world held its breath as the threat of nuclear annihilation seemed about to be realized.

This period saw the end of colonialism, which had a great impact on the missionary enterprises of all the churches. It was the time when Christian Democracy emerged in countries recently under Fascist dictatorships, and it was the time when the Western world finally had to face the horror and the implications of the Holocaust. These and other factors led politicians and churchmen to believe that a new age was dawning that needed new solutions and approaches.

If these are the contexts, what are the issues the council dealt with? Distinctive of Vatican II was the broad scope of the issues it addressed. It dealt with the use of the organ in church services; the place of Thomas Aquinas in the curriculum of seminaries; the legitimacy of stocking nuclear weapons; the blessing of water used for baptisms; the role of the laity in the church's ministries; the relationship of bishops to the pope; the purposes of marriage; priests' salaries; the role of conscience in moral decision-making; the proper clothing (or habit) for nuns; the church's relationship to the arts; marriage among deacons; translations of the Bible; the boundaries of dioceses; the legitimacy (or illegitimacy) of worshiping with non-Catholics; and so on, almost, it might seem, into infinity.

All the issues the council addressed must of course be taken seriously. Nonetheless, some are of more general significance than others. The best place to begin is with the topics dealt with in the sixteen final documents of the council. They indicate sixteen areas of special concern—liturgy, education, ecumenism, and the rest. That is obvious but nonetheless important to keep in mind. As I suggested, however, during and after the council nobody thought that what Vatican II said about the media compared in importance with what it said about church-state relations or about the church's relationship to Muslims and Jews.

What, then, were the most important issues at the council? The desire to recognize the dignity of lay men and women and to empower them to fulfill their vocation in the church was certainly among them. Although disagreements arose as to particulars, the decree dealing with the apostolate of the laity sailed through the council with relatively little difficulty because of an across-the-board agreement on the fundamental direction it took. But in that regard the decree was an exception.

Generally speaking, the most important issues were the most hotly contested. This almost invariably meant that some bishops rightly or wrongly perceived them as deviating from previous practice or teaching to such an extent as to be dangerous, or illegitimate, or heretical. The amount of time the council spent dealing with an issue, whether on the floor of the council or in meetings in other venues, signaled the importance attached to it. The time spent was often in direct proportion to the degree to which the issue seemed to violate received teaching or practice.

Three issues were in this regard so sensitive or potentially explosive that Pope Paul withheld them from the council's agenda—clerical celibacy, birth control, and the reform of the Roman Curia (the central offices of the Vatican). To these three must be added the Synod of Bishops, which Pope Paul created during Vatican II without having made any provision for the council to act on the measure or participate in its formulation. These four issues, supposedly not issues *of* the council, were nonetheless issues *at* the council, and thus are important for understanding what happened.

The first issue protractedly debated, however, was the place of Latin in the liturgy, which intermittently occupied the council for several weeks. This issue, important in its own right, also had deeper ramifications. It was a first, awkward wrestling with the question of the larger direction the council should take—confirm the status quo or move notably beyond it. The council resolved the question of Latin by taking a moderate, somewhat ambiguous, position. After the council that position got trumped by the most basic principle Vatican II adopted on the liturgy—encouragement of the full participation of the whole assembly in the liturgical action. This is a good illustration of a wider phenomenon of the council. Sometimes the inner logic or dynamism of a document carried it beyond its original delimitations.

The relationship of Tradition to Scripture also emerged early on as a hot issue, and it continued to be such all through the council. Underneath the contention on this seemingly technical theological question lurked questions of wider significance—first, the prescriptive value of earlier doctrinal statements (in this instance, the decree of the Council of Trent on the subject), and second, the way the teaching authority of the church relates to Scripture. Closely associated with the Scripture-Tradition question, moreover, was the question of how far modern methods of literary and historical interpretation were legitimate as applied to the Bible.

Few issues ignited such bitter controversy both inside and outside the council as the relationship of the church to the Jews, and then to other non-Christian religions. Few of the documents, that is to say, bumped along on such a rough road as *Nostra Aetate*. The relationship of the Catholic Church to other Christian churches and communions also had a rough ride, but not nearly so rough as the relationship to the Jews. The latter was peculiarly difficult partly because of its potentially political implications in the Arab world, and partly because of negative statements about "the Jews" in the New Testament. John's gospel, for instance, consistently describes "the Jews" as Jesus' enemies.

The declaration On Religious Liberty traveled a similarly difficult path. Its advocacy of forms of separation of church and state, as well as the kind of primacy it gave to conscience over obedience to ecclesiastical authority, aroused fierce opposition, which threatened the document's viability. The constitution On the Church in the Modern World, *Gaudium et Spes,* sparked controversy of a different kind, not only because of some of the particular issues it addressed, such as the stockpiling of nuclear weapons and the aims of marriage (with its implications for birth control), but also because of its seemingly sprawling scope, its lack of precedent in any previous council, a tone some judged too optimistic, and the sociological or empirical approach it sometimes seemed to be basing itself upon.

The document on the church prepared before the council convened was in effect rejected at the end of the first period. It was sent into the repair shop for what amounted to such a thorough revision that it emerged essentially a new document, *Lumen Gentium.* Although the new document met criticism on many points and was revised accordingly, none of its provisions turned out to be more contentious and more central to the council's agenda than the relationship of the bishops, or episcopal hierarchy, to the papacy. The technical expression for the relationship the council advocated was "collegiality." What kind of authority did the bishops have over the church at large when they acted collectively, that is, collegially; how was that authority exercised in relationship to the pope; and how was collegiality different from "Conciliarism" (supremacy of council over pope), a position condemned in the fifteenth century and repeatedly condemned thereafter? Closely connected with this issue was the more technical question of how bishops related to the sacrament of orders. Also implied was the question of what voice others in the church, including the laity, rightly have in decision-making.

As the council hammered out the positions that eventually prevailed on these issues, it was carried along by an overwhelmingly large majority of bishops. Nonetheless, a small minority—10 to 15 percent—adamantly opposed the trends and made their influence felt in various ways. Tempers flared. Harsh words were exchanged, accusations made. The leaders of the minority emerged early and remained constant. Although throughout the council the other bishops who at any given moment made up the body of this minority were not always the same—the bishops were, after all, individuals with individual outlooks and convictions—the percentage remained fairly consistent. This struggle between majority and minority, so easy to oversimplify, constitutes an essential component of the history of Vatican II—and a component not even hinted at in the serene language of the documents.

Those are, in any case, the issues scholars rightly consider hallmarks of the council. As we travel though the council's story and examine the documents Vatican II left as its most palpable legacy, these are the issues that emerge most clearly and characteristically. They are the upfront issues. But can we go deeper? Are there issues under these issues, issues of which these were a surface manifestation? I believe there were at least three: (1) the circumstances under which change in the church is appropriate and the arguments with which it can be justified; (2) the relationship in the church of center to periphery, or, put more concretely, how authority is properly distributed between the papacy, including the Congregations (departments or bureaus) of the Vatican Curia, and the rest of the church; and (3) the style or model according to which that authority should be exercised. These issues are a key to understanding Vatican II. They are, moreover, critically important for anybody who is interested in grasping the tensions and conflicts within the Catholic Church today. In their abstract formulation these topics sound perennial, yet in their concrete manifestations they are current and urgent.[7]

In this book I am concerned with these issues only insofar as they help explain the dynamics of the council and thence Roman Catholicism. In different and more secular forms, however, many other institutions—schools, certain businesses, nations—must face them as well. They are about identity—how to maintain it while dealing with the inevitability of change, and then how to make it effective in new but recognizably authentic ways. In that perspective the council serves as a case study, a paradigm. The issues transcend their religious articulation. But it is with their religious articulation that this book is concerned.

As the council was coming to a close, John Courtney Murray, an American Jesuit and perhaps the single most important *peritus* at the council on the church-state problem, put his finger on the first issue, calling it "*the* issue under the issues."[8] Murray termed it "development of doctrine." By that he meant the problem of elaborations of church teaching that went beyond, or might even seem to contravene, previous teachings: in a word, the problem of change in an institution that draws its lifeblood from a belief in the transcendent validity of the message it received from the past, which it is duty-bound to proclaim unadulterated.

Murray's position on the church-state question illustrated, in his opinion, the problem of "development" because at least on the surface it flew in the face of the repeated condemnations of "separation of church and state" pronounced by popes since the early years of the nineteenth century. It also differed from the official stance on church-state relations supported in Murray's day by the highest of the Vatican's Congregations, the Supreme Congregation of the Holy Office (today known as the Congregation for the Doctrine of the Faith). As it turned out, the general orientation Murray favored prevailed in the council, but only after a bitter struggle.

The majority of the bishops of the council were satisfied with the arguments for the legitimacy of this "development." But the problem recurred again and again throughout the council, to the point of being a pervasive feature of many of its deliberations. When Pope John XXIII spoke about what he had in mind for the council, he sometimes used the term *aggiornamento,* an Italian word meaning bringing up to date. The word caught on and came to be a shorthand expression (certainly an inadequate one) to describe what the council was about. *Aggiornamento* injected the problem of change into the council in an unavoidable way, but even without it, the problem of the relationship of past to present would most surely have arisen and been just as pervasive and troubling. Nonetheless, for reasons that will become clear, the sixteen final documents of the council give no sense of before and after; nor do they indicate, except occasionally in a soft way, that what they are saying changes anything that earlier seemed normative.

As with the church-state issue, the problem of change often arose in connection with the teaching of a papal encyclical or of other documents emanating from the Holy See, the Vatican. In its own way it implicated, therefore, the second issue-under-the-issues, the relationship of center to the rest of the church. The question that underlay this issue was, put bluntly, whether the church had sidelined the authority of bishops and become too centralized for its own good. As indicated, the issue erupted most explicitly in the debates over collegiality. Two venerable traditions in the church could be traced back to the earliest centuries—the special leadership role of the bishop of Rome and the leadership role of other bishops, especially when assembled either in local or provincial synods or in ecumenical councils.

Only when the leadership role of the papacy began to be formulated in an ever more monarchical framework, beginning in the Middle Ages but taking more explicit form in the nineteenth century, did the relationship between these two traditions become particularly problematic. More specifically, how would the church reconcile the definition of papal primacy in Vatican Council I with a sharing of authority with the bishops? This was by no means an abstract problem or one remote from the day-to-day workings of the council. It played itself out in the tensions that emerged between the Curia and the bishops and, more dramatically, between Pope Paul VI and the bishops, who were assembled in a basilica a hundred yards away from his quarters.

What precisely was the role of the pope when a council was in session? Paul VI, as mentioned, removed four problems from the agenda of Vatican II. Was this to avoid unseemly verbal brawls, or was it because the council could not be trusted to arrive at the right conclusion? After a certain point in the council bishops began running to the papal apartments for solutions to problems that one might legitimately have expected them to solve on the floor of St. Peter's. The complicated and murkily delineated procedures of the council almost forced the bishops to run to the pope, but the problem was broader than that.

Indeed, the issue went beyond the relationship of pope to bishops. It entailed the relationship of the Vatican Congregations, especially the Holy Office, to the bishops, who sometimes felt that the Congregations dealt with them in high-handed fashion, to the point of trampling on prerogatives they believed were theirs by virtue of their office. Resentment of the Curia surfaced often during the council and sometimes exploded. In this perspective, the so-called politics of the council were not an interesting sideshow. The drama of the politics was part of the council's substance, intrinsic to its meaning.

But the problem of the distribution of authority in the church extended even further, beyond bishops to priests and lay persons, who were exhorted to exercise initiative and take a role in decision-making. When *Lumen Gentium* described the church as "the people of God," it implicitly touched on this issue by modifying the traditional and exclusive focus on a top-down hierarchical model with a more horizontal one. Once again, however, the sixteen official documents give no hint that center/periphery was a hot point of contention and an almost ubiquitous issue.[9]

In the church the relationship of law to inspiration and initiative is connected to the relationship of center (law) to periphery (inspiration and initiative). In classic religious terms this is the relationship of order to charism, that is, of obedience to gifts of the Spirit. For the life of the church to be healthy, it is generally agreed, these two aspects must balance each other in an equilibrium. Many at the council felt that the enforcement of order by the central administration of the church had been all too predominant up to that point. At Vatican II, therefore, charism for the first time in history enters into the vocabulary of a council.

No matter where authority in the church is located, in what manner is it to be wielded? That is a third issue-under-the-issues, suggested by the word "charism." Here the council becomes more explicit by introducing a new vocabulary and literary form. Words like "charism," "dialogue," "partnership," "cooperation," and "friendship" indicate a new style for the exercise of authority and implicitly advocate a conversion to a new style of thinking, speaking, and behaving, a change from a more authoritarian and unidirectional style to a more reciprocal and responsive model. This change effected a redefinition of what councils are and what they are supposed to accomplish. Vatican II so radically modified the legislative and judicial model that had prevailed since the first council, Nicaea, in 325, that it virtually abandoned it. In its place Vatican II put a model largely based on persuasion and invitation. This was a momentous shift.

If this third issue is so explicit in the special vocabulary of the council, how can it be an issue *under* the issues, which would imply hidden from view? Like Edgar Allen Poe's "Purloined Letter," it is hidden in plain sight. It is so obvious that little attention had been paid to it except by vague references to the council's "pastoral language." I believe, however, that this is the issue captured by the expression "the spirit of the council," that is, an orientation that goes beyond specific enactments.[10]

What is clear, in any case, is that style was a big issue at the council, an issue fought on the seemingly superficial battleground of the vocabulary and literary genre of the documents, with protagonists perhaps not always realizing the profound implications of what was at stake. The literary style, that is to say, was but the surface expression of something meant to sink into the very soul of the church and of every Catholic. It was much more than a tactic or a strategy, much more than simply the adoption of a more "pastoral language." It was a language-event. The language indicated and induced a shift in values or priorities. To that extent it indicated and induced an inner conversion, which is the most profound aspect of this third issue-under-the-issues in Vatican II. This conversion found outward expression in a certain style of behavior especially incumbent upon church leaders. The council's language-choice largely explains why "the call to holiness" emerged as such a strong and pervasive theme at the council and is one of its most distinctive marks.

These three issues-under-the-issues are not perfectly distinct from one another; nor are they distinct, of course, from the more specific issues like religious freedom or the full participation of the community in the liturgical action. On superficial glance, Vatican II might seem like a collection of issues without much relationship with one another. But on closer inspection it manifests a truly remarkable network of connections and a coherence unlike any previous council, due in no small measure to the new literary style the council adopted.

These three issues-under-the-issues, moreover, provide lenses for interpreting the council. They are a first step toward a hermeneutic that transcends an often myopic, sometimes almost proof-texting, approach to the council that focuses on the wording of the documents without regard for contexts, without regard for before and after, and without regard for vocabulary and literary form. The result is often a minimal interpretation of the council, an interpretation that fails to see the council as the new moment it wanted to be in the history of the Catholic Church.[11]

By their very nature these issues do not admit of definitive resolution one way or the other. Their essence is to be in tension. Each of them pulls in opposite directions. Both directions have validity; neither is absolute. The church, like any organization, must deal with the tension, not deny it. If the institution is to be healthy and effective in carrying out its missions, it must maintain and exploit the dialectic between continuity and change, between center and periphery, between firmness and flexibility.

Decades have now passed since the council. Today we are in a more decidedly postmodern, postcolonial, multicultural world than in the 1960s. What perspective does that situation provide on the council and its issues?

In 1979, five years before his death, the German Jesuit theologian Karl Rahner spoke of Vatican II as opening a third epoch in Christian history.[12] The first epoch was the brief period of Jewish Christianity, which began to end as early as Paul's preaching to the Gentiles. The second epoch ran from that time until Vatican II, the period of Hellenism and the European church. The third period, the postcouncil present, is the period of the world church.

Did the council really initiate this new period? At first glance it would seem not. What is striking about Vatican II is not any prominent role played by "the new churches" of former colonies but its dominance by Europeans.[13] The leading figures were almost exclusively from the Continent, and those few who were not, like Murray or Paul-Émile Léger, archbishop of Montreal, were European in the broad sense. The council was even more deeply Eurocentric in that the issues it dealt with originated in the history of Western Europe—the Roman Empire, the Gregorian Reform, the Reformation, the Enlightenment, the French Revolution, the Risorgimento, the loss of the Papal States, the Nazis, the Holocaust, Christian Democracy.

Europe, its concerns and the legacy of its history, provided the framework within which Vatican II operated. The story of the council is almost exclusively the story of Europeans fighting over issues arising out of European history. The history and tradition of Christianity as the council knew it was the history and tradition of Christianity in the West, with an occasional nod to the history and tradition of the Christians of the Middle East when prodded, or shamed, into looking in that direction by the bishops from there. Those bishops, whose traditions had not been shaped by the course of Western history, frequently pointed out to the council fathers how parochial their outlook was.

Yet in revisiting that history and tradition the council was engaged sometimes, maybe not always wittingly, in transcending its European determinations. The debate over Latin was a revisiting of the debates of the sixteenth century, but the outcome had world-church repercussions. The softening of the role of Aquinas in the curriculum of seminaries, and consequently in theological discourse, revisited the nineteenth century and seems to have had principally in view a greater openness to other European philosophies. But it also opened a window to non-European philosophies and approaches.

Of direct import, of course, were the council's specific recommendations for adaptation to local customs and cultures. In the constitution On the Sacred Liturgy, the first document the council approved, occurs the symptomatic line: "The art of our own times from every race and country shall also be given free scope in the church." Such explicit openness and adaptation were not quite leitmotifs in the council, but they occurred just often enough to signal that a wider vista was trying to break through.

I

Big Perspectives on a Big Meeting

Fʀoм the moment Angelo Giuseppe Roncalli was elected pope on October 28, 1958, he surprised people. This began with his first act, taking the name John, a name no pope had borne since the fifteenth century. When immediately after his election he appeared on the balcony of St. Peter's basilica before an immense crowd gathered below in the piazza, he struck in his rotund appearance a great contrast with his predecessor, the slender and dignified Pius XII. A photo of John taken when he was nuncio (papal ambassador) in Paris began to be reprinted—in it, he held a cigarette in his hand. It soon became known, moreover, that unlike Pius, who was circumspect in speech and reserved in manner, John was spontaneous and even liked to tell jokes. Early on he made changes in Vatican protocol that suggested he wanted a somewhat less formal atmosphere to prevail.

Nothing he did in those early days of his pontificate, however, prepared the world for his announcement on January 25, 1959, less than three months after his election, that he intended to convoke a council. Ten days earlier he had tested the idea with his secretary of state, Cardinal Domenico Tardini, who responded with enthusiasm.[1] The announcement took everybody else by surprise, including the other cardinals of the Curia, and it left most people stunned. After the definitions of papal primacy and infallibility at Vatican Council I, some theologians predicted that there would never be another council because it seemed to them that now the

Pope John XXIII. Photograph by Hank Walker / Time & Life Pictures / Getty Images.

pope could solve all problems. We have since learned that in the early 1920s Pius XI and again in the early 1950s Pius XII seriously considered calling a council, which they intended as a resumption and completion of Vatican I, interrupted by the seizure of Rome by Italian troops in 1870 and never officially closed.[2] But in 1959 those initiatives were well-guarded secrets, and it seems that John XXIII did not know of them until after he made his announcement. In any case, he consistently maintained that the idea came to him as a spontaneous inspiration.[3]

But a council to do what? The pope made no mention of Vatican I, and he almost certainly never conceived of his council as a resumption of that earlier convocation. On July 14 he put all doubts to rest when he informed Tardini that the council would be called Vatican II. This meant that it would be a new council and therefore would not have to carry out, even in revised forms, the unfinished agenda of the earlier one. Vatican II could pursue its own path.

But what was that path to be? Of the twenty councils that the Catholic Church at that point recognized as ecumenical, the better known, like the Council of Trent, had been convoked to deal with a crisis. Although serious issues emerged as preparations for Vatican II got under way, in 1959 no obvious crisis troubled the Catholic Church. In fact, except in those parts of the world where Christianity was undergoing overt persecution, mainly in countries under Communist domination, the church in the decade and a half since the end of World War II projected an image of vigor and self-confidence.

Why, then, a council, and what was it supposed to do? In his announcement on January 25 the pope, after speaking of the need to reaffirm doctrine and discipline, mentioned almost in passing two aims that were tantalizingly vague. The first was to promote "the enlightenment, edification, and joy of the entire Christian people," and the second was to extend "a renewed cordial invitation to the faithful of the separated communities to participate with us in this quest for unity and grace, for which so many souls long in all parts of the world."[4] These aims could be dismissed as pious generalities, and they more than suggest that at this point the pope himself was unclear about the specifics with which the council might deal. Nonetheless, in their context they were remarkable for two reasons.

First, they were couched in altogether positive terms. Especially from the beginning of the nineteenth century up until John XXIII's pontificate, the popes and the Holy See usually framed public statements in negative terms of warning or condemnation. Even when proposing a positive solution to some issue, they generally did so to provide antidotes to "the evils of the times." There was no hint of such negativity in John's announcement. The significance of this fact would become clear only later with some of his subsequent statements, and especially in the light of his allocution on October 11, 1962, opening the council. These positive terms were an adumbration of the approach he wanted the council to adopt. In his diary for January 20, he said he intended the council as an invitation to spiritual renewal for the church and for the world.[5]

Second, John's stated aims quite directly extended a hand in friendship to the other Christian churches, and they did so, it seemed, without strings attached. As is clear from John's diary, he chose January 25 to make the announcement because he was at the basilica of St. Paul to close the Church Unity Octave, a week of prayer for Christian unity that originated in the United States in 1908 with an Anglican priest and had become widely popular even in Catholic circles.[6] John's invitation was not "to return" but "to participate." In his heart of hearts, John, like all Catholics of that time, probably harbored the hope that the council would lead to a "return," but for whatever reason he did not thus express himself. From the very beginning, in any case, the council turned its eyes in part to persons outside the parameters of the Roman Catholic Church. The pope's "invitation" was a gentle but significant departure from papal policy of eschewing ecumenical encounters that had been strongly reaffirmed and insisted upon by Pius XI in 1928 in his encyclical *Mortalium Animos* and asserted in less stringent terms by Pius XII as late as 1950 in *Humani Generis.*[7]

The Biggest Meeting

With that brief announcement, Pope John XXIII launched a process that would culminate in what was quite possibly the biggest meeting in the history of the world. Initially the pope and council planners had hoped that Vatican II could complete its business in one or at most two periods lasting several months, but the council actually extended over four years. True, it was formally in session only ten or so weeks a year, but the work of the leading figures at the council was so intense in the months that intervened between the formal periods that that time must also be counted as an integral part of the council.

Four years does not seem long when compared, for instance, with the

Council of Constance, which also lasted four years, or with the Council of Trent, which stretched over seventeen. But for Trent the numbers are deceptive because of the long intervals between the three periods in which the council was actually in session, which again amounted to about four years. Unlike those councils, which met without any preparations, Vatican II was prepared for on such a massive scale that the two and a half years that elapsed between the announcement and the opening of the council must be considered part of it. Unlike Constance, Trent, and a few others, most councils lasted no longer than two or three months. The important Fourth Lateran Council, in 1215, completed its business in three sessions and lasted only three weeks.

The preparations for Vatican II moved in two distinct phases, the first of which opened in May 1959 with the appointment of an Ante-Preparatory Commission whose task was to gather opinions from bishops and others about issues needing action.[8] The results of this consultation provided the materials to be used in the second, "preparatory" phrase, when those materials were sifted, organized, and formulated into texts to be presented to the council when it opened. The Ante-Preparatory Commission originally planned to send a questionnaire to all those who were eligible to participate as voting members—clerics with the rank of bishop or higher and the superiors-general of the religious orders of men. But Cardinal Tardini, whom Pope John had appointed head of the commission, decided instead on a letter, presumably because it would be less prejudicial regarding subjects to be discussed. John approved the change. The letter, dated June 18, 1959, was sent out over Tardini's signature.[9]

In direct language the letter stated simply: "The Venerable Pontiff wants to know the opinions or views and to obtain the suggestions and wishes of their excellencies, the bishops and prelates who are summoned by law (Canon 223) to take part in the ecumenical council. . . . These [suggestions, etc.] will be most useful in preparing the topics to be discussed at the council." The letter exhorted the bishops to offer their ideas "with complete freedom and honesty . . . on anything Your Excellency thinks should be treated in the council."[10]

The letter went to 2,598 ecclesiastics and elicited 1,998 responses (77 percent). The responses varied in length from six lines from the bishop of Wollongong in Australia to twenty-seven pages from the cardinal archbishop of Guadalajara, Mexico. When printed after the council the responses filled eight large-format volumes, totaling well over 5,000 pages.

Meanwhile, Tardini had asked the Congregations of the Curia, such as the Congregation of Rites and the Holy Office, to submit their suggestions, which came to another 400 pages. He asked the same of all institutions of higher learning in Rome and around the world that held papal charters. Among those from North America that responded were The Catholic University of America, the University of Laval, and the Pontifical Institute of Mediaeval Studies, Toronto.[11] All told, the documentation from the ante-preparatory phase filled twelve volumes. Of all the previous councils, none had a consultation in any way comparable in scope. Moreover, no prior council had such a thorough, systematic preparation. Most had none.

By and large the responses called for a tightening of the status quo; for condemnations of modern evils whether inside the church or outside; and for further definitions of doctrines, especially those relating to the Virgin Mary.[12] The bishops registered widespread concern about Communism, with many asking for yet another explicit condemnation of the movement. A few responses were more venturesome, particularly in asking for greater responsibilities for the laity in the church and for an extension of the use of the vernacular in the Mass, despite Pius XII's recent cautions in that regard. A very few bishops from non-Western countries or regions asked for modification or abrogation of celibacy for priests.[13] By late spring 1960, all the responses had arrived that were going to arrive, and on June 5, 1960, Pope John officially closed the ante-preparatory phase and inaugurated the preparations proper.

He then set up ten Preparatory Commissions to compose documents on subjects that had emerged from the consultation. These commissions were headed by cardinals who, with one exception, were prefects of a Congregation of the Curia. (The exception was the Commission on the Apostolate of the Laity, for whose subject there was no corresponding Congregation.)[14] Thus the materials were categorized to correspond to the official remit of the various Vatican bureaus. This decision had the practical merit of making use of organizational machinery already in place, but it also delivered the materials into the hands of "the center." A Central Preparatory Commission oversaw the work of the others. Besides these commissions, John established a Secretariat for Christian Unity, whose task at this stage was restricted to not much more than communication with other Christian bodies.

The commissions were composed of members properly speaking and consultors. The members, who were of at least episcopal rank or its equivalent, had the right to vote and to express their opinions freely, whereas the consultors, the *periti,* did not vote and, at least in theory, could speak only when spoken to. Thus eventually some 850 clerics ranging in rank from simple priests to cardinals worked together for two years. Their task was to produce documents to be submitted to the council for ratification. The commissions worked with varying degrees of intensity, with greater or lesser recourse to the results of the ante-preparatory consultation, and, as it turned out, with little coordination from the commission entrusted with that responsibility. Although the majority of the members and consultors lived outside Rome, the burden of the work fell on the Roman members, many of whom belonged to the Roman Curia or were professors at Roman institutions.

Like the Ante-Preparatory Commission, these Preparatory Commissions generated an immense documentary output: seven volumes in all. This number is almost minuscule, however, when compared with the official documentation generated by the council itself, thirty-two volumes, many of which run to more than 900 pages. In sheer mass its closest competitor is the seventeen volumes for the Council of Trent. Unlike other councils, Vatican II also generated hundreds of unofficial documents of considerable size and importance such as diaries and private correspondence, only a portion of which have been published.[15] To these must be added the reports and commentaries in newspapers and journals of various kinds.

The quantity of that documentation reflects the immensity of almost every other aspect of the council. On July 15, 1962, the Vatican Secretariat of State sent out about 2,850 invitations to persons with a right to participate fully in the deliberations of the council—85 cardinals, 8 patriarchs, 533 archbishops, 2,131 bishops, 26 abbots, and 68 superiors-general of religious orders of men. All but a few hundred, impeded by ill health or their governments' refusal to let them attend, showed up for the opening of the council.

After the opening days, the number of people present in the basilica varied considerably, but generally there were about 2,400 council fathers participating at any given time. Their average age was sixty. Between the opening and closing dates, 253 of the council fathers died and 296 new ones were added. A total of 2,860 attended part or all of the four periods. In contrast, about 750 bishops participated in Vatican I. The Council of

Bishops in St. Peter's, October 11, 1962. Photograph by David Lees / Time & Life Pictures / Getty Images.

Trent, the least well attended of all the councils, opened with just twenty-nine bishops. Even later, at its largest sessions, the number of voting members at Trent barely exceeded 200.

The bishops who attended Vatican II came from 116 different countries, with more or less the following geographic distribution: 36 percent from Europe, 34 percent from the Americas, 20 percent from Asia and Oceania, and 10 percent from Africa.[16] The Communist governments of China, North Korea, and North Vietnam prohibited entire episcopates from attending, and European governments behind the Iron Curtain also made participation difficult or impossible. With about 7 percent of the world's Catholics, North America was somewhat over-represented in that it provided more than 12 percent of the bishops.

Many of the "council fathers," as they came to be known, brought with them a secretary or a theologian or both. Meanwhile, the pope named theological experts to the council to help the bishops. By the time the council was over, 484 such *periti* had been appointed by either John XXIII or Paul VI, with many of them serving for all four periods of the council.[17] Representatives of the media were present in great numbers—by the opening day of the council, the Vatican had distributed about a thousand press cards to journalists. To these numbers must be added some fifty to well over a hundred "observers and guests" from other churches and, beginning in 1963, a relatively small number of lay "auditors." Other individuals or groups having direct, indirect, or intermittent business with the council raised to an estimated 7,500 the number of people present in Rome at any given time because of Vatican II.

The meetings were held in the central nave of St. Peter's basilica. Despite the huge proportions of that space (2,500 square meters), it was barely sufficient to hold all the attendees. The nave was outfitted to provide 2,905 spaces: 102 for cardinals, 7 for patriarchs, 26 for the General Secretariat of the council, 2,440 for the bishops and archbishops, 200 for the *periti,* and 130 for observers and guests from the other churches. The observers and guests sat in a tribune reserved especially for them, right under the statue of St. Longinus, nearer to the presiders' table than even the cardinals—the best seats in the house. Two catering stations or coffee bars (no alcoholic beverages) were set up in the basilica, and lavatories were installed both inside and outside St. Peter's.

The meetings were of two types. During the four periods of the council, there were ten Public Sessions, to which were admitted as many people as were specially invited or managed to obtain tickets. Among these sessions were the opening ceremonies for each of the four periods. Then there were 168 actual working sessions, officially known as General Congregations, in which documents were presented, discussed, emended, and voted on. These working sessions began with a Mass at nine in the morning. Since the Masses were sometimes celebrated in rites other than the so-called Latin or Roman, the only rite familiar to many bishops, they provided attendees with an informal education in liturgy. After Mass the bishops took up the business of the day until the session adjourned at midday. Although the council did not meet in the afternoon, bishops were fully occupied in studying the documents, working on the commissions, and attending other official, semi-official, or unofficial gatherings related to the council, of which there were many. For the bishops and the *periti,* the council was anything but a "Roman holiday."

To ensure that everyone present with a right to speak could do so handily and audibly, thirty-seven microphones were installed in the basilica in such a way that no speaker would have to walk more than twenty yards to find one. Douglas Horton, one of the Protestant observers, noted in his diary for October 23, 1962: "For the council the great pile of St. Peter's is skillfully wired for sound so that with microphones in strategic places even a whispered note can be heard in the remotest part."[18] Every effort was made, therefore, to guarantee full participation.

The council was an extremely expensive enterprise, but just how much it cost is still not clear. The new installations in St. Peter's—the lavatories, coffee bars, furnishings for the seating arrangements, the purchase and installation of the public address system, and so forth—cost close to a million dollars, which in the 1960s was a lot of money. There were, besides, the labor costs for the large staff needed to keep the basilica clean and the meetings orderly. Only slightly more than half the bishops could pay their own way, which meant that the Vatican had to pick up the expenses for the rest. Most bishops brought a secretary and a theologian, so that the Vatican had to pay for transportation and lodging for as many as 3,000 participants over the four years of the council.

At the beginning of Vatican II the German episcopal conference contributed a million marks (about a quarter of a million dollars), and once the council got under way the North Americans were particularly generous in trying to ease the financial burden on the Vatican. During the council the question of cost was never raised as a reason for curtailing the agenda or for speeding up the discussions. Nonetheless, Vatican II was a tremendous strain on the finances of the Holy See, a fact that surely strengthened Paul VI's resolve to close the council after a fourth period.[19]

Except for its opening session in 1962 and its closing session in 1965, Vatican II did not attract the huge crowds drawn to events like the international Olympic Games. It was not the biggest gathering in the sense of number of people assembled at a given moment. But it was the biggest *meeting,* that is, a gathering with an agenda on which the sustained participation of all parties was required and which resulted in actual decisions. It was a gathering the likes of which had never been seen before.

The Council and the Councils

The sixteen final documents of the council run in a standard edition in Latin to slightly over 300 pages.[20] In the same edition the documents of the Council of Trent run to about 130 pages, and the documents of those two councils together almost equal the documents of the other nineteen ecumenical councils put together. These numbers not only point to the sheer size of almost everything connected with Vatican II but also prompt the more general question of how Vatican II compared with previous councils.[21]

The one feature common to all the councils is that they were assemblies, principally of bishops, that made authoritative decisions binding for the whole church. The participants arrived at their decisions, it is traditionally believed, under the special guidance of the Holy Spirit. In all other respects, the councils differ considerably among themselves.[22] They fall, however, into two clearly distinct groups. The first eight were all held in Greek cities in Asia Minor, were conducted in Greek, and were convoked by the emperor or empress. No pope attended any of them; indeed, while papal and Western influence on these councils varied, it was often small and rarely determinative. The emperor Constantine called the first of these Eastern councils, the Council of Nicaea, to bring peace to the church in the face of the Arian heresy. The last of them was Constantinople IV, in 869–870, convened to deal with the aftermath of the so-called Photian schism.

The remaining thirteen councils were all held in the West (in Italy, France, or Switzerland), were conducted in Latin, and were convoked by the pope, with the Council of Constance a special case. Except for the

Council of Ferrara-Florence-Rome, in 1438–1445, and to a much lesser degree Lyons II, in 1274, only Westerners participated in them. At the Fifth Lateran Council, 1512–1517, two of the bishops held sees in present-day Haiti and the Dominican Republic, whereas at the later Council of Trent, 1545–1563, no one attended from outside Europe. In fact, until the late arrival (November 1562) of a small but important delegation of French bishops, Trent was made up almost exclusively of bishops from Italy, Spain, and Portugal. Of the approximately 750 bishops who opened Vatican Council I in 1870, 121 came from the Americas, 41 from Asia, 18 from Oceania, and 9 from Africa. Except for the North and South Americans, none of these attendees were native-born. The overwhelming majority, therefore, were European, with 40 percent of the total assembly from Italy. At Vatican II, 64 percent of the bishops came from outside Europe.

Bishops have always been the determining presence at the councils, but at times others have also played important roles. King Philip IV of France, though he could not fully accomplish his agenda, was the dominant person associated with the Council of Vienne, 1311–1312, and Emperor Charles V was as responsible for the eventual convocation of the Council of Trent as any single individual. Although some 400 bishops attended Lateran Council IV in 1215, the 800 abbots and heads of cathedral chapters who also attended vastly outnumbered them.

In the latter part of the Middle Ages professional theologians were invited to the councils, and in a few instances they even had the right to vote. At the Council of Trent they constituted an official institution called the Congregation of Theologians, whose task was to discuss and formulate the issues for the council and then communicate the resulting documents to the bishops, who made the final determinations. Theologians sometimes addressed the council but did not vote on its formal documents.[23] At Vatican II, theologians accredited to the council had places reserved for them in St. Peter's, but their contribution was strictly confined to helping prepare the documents of the council in the various commissions, where they were outnumbered by the bishops.

During the Middle Ages, kings and major nobles sent their representatives to councils, as sometimes did a few cities. At Lateran IV, for instance, Pope Innocent III insisted that the whole church, ecclesiastical and lay, be represented, and he invited kings, princes, and city magistrates. At Lateran V, 1512–1517, twenty-six secular rulers, nobles, and knights were listed as participants, a number that does not include the representatives sent by the great monarchs. During the Council of Trent the lay members spoke to issues that concerned them, which included a long address by Augustin Baumgartner, the Duke of Bavaria's ambassador to the council, advocating the abolition or at least the attenuation of clerical celibacy. In its last session Trent sternly reminded secular rulers of their duty to enforce the decrees of the council and to punish anybody who resisted them.

Lay people enjoyed their strongest position in the first eight councils, held at the invitation and under the aegis of the emperors, who for all practical purposes sometimes set major items on the agenda.[24] The opening session of the first ecumenical council, Nicaea, was held in the imperial palace, where Constantine delivered the inaugural address. The council lasted about a month. We are told that on at least one occasion Constantine assisted at the debates. He ratified the decisions of the council by making them legally binding throughout his empire, and, except where it would impinge on the rights and duties of the bishops, he took full responsibility for their implementation.[25] At the Council of Chalcedon, in 451, the nineteen envoys of the emperor sat on a raised platform in the center of the assembly. Although they did not vote, they in effect chaired the meeting by setting the order of the day and guiding the discussion. The empress Irene convoked Nicaea II, attended the opening session, and arranged for the final session to be held in her presence in the Magnaura palace.

Until Vatican Council I, therefore, the presence of the laity was taken for granted, and secular leaders were crucially important as enforcers of the councils' decrees. Although in the bull of convocation of Vatican I, Catholic monarchs were urged to promote the success of the council, they were not invited to attend or participate, and no lay person of any status took an active part in the council.[26] This exclusively clerical precedent became prescriptive in 1917 in the Code of Canon Law (Canon 223), and it was therefore operative for Vatican II in Pope John's letter to the bishops and to the others "authorized by law to take part." Nonetheless, the council later admitted a few lay men as "auditors," and by the third period there were twenty-one of them. During that session three lay men addressed the council on the topics of the lay apostolate (in English), world poverty (in Latin), and the mission of the laity in the modern world (in Spanish). Also at this session, women auditors were admitted for the first time, though the seven lay women and eight women from different religious communities did not address the council.[27]

The Popes and the Councils

The long history of the popes' relationship to the councils falls into three fairly distinct periods.[28] The first consists of the initial eight councils. These were, as mentioned, convoked by the emperor or empress. No pope ever attended. While their office and their envoys were always shown special deference, the popes played their varied roles from a distance.[29] Pope Silvester sent two priests to represent him at Nicaea, where it seems they made no significant contribution. A half century later no Western bishops or papal envoys were present at Constantinople I. Pope Celestine had an important though indirect influence on the Council of Ephesus, in 431, by throwing his support to Cyril, patriarch of Alexandria. Cyril turned out to be the most powerful figure at the council but not particularly because of Celestine's support.

Pope Leo the Great played a direct role at the Council of Chalcedon, in 451, which Emperor Marcian convoked only after consultation with Leo. Leo insisted that his legates preside at the council, though the imperial commissars for the most part ran the assembly. Leo's *Tome,* his statement of orthodoxy drawn up before the council, was shown due regard in the creed that the council finally issued. A hundred years later Pope Vigilius boycotted the next council, Constantinople II. Some months after the council, while virtually a prisoner of Emperor Justinian, he accepted its decrees and was then free to return to Rome.

Emperor Constantine IV actively sought the collaboration of Pope Donus and then of his successor, Pope Agatho, in negotiations that culminated in the sixth ecumenical council, Constantinople III, in 681, which condemned Monothelitism. Legates of Agatho carried to the council a profession of faith drawn up by a Roman synod headed by the pope. In its eighth session, held like all the others in the imperial palace, the council adopted Agatho's teaching.

A century later, in 786, the empress Irene, acting as regent for her son, summoned the pope and the three Eastern patriarchs to Nicaea II. Pope Hadrian gave his approval to the convocation and sent two legates, who enjoyed a place of special honor at the council. At the second session Hadrian's letters condemning the Iconoclast heresy were read out, and they formed the basis for the council's decree. At the last council held in the East, Constantinople IV, 869–870, the papal legates played a decisive role in the central issue, viz., the deposition of the bishops and priests ordained by Photius, the former patriarch. This council, poorly attended, is special in that, although held in the East with Greek as the official language, it is recognized as legitimate not by the Greeks but only by the Latins.

The second period begins with Pope Calixtus II's convocation of a council in Rome two and half centuries later, in 1123, to deal "with various important matters." Close to 300 bishops and others gathered at the Lateran basilica, the pope's cathedral. As far as we know, none of them came from the East. The gathering did not differ much from similar synods held earlier in Rome and elsewhere under papal patronage, and its ecumenical status was confirmed only later by the tradition of the Catholic Church. The next three councils were also held at the Lateran, followed by three in France—two in Lyons and the last in Vienne. The councils had by this point become an exclusively Western institution. Moreover, in 1075, Pope Gregory VII had laid down in his famous *Dictatus papae* the principle that no council could be considered ecumenical except by order of the pope, and the principle worked its way ever more deeply into the tradition of canon law.

At these seven councils a general harmony prevailed between the pope and the assembly over which he presided. Even with the increasing importance of the College of Cardinals as an advisory body, popes still felt the need to refer more important matters to the deliberation of councils, which they convoked without misgiving during this period. The average rate of convocation was about once every thirty years. The last council, Vienne, is an exception in that King Philip IV of France put pressure on an unwilling Pope Clement V to convoke it, and the king forced his agenda on the pope.

Vienne was thus a harbinger of the third period, in which popes began to fear councils as instruments that could be used against them. The next council, Constance, saved the papacy by resolving the scandal of the Great Western Schism, in which three men claimed to be the legitimate pope. It was able to accomplish this feat, however, only by the extreme measure of deposing two of the men and forcing the third to resign. The council then proceeded to elect a new pope, Martin V. In its course, moreover, it issued the decree *Haec Sancta;* though scholars still debate its interpretation, its wording made clear that in serious matters, perhaps almost as a last resort, a council can take measures even "against the papal dignity."[30] The council also claimed as part of its mandate reform of the church "in head and members," with "head" meaning papacy. It later issued the decree *Frequens,* which bound the popes to convoke a council at stated intervals.

Pope Martin V obeyed *Frequens* by convoking a council at Pavia and then Siena, which he dissolved because of poor attendance. Shortly before his death he convoked another council, this time at Basel. Under his successor, Eugene IV, Basel got out of hand: it asserted the supremacy of councils over popes as the regular constitution of the church and elected its own pope, Felix V, to displace Eugene. Eugene finally finessed the situation by convoking another council that met first at Ferrara and then at Florence, after which the council at Basel gradually lost support.[31]

The damage, however, had been done. Conciliarism had arrived on the scene.[32] The term has been used in different ways, but when taken in its most radical sense it meant that councils were supreme over popes in the government of the church even outside emergency situations like the Schism. Conciliarism in that sense became a full-fledged theory, and though in that extreme form it never won wide support in the church, in different guises it had a long lifespan. At Vatican II opponents of the doctrine of collegiality saw it as Conciliarism in disguise, a subversive idea that even in its more moderate forms the solemn definitions of papal primacy and infallibility at Vatican I had once and for all laid to rest.

Meanwhile, in 1460, after the papal success with the Council of Florence, Pope Pius II published the bull *Execrabilis* forbidding appeals from a pope to a council. In 1483 Sixtus IV in essence repeated the provisions in *Qui Monitis,* and in 1509 Julius II again repeated them in *Suscepti Regiminis.* For Julius, *Suscepti Regiminis* turned out to be more than an academic exercise. Two years later a council at Pisa threatened to depose him. He salvaged the situation by calling his own council, Fifth Lateran, 1512–1517, thereby defusing the crisis.

The Council of Trent, convoked to address the Reformation, was delayed for a generation in part because Pope Clement VII feared that Emperor Charles V would use the council to depose him.[33] Many bishops at Trent hoped to impose reforms on the papacy, especially concerning the granting of dispensations from the canonical requirement that bishops reside in their dioceses and not hold more than one bishopric at the same time, the keystone of the Tridentine reform. They were consistently frustrated in this regard by the papal legates who presided at the council and who were under strict orders not to let such restrictions of papal authority come to the floor.[34] Aside from that issue, however, the fathers assembled at Trent, though under pressure from different sources, set their own agenda and pursued it.

Three hundred years passed before Pope Pius IX called another council, in 1870. Meanwhile, in 1854 he had solemnly defined on his own authority the dogma of the Immaculate Conception, the first such papal definition in history. At Vatican I the definition of papal infallibility was thus to some extent a ratification of a *fait accompli.* In any case, at Vatican I the pope, though he had to deal with objections from some bishops, was securely in charge of the agenda. Moreover, the definitions of primacy and infallibility persuaded some commentators that Vatican I was the council that ended councils.

Nonetheless, the Code of Canon Law of 1917 made provision for councils. It asserted the ancient tradition in Canon 228: "An ecumenical council enjoys supreme power over the universal church." Yet in Canon 222 it unambiguously put all authority in councils in the hands of the pope: "There is no such thing as an Ecumenical Council unless it is convoked by the Roman Pontiff. . . . It is the right of that same Roman Pontiff to preside at the council either in his own person or through others designated by him. It is also his right to establish and designate the matters to be treated and the order to be observed, and it is his right to transfer the council, suspend it, dissolve it, and confirm its decrees."[35]

But just how was Canon 222 to operate in the concrete circumstances of Vatican II? What about the "liberty" of the council (to use the traditional term)? Was the council simply a consultative body for the pope, or even a body whose direction was to be set by the dictates of a Vatican Congregation like the Holy Office and its orthodoxy scrutinized and judged by it? As every well-informed participant in the council knew, this was hardly the role councils had played in the church.

The Gregorian Reform of the eleventh century marked a turning point in the way papal authority was viewed and exercised. It began a long process of centralization that, despite flagging somewhat from the late Middle Ages until the French Revolution, picked up speed and practical implementation in the nineteenth century and the first half of the twentieth.

On the theoretical level, this centralization was justified by the claim that the popes possessed "plenitude of power," now understood, not in the traditional sense of whatever authority was necessary to fulfill the duties prescribed for the office, but in a new sense of complete authority in the church. Whatever power anybody else might hold, including the bishops, came from the pope. On a practical level, the centralization was justified by the increasingly one-world situation brought about by modern means of communication and travel. The result, in any case, was that the popes—or usually the Congregations of the Curia—increasingly made all important decisions. Theological textbooks before Vatican II described the papacy as a monarchy, and papal-centric readings of church history supported the monarchical model to the exclusion of all others.

Notably absent from the model were the collegial aspects of church history that prevailed well into the modern era—not so much in the relatively rare ecumenical councils as in the many hundreds of local and provincial councils or, as they are sometimes called, synods.[36] The biblical precedent for councils lay in the Jewish Sanhedrin, the national council of priests and elders that regulated religious matters in Israel. The first recorded gathering of Christian leaders, which implicitly followed the Jewish pattern, was the gathering of apostles and elders in Jerusalem described in *Acts of the Apostles,* 15:6–29.

During the next two centuries Christian leaders in different localities continued to meet to settle disputes and otherwise give direction to Christian communities. These assemblies, whose ultimate origin was the community gathered in worship, retained some liturgical forms, but they increasingly followed the procedures and protocol of the corresponding political bodies of the Roman Empire. Nonetheless, the fact that every session of Vatican II began with the celebration of Mass and the solemn enthronement of the book of the gospels reveals the importance and continuing impact of that aspect of councils' origins. These liturgical acts were not superficial ornaments. They pointed to the conviction that the council was above all a sacred gathering.[37]

By the middle of the third century, local councils for which we have records had proliferated and met, usually without reference to the bishop of Rome, in cities as widespread as Alexandria, Antioch, and Rome. At least eight synods met in the province of Africa and five in the province of Rome, for instance, within the ten-year period 250–260.[38] In the fourth century, with Christianity now legal, a council seemed to be meeting someplace in the Greco-Roman world at a rate of about every five years—Jerusalem, Milan, Cordova, Orange, Carthage, Mileve, to name only a few. Between 306 and 711, at least thirty-five councils were held in Spain, seventeen of them in Toledo alone.[39] The Synod of Whitby in Northumbria, in 664, critical for the development of Christianity in Britain, is justly famous.

The pattern continued through the Middle Ages, with northern Europe now the scene for many councils. In its Twenty-fourth Session, on November 11, 1563, the Council of Trent decreed that provincial councils, convoked by the metropolitan bishop, were to be celebrated every three years. Although the rhythm of that prescription was unrealistic, provincial councils were frequent in the modern period. They became much less so after Vatican I, despite the provision for them in the 1917 Code of Canon Law (Canons 281–282).[40] In the United States, for instance, seven provincial councils were held in Baltimore between 1829 and 1849, followed by three plenary councils in 1852, 1866, and 1884, but then no more. Provincial, national, and diocesan councils were from early times a vital, normal, and ongoing part of church life.[41]

Some Distinguishing Characteristics of Vatican II

Councils thus differed among themselves and in their relationships to the papacy, with the first eight a striking contrast to those that followed. Even when the differences among some of them, like the first three Lateran councils (held in Rome in 1123, 1139, and 1179), do not seem so great, every council had distinctive characteristics. Those of Vatican II are so extraordinary, however, that they set the council apart from its predecessors almost as a different kind of entity. The most obvious of these characteristics is of course the council's massive proportions, its remarkable international breadth, and the scope and variety of the issues it addressed. That is, however, only the tip of the iceberg.

The decision to admit non-Catholic observers as an integral body was not only unique in the annals of ecumenical councils but also allowed the deliberations of the council to be reviewed by scholars and churchmen who did not share many of the basic assumptions upon which Catholic doctrine and practice were based. As events proved, this decision stimulated a more searching scrutiny of the deliberations and decisions, and it was important for not allowing the attention of the council to focus on issues of concern only to Roman Catholics—or only to Roman Catholic prelates. The number of observers or guests actually present at the council rose to 182 at the end.[42]

Moreover, the media took an aggressive interest in the council. Until

Trent, 1545–1563, the deliberations of the councils were almost the exclusive concern of those who participated in them. How many people knew or cared what happened, for instance, at Lateran III, in 1179? True, the Council of Constance, 1414–1418, which resolved the Schism that resulted when three men claimed to be the legitimate pope, directly affected some segments of the general population, but it was the invention of the printing press later in that century that changed the public's relationship to the councils. Trent and especially Vatican I had to contend with a general and rapid dissemination of information and propaganda, much of it unfavorable. Even so, at this point only a small percentage of the world's population was informed of the proceedings.

By the time of Vatican II, however, radio and television transmitted news around the globe at the very moment any important event occurred. The mere spectacle of Vatican II made it newsworthy even apart from anything else that happened. The extraordinary popularity of Pope John XXIII among Catholics and non-Catholics alike excited interest in "Pope John's council." *Time* magazine named John "man of the year" for 1962, the year the council opened, and his picture appeared on the cover.

Once the council got under way, the media and the public were captivated by two phenomena in particular: the ill-kept secret of the sometimes acrid debates and confrontations in the council; and the emerging possibility of changes in posture and practice that just a few months earlier had seemed set in stone. The Catholic Church had presented itself internally and to the world at large as the church that did not change. It took great care, as well, to show a united front on all issues and to deal swiftly and discreetly with any occurrences within the church that might seem to suggest otherwise. Yet despite efforts to hide or disguise them, the debates and disagreements in the council entered the public forum. They shocked some, delighted others, and made clear to all that Catholicism was not the monolith they thought they knew. All at once the church had a new image.

The actions of the council thus came to be discussed and debated in the media, and newspapers like the *New York Times,* the *Washington Post,* and their counterparts in other countries gave them consistent and generally sympathetic coverage.[43] Henri Fesquet's reports in *Le Monde* (Paris), later published as a book, were notably judicious and well informed.[44] In the English-speaking world, the "Letters from Vatican City," written by Francis Xavier Murphy under the pseudonym Xavier Rynne and published in *The New Yorker,* provided a gossipy but engrossing account of what was going on. Although blatantly biased and composed in haste under tight deadlines, the "Letters" got the basic story straight. They were read avidly by a wide public during the four years the council was in session and were extremely influential in the interpretation they provided.

There is no doubt that the attempt to satisfy some of the expectations, objections, and problems raised by the media affected the direction of the council and gave encouragement to its progressive wing. Even before the council opened, Hans Küng, a young Swiss theologian, published *The Council, Reform, and Reunion* (1960). The book, translated into eight languages, was the most influential among the publications in the preparatory years that tried to move people's imagination into larger issues the council might address and open possibilities beyond a mere tinkering with the status quo, which most bishops seemed to have in mind.

With the new ease of communication, Vatican II's decisions could be implemented with a speed and directness no previous council could come close to mustering, even if it had wanted to. As it turned out, some of the decisions had an immediate impact on the life of the ordinary believer. This was, again, something special to Vatican II. When believers entered their church for Mass on November 29, 1964, the first Sunday of Advent, they encountered something very different from what they had experienced all their lives up to the previous Sunday. With Vatican II still in session, the council managed to begin implementing unmistakable changes in the Mass, such as use of the vernacular in many of its parts.

For centuries Catholics had been warned against reading the Bible.[45] Although that caution had diminished in the years immediately before Vatican II, it now disappeared completely as Catholics were urged to read and study the Bible, even in company with their Protestant neighbors. Forbidden since the sixteenth century to attend even funerals and weddings in Protestant churches, Catholics were now urged to join hands with those of different faiths in various causes. They were exhorted to join in "dialogue" or conversation with their non-Catholic neighbors, even about religious matters.

The decisions of previous councils were directed almost exclusively to the clergy; even when they had some import for the lives of ordinary Christians, they were implemented so slowly and often so haphazardly as to be virtually imperceptible. The very opposite was true for Vatican II, and the rush "to implement the council" was keenly felt in Catholic communities. No other council could compare with it for direct impact on the life of every Catholic and with the sometimes considerable adjustments in religious practice and general attitude that the changes required.

Moreover, for many Catholics the adjustments they were asked to make seemed to carry the message that old rules no longer applied. But which ones and to what extent? These questions, shocking in themselves to many Catholics schooled in the idea that the church did not change, were debated not only in classrooms and rectories but at the dinner tables of working-class families. Whereas "reform" was traditionally a code for a stricter or at least more precise discipline, Vatican II seemed to aim at loosening what had become too tight.

These factors, plus the originally indeterminate aims of the council, contributed to another of Vatican II's most important and distinguishing characteristics: the great scope of its concerns. The council wished to "speak to all men and women," as the constitution on the Church in the Modern World succinctly stated. Vatican II took greater note of the world around it than had any previous council, and it assumed as one of its principal tasks dialogue or conversation with that world. The council's concerns were thus further broadened beyond the confines of the Catholic Church, in a manner unprecedented among previous councils.

Aggiornamento, Ressourcement, and Development of Doctrine

Whence the impulse acknowledging that change was legitimate and even good? The mentality with which many of the most influential bishops and theologians approached their task at Vatican II was more historical than at any previous council. The prevalence of this mentality is another of Vatican II's distinguishing characteristics. Marie-Dominique Chenu, a Dominican who, though not a *peritus,* would be influential at the council, described the principles that underlay the theological ferment in the middle years of the twentieth century at the Dominicans' house of studies, *Le Saulchoir* in Étiolles, near Paris. He succinctly expressed the great shift taking place much more broadly in Catholic theology: "Since Christianity draws its reality from history and not from some metaphysics, the theologian must have as his primary concern . . . to know this history and to train himself in it."[46]

In certain circles this mentality, the result of the great impetus to historical studies that began in the nineteenth century and never abated, deeply affected the study of every aspect of church life and doctrine. The leading voices at the council were much more aware of the profound changes that had taken place in the long history of the church than were their counterparts in earlier councils. They were persuaded that at least some of these changes could be explained as expressions of a given culture and thus were not irreversible. Moreover, it was now more obvious than ever that some doctrines taught by the church in the twentieth century, such as the Immaculate Conception of the Virgin Mary, were unknown as such in the church of the apostolic or patristic periods.

This keener sense of history was operative in at least three important ways at the council, which can be captured by three words current at the time—*aggiornamento* (Italian for updating or modernizing), development (an unfolding, in context sometimes the equivalent of progress or evolution), and *ressourcement* (French for return to the sources). One basic, crucial assumption underlay all three as they were understood in the council: the Catholic tradition is richer, broader, and more malleable than the way in which it had often, especially since the nineteenth century, been interpreted. The bishops who had appropriated that assumption not as an abstract truth but as a license to reexamine the status quo emerged at Vatican II as leaders of the majority. They reacted against interpretations of Catholicism that in their view reduced it to simplistic and ahistorical formulas.

The three words overlap in their meanings, but in general they look, respectively, to the present *(aggiornamento),* the future (development), and the past *(ressourcement).* They all are concerned with change and, in the context of a reluctance to admit change, operate as soft synonyms for it and soft synonyms for reform. They signal the abandonment of the so-called classicist worldview that saw human living in static, abstract, and immutable terms.[47] R. G. Collingwood designated that mind-set "substantialism," by which he meant a historiography "constructed on the basis of a metaphysical system whose chief category is the category of substance," which resulted in a mentality that saw great social entities like the church sailing like a hermetically sealed and fully defined substance through the sea of history without being affected by it.[48]

Of the three terms, *aggiornamento* was the most often invoked to describe what Vatican II was all about. Those who interpreted the council as essentially an *aggiornamento* found good validation of their position in John XXIII's opening allocution to the council, *Gaudet Mater Ecclesia,* when he said: "[The church] by making appropriate changes [*opportunis inductis emendationibus*] . . . will lead individuals, families, and peoples to turn their minds to heavenly things." And later: "the church should never depart from the sacred patrimony . . . But at the same time she must ever look to the present, to the new conditions and new forms of life introduced into the modern world that have opened up new avenues to the Catholic apostolate."[49]

In a number of its decrees Vatican II determined that some expressions of religious practice be changed to conform to the "new era" in which the council was taking place. The very first sentence of the very first document the council approved and promulgated, the constitution On the Sacred Liturgy, states: "The council has set out . . . to adapt to the needs of our age those institutions that are subject to change."

In principle this was nothing new. In 1215, for instance, Lateran IV legitimated changes if they were undertaken for reasons of "urgent necessity or evident utility."[50] In the twentieth century, moreover, the Vatican showed no reluctance to make use of new inventions and conveniences. It adopted microphones and amplifiers, for instance, before the House of Commons and typewriters before the British Foreign Office. In 1931, when radio was still in its infancy, Pius XI inaugurated Vatican Radio.

But the *aggiornamento* of Vatican II moved on a different, more sensitive plane. Four things are special about it. First, the changes made in the name of *aggiornamento* sometimes touched on things ordinary Catholics considered normative, and hence they sometimes had a startling impact. Second, no previous council had ever taken the equivalent of *aggiornamento* as a leitmotif, as a broad principle rather than as a rare exception. Previous councils had, rather, insisted on the unchangeable character of religious practice and doctrinal formulations and on the necessity of eradicating any "novelty." For certain, neither John XXIII nor the bishops at Vatican II invested *aggiornamento* with a radical meaning, yet by applying it in such an unprecedentedly broad way, the council gave it a special character and imbued it with a special force.

Third, *aggiornamento* made clear that Catholicism was adaptive even to "the modern world," not simply by making use of modern inventions like the radio but by appropriating certain cultural assumptions and values. This was a shift from the integralism that marked most Catholic thinking from the early nineteenth century well into the twentieth and saw almost everything stemming from the Enlightenment and the French Revolution as incompatible with the church. It was a sign of the end of the long nineteenth century.

How and why this shift took place is difficult to explain except in the most general terms, but it was well under way in a few circles as early as the 1920s. In 1922 Jacques Maritain, the Catholic philosopher, published his *Antimoderne,* which despite the title was both a symptom of change in attitude and a catalyst for it. According to Maritain, Catholicism possessed a "bold ability to adapt itself to the new conditions erupting suddenly in the life of the world."[51] *Aggiornamento* was a practical expression of that bold ability. It turned out to be, moreover, the best known of the euphemisms employed to win assent to some of the council's decisions and to lessen their shock.

Fourth, this broad adoption of a principle of deliberate reconciliation between the church and certain changes taking place outside it provided an entry point into a more dynamic approach to church life and teaching. It implied a continuation after Vatican II of the dynamism that characterized the council itself, which meant that the documents were not an end point but a starting point.

This dynamism was even more relevant to the concept of "development." In fact, "development of doctrine" was "*the* issue under all issues" at Vatican II, according to John Courtney Murray.[52] It was certainly the key issue in the bitter battle on the floor of the council over the church-state issue, Murray's specialty, but it was crucial for other issues as well, including the behind-the-scenes drama over designating the Virgin Mary "Mother of the Church." By the time of Vatican II, almost all theologians admitted that some form of "development" had taken place in the teaching of the church through the centuries. John Henry Newman's *Essay on the Development of Christian Doctrine* (1846) was the classic statement on the subject. Received with suspicion in Catholic circles when first published, it was by 1962 widely accepted as close to the definitive book on the subject.

Development was usually understood as movement further along a given path, as with the definition of the Assumption of Mary (1950) following the earlier definition of her Immaculate Conception (1854), leading to the hope expressed by many on the eve of Vatican II for further Marian definitions at the council. It was thus a cumulative process in which the tradition became ever richer—or, from another angle, ever heavier, with ever more to bear and to explain.

The idea was used to explain and justify the growth in papal authority from the earliest times until its culmination in Vatican I, as from the acorn comes the oak. It took the present as the norm for understanding the past. It searched the past to find evidence to confirm the present—and sometimes to "develop" it into the future for more of the same.

Development suggested progress, especially as a further clarification or a greater efflorescence. The council subscribed to this understanding, for instance, in its decree on Revelation, *Dei Verbum:* "The Tradition that comes to us from the apostles makes progress in the church with the help of the Holy Spirit. There is a growth in insight into the realities and words that are being passed on." Tradition, in this definition, is not inert but dynamic.

The problem Murray ran into in the council was that the doctrine of church-state relationships that he and his colleagues advocated seemed to critics not a further step along the path but an abandonment of the traditional path for a different (and, indeed, forbidden) path. The popes had repeatedly condemned separation of church and state, and now the council proposed it as a legitimate "development" of Catholic—indeed, of papal—teaching. This seemed like legerdemain—or, worse, backpedaling. Hence the vigorous and sustained opposition to the ideas proposed in the declaration On Religious Liberty.

If development takes the present as its starting point and looks to the future for even greater fulfillment, *ressourcement* is skeptical of the present because of what it has discovered in the past. It entails a return to the sources with a view not to confirming the present but to making changes in it to conform it to a more authentic or more appropriate past, to what advocates of *ressourcement* considered a more profound tradition. The word was a neologism coined by the poet Charles Péguy early in the twentieth century. Several decades later, Yves Congar gave it a certain currency, and by the mid-twentieth century, scholars in France associated with a phenomenon known as the new theology, "la nouvelle théologie," had claimed it as their own.[53]

Unlike development, a theory that was first straightforwardly proposed only in the nineteenth century, *ressourcement* had enjoyed *avant la lettre* a truly venerable history in the Western church beginning with the Gregorian Reform of the eleventh century. At the midpoint of that century a series of reforming popes spearheaded a vigorous campaign of change in the name of restoring a more ancient canonical tradition. As the dust began to settle after the bitter and bloody battles that the campaign ignited, the principle, even though not explicitly invoked, undergirded the important legislation of Lateran councils I and II regarding especially the election of bishops and clerical celibacy. The reformers understood their position on these two matters as reassertions of the normative practice of an earlier era, which implied a mandate to reinstate the older practice.

Ressourcement was in its Latin form the motto of the great humanist movement of the Renaissance—*ad fontes*, "to the sources!" The Renaissance return to the sources, especially to the Bible and the Fathers of the Church, was what inspired humanists like Erasmus because they believed it would lead to a reform of theology, piety, and education. Return to the sources is what drove the Protestant Reformers, as they sought to restore the authentic Gospel that in their opinion the papal church had obscured and perverted. In Catholicism in the nineteenth century it lay behind Leo XIII's encyclical *Aeterni Patris* (1879), initiating the revival of the study of Thomas Aquinas, and it lay behind the conservative origins of the Liturgical Movement with Prosper Guéranger in the monastery of Solesmes. In brief, some form of *ressourcement* lay behind every reform movement in Western Christianity—and behind every reform movement in Western culture—at least up to the Enlightenment.

On the eve of Vatican II, the call to return to the sources, now explicitly under the name *ressourcement*, drove much of the theological ferment in France that caused grave concern in Rome and elicited from the Holy Office silencings and condemnations. Stigmatized by its opponents as "la nouvelle théologie" and therefore a "novelty," it was viewed by its proponents as just the opposite, as a recovery of an older theology, which to a large extent was the theology of the Bible and the Fathers of the Church.[54] "La nouvelle théologie" replayed in remarkably similar terms the concerns and themes that had preoccupied Erasmus and other humanists in the sixteenth century.

Just as Erasmus had wanted to displace medieval Scholasticism with a biblical/patristic theology, the twentieth-century *ressourcement* wanted to do essentially the same. It contravened the earlier Thomistic and, more broadly, Neo-Scholastic *ressourcement* that originated with Leo XIII in 1879 and that now was considered normative in Catholic theological discourse.[55] In his 1950 encyclical *Humani Generis*, Pius XII expressed his displeasure at those who criticized Thomism and wanted "to bring about a return in the explanation of Catholic doctrine to the way of speaking used in Holy Scripture and the Fathers of the Church." He challenged the principle of *ressourcement* by affirming that the task of theology was to discover how the present teachings of the church's Magisterium are found in the past, which is precisely the opposite of what *ressourcement* implied.[56] Within a short time proponents of the "new" theology were being removed from their teaching posts.[57]

The critics of "la nouvelle théologie" had a point, for *ressourcement* implied something potentially more radical than development. Development took the present as a lens to understand the past, and thus was in danger of falling into the historical fallacy of presentism, reading the present into the past. *Ressourcement,* on the contrary, took the past as a norm for judging the present. Whereas development was conceived as movement along the same path, *ressourcement* looked to the past for norms or practices or mind-sets to be used in changing, correcting, or at least qualifying the direction things were moving in the present. The Gregorian reformers of the eleventh century, for instance, were convinced that the church had been on the wrong path by letting lay men choose bishops. They plowed ancient canonical sources and discovered the principle of the free election of bishops, which they saw as the remedy for the present.[58]

While development is understood as movement along a given path, *ressourcement* equivalently says: we are no longer going to move along Path X. We are going back to the fork in the road and will now take, instead, Path Y, a better path. Or, we are just going to stop where we are for a while, or even permanently settle down at this point and not go a step further, declaring a dead-end. This is what happened at the council when it resisted the impetus to define further doctrines about Mary.

Development and *ressourcement* are both about corporate memory, the memory constitutive of identity. What is true for individuals is true for a social body. What such bodies choose to remember from their past makes them what they are. The great battles in the council were battles over the identity of the church, not over its fundamental dogmas but over other aspects of its tradition, especially its more recent tradition. The great questions were: How malleable is the tradition of the church? What are the patterns of change related to it? What are the legitimate limits of those patterns? The way to dodge such troubling questions, of course, is to deny change.[59] An underlying assumption of those trying to deal with change at Vatican II was that appropriate change meant not losing or changing one's identity but enhancing it or even salvaging it from ossification. Such change entailed a process of redefinition that was both continuous and discontinuous with the past.

The theologians of "la nouvelle théologie" like Henri de Lubac and Yves Congar were rehabilitated at Vatican II. Partly because of them the principle of *ressourcement* became operative in the council. In different forms, however, it was before the council even more widely operative in Catholic theology, well beyond "la nouvelle théologie," and it found expression in the council in a variety of ways. In its document on religious life, for instance, the council urged members of religious orders to return to their origins and draw from them principles and energy to make changes in the present. *Ressourcement* was the principle that validated collegiality. But *ressourcement* influenced the council in a more pervasive way that transcended all particular instances of "returning to the sources." This was evident in Vatican II's adoption of a style of discourse more closely resembling the style of the Fathers than the style used by previous councils. If we are looking for special characteristics of Vatican II, this has to rank high, maybe even first, among them.

Genre, Form, Content, Values: "The Spirit of the Council"

Through the centuries councils have made use of a range of literary genres, most of which have borrowed from the discourse of Roman antiquity. The genres in large measure were, or closely resembled, laws and judicial sentences. While ensuring correct belief in the church and enforcing appropriate behavior, especially of the clergy *(fides et mores)*, the laws were not and could not be separated from securing public order in society at large, and for that reason secular authorities undertook their enforcement. They were "the law of the land" as well as the law of the church.

Two fundamental assumptions were in play. First, councils were judicial bodies that heard cases and rendered judgment, with anybody found guilty duly punished. Second, they were legislative bodies that issued ordinances, to which were attached, as with any law, penalties for failure to comply. This pattern in fact antedated Nicaea, for it is found in regional councils from at least the middle of the third century. The procedural models the bishops began to adopt early on were those followed throughout the empire by local assemblies and municipal councils. Bishops, who were drawn principally from the local notables, fell into this pattern for their meetings as almost second nature. Although the Roman Senate was a special case, it stood in the same procedural tradition.[60]

At Nicaea the analogy with the Senate was strengthened by the presence of the emperor himself. Thus councils adopted the legislative and judicial patterns of the Roman Empire, which would persist down through the centuries. In the Latin councils in the West, the role of the emperor and other lay rulers would be much diminished, but what would remain fundamentally unchanged was the assumption that a council was, like the Roman Senate, a legislative-judicial body. It was this model that Vatican II implicitly rejected for itself; in so doing, it redefined what a council was. Although this is a change of momentous import, its implications have gone largely unexplored. This inattention has contributed to confusion and disagreement over how to interpret the council.[61]

Among the many literary forms used by councils through the centuries were confessions of faith, historical narratives, bulls and letters, judicial sentences against ecclesiastical criminals, constitutions, and various kinds of "decrees." Especially in the early councils the most respected and important form was the creedal statement. The genre employed most characteristically by Nicaea and by many subsequent councils, however, was the canon, usually a relatively short, prescriptive ordinance that often carried with it punishment for failure to comply. The punishment was usually an anathema, that is, a ban or an excommunication. Canon 27 of the Council of Chalcedon, in 451, illustrates the point: "The sacred synod decrees that those who carry off girls under pretext of cohabitation, or who are accomplices or cooperate with those who carry them off, are to lose their personal rank if they are clerics, and are to be anathematized if they are monks or layfolk."[62]

Although most of the other forms employed by councils betray in their context the assumption that a council is a legislative-judicial body, the canon, as the example from Chalcedon shows, directly and unmistakably manifests that assumption. The Council of Trent issued about 135 such canons relating to doctrine, to say nothing of its similar prescriptions regarding ecclesiastical discipline or "reform." Canon 1, on the Mass, is typical of Trent's doctrinal canons: "If anyone says that a true and proper sacrifice is not offered to God in the Mass, or that the offering is nothing but the giving of Christ to us to eat, let him be anathema."[63]

Even such doctrinal canons strike not at what a person might believe or think or feel but at what they "say" or "deny," that is, at some observable behavior. They are not concerned with interiority as such. Like any good law, canons and their equivalents were formulated to be as unambiguous as possible, drawing clear lines between "who's in" and "who's out." They sometimes depict those who are "out" as full-fledged enemies, as did the decree of Lateran V, in 1512, against the cardinals who had attempted to depose Pope Julius II: "We condemn, reject, and detest . . . each and every thing done by those sons of perdition."[64] The Council of Constance (1418) denounced John Wyclif as a "profligate enemy" of the faith and a "pseudo-Christian," and it handed over his disciple Jan Hus to be burned at the stake.[65]

True, these are extreme examples, but for that reason they best illustrate the point. Although allowance must be made for many differences, the councils from Nicaea to Vatican I had a characteristic style of discourse. That style was composed of two basic elements. The first was a literary genre—the canon or its equivalent. The second was the vocabulary typical of the genre and appropriate to it. It consisted in words of threat and intimidation, words of surveillance and punishment, words of a superior speaking to an inferior—or to an enemy. It consisted in power-words.

Although canons and the like deal with the exterior, insofar as they are inspired by Christian principles they must be presumed not to be devoid of relationship to inner conversion. Even a coerced change in behavior can sometimes be the first step in a change of heart. Moreover, strict laws and harsh punishment are sometimes required if a long-standing abuse is to be rooted out. The bishops at Trent knew they could not reform the episcopacy (that is, themselves) without strong sanctions. They acted accordingly—and to good effect. Nonetheless, their language is that of adversarial relationships. It is a language concerned with public order.

The manner in which the canons expressed themselves reinforced social disciplining as an ecclesiastical style, as the way the church "did business." The language projected an image of the church as a stern master, and the image in turn promoted the reality and helped it self-fulfill. Such language was not confined to councils. In the nineteenth and twentieth centuries, papal pronouncements such as Pius IX's *Syllabus of Errors* (1864) and Pius X's *Lamentabili* and *Pascendi* (1907) made ample use of it. But Vatican II eschewed such language. It issued no canons, no anathemas, no verdicts of "guilty as charged." In so speaking it marked a significant break with past councils.

Another language-tradition was in play as well. From the early centuries, concepts from Greek philosophy also influenced conciliar language. Especially in the High Middle Ages, when such masters as Abelard, Peter Lombard, and Thomas Aquinas developed the great change in theological method known as Scholasticism, the dialectical and analytic aspects of the Western philosophical tradition began to play an even greater role in council pronouncements. Dialectics is the art of proving a point, of winning an argument, and of proving your opponent wrong. It expresses itself in the syllogism, in the debate, in the disputation. Even when aiming at reconciliation, it has an adversarial edge to it. It is, further, an appeal to the mind, not to the heart. Its language is abstract, impersonal, and ahistorical. It cannot succeed in its goal without a precise, technical vocabulary and the use of unambiguous definitions. In that regard it is similar to the legislative-judicial tradition. Both are intent on drawing firm lines of demarcation.

Vatican II, however, largely eschewed Scholastic language. It thus moved from the dialectic of winning an argument to the dialogue of finding common ground. It moved from abstract metaphysics to interpersonal "how to be." It moved from grand conceptual schemes or *summae* with hundreds of logically interconnected parts to the humble acceptance of mystery. In so doing it largely abandoned the Scholastic framework that had dominated Catholic theology since the thirteenth century.

The shift in language did not go unnoticed or unchallenged in the council, as we shall see, but neither its advocates nor its adversaries ever articulated clearly the implications of this change to a more "pastoral" language (as it was generally described). The shift affected not one or two documents of the council but, with varying degrees of consistency, all of them. It modified the existing value system. It implicitly said, for instance, that it is more valuable to work together as neighbors than to fight over differences, as we have up to now been doing.

The style of discourse the council adopted was, like that of previous councils, also made up of two essential elements, a genre and a vocabulary appropriate to it. That style, while operative to a greater or lesser extent in all the documents, is best exemplified in the four constitutions. Even in those most authoritative documents, however, the new style suffers interruptions, deviations, and admixtures. Long sections are simply expository. Nonetheless, this style is different from that of previous councils.

The genre can be precisely identified. It has been known and practiced in many cultures from time immemorial, but it was clearly analyzed and carefully codified by classical authors like Aristotle, Cicero, and Quintilian.[66] It is what the Roman authors called the *ars laudandi,* the panegyric, and its home is in what is traditionally known as humanistic culture. Panegyric is the painting of an idealized portrait in order to excite admiration and appropriation. It was an old genre in religious discourse, used extensively by the Fathers of the Church, revived in the Renaissance, and revisited in the twentieth century by the proponents of "la nouvelle théologie." It was a literary rather than a philosophical or legal genre, and hence it had altogether different aims and rested on different presuppositions. Panegyric was, in the technical sense, a humanistic genre because it was cultivated in the humanistic or literary tradition.[67]

The purpose of the epideictic genre, the technical name for panegyric in classical treatises on rhetoric, is not so much to clarify concepts as to heighten appreciation for a person, an event, or an institution and to excite emulation of an ideal. Its goal is the winning of internal assent, not the imposition of conformity from outside. It teaches, but not so much by way of magisterial pronouncement as by suggestion, insinuation, and example. Its instrument is persuasion, not coercion. If most Fourth of July speeches are secular examples of the genre at its worst, Lincoln's Gettysburg Address and his Second Inaugural are examples of it at its best. Lincoln tried simply to hold up for appreciation what was at stake in the war. By implication he praised it as noble and worthy of the great cost, and then invited the nation to move on. By depicting the attractiveness of certain ideals and values, he hoped to inspire his audience to strive to achieve them. He employed a rhetoric of invitation.[68]

Although the documents of the council are far from being literary masterpieces and, as committee documents, are not stylistically consistent, in their general orientation they fit the epideictic mold. That is a critical element in their style. They hold up ideals, then draw conclusions from them and often spell out practical consequences. This is a soft style compared with the hard-hitting style of canons and dialectical discourse.[69] It is rightly described as "pastoral" because it was meant to make Christian ideals appealing. Yet in the context of the council, "pastoral" is itself a soft word, a euphemism that obscures the significant shift in values and in the styles of relationships that the documents promoted. As expressions of a rhetoric of invitation and dialogue, the documents encourage conversion, an interior change that is induced by and then expressed by a new way of speaking and behaving. The shift in style entails a shift in value-system.

New way of speaking? The implications are profound. To learn a new language so as genuinely to live within it entails an inner transformation. Much more is at stake than learning new words for one's old concepts. To properly speak a new language means to enter fully into the values and sensibilities of a culture different from one's own and to appropriate them. One gestures, shrugs, bears oneself differently, and responds differently to situations to the point of, to some extent, becoming another person.

As a form of the art of persuasion, the panegyric-epideictic genre looks to reconciliation. While it raises appreciation, it creates or fosters among those it addresses a realization that they all share (or should share) the same ideals and need to work together to achieve them. To engage in persuasion is to some extent to put oneself on the same level as those being persuaded. Persuaders do not command from on high. Otherwise, they would not be persuading but dictating. Persuasion works from the inside out. To be successful, persuaders need to establish an identity between themselves and their audience and make clear that they share the same concerns and even the same sentiments, such as hope, joy, and sadness. The genre, moreover, wants to lift its audience to big issues. Implicit in it, therefore, is an invitation to rise above all pettiness and to strive for an expansive vision and a generous spirit.

These traits are characteristic of the style of discourse of Vatican II. The fathers of the council did not set out to "talk epideictic," but they wanted to adopt a style different from that of theological textbooks and most ecclesiastical pronouncements, a style more consonant with the style of the Fathers of the Church, as they often insisted during the council. However we might explain it, the documents of the council fit the epideictic pattern and therefore need to be interpreted accordingly. They must be analyzed according to their genre, their literary form.

The most concrete manifestation of the character of the new genre is the vocabulary it adopted. In fact, nowhere is the contrast between Vatican II and the preceding councils more obvious than in its vocabulary—in the words it most characteristically employed and in the words it eschewed. What kind of words are absent? Words of alienation, exclusion, enmity, words of threat and intimidation, words of surveillance and punishment. Although in the documents of Vatican II the hierarchical character of the church is repeatedly stressed and the prerogatives of the pope reiterated almost obsessively, the church is never described as a monarchy or the members of the church as subjects—a significant departure from previous practice. Definition (or, more technically, "determination") is the goal of the dialectical process that is at the heart of the Scholastic method. Vatican II issued no doctrinal definitions, even though that was what people expected because that was what councils had always done.

What kind of words are present? Words untypical of the vocabulary of councils. They cannot be considered casual asides or simple window-dressing—"mere rhetoric." They are used far too insistently and too characteristically for that. They do not occur here and there but are an across-the-board phenomenon. Genre and vocabulary together provide us with the lenses that bring the picture of Vatican II into sharp focus. They allow us to determine patterns that provide a horizon of interpretation.

Taken together, moreover, they constitute a style of discourse that reveals the inner values of the person speaking: "Out of the abundance of the heart the mouth speaks." In this instance the mouth speaking is that of the council. The council is speaking for the church and thus manifests what it holds to be the church's inner reality. It thereby indicates how the church will, ideally, behave and "do business." The council is speaking about the very identity of the church. It *teaches* by means of its style.

I divide the new words into categories, but the categories are imperfectly distinct from one another. They overlap and crisscross, making the same or related points. One category consists of horizontal-words, or even equality-words. The most widely invoked of such expressions and the one that remains the best known, despite its problematic implications, is "people of God." Others are "brothers and sisters" and "the priesthood of all believers." The most bitterly contested of such words during the council was "collegiality." These expressions contrast with the exclusively vertical or top-down words of previous councils; when the latter appear in Vatican II, as they often do, the horizontal-words provide a balance and a counterpoint.

Collegiality is especially important. Although it can be taken, as here, as an image expressing a general orientation, in the council it also had specific content. It well exemplifies the illegitimacy of separating style from content. Style is the ultimate expression of meaning. It does not adorn meaning but is meaning. It is a hermeneutical key par excellence. No one doubts that a poem must be interpreted differently from a scientific treatise.

Then there are words of reciprocity, such as "cooperation," "partnership," and "collaboration." Striking in the constitution On the Church in the Modern World is the bold statement that just as the world learns from the church, the church learns from the world—in a relationship of mutuality. The words "dialogue" and "conversation" abound. Dialogue manifests a radical shift from the prophetic I-say-unto-you style that earlier prevailed and indicates something other than unilateral decision-making. Collegiality, too, belongs in this category.

Humility-words recur, beginning with the description of the church as a pilgrim. The council silently effected the redefinition of the triad prophet-priest-king by seeing prophet not only as a proclaimer of the truth of the Gospel but also as a partner in dialogue. It did so by affirming the priesthood of all believers while retaining a special identity for the "presbyter," and by insisting that, while those entrusted with authority cannot shirk it, they are in the last analysis servants. "Servant" is not a power-word.

Even though the word "change" scarcely appears as such in the council documents, other words that imply historical movement of one kind or another show up almost for the first time in Vatican II—words like "development," "progress," and even "evolution." The most familiar change-word associated with Vatican II is John XXIII's *aggiornamento*. By admitting the change-principle, the council implicitly admitted the open-ended character of its own pronouncements. Related to the dynamism and open-ended modality implied in the change-words are the empowerment-words or statements, as when the constitution On the Sacred Liturgy insists that the fundamental principle to be observed and promoted is "the full and active participation by all the people." The decree On the Apostolate of the Laity is a call to action.

The final category is interiority-words. Among these are "charism" as well as "joy and hope, grief and anguish," the opening words of the constitution On the Church in the Modern World. The constitution continues: for the followers of Christ all that is human finds an echo in their hearts. Most impressive among interiority words is "conscience": "Deep within their consciences individuals discover a law that they do not make for themselves but that they are bound to obey, whose voice, ever summoning them to love and to do what is good and avoid what is evil, rings in their hearts."[70] Vatican II was about the inward journey. Perhaps the most remarkable aspect of *Lumen Gentium* is chapter five, "The Call to Holiness." *Lumen Gentium* thus set the agenda, leading the way for the call to holiness to become one of the great themes running through the council. The documents of Vatican II are thus religious documents in a way notably different from those of previous councils.

Holiness, the council thus said, is what the church is all about. This is an old truth, of course, and in itself is not remarkable. Yet no previous council had ever explicitly asserted this idea and certainly never developed it so repeatedly and at length. The genres and vocabularies of those councils, the assumption that they were judicial-legislative bodies, precluded such a theme. The call to holiness is something more than external conformity to enforceable codes of conduct. It is a call that, though it must have external form, relates more directly to the higher impulses of the human spirit, which in the council often got specified in commitment to the service of others in the world.

When both genre and vocabulary are taken into account they convey a remarkably consistent message. The message is that a model-shift has occurred or, better, is struggling to occur. Genre together with its appropriate vocabulary also imbues Vatican II with a coherence lacking in previous councils. The enactments of councils before Vatican II have been a collection of discrete units, a collection of enactments, which on the surface have little connection with one another. Under the surface a connection can sometimes be discerned. It is possible, for instance, to construct a picture of the "ideal bishop" according to the decrees of the Council of Trent, but that ideal must indeed be constructed from a mass of enactments that do not immediately reveal the pastoral ideal that lies behind them.[71] The decree on bishops of Vatican II, on the contrary, sets out ideals for bishops to strive for. Moreover, those ideals correspond to ideals set out in other documents of the council.

The documents of Vatican II thus have a coherence, sometimes interrupted by elements from outside the guiding vision, that is ground-breaking for ecclesiastical assemblies up to that point. The council shaped and reshaped the documents to make them consistent with one another—on the level of style, yes, but also on the level of principle, to which the style gave expression. The intertexual character of the documents is pervasive and deliberate. It is no accident, for instance, that the fundamental principle of the constitution *Sacrosanctum Concilium* is "the full participation" of everyone in the congregation in the liturgical action and that the most memorable description of the church in the constitution *Lumen Gentium* is "the people of God."

This coherence was immediately recognized by commentators on the council and was often expressed in the vague term "spirit of the council." "Spirit" here meant an overriding vision that transcended the particulars of the documents and had to be taken into account in interpreting the council. The vagueness of "spirit" is brought down to earth and made verifiable when we pay attention to the *style* of the council, to its unique literary form and vocabulary, and draw out their implications. Through an examination of "the letter" (form and vocabulary) it is possible to arrive at "the spirit."

2

The Long Nineteenth Century

Vatican II was for Roman Catholicism not only "the end of the nineteenth century" but also the fulfillment of certain aspects of it.[1] For Catholics the century was a long span during which the church at its grass roots and away from "the center" largely rebounded from the devastations of the French Revolution. In many parts of the world Catholicism showed an extraordinary vigor, and in France itself the church, despite struggling with powerful political and ideological adversaries, flourished. In almost every Catholic country vocations to the priesthood began to climb to pre-Revolutionary levels. The religious orders of men and women, which were virtually extinct by 1800, grew at an astounding rate. Missionaries from Europe arrived in Asia and Africa in unprecedented numbers and reported many conversions.

Programs of catechetical instruction got under way that resulted by the mid-twentieth century in perhaps the best-catechized Catholic population in the history of the church. An almost incalculable number of popular magazines and learned journals were launched, and Catholic schools at every level of instruction sprang up wherever Catholics were present in any numbers. Although in Europe Catholics were opposed to the intellectual mainstream, significant thinkers emerged and sowed the seeds for important movements that would bear fruit in Vatican II.

Nonetheless, ecclesiastical leadership, especially the papacy, felt beleaguered and on the defensive. The French Revolution had been a traumatic experience, in some ways more traumatic than the Reformation, for it erupted in Catholic France and its ripple effects were felt most keenly in other Catholic countries like Spain and Portugal, as well as in the states of continental and peninsular Italy.[2] In the Papal States it created a severe and protracted political crisis that centered largely on the Risorgimento.

The Risorgimento (Italian for resurgence) was a popular movement aimed at Italian political unification. It entailed the elimination of smaller units like the Papal States and the establishment of Rome as the capital of the new nation. The political crisis for the papacy culminated in 1860–1870, when first the States and then Rome were seized by the forces of the Risorgimento. The crisis festered, however, for another sixty years until the "Roman Question" (the papacy's relationship to the city of Rome) was finally settled in 1929 with the creation of Vatican City as a sovereign state and the papacy's surrender of claims to Rome.

Not only had the French Revolution shaken and temporarily abolished the monarchies on the Continent, but in so doing it had also shaken to its foundation the old marriage of throne and altar, that is, state support of the Catholic Church to the exclusion of all others. Even more devastating was the ideology that carried these events forward. Behind the Revolution lay the Enlightenment, which on the Continent was rabidly anticlerical, anti-Christian, and especially anti-Catholic. Some Catholics tried to come to terms with the new thinking, and their importance in what is termed the Catholic Enlightenment is now being increasingly recognized. Yet they were relatively few. Voltaire's wish for the church was shared by other *philosophes:* "Obliterate the dreadful thing!"—*Écrasez l'infâme!*

Modernity is a handy catchword for summing up what was at stake. The thinkers of the Enlightenment turned their backs on the past, turned their faces resolutely to the future, and looked forward to ever better things to come. Among those things was a new era of liberty, equality, and fraternity. Religion and monarchy would no longer shackle the human spirit. Freedom of expression and freedom of the press were rights that could not be denied. No more religious dogma, for Reason was the only god to be adored. No more hierarchy or privilege by reason of birth. No more kings—or at least no more kings without severe constitutional restraints. The list could go on, but progress toward a better future undergirded the mentality. Modernity implied, therefore, a view about historical change.

Modernity was thus not simply the present state of things, the point in time at which life was now being lived. It had become an ideology, or perhaps several ideologies, all of them antagonistic in some measure to Catholicism. "Liberalism" was the name by which such passionately held views were commonly known in the nineteenth century. Especially for the papacy, Liberalism stood for all that was wrong with the modern world. It stood for the philosophies responsible for overturning the right order of society and for causing morality to plummet to unheard-of depths of degradation.

Liberalism had to be answered. Culture wars of the first order broke out.[3] The papacy's search for a response to the enemy helped generate one of the most important yet little commented-upon changes in Catholicism in the modern era: the popes became teachers. Or, better put, they became teachers in a newly professed and more expanded way. Their principal vehicle for doing so was the papal encyclical. They used that medium to propose, expound, and elaborate theological and doctrinal positions in a manner unprecedented. By definition an encyclical is a circular letter, and as such it was used by popes and others from ancient times. But in the nineteenth century its significance changed to such an extent that it emerged as virtually a new genre. Benedict XIV's *Ubi primum,* issued in 1740, was the first.[4]

How did the encyclical differ from the genres previously favored by the popes for their pronouncements? In one way or another, the premise for the earlier genres like bulls and briefs was that the pope was a judge or a dispenser of favors. He decided cases among contending parties, conferred benefits, issued executive orders regarding liturgical practice and similar matters, and on relatively rare occasions condemned heretical or offensive opinions. Insofar as the pope "taught," he did so principally by condemning a wrong opinion without providing a correct one or developing an alternative. A famous example of this type of teaching is Leo X's bull *Exsurge, Domine* (1520), condemning Martin Luther—it is simply a list of Luther's forty-one errors. The papal encyclicals of the nineteenth century certainly did not hesitate to condemn errors, and their often negative tone is an important aspect of their significance for Vatican II. But they also elaborated on the topics as would a teacher in the classroom. Addressed to all the bishops of the Catholic world, they enjoyed the status of authoritative doctrinal pronouncements.

The popes' increased use of the genre is indicative of its growing importance. From the two issued at the end of the eighteenth century by Pius VI over the course of twenty-four years and the one by his successor over twenty-three years, we move to thirty-eight by Pius IX in mid-century and then to seventy-five by his successor, Leo XIII. Many of these encyclicals, it is true, dealt with local problems or situations. But the simple increase in number indicates a new mode of papal teaching authority that committed the popes to an increasingly large number of positions on a wide range of issues. Moreover, even before but especially after the definition of infallibility, what popes said in their encyclicals tended to assume an irreversible quality.

As a consequence, Catholics increasingly looked to "Rome" not only as a court of final appeal but for answers to all questions. The invention of the telegraph and the telephone facilitated such appeals. "Rome" responded by issuing ever more pronouncements on a growing number of issues, most often through decrees of the various Congregations of the Curia, especially the Holy Office. That Congregation was the direct descendent of the Roman Inquisition, created in 1542 by Pope Paul III to deal with the spread of Lutheranism in the Papal States. By the twentieth century it was, literally, the "supreme" Congregation—*Suprema Congregatio*—the top office of the curial bureaucracy through which other Congregations often had to pass their decisions before they could act upon them. For the internal affairs of the church, the cardinal in charge of the Holy Office wielded power second only to that of the pope, in whose name he in fact exercised his authority. He was responsible, he could well believe, for the orthodoxy of the church.

These developments of the papal teaching authority, the Magisterium, are of great importance for Vatican II. Bishops at the council correctly perceived that the direction the council was headed on some important questions modified or seemingly contradicted the teaching found in papal and curial documents between 1832 and 1958. Encyclicals were the best known and most authoritative of these documents, but in the wake of the encyclicals the popes made use of other, similar forms, such as addresses to groups of pilgrims, to express their teaching and their views. Such forms of papal communication were virtually unknown until as late as the twentieth century. At that point they burst upon the scene in full force. The speeches and other documents of Pius XII, for instance, fill twenty volumes of five to six hundred pages each.[5] At the same time, the popes at least tacitly encouraged the Congregations of the Roman Curia, especially the Supreme Congregation of the Holy Office, to issue judgments on different matters.

"The Magisterium" increasingly came to mean not so much the teaching authority of the church as specifically the teaching authority of the popes and their Congregations.[6]

For Catholics the greatest ecclesiastical happening of the long nineteenth century was the almost unmitigated triumph of Ultramontanism, the concentration of authority in the papacy and the unquestioned recognition of other papal prerogatives. This was true not only on a high theological level but also on the level of a corporate consciousness that reached down to ordinary Catholics in the pews and touched them deeply. For the first time in history, thanks to the modern media, Catholics knew the name of the reigning pope and could recognize his face.

The Beleaguered Papacies of Gregory XVI and Pius IX

Nineteenth-century Europe experienced a see-saw effect between forms of republican government and restored monarchy, with France providing the most vivid and familiar example of the oscillation. In these upheavals nationalism became part of the Liberal ideology, and nowhere did it have more practical repercussions than in Italy. There, it looked to uniting the different political entities into one Italian nation. It animated the Risorgimento. Nowhere, therefore, was it more threatening to the church, for it implied the end of the Papal States, that huge swath of territory that stretched from the Kingdom of Naples all the way northeastward almost to Venice. For the popes, the struggle to maintain the States became a major focus in the struggle against "the modern world" and all that it stood for.

The church in Italy had been spared the destruction and carnage that during the Revolution in France took the lives of countless priests and nuns. Only with Napoleon did the popes experience palpable attacks on their status and their person. In 1796 French armies under Napoleon bore down on Italy, occupied the Papal States, seized for France many valuable works of art and other cultural artifacts, and finally forced Pope Pius VI to flee Rome, a virtual prisoner of the French. The pope died in 1799 in France at Valence.

In 1809 Napoleon officially annexed the Papal States to his empire. Pius VII, like his predecessor, Pius VI, soon found himself a prisoner in France. Only in 1814, when Napoleon was himself about to be deposed and exiled, was the pope able to return to Rome. Soon thereafter the Congress of Vienna restored the old order to Europe. It reinstated the French monarchy. and returned to the pope his kingdom. Europe had put behind it the Revolution and all that it stood for. It had restored, as best it could, the *ancien régime.*

But the reality of the situation was different—monarchies would never be quite the same or quite so stable. The pope had been restored to his kingdom, but his rule was ominously insecure. Especially in important cities like Ancona, Ravenna, Ferrara, and Bologna, the intellectuals, a well-to-do bourgeoisie, and the new professional and urban classes had little tolerance for "the government of priests" that almost totally excluded them from political power. This theocratic absolutism provoked ever fiercer resentments. Secret societies seemed to spring up everywhere and provided organization of a sort to "the Liberals." Because of the inadequacies of the papal police and even their collusion, these groups sometimes functioned almost openly.

Only with Gregory XVI (1831–1846) did the crisis explode. Elected after a difficult conclave that lasted fifty days, Gregory immediately faced insurrectionist armies that threatened Rome itself. The situation was truly desperate, with the Papal States on the verge of complete collapse. After a brief, vain attempt to put down the rebellion with the papal army, Gregory saved the situation only by calling on Austria to send in troops to defeat the rebels—and to stay thereafter to maintain order. France then sent soldiers to do the same, and the two armies did not withdraw until eight years later.

The pope's own subjects violently challenged his authority, and Gregory did not have the resources on his own to maintain his position. Most outside observers were convinced of the inability of the papal government to deal effectively with the economic, social, and political imperatives of the situation. The more the pope clamped down, the stricter the censorship of the press, and the more active the surveillance by the papal police, the worse the situation seemed to get.

For Gregory, the culprit responsible for this evil as well as for the general depravity of the times was "the terrible conspiracy of impious men," as he said in his first encyclical, *Mirari Vos.* These men were inspired by false principles and, worse, propagated them. He published the encyclical in 1832, a year after his election and just shortly after "the conspiracy" had been put down by the desperate expedient of calling in foreign troops. "Eventually," Gregory wrote, "We had to use Our God-given authority to restrain with the rod the great obstinacy of these men."

Although the encyclical began with the allusion to the rebellion in the Papal States, it was in fact occasioned by the writings of a few French Catholics, principally Felicité Robert de Lamennais, a prominent French priest who was trying to move the church away from what he considered outmoded ideas and an attachment to despotic regimes. Gregory did not mention Lamennais by name, but his were the false teachings the pope excoriated. Among them was the idea that changes needed to be made in the church. To this idea Gregory replied, "Nothing of the things appointed ought to be diminished, nothing changed." He dismissed as absurd the call "to propose a certain 'restoration and regeneration' for the church as though necessary for her safety and growth, as if she could be subject to defect or uncertainty or other misfortune." In particular he warned against "the abominable conspiracy against clerical celibacy . . . promoted by profligate philosophers, some of whom are even clerics."

One of the worst evils of the day was freedom of conscience: "The shameful font of indifferentism gives rise to the absurd and erroneous proposition that claims freedom of conscience must be maintained for everyone. It spreads ruin in sacred and civil affairs, though some repeat over and over again with the greatest impudence that some advantage accrues to religion from it. . . . Experience shows, even from earliest times, that cities renowned for wealth, dominion, and glory perished as a result of this single evil, namely immoderate freedom of opinion, licence of free speech and desire for novelty." In the next paragraph, not surprisingly, Gregory denounced freedom of the press.

The pope devoted more space to the obedience owed to princes than to any other subject. Among those princes he of course included himself, at the time so sorely pressed by the disobedience of his subjects. "Both divine and human law," he said, "cry out against those who strive by treason and sedition to drive the people from confidence in their princes and force them from their government." "Shameless lovers of liberty" even went so far as to advocate separation of church and state.[7]

The encyclical was a manifesto of attitudes and positions that characterized the papacy for the next fifty years and, in less extreme forms, even beyond. Better known than *Mirari Vos*, however, is the *Syllabus of Errors*, promulgated in 1864 by Gregory's successor, Pius IX (1846–1878). The scope of the *Syllabus* was broader but moved along the same lines, condemning eighty errors. Among the condemned opinions was the idea that "in our times" it was no longer proper or expedient for Catholicism to be the established religion of the state, with all others banned, as well as the opinion that non-Catholic immigrants into a Catholic country be allowed openly to practice their religion. Condemned as well was the opinion that people have full liberty to express their ideas. The final opinion the *Syllabus* rejected was the often-cited and resounding conclusion to the list: "That the Roman Pontiff can and should reconcile himself and make peace with progress, with Liberalism, and with modern culture."[8]

Gregory XVI and Pius IX assumed the roles of prophets in denouncing the evils of the times. They were hardly alone among religious figures in their fear of Liberalism, though that term meant somewhat different things in different contexts; nor by any means were all those who denounced it Catholics.[9] Protestant countries had not, however, experienced the chaos and radical upheavals of the Revolution and its wake the way Catholic countries had. Thus religious leaders there espoused some values found in the mix called Liberalism, such as elected governments and freedom of the press. To most Catholics, by contrast, Liberalism meant social and political subversion and its inevitable consequence, chaos. Where to turn to stabilize both church and society?

To the papacy. This was the answer given by Count Joseph de Maistre in *Du pape* (1819). De Maistre, though earlier influenced by Enlightenment ideas, renounced them after the Revolution to become an effective apologist for monarchy and for the supreme authority of the papacy. His argument was simple: there can be no order in society without religion, no religion without Catholicism, no Catholicism without the papacy, no effective papacy without sovereign and absolute papal authority.[10]

Although de Maistre's book was important in stimulating the increasing attention paid to papal prerogatives in the nineteenth century and to efforts to strengthen and expand them, in 1831 it got a boost with the election of Bartolomeo Alberto Cappellari as Pope Gregory XVI. In 1799 Cappellari published *The Triumph of the Holy See and the Church over the Attacks of Innovators,* which did not receive much attention until he became pope.[11] But after 1831 the book was frequently republished and translated. In it he explicitly adopted for the church the secular political concept of sovereignty. God himself was the sovereign ruler. This meant that the pope's sovereign fullness of authority—legislative, judicial, and executive—demanded absolute obedience. As revolutions were upsetting Europe, Cappellari exalted the church as immutable, infallible, and monarchical. Once he was elected pope as Gregory XVI, he did his best to act in accordance with these convictions.

The books by de Maistre and Cappellari were followed by others like them, creating a powerful wave that reached a crest in 1870 with Vatican I's definitions of primacy and infallibility. The definitions were the Magna Carta of the center. Ultramontanism increasingly came to define what it meant to be a Roman Catholic.[12]

The final paragraph in the long section of Vatican I's decree dealing with primacy could hardly be more categorical:

> So, then, if anyone says that the Roman pontiff has merely an office of supervision and guidance, and not the full and supreme power of jurisdiction over the whole church, and this not only in matters of faith and morals but also in those that concern the discipline and government of the church dispersed throughout the whole world; or that he has only the principal part but not the absolute fullness of this supreme power; or that this power of his is not ordinary and immediate both over all and each of the churches and over all and each of the pastors and faithful; let him be anathema.[13]

Pope Leo XIII (1878–1903)

In 1870 Italian forces seized Rome from the army of Pius IX, who was forced to surrender the city. Thus the nation of Italy was born as a constitutional monarchy with Rome as its capital. Pius, bitterly resentful, retreated to the Vatican area of the city, where the new government let him have full rein, undisturbed. He declared himself "the prisoner of the Vatican." When he died eight years later, the Italian government did its utmost to convey to the cardinals its intention to help ensure a peaceful and legitimate conclave, thus there was no need to hold the assembly outside Italy. Given the Vatican's location right in the capital of the new nation, there was, in fact, no way the Holy See could operate without the cooperation of the Italian government.

Despite the accommodations that the two sides had to make to each other, suspicion and distrust continued strong and fundamentally unabated. Even years after his election, Leo XIII, Pius's successor, on occasion felt so direly threatened, though without much evidence, that he seriously contemplated moving the papacy outside Italy.[14] Leo, not as intransigent as Pius, nonetheless continued Pius's policy of forbidding Italian Catholics to engage in any behavior that might suggest the legitimacy of the new nation, including holding public office and voting in elections.

As opposed to Liberalism in all its forms as were his predecessors, he nonetheless made decisions that mitigated some of their more extreme positions. Long before his election he seems to have come to the conclusion that condemnations of modern philosophies were insufficient unless some alternative was provided. This belief was behind the encyclical *Aeterni Patris,* which he issued the year after his election. In that document he in effect prescribed the study of the "philosophy" of Thomas Aquinas in Catholic schools and seminaries.[15] Aquinas was to replace the eclecticism that prevailed in those institutions and to put an end to the abuse that allowed professors to choose the authors to be studied: "A multiform system of this kind, which depends on the authority and choice of any professor, has a foundation open to change, and consequently gives us a philosophy not firm, stable, and robust like that of old but tottering and feeble."

Leo extolled the many benefits that would accrue to the church and society from the study of Thomas, who was "the special bulwark and glory of the Catholic faith." Among those benefits the political loomed large. Thomas provided the principles for guiding society aright—principles "on the true meaning of liberty, which at this time is running into license, on the divine origin of all authority, on laws and their force, on the paternal and just rule of princes, on obedience to the higher powers."[16]

Few papal pronouncements have had such success in securing a course of action, even though Leo and his advisers were, from our later perspective, woefully ignorant about the character and scope of medieval learning. The encyclical rode the tide of nineteenth-century Romantic enthusiasm for the Middle Ages that was by no means confined to Catholics, and it provided a stimulus for Catholics to claim the Middle Ages, now the "Ages of Faith," as peculiarly their own. Thus began the powerful Neo-Thomist movement in Catholicism.[17] Although it started as a conservative movement, it sparked Catholic research into the philosophies and theologies of medieval Scholasticism and led to results unexpected by its originators, which included the discovery that those phenomena were much richer and more complex than originally envisaged. Thomism, originally a club with which to beat modern philosophers beginning with Descartes, took on a life of its own, especially in France, Belgium, and Germany, and produced outstanding scholars.

Influential though Leo's encyclical was, it was not until after Vatican II that it had any real impact on the theological textbooks used in seminaries around the world. Although those books ultimately based their approach on the "commonplaces" *(loci communes)* applied to theology by Philipp Melanchthon, Melchor Cano, and other theologians of the sixteenth century, they took their classic shape in Rome in the mid-nineteenth century during the pontificate of Pius IX. Distinguished especially by their positivistic approach, their hostility to the principle of immanence, their abstraction from historical context, and their propositional formulation of truths, these "manuals," as they were sometimes called, stood apart in almost determined isolation not only from other forms of contemporary scholarship but to a large extent even from Neo-Scholasticism itself.[18]

Leo's travels throughout Europe before he became pope had made him keenly conscious of social unrest and the oppression of the working classes by their employers, aided and abetted by the *laissez-faire* economics that was often part of the Liberals' philosophy and agenda. The unrest of the 1880s that threatened anarchy and the growing influence of Socialism and Communism, already condemned by both Gregory XVI and Pius IX, led the pope to react as both a traditionalist and an innovator. He showed himself favorable to organizations of the working classes that strove to ameliorate their situation. He became convinced that limits had to be placed on the power of capital to dictate terms of employment without any considerations of just wages and humane working conditions.

On May 15, 1891, Leo issued the encyclical *Rerum Novarum,* "On the Condition of the Working Classes." While it proclaimed private property as a natural right, it insisted on its limits, on the necessity of a just wage for a day's work, and on decent working conditions; perhaps most remarkable, it accepted that workers had a right to organize themselves to achieve these goals. This meant that to some extent the social order was to be formed by movements coming from below as well as by authority and power descending from above. *Rerum Novarum* is a long encyclical in which points are argued and fully developed. Although it reckons Socialism and Communism as nonsolutions and as dangerous movements, it speaks in a placid style, free from rant.

Some Catholics denounced the encyclical as a betrayal by the church, which was supposed to stand with the establishment and never countenance something as dangerous as workers organizing themselves. According to them, moreover, Leo overstepped the bounds of his office by addressing questions outside the realm of faith and personal morality. With the encyclical, however, he managed to make his voice heard and set a precedent for similar interventions on social issues by Pope Pius XI in 1931 and John XXIII in 1963. All three popes addressed "modern" questions in ways that were something other than condemnations of the status quo and hankerings for the good old days of the *ancien régime.*

But Leo, a firm supporter of the *Syllabus of Errors,* was by no means innocent of such hankerings. In 1881 he published *Diuturnum,* an encyclical "on the origins of civil power." Although the document concedes that legitimate government can take different forms, on the surface it reads almost like a tract on the divine right of kings. Condemned again and again in it was the proposition that authority in the state is owed to the will of the people, for all such authority comes from God: "It will behoove citizens to submit themselves and to be obedient to rulers, as to God. . . . And by this means authority will remain far more firmly seated in its place."[19]

Yet eleven years later, Leo published *Au Milieu.* In that encyclical he urged French Catholics to unite and, though he does not say so explicitly, to take roles in the Third Republic, for only thus could its unjust and anti-Catholic laws be undone. *Au Milieu* is a cautious letter, clear in its condemnation of separation of church and state as an "absurdity," and it made little impact on the audience it addressed. Nonetheless, the letter is significant in its repeated statements that in the abstract, all three forms of government that France experienced in the nineteenth century—empire, monarchy, and republic—were good.[20] In 1901, two years before his death, Leo resolved a bitter dispute among Catholics by allowing the legitimacy of the term "Christian Democracy" while insisting on a conservative definition of it.[21]

Pius X (1903–1914)

In 1905 Leo's successor, Pius X, had to deal with a new anticlerical government in France, and in 1910 he had to deal with the same in Portugal. These new governments breathed the fire of a rabid anticlericalism and moved far beyond anything that could be considered neutral regarding Catholicism. As only to be expected, the pope responded in each case with encyclicals reminding the bishops that "the Roman Pontiffs have never ceased, as circumstances required, to refute and condemn the doctrine of the separation of church and state."[22]

In *Vehementer Nos,* his encyclical in 1906 to the French clergy and lay people on the occasion of the actions of the new government, he reiterated the hierarchical structure of the church, "a society comprising two categories of persons, the pastors and the flock." The duty of the former, which holds all authority in the church, is to direct "the multitude." It follows that "the one duty of the multitude is to allow themselves to be led and, like a docile flock, to follow the pastors."[23]

Just two year earlier Pius had launched a project for the codification of canon law, completed in 1917, which had a great impact on how the church conducted itself. The Code of Canon Law was the first such one-volume, handy organization of ecclesiastical ordinances in history, and it in effect ended the tradition of customary law in the church. It professed to do nothing more than put existing legislation into a manageable order, but, produced in the wake of Vatican I and under the vigilant eye of Pius X, the code invariably interpreted that legislation in ways that shored up or even augmented papal authority, as in Canon 222 giving the popes control of councils.

Similarly symptomatic of this tendency was Canon 329, which affirmed that the pope appointed bishops in the church. Although the Holy See continued to respect the provisions of concordats and long-standing local traditions that qualified this bald assertion, the canon marked the definitive abandonment of the traditional principle of free election of bishops, for which the popes had at times fought so bitterly. Thus the code of 1917, when viewed in its full scope, marked "the culmination of the process of centralization in the life of the church."[24] One of its unintended consequences, moreover, was an intensification in the church of a juridical approach to a wide variety of issues, including many that fell outside the scope of the code proper.

Besides the emergence of an aggressive Liberalism, the church in the nineteenth century also had to contend with the new enthusiasm for historical approaches to almost every academic discipline. This development, long in the making, moved the discipline of history from its older base in rhetoric and moral philosophy to more controlled methods of research, which at a certain point began to be described as "scientific." The methods professed objectivity in evaluating evidence and freedom from contamination by apologetic concerns and by what the maintenance of received opinions might require. History was no longer an edifying tale celebrating past achievements or deploring past failures. It strove to be a critical discipline that analyzed the past especially in terms of changes that explained the present.

Several Catholic historians emerged with prominence, including Johannes Jansen, Johann Ignaz von Döllinger, Louis Duchesne, and Lord Acton, but the greatest lights were German Lutherans, French and Italian Liberals, and others unfavorably disposed toward the Catholic Church. Try as they might to be objective, these historians operated out of assumptions about religion and Christianity that made it difficult for them to appreciate Catholicism and more often than not made them outright hostile to it.

Since the sixteenth century, moreover, Catholic historical writing had emphasized the continuity of the church with its past, whereas Protestant or Liberal historians were just as obsessed with discontinuities. Luther, Calvin, and other Reformers accused the church of being so discontinuous with the past that it had perverted the Gospel message. Catholics responded with vehement denials and worked, as the documents of the Council of Trent show, to prove that what the church did and taught was essentially identical with the apostolic age. These two historiographical traditions, in both extreme and modified forms, continued strong well into the twentieth century and, in some circles, up to the present. One focused on change, the other on continuity, sometimes to the point of effectively denying change or, more generally, being oblivious to its import—R. G. Collingwood's "substantialism."[25]

In the nineteenth century a major crisis occurred with the definition of papal infallibility. As the council was being prepared, word spread that it would not only define papal infallibility but also declare the *Syllabus* a dogma. The historical problems such definitions implied were countless. They stirred Döllinger, priest and professor of church history at the University of Munich, to write, under pseudonyms, formidable criticisms of the council and infallibility: *Letters of Janus* (1869) and *Letters of Quirinus* (1869–1870). When after the council he refused to accept the definition of infallibility, he was excommunicated by the archbishop of Munich, an act that precipitated the formation of a Catholic Church in schism from Rome—the Old Catholic Church. Most of the original members of that church were from the intelligentsia, with historians the largest single profession represented. Two-thirds of Catholics teaching history in German universities became Old Catholics, "a disaster for the Roman Catholic study of history."[26]

Bismarck, the German chancellor, did not lack reasons for trying to bring Catholics to heel in the new German Reich, but the definitions of papal primacy and especially papal infallibility provided him with yet another excuse to launch his persecution of Catholics, the *Kulturkampf*. In 1874 he published a circular letter in which he maintained, among other things, that the council's definitions had made the bishops nothing more than tools *(Werkzeuge)* of the pope, who now had more power than any absolute monarch of the past.

The German bishops answered him in a joint statement in early 1875 in which they insisted that the church could not be compared to an earthly kingdom nor the pope to an earthly king, that the bishops' authority was not in any way diminished by the decree on papal primacy, and that papal infallibility extended only to what Scripture and Tradition taught. In sum, the definitions had changed nothing, "not the least thing."[27] They were, it seems, a non-happening.

Even more threatening than the work of church historians was the application of the new methods to the most sacred text of all, the Bible.[28] David Friedrich Strauss of the University of Tübingen was more a disciple of Hegel than a historian or exegete, but in 1835 he wrote *Leben Jesu*, in which he applied "myth theory" to the life of Jesus. Strauss denied the historical foundation of all supernatural elements in the gospels. His book, roundly denounced by Protestant and Catholic clergy, created a sensation. Despite its glaring faults it could not be ignored, and the discussion that swirled around it deeply affected subsequent biblical scholarship.

Some twenty years later another "life of Jesus" appeared, this time from the former seminarian Joseph Ernest Renan in France. This *Vie de Jésus* similarly rejected the possibility of supernatural elements in the story of Jesus and portrayed him as simply a charming Galilean preacher. In 1862 Renan was named professor of Hebrew at the Collège de France, but the uproar over his book was so great that he was dismissed two years later, the very year an English translation was published in London.

Other scholars began making use of historical, archeological, and philological approaches but came to far less radical conclusions. Among them was Marie-Joseph Lagrange, a French priest of the Dominican order, who after philological studies at the University of Vienna single-handedly founded in 1890 a center of biblical studies in Jerusalem, l'École Biblique.[29] It was the first school and research institute in the Catholic world that programmatically made use of the new methods, and in 1892 it began publishing its own journal, *Revue Biblique*. Although controversy dogged Lagrange's steps, he emerged in learned circles as the leading Catholic exegete.

In 1893 Leo XIII issued *Providentissimus Deus,* an encyclical on the study of the Bible in which he commended the time-tried methods and warned of the dangers of the new. In this long document he never once encouraged the reading of the Bible by the laity. In 1902, the year before his death, he established the Pontifical Biblical Commission, whose function was, according to its founding documents, to promote a thorough study of the word of God and ensure that it "be shielded not only from every breath of error but even from every rash opinion." The commission began issuing responses, uniformly conservative, to questions about specific interpretations. In 1906, for instance, it rejected the proposition that Moses was not the author of the first five books of the Bible, the Pentateuch, an issue that had become almost a litmus test of orthodoxy for exegetes.[30]

Advocacy among Catholics of a sometimes undiscriminating adoption of the new critical methods of exegesis became part of an amorphous and much broader phenomenon known as Modernism.[31] The term originated in 1904 with Umberto Benigni, a minor official of the papal Curia who, besides being an ardent monarchist, was an archenemy of every philosophical and historical approach to problems that did not fit with his ultraconservative presuppositions. The term that gave birth to the definition of Modernism could thus not have come from a more hostile source. From the very beginning it prejudiced the understanding of what was at stake and almost hopelessly confused the issues.

This broadly inclusive label helps explain why it is difficult to find a common thread linking the so-called Modernists beyond their desire to help the church reconcile itself with what they felt was best in intellectual culture as it had evolved into the present. They were the protagonists or beneficiaries of a little-noticed but remarkable outburst of Catholic intellectual ferment that especially in France had been under way since the 1880s. A general but not universally accepted premise of the movement (if it can be called that) was the pervasiveness of change and the need to reckon with it. This implied a teleological attitude toward history, finding the meaning of the historical process in its issue rather than in its origins.

The Modernists were skeptical of metaphysics and critical of the intellectualism of Scholasticism/Thomism. Some saw democracy as the system to which society had evolved. They advocated a Christian Democracy in which the laity, freed from the supervision of the hierarchy, would assume their rightful responsibility for the common good. Still others saw Christian truth as founded on intuition and religious experience that were then articulated into symbols and rituals.

The storm broke on July 3, 1907. On that day the Holy Office issued the decree *Lamentabili,* which formulated and condemned sixty-five propositions supposedly held by the Modernists. Number 11, for instance, denied that the Bible was inspired to the extent that every part of it was utterly free from error, and number 44 asserted that marriage evolved as a sacrament only later in Christian history. Symptomatic of the supposed threat of Modernism was the condemnation of the proposition: "The state to which learning has progressed demands a reform of Christian teaching about God, creation, revelation, the person of the Word Incarnate, and of redemption.[32]

Two months later came Pius X's encyclical *Pascendi Dominici Gregis.* The pope presented a synthesis of the teachings of the Modernists in which he described the heresy as resting on two false principles, the rejection of metaphysical reason, which led to skepticism regarding rational proofs for God's existence, and the rejection of the supernatural, which led to the idea that Christian doctrine was derived solely from religious experience. The matter was extraordinarily grave, Pius said, because the "partisans of error" were to be found not among the church's enemies but "in her very bosom and heart." For that reason they were "the most pernicious of all the adversaries of the church."

Pius recognized the multiformity of the Modernist movement, commenting that the "Modernist sustains and comprises within himself many personalities; he is a philosopher, a believer, a theologian, a historian, a critic, an apologist, a reformer." Modernists hold that "dogma is not only able, but ought to evolve and to be changed, for at the head of what the Modernists teach is their doctrine of evolution. To the laws of evolution everything is subject—dogma, church, worship, the books we receive as sacred, even faith itself." According to them the conserving force in the church is Tradition, which is represented by figures holding religious authority, but then comes "that most pernicious doctrine that would make of the laity a factor of progress in the church."

The Modernists, Pius continued, also teach that "ecclesiastical government requires reformation in all its branches, but especially in its disciplinary and dogmatic parts . . . a share in ecclesiastical government should therefore be given to the lower ranks of the clergy and even to the laity, and authority should be decentralized. The Roman Congregations, especially the Congregations of the Index and the Holy Office, are to be reformed." In view of its thoroughgoing perversity, Modernism is not so much a heresy as "the synthesis of all heresies."

What are the remedies to be applied? First, greater insistence on making the philosophy of St. Thomas the base upon which the theological edifice was to be built. Second, anybody found "to be imbued with Modernism" as well as anybody found "criticizing Scholasticism, the Holy Father . . . [or showing] a love of novelty in history, archaeology, biblical exegesis" was to be excluded "without compunction" from all teaching positions. Third, bishops should censor all publications, drive out of their dioceses, "even by solemn interdict, any pernicious books that may be in circulation there," and make sure booksellers not stock them. Since Modernists used public gatherings to spread their ideas, priests were to be forbidden to gather for meetings except on very rare occasions, for just reasons, and only with the bishop's permission. Each diocese was immediately to establish a "Vigilance Council" whose function was to inform the bishop of anything or anybody possibly tainted with the heresy. To ensure observance of these provisions, all bishops and heads of religious orders were every three years to submit a sworn report on how they were being implemented.[33] Three years later, to ensure the uprooting of the heresy, Pius made all clerics, especially teachers of philosophy and theology, swear a long oath to uphold provisions of *Lamentabili* and *Pascendi*. The oath was abrogated only in 1967.

For the sweep of its accusations, the accusatory style of its language, and especially the severity of its provisions, *Pascendi* had few, if any, precedents in documents emanating from the papacy. A veritable purge followed. No doubt, some of the tenets of the Modernists could not be squared with Christian belief no matter how broadly that belief might be interpreted, but in the wake of the encyclical the innocent got stigmatized and their careers ruined. The definition of Modernism was so general, virtually equated with "any novelty," that it could be applied to almost any work of any philosophical or historical school. Excommunications, dismissals from office, and banning of books reached epidemic proportions. The young Angelo Roncalli, future pope John XXIII, was investigated for a lecture on faith and science that he delivered at the seminary in Bergamo.[34]

In the meantime Benigni, favored by the pope and now holding office in the Vatican's Secretariat of State, organized a secret society that soon spawned cells in a number of countries. This *Sodalitium Pianum* (Sodality of Pius V), commonly known as *La Sapinière,* sponsored the most extreme Ultramontanist and monarchist publications. Through its founder, it established an international network of informers to expose people who did not share Benigni's views.[35] Pius's successor, Benedict XV, finally suppressed *La Sapinière* in 1921, but Benigni had meanwhile published the names of suspects in his organization's journals.

Two years after *Lamentabili* and *Pascendi,* Pius founded in Rome the Pontifical Biblical Institute, which was modeled somewhat on the École Biblique in Jerusalem but intended as a conservative counterweight to it.[36] With that aim he entrusted the institute to the Jesuits and gave it authority to grant pontifical degrees. For some years the Biblicum, as it is generally known (Pontificium Institutum Biblicum), lived up to the conservative hopes Pius placed in it, but with the passing of the years the professors had to come to terms with the new methods and utilize them. In that regard they represent a pattern in Catholic "sacred studies" that would be verified in every field.

The Liturgical Movement, for instance, which had gained so much strength by the middle of the twentieth century and led to the changes in worship initiated by Vatican II, could not have had a more conservative, restorationist origin.[37] Prosper Guéranger (1805–1875) was a key figure, representative of the generations that after the French Revolution felt a heavy responsibility for trying to repair the ravage. Convictions were widespread in these generations that the eclipse of community resulting from the rise of individualism was a great source of evil in the modern world. Remedies were to be found in past models.

In 1833 Guéranger, Benedictine monk and zealous Ultramontanist, refounded the monastery of Solesmes in France with the idea of providing a model of Christian community united around the liturgy of the church, whose beauty would raise to God the souls of all who participated in it or witnessed it. In so doing, Guéranger made the official liturgy of the church—the Mass and the liturgical hours like Lauds and Vespers—the center of worship and moved piety away from the many other services and devotions like novenas and Stations of the Cross that had proliferated in Catholicism since the late Middle Ages.

Guéranger reached an international audience with his immensely important publications, especially *L'année liturgique* (1841–1866), a nine-volume devotional commentary on the feasts and solemnities of the church year that appeared in English translation in 1867–1871. At about the same time at Solesmes, Augustin Gontier, Paul Jausions, and later other monks such as Joseph Pothier worked to replace the "theatrical" music of the baroque and Romantic eras with the almost forgotten Gregorian Chant as the genuine music for the liturgy.

The monk symbolized for most people in the nineteenth century the quintessence of the Middle Ages; hence Solesmes and the other monasteries it directly or indirectly generated fitted nicely into the Romantic revival of gothic in all its forms and the creation of the image of the medieval period as the Age of Faith.[38] Monasteries more or less modeled on Solesmes or at least indirectly inspired by it sprang up in Belgium, Germany, and elsewhere, including North America, where Conception Abbey in Conception, Missouri, and St. John's in Collegeville, Minnesota, would later be important in the Liturgical Movement. Such monasteries revived the notion of the monk-scholar whose life outside the hours spent celebrating the liturgy were spent on the study of texts, which made some of the monks formidable historical scholars, not always unaffected by the new methods. As the texts were studied, the patristic era began to replace the Middle Ages as the more normative liturgical model.

Just as when Pius X founded the Biblicum in Rome he had an impact on the future of scholarship that frustrated the ultraconservative goal he had in mind, he played a similar role in the Liturgical Movement. He issued a series of decrees whose ultimate goal was to rally the faithful against the spirit of the age by fostering modes of worship that purportedly prevailed in the Middle Ages or patristic era and that would effect the spiritual regeneration of society.[39] Implicit in the decrees, therefore, was the principle that changes could legitimately be made to make the present conform to a normative past.

During the second half of the nineteenth century, the cry for "sacred music" in the liturgy, as clearly distinct from profane music, swelled ever stronger in certain circles in France, Germany, and Italy. This development prompted Pius X to issue in 1903 an important document titled *Inter*

Sollicitudines, which called for the use of Gregorian Chant in ordinary parishes and for the congregation's participation in singing it. In second place the document commended the sacred polyphony of Palestrina and his successors.

Because Gregorian Chant and polyphony were musical styles with which very few people were familiar, this provision was not easily or widely implemented. Nonetheless, by asserting that his goal was to move the members of the congregation from a passive to a more active role in liturgical celebrations, from praying their rosary during Mass or reading their novena prayers to paying attention to the liturgical action itself, he enunciated a principle that the decree on the liturgy at Vatican II would take to its logical conclusion.[40]

If Pius X's promotion of chant and polyphony had only limited success in influencing how Catholics worshiped, his success in promoting frequent, even daily, reception of the Eucharist was close to spectacular. During his pontificate, the Holy See issued a number of documents related to the Eucharist, the most important of which was *Sacra Tridentina Synodus,* published on December 20, 1905. By making frequent reception of the Eucharist the norm for Catholic piety, the decree definitively settled a longstanding debate between those advocating frequency and those opposed to it. In 1917 the substance of the decree was incorporated into the Code of Canon Law (canon 863), an indisputable indication of its importance.

At the time the decree was promulgated, most Catholics received the Eucharist only once, twice, or a few more times per year, but by the eve of Vatican II weekly reception had become standard for large numbers in a typical Sunday congregation. Daily reception was no longer uncommon or considered strange. For many people, "going to Mass" now regularly included receiving Holy Communion. This change in the pattern of worship, gradual but dramatic, gave "active participation" a truly substantive form.

The Benedictines continued to play a crucial role in the Liturgical Movement, but by the second and third decades of the twentieth century others were studying ancient liturgical sources and relating them to the present, a development similar to the revival of patristic studies that occurred at the same time. Moreover, the intimate relationship between liturgy and ecclesiology was becoming ever clearer: how one understood liturgy was key to how one understood church, and vice versa. In that regard scholars began to call upon the pioneering work of theologians like Johann Adam Möhler (1796–1838) and Franz Anton Staudenmaier (1800–1856) of the so-called Tübingen School and Matthias Scheeben (1835–1888) of Cologne, who laid the groundwork for the connection.[41]

If Guéranger deserves credit for originating the revival of interest in the liturgy, the Belgian Dom Lambert Beauduin (1873–1960) deserves credit for launching the movement and promoting effective measures to bring it to Catholics in the pews.[42] At an important conference at Malines in 1909 he called for full and active participation of all the faithful in every aspect of the church's life and ministry, especially in the liturgy. That same year he helped launch in both a French and a Flemish version a monthly entitled *Liturgical Life,* which soon had more than seventy thousand subscribers. With the support of Cardinal Désiré Joseph Mercier of Malines, he developed a plan to have the Roman Missal translated into the vernacular, thus putting it in the hands of the laity. For the first time, therefore, the laity could follow the service by reading in their own language the same text as the priest. Beauduin saw the liturgy, moreover, as a medium in which Anglicans, Orthodox, and Catholics could meet in friendship. Thus, like Mercier, he was a Catholic pioneer in ecumenism. What especially drove Beauduin and other leaders of the movement, however, was the conviction that the liturgy, when properly and fully appropriated by the faithful, was not simply in principle the center of the devotional life of Catholics but the church's most powerful instrument for the spiritual rebirth of society at large.

Inspired by the Belgian example, other countries translated the Missal into the vernacular. By the early decades of the twentieth century, therefore, the movement was having an impact on ordinary Catholics, who were exhorted to "pray the Mass," that is, follow the words and actions of the ceremony and not use the time to read other prayers or simply daydream. In 1932 Joseph F. Stedman, a priest of the diocese of Brooklyn, published *My Sunday Missal,* an inexpensive and easy-to-use little volume that fast became a best seller. By the 1940s it had found its way into the hands of millions of English-speaking Catholics around the world. Soon translated into all the major European languages, as well as into Chinese and Japanese, it (and the other books like it) began a momentous shift in how ordinary Catholics understood what they were doing when they "attended Mass."[43] For many people the next logical step after reading the prayers of the Mass in the vernacular was to ask why the priest was still required to read them in Latin.

Decades before Leo XIII published *Aeterni Patris* decreeing St. Thomas, and therefore the Scholastic system, as normative for Catholic theology, Jacques-Paul Migne, a diocesan priest and publishing entrepreneur, was busy in Paris bringing forth monumental editions of different kinds of ecclesiastical texts. None of these editions could compare in impact with his monumental *Patrologia*. Divided into two parts, the *Patrologia Latina* (1844–1864), a corpus of Latin Christian writings from the second to the early thirteenth century, ran to 221 volumes, and the *Patrologia Graeca* (1856–1866), a corpus of Greek writings (with facing Latin translations) from the late first century until 1439, ran to 162 volumes. For the first time scholars had at their disposal in easily accessible form a magnificent range of authors and texts, many of which they earlier could have consulted only in partial and widely scattered selections. Now every library of any substance possessed these texts not as rare books stored carefully away but as resources sitting on open shelves.

Nothing was more important than Migne's *Patrologia* in promoting the study of the Fathers from this time forward. As that study was pursued, the discrepancies in style, focus, and even content between patristic and Scholastic theology became even clearer and reached a point of special acuity by the middle of the twentieth century in "la nouvelle théologie." The denigrating term "new theology" originated in 1942, it seems, with Pietro Parente, an assessor in the Holy Office, who would play an important role in Vatican II. A few days before his negative judgment appeared in the Vatican newspaper, *L'Osservatore Romano,* the Holy Office placed Chenu's work *Une école de théologie: Le Saulchoir* on the Index of Forbidden Books.[44]

Nonetheless, the movement continued to grow. In an article in *Études* in 1946, Jean Daniélou, a French Jesuit theologian, sounded the manifesto for the "new theology."[45] What the present age required, according to Daniélou, was a theology that not only encompassed the great mysteries of the Christian faith but also, unlike Neo-Scholasticism, provided spiritual nourishment. Such a theology would take account of the turn of modern thought to historicity and subjectivity and would draw its Christian inspiration from a return to three great, interlocking sources—the Bible, the liturgy, and the Fathers. In his book *Bible et liturgie,* published five years later, Daniélou illustrated at some length what he meant.[46]

The *ressourcement* of the "new theology" was thus broader than a return to patristic sources, and the force driving it was the quest for texts that would nourish the soul. Yet study of the Fathers and assimilation of their approach to doctrine that emphasized its relevance for one's spiritual life held a preeminent place in the theological ferment that animated especially Jesuit and Dominican theologians in France in mid-century. The year after Daniélou wrote, his Jesuit colleague Henri de Lubac put the matter succinctly: "Let us abide by the outlook of the Fathers."[47] The two of them had just a few years earlier launched a new series of volumes that published patristic texts with facing French translations. It bore the suggestive title *Sources Chrétiennes* (Christian Sources).

This adaptation of patristic outlook and language became widespread among younger theologians in Europe. It was an alternative or an antidote to what they saw as the spiritually arid and overly intellectualized theology officially promoted by the church. It was, for one thing, more in accord with the "turn to the subject" that had preoccupied philosophers ever since Kant and that provided an opening for religious experience in theological method.

In September 1962, just before the council was to open, Cardinal Frings of Cologne sent a memorandum to Cardinal Amleto Cicognani concerning the first seven documents the council fathers had received for discussion and decision in the opening weeks of Vatican II. In the memorandum Frings argued that the texts should avoid the style of textbook theology and "speak instead the vital language of Scripture and the Church Fathers." The author of Frings's memorandum was Joseph Ratzinger.[48]

Patristic theology originated in pastoral settings and was for the most part embedded in sermons or occasional treatises. It was based primarily on the principles of classical rhetoric, the art of touching hearts and minds in order to win inner assent. It was thus "pastoral" and spiritual, not academic, in its orientation. It focused on the big truths of faith like the Trinity and the Incarnation and proposed an ideal of the Christian life based on the Beatitudes and the Gifts of the Holy Spirit. The Greek Fathers in particular emphasized the great dignity of creatures created in the image and likeness of God and, by the Incarnation, raised to an even greater dignity, a deification, through grace.

An important study of the patristic era, published in 1833, long before Migne's editions, was *The Arians of the Fourth Century,* by the young Anglican divine John Henry Newman. His research and wide reading alerted Newman to the difference between patristic positions on dogmatic matters and the nineteenth-century teaching of both Roman Catholicism and Liberal Protestantism. Newman's background in the Fathers helped him much later in life to reinstate the human subject in theological discourse, especially in his book *A Grammar of Assent* (1870), which presaged and influenced later developments in theology along that line.[49]

Newman's conversion to Catholicism in 1845 was followed almost immediately by his *Essay on the Development of Christian Doctrine,* in which he used different analogies to show how teachings evolved while remaining fundamentally true to their origins. The book, still the classic on the subject, is ironical in that it led Newman into a church that on the official and unofficial level was denying that such evolution took place. In 1904 the highly respected and prolific Jesuit Louis Billot, for instance, published the first edition of *On the Immutability of Tradition against the Modern Heresy of Evolutionism (evolutionismum),* which was reprinted several times over the next few decades.[50] Newman's book, however, had put the problem of change on the stage of theological debate to a degree unknown before. The problem would remain there to become a central point of contention in Vatican II. The book appeared just ten years before Darwin's *On the Origin of Species.*

By the middle decades of the twentieth century, the problem for Catholicism of historical approaches to sacred subjects was made even more acute by a proliferation of important studies done from a historical perspective. In 1932, for instance, the Austrian Jesuit Josef Andreas Jungmann published a book confirming that the form of the sacrament of Penance as practiced in the medieval and modern church was unknown in the patristic era.[51] Sixteen years later, in 1948, he published his ground-breaking and highly influential *Missarum Solemnia,* a study of the history of the Mass of the Roman rite showing the changes that accrued to it over time. The fact that the book was almost immediately translated from the original German into other major languages, including English, shows how important it was seen to be.[52] In this instance, as in others, the logical conclusion: if it was not always thus, it need not always be thus.

In 1955 Brian Tierney published *Foundations of the Conciliar Theory,* in which he showed, among other things, that in the Middle Ages reputable canonists assumed that responsibility for the good of the church was distributed among various offices and corporations, each of which had its own intrinsic (not delegated) authority.[53] The episcopal office reigned above the others. Bishops, especially when assembled in synod or council, were along with the pope the most important repositories for ecclesiastical authority. Tierney implicitly demonstrated that the "Conciliarism" that saved the papacy at the Council of Constance could not automatically be identified with the Conciliarism that claimed a council was in every circumstance superior to the pope.

The return to the sources was thus throwing light on the church itself. If Tierney's study concerned the structure of authority in the church, Yves Congar's book on reform in the church, published just a few years earlier, looked more to its inner mystery and spiritual message.[54] In it Congar showed that reform had been a recurring—and healthy and necessary—feature of church life through the ages. He then argued that at present the church needed to "adapt and revise" certain aspects of its life. To suggest that the church needed "reform," even as cautiously as Congar put it, was bold in the 1950s because the term had become so closely associated with Protestantism. Although Congar was not concerned with church structures as such, he consistently referred to the church as "the people of God," which would become a favorite image for the church at Vatican II.

The historical approach made significant inroads into the Neo-Thomist movement. In 1919 Étienne Gilson published his first book on Aquinas, inaugurating a long and brilliant career of studies on aspects of medieval philosophy and theology that showed its diversity and historical development.[55] Ten years later he helped found an academic center in Toronto that in 1939 became the Pontifical Institute of Mediaeval Studies, where historical methods were applied to every facet of medieval life. Gilson's admiration for Thomas never wavered, but he helped move him from the status of an icon to a figure in real history. As his friend Henri de Lubac relates it, Gilson despised the approach taken by seminary textbooks for "its out-of-date methods, its lack of historical sense, the ignorance of or the snobbish inability to understand the latest research, the need to create heretics to cut up—in short, he criticized a spirit that was taking shape in systems that were becoming more rigid the more unfaithful they were to tradition, a spirit quite other than the Angelic Doctor's." Gilson's spontaneous expression of his views, which underscores how little impact even the best of Neo-Thomism had on seminary instruction, took place in 1959, the year Pope John announced the council.[56]

Gilson's career was so spectacular that it overshadowed that of other important Catholic scholars like Martin Grabmann and Joseph de Ghellinck, who took a similarly historical approach. By the 1940s leadership in this tradition passed especially to French Dominicans like Marie-Dominique Chenu. In the meantime Jacques Maritain, another layman like Gilson but, unlike him, a convert to Catholicism, spearheaded a different trajectory that applied Thomistic principles to contemporary problems in ways that foreshadowed themes of Vatican II. A prolific writer, he became an immensely influential figure among Catholics but was also respected by many of his secular peers. As his career took off, he spent almost as much time in North America, especially in the United States, as he did in France.

Maritain's *Antimoderne* argued that Catholicism was by definition adaptable to different cultures and situations.[57] Time marches on, he in effect said, and it was silly to try to remake the world in a medieval pattern, as he believed many Catholics were hoping to do. In *True Humanism,* one of his most popular books, he used a broad brush to contrast a "Christian humanism" with other varieties current in the world. He exalted it as the only humanism that reveals and makes operative the full dignity of the human person. It was a humanism that, for all its transcendent dimension, implied engagement with the world in which we live.[58]

His wife, Raïssa, was a daughter of Russian Jewish immigrants to France, and this made him an especially potent spokesman against anti-Semitism well before the Holocaust.[59] From 1945 to 1948 he was French ambassador to the Holy See, where he formed a life-long friendship with Giovanni Battista Montini and tried to persuade Pius XII to issue a forthright condemnation of the Holocaust.[60] As a passionate defender of the doctrine of natural rights, he collaborated in the formulation of the United Nations Universal Declaration of Human Rights in 1948.

Meanwhile, yet another development gained momentum among scholars devoted to Thomas. In 1922 the Belgian Jesuit Joseph Maréchal came out with his five-volume work *La pointe de départ de la metaphysique,* which launched an influential movement soon known as Transcendental Thomism. Like others at the time, Maréchal opened the door to a more subject-oriented and historically sensitive theology. He made possible even for Thomists an appropriation of a philosopher like Martin Heidegger, whose starting point was the human person as existing in time and history and as concerned with what that situation meant for life's choices. By the 1950s Karl Rahner had become the most notable exponent of this brand of Thomism. Other Dominican and Jesuit theologians, however, vigorously opposed their confreres like Chenu and Rahner, who to them seemed to be purveying precisely the errors from which the founders of the Neo-Thomist movement had wanted to protect Catholic theology. They assessed what they saw as thinly disguised Modernism.

Writing at the same time as Maréchal was the Jewish philosopher and religious thinker Martin Buber. Early on Buber published two works that radically challenged the objective and impersonal frame of reference in which Western philosophy traditionally addressed even human issues—*I and Thou* (1923) and the essay "Dialogue" (1929). In later works Buber went on to criticize Aristotle and Aquinas for the abstract character of their systems, which removed individuals from real-life situations where they faced choices: "Aquinas knows no special problem and no special problematic of human life, such as Augustine experienced and expressed with trembling heart."[61]

For the abstractions of great philosophical systems Buber substituted relationships in which mutuality and the sharing of experience and beliefs were the hallmarks. In such relationships the privileged form of communication was dialogue. He defined dialogue in different ways but most tellingly as "conversation . . . from one open-hearted person to another open-hearted person."[62] Just as in "la nouvelle théologie" rhetoric was opposed to dialectic, in Buber dialogue is also opposed to dialectic as its polar opposite. Dialogue is for him not a ploy, not a technique, but the surface expression of core values.

Buber's works attracted a wide readership, and they directly and indirectly influenced Catholic thinkers. The year before the council opened, the young theologian Hans Urs von Balthasar published *Martin Buber and Christianity,* in which he praised Buber as "one of the most creative minds of our age" and "the originator of the 'dialogical principle.'"[63] But the idea was in wide circulation. In 1960 the American Jesuit theologian Gustave Weigel noted that "dialogue" was appearing so frequently in newspapers and journals that it was beginning to seem "cultish and faddish." Weigel wrote before Vatican II opened, before dialogue assumed such a prominent and symptomatic role in the council, and before it acted as catalyst for other horizontal words like "partnership" and "cooperation." No single word, with the possible exception of *aggiornamento,* would be more often invoked to indicate what the council was all about.

From Pius XI to the Eve of Vatican II

On February 6, 1922, Achille Ratti was elected pope on the fourteenth ballot and took the name Pius XI. Intelligent and resolute, he had to face the worldwide economic and social unrest caused by the Great Depression, as well as the difficult political situations that followed World War I and led to the rise of Communism in Russia and Fascism in Germany and Italy. The very year Pius was elected, Mussolini staged his famous March on Rome and was invited by King Victor Emmanuel III to form a government, soon transformed into a dictatorship. The pope at first welcomed this turn of events as stabilizing the political situation, and he was able finally to resolve with Mussolini's government "the Roman Question," which meant the establishment of Vatican City in 1929 as an independent, sovereign state. In the concordat that was part of the agreement, Catholicism was granted special status as the official religion of Italy, even though other churches were permitted to function.

Some commentators interpreted these developments as another sign of the propensity of the Holy See to favor despotic, right-wing regimes. In 1926, however, Pius condemned in France the rabidly monarchist and nationalistic movement *Action Française* and was soon disillusioned by Mussolini and even more so by Hitler. His encyclical *Mit brennender Sorge,* smuggled into Germany in 1937, was an indictment of the regime. When his pontificate ended in 1939, the relationship between the Holy See and those two governments, right on the eve of World War II, was extremely tense. Pius was perhaps even more afraid of Communism, and he saw the church as the only real bulwark against it. His encyclical *Quadragesimo Anno* (1931) offered a critique of both capitalism and socialism, including Communism, and was an important and fitting follow-up to Leo XIII's *Rerum Novarum.*

Consonant with that encyclical was the pope's enthusiasm for "Catholic Action," which he defined as the participation of the laity in the work of the hierarchy—in works of social assistance, in the marketplace, and in the founding of Catholic journals and newspapers. Although he never devoted an encyclical exclusively to the subject, he returned to it again and again in his addresses and correspondence. He encouraged different forms of action for different countries, and without doubt he gave impetus to the proliferation of lay organizations throughout the world, thus laying the groundwork for the focus on the laity that would prevail at Vatican II.

Although a number of younger Catholic scholars, almost all of them clerics, were pursuing studies that could be considered at least tinged with Modernism, they were doing so in a discreet way that allowed them to escape condemnation. Pius XI was not constrained, therefore, to issue any blanket condemnations along the lines of the *Syllabus* or *Lamentabili.* On specific issues, however, he took a strong line. Two proscriptions would be particularly significant for what happened at Vatican II. In 1928 he condemned the ecumenical movement with the encyclical *Mortalium Animos,* and in 1930 he condemned all forms of birth control in *Casti Connubii.*

In *Mortalium Animos* he insisted that it was unlawful for Catholics to support the ecumenical movement. He recalled that the evangelist John himself "altogether forbade any intercourse with those who professed a mutilated and corrupt version of Christ's teaching."[64] He called for the dissidents to return to the true church. The encyclical, besides condemning Catholic participation in ecumenical endeavors, indirectly reinforced the provisions of Canon 1258 of the Code of Canon Law promulgated in 1917: "It is absolutely forbidden for Catholics to be present at or take part in any non-Catholic religious service." The canon made an exception only for those rare cases where a Catholic's political office required simple physical presence at solemn occasions like a state funeral. Reputable Catholic theologians took the principle of the canon to the extreme, for instance, of forbidding Catholic nurses attending a dying Protestant patient to summon a minister of the person's church.[65]

Casti Connubii was a long and wide-ranging encyclical that dealt with a number of issues connected with marriage. While it spoke in positive terms about the beauty of the sacrament, it was especially intent on condemning "the pernicious errors and depraved morals" of the age that were to be found "even among the faithful." It insisted at great length that the marriage bond could never be dissolved. What caused the encyclical to become one of the most cited even today is the relatively short but pointed and absolute condemnation of birth control.

In that regard it is not so unrelated to *Mortalium Animos* as it might at first seem. Earlier in 1930 at the Lambeth Conference, the Church of England became the first church officially to accept the morality of "artificial contraception," that is, the use of prophylactics. *Casti Connubii* was in part a response to that decision and a rejection of it as a departure "from the uninterrupted Christian tradition." Therefore, "the Catholic Church . . . standing erect in the midst of the moral ruin that surrounds her . . . raises her voice in token of her divine ambassadorship and proclaims anew: any use whatsoever of matrimony exercised in such a way that the act is deliberately frustrated in its natural power to generate life is an offence against the law of God and of nature, and those who indulge in such are branded with the guilt of a grave sin." The language of this passage was so solemn that some theologians interpreted it as an infallible pronouncement.[66]

The teaching, though accepted by theologians, caused problems for confessors and their penitents that were exacerbated in 1960, when "the pill" became available over the counter in the United States and two years later in Europe.[67] A few theologians began to speculate that the pill created a new situation and therefore put the teaching of *Casti Connubii* in question. Others were troubled by the moral implications of the population explosion. Just at the time the council opened, therefore, the birth-control issue came to the fore with new urgency. By this time even for Catholics, Freud lurked in the background and subtly or not so subtly influenced all discussions of sex.

Pius XI was succeeded by Eugenio Pacelli, who also took the name Pius and who, just six months after his election in March 1939, had to deal with the horrors of World War II and the difficult choices it often posed for the Holy See.[68] The fact that Pius XII did not condemn the Holocaust in outright terms has been the subject of great controversy. At Vatican II, it contributed to the difficult course of *Nostra Aetate,* the decree dealing with the relationship between Catholics and Jews.

On Christmas Eve 1944, just as World War II was drawing to an end, Pius XII delivered a surprise in a radio address transmitted around the world.[69] He devoted the first part to a commendation of democracy as a form of government appropriate for the times: "Taught by bitter experience, people today more and more oppose monopolies of power that are dictatorial, accountable to no one, and impossible to reject. They want a system of government more compatible with the dignity and the liberty due to citizens." He speculated that "the future belongs to democracy."

This was the first time in history that a pope had publicly and at length praised democracy, and the address was rightly taken by young Catholics in Europe and Latin America as an encouragement to strike out in politics in ways that earlier were viewed by the Vatican with suspicion, if not hostility. Perhaps just as important, Pius's repetition again and again of the words "dignity" and "liberty," not prominent in papal vocabulary up to that point, adumbrated their prominence in the council.

Within a few years of the end of the war, all the countries of Western Europe that had been engaged in the conflict had adopted or confirmed a parliamentary form of government. The pope's message was surely not responsible for this turn of events, but neither was it irrelevant to it. The message was even more surely not a call for such a model of governance in the church. Nonetheless, by the time the council met, the leaders of the majority, both bishops and theologians, came to it with a political sense sharpened by a democratic experience. They happened to be the leaders keen on collegiality.

The pontificate of Pius XII set the immediate stage for the council. The tensions in his reign presaged the tensions in the council. Of his forty encyclicals, four are particularly important in that regard. The first was *Divino Afflante Spiritu,* 1943, in which he gave remarkably strong approval, to the literary, philological, and historical methods of biblical exegesis that had been developing since the nineteenth century.[70] In commending those methods the encyclical in effect dismissed the traditional "allegorical" senses of Scripture and instated the literal sense, the sense that could be determined by properly historical methods. Prepared for the most part by a German Jesuit, Augustin Bea, then the rector of the Biblicum, it marked a significant departure from the hostility to those methods that had prevailed especially since Pius X's crusade against Modernism. Its positive tone and its suggestions that contemporary exegetes might carry understanding of the biblical text beyond levels achieved in the past were just as striking. At points it hinted at something like *aggiornamento.*

The encyclical did not convince everybody of the legitimacy of the new methods, and suspicions about Catholic exegetes who employed them continued strong in some circles, with the Biblicum targeted as a hotbed of heterodoxy, even though Pius XII had explicitly praised it in *Divino Afflante.* In 1961, for instance, on the very eve of the council, Cardinals Pizzardo and Ruffini expressed themselves by word and deed in ways that seemed to repudiate much of what the encyclical allowed. Even more significant, the Holy Office under Cardinal Ottaviani issued a warning *(monitum)* in the same vein. Antonino Romeo, a professor at the Lateran University in Rome, launched a bitter attack against the "new methods," and at the end of that academic year the Holy Office suspended from teaching two professors at the Biblicum, Stanislas Lyonnet and Maximilian Zerwick.[71] (Romeo lost friends and gained notoriety during the council for describing it as "a sinister comedy of three thousand good-for-nothings with gold crosses on their chests.")[72]

The encyclical energized Catholic biblical scholarship, which by the time the council opened flourished in Germany, France, and Belgium. In France in particular Catholic biblical scholars, while intent on producing studies on the Bible that satisfied the most rigorous standards of their profession, were just as intent on showing the relevance of the Bible for the spiritual life of Catholics. Their enterprise was, therefore, more than purely academic.

Also in 1943 Pius published *Mystici Corporis,* an encyclical on the church as the Body of Christ. Written principally by another Jesuit, Sebastian Tromp, professor at the Gregorian University in Rome, the encyclical built on research into the patristic tradition of ecclesiology represented by Émile Mersch's work *Le Corps mystique du Christ* (1933).[73] While the encyclical described the relationship between head and members in hierarchical and juridical terms, it also softened the approach to the church that had prevailed since the Reformation, in which the basic analogy was the state. In contrast, the encyclical insisted on the role of the Holy Spirit in the church and thus on the balance that needed to hold between the hierarchical structures and the charismatic gifts of the Spirit. It identified the Mystical Body with the Roman Catholic Church and taught that membership in the church was restricted to those who were baptized, professed the true faith, and were in communion with the pope.[74]

Did one, then, have to be a practicing Roman Catholic to be saved? Leonard Feeney, a Jesuit who in the 1940s ran a center for the few Catholic students then attending Harvard University in Cambridge, Massachusetts, answered in the affirmative in such a vociferous and uncompromising way that he attracted the attention and aroused the displeasure of the president of the university, who protested to the archbishop of Boston. The archbishop referred the matter to the Holy Office, which replied on August 8, 1949, that it was possible to be saved by implicit desire *(voto vel desiderio)* in the case of persons of good will who would join the church if they only knew it was the one, true church of Christ.[75]

The teaching of the Holy Office was in keeping with a long tradition of Catholic theology, but the more rigorist interpretation also had a long history. The encyclical and the Feeney controversy are only two instances of the great interest in the church and the lively discussion about its nature and role in the decades immediately before the council opened. They helped pave the way for the centrality that *Lumen Gentium* assumed in the council and also for the discussion of the vexed question of Catholicism's relationship to other Christian churches and other religions.

In November 1947, Pius published *Mediator Dei,* the first papal encyclical devoted entirely to the liturgy. With this long document the pope in effect gave his blessing to the Liturgical Movement, which not only sought to promote devotion to the liturgy but also looked to change it in ways that would make it more attractive, more effective in accomplishing its purposes, and more clearly in accord with its true character. The blessing was not unreserved. The pope condemned many "abuses" in the liturgy, sometimes in scolding terms.[76]

The encyclical did not, therefore, satisfy the more sanguine hopes of the movement; nor did it succeed in lifting the suspicion that many theologians and bishops entertained about it. It was, nonetheless, something to which liturgists could appeal to make a case for their enterprise. In it Pius allowed, for instance, that the liturgy "grows, matures, develops, adapts, and accommodates herself to needs and circumstances." He also granted that "in certain rites" (presumably not the Mass) more use might be made of the vernacular.[77]

Pius took seriously some of the implications of *Mediator Dei* and the next year set up a secret commission to advise him on the feasibility of a general reform of the liturgy. Shortly thereafter he took action that included a modification of the fast required before receiving the Eucharist, which thus made possible the celebration of Mass in the evening. In two decrees, 1951 and 1955, he completely reorganized the liturgies for the Sacred Triduum, that is, for the last three days of Holy Week. This reform entailed, among other things, moving the liturgies for Holy Thursday from early morning until evening and the liturgy for Holy Saturday from early morning to just before midnight so that it would be a true vigil of Easter.[78] This was, again, *aggiornamento* before *aggiornamento*. But it was more fundamentally the fruit of *ressourcement*.

The fourth encyclical, *Humani Generis,* appeared on August 12, 1950, a startling contrast to the other three. It was an unremitting condemnation of a number of "false opinions" and "novelties" that threatened to undermine Catholic truth. In comparison with the three encyclicals just discussed, its pervasively negative and accusatory tone came as a shock. The encyclical marked the beginning of a cautious and fearful final phase of Pius XII's pontificate.[79] Although much more measured in its condemnations than *Lamentabili* and *Pascendi,* it otherwise resembled them and was inspired by the fear that Modernism had risen from the grave. "Where is the new theology leading us?" asked the important Dominican theologian Reginald Garrigou-Lagrange in 1946. "To Modernism," was his answer.[80]

Some passages of *Humani Generis* seemed to step back from positions

Pius had taken in the earlier encyclicals—or at least they gave comfort to those who were opposed to those positions in the first place. The most repeated complaint of the encyclical was that theologians were not giving due respect to the official teaching of the church, especially as expressed in papal encyclicals. Pius returned again and again to criticisms by theologians of Thomistic/Scholastic theology and of the Aristotelian philosophy that undergirded it. Some such theologians, "desirous of novelty," dally with other philosophies like existentialism and "a certain historicism." They are imbued with an "irenic" aim that would try to minimize the differences between Catholicism and the "dissident" Christian groups. To promote that goal some of them want "to bring about a return in the explanation of Catholic doctrine to the way of speaking used in Holy Scripture and by the Fathers of the Church." When Catholic teaching "has been reduced to this condition, a way will be found [they think] to satisfy modern needs, a way that will permit dogma to be expressed also by the concepts of modern philosophy."[81] For Pius the style issue was, obviously, crucial.

The encyclical also singled out specific errors for condemnation. Some theologians were saying, for instance, that they were not bound to accept "that the Mystical Body of Christ and the Roman Catholic church are one and the same," as Pius had taught. Others were denying the gratuity of the supernatural order, or wanted to modify the doctrine of transubstantiation, or gave undue credence to the theory of evolution. In that last regard the encyclical deplored "too free interpretations" of the first eleven chapters of the book of Genesis, and it asserted that Catholics could not embrace the opinion that after Adam there were human beings who did not descend from him.

Like most such documents, *Humani Generis* spoke in general terms and named no names. The superiors-general of the Jesuits and Dominicans, however, lost no time in taking action against the offenders within their orders in the most wide-ranging clamp-down on theologians since the Modernist ordeal. France was the epicenter of the crisis, and in the years following the encyclical Henri de Lubac, Yves Congar, Marie-Dominique Chenu, and a number of others were removed from their teaching positions and forbidden to publish, at least on certain topics.[82] From 1951 until the opening of the council, Karl Rahner was intermittently censored and forbidden to publish. In 1962, just before the council opened, he was notified that anything he wrote had to be censored in Rome before it went to press.

On June 30, 1952, the Holy Office, echoing a talk by Pius XII, issued an "instruction" on the use of modern art in churches that underneath the generic wording was really a warning against its "aberrations" and "contaminations."[83] The next year it came close to publishing a condemnation of Graham Greene's novel *The Power and the Glory*, about an alcoholic priest.[84] In 1955 John Courtney Murray was forbidden to write on his speciality, church-state relations, and Jacques Maritain came under severe attack for his similar views.[85]

During his lifetime Pierre Teilhard de Chardin, the Jesuit paleontologist, was forbidden to publish any of his spiritual or theological works. Through his literary executor, however, his writings began to appear after his death in 1955 and attracted great notice. On June 30, 1962, within months of the council's opening, the Holy Office found these works to be filled with grave philosophical and theological errors, presumably related in one way or another to his theories about evolution and the expanding universe. It exhorted prelates and heads of academic institutions to protect the faithful from the dangers they posed to Catholic doctrine.[86]

Thus the Supreme Congregation of the Holy Office, headed by Cardinal Pizzardo and then by Cardinal Ottaviani, had by the time of the council screwed the lid on tight. Its actions were bitterly resented not only by theologians but also by a number of bishops, who felt that "Rome" was overstepping its bounds. Bishops complained that they were being treated like mere executors of the orders of the Holy See, mere *Werkzeuge,* to use Bismarck's term. What they resented as much as the punishment of theologians was the autocratic style in which it was meted out. As H.-M. Féret, one of the French Dominicans whose work was condemned, said: "I do not see any means of reconciling with the spirit of the Gospel a system that condemns someone as a result of secret denunciations, that gives that person no way of defense, and that provides no way of knowing the context of the condemnation."[87]

In 1954 the Belgian historian Roger Aubert published a small book summarizing the state of Catholic theology at mid-century.[88] He singled out the ferment in biblical, patristic, and liturgical studies, the new concern for ecumenism, an openness to existentialism and other modern philosophies, and a reconciliation with "the modern world." These were largely northern European phenomena. He did not mention their opposite number, known in the parlance of the day as "Roman theology." Roman theology was relatively untouched by these phenomena or inimical to them and was characterized by juridical and ahistorical methods. It was often indistinguishable from the approach taken by the theological manuals of seminaries, many of the most widely diffused of which were written by professors in Roman institutions. In the eyes of its critics, besides its other many faults, Roman theology amounted to an academic mind-game, irrelevant to life. The drama of Vatican II played itself out in the tension between these two theological poles. This tension was another facet of the tension between center and periphery.[89]

Roman theology was powerfully operative in the Congregations of the papal Curia, especially in the Holy Office. But the officials of the Curia did not create this theological style. They had learned it in Roman institutions, where the "Roman approach" was inculcated. Even its critics realized, however, that there were in this regard important differences among the ecclesiastical institutions of higher learning in Rome. They were not all equally Roman. In order of descending Roman density, the more important schools were the Lateran University, the Angelicum (the Dominican institution), the Gregorian University, and the Biblicum.

The Lateran and the Biblicum stood at the opposite ends of the spectrum. During the last years of the reign of Pius XII and during the council itself, they were openly at war, with the Lateran the aggressor. The situation came to such a pass that in a courtesy visit to the Lateran on October 31, 1963, Paul VI gently but publicly and unmistakably communicated to the teachers and students that he wanted them not only to work in harmony with the other Roman institutions but also to put a stop to their polemics.[90]

In the 1950s, therefore, behind the placid façade that Catholicism presented to the world, a clash of epic proportions was waiting to happen. Pius XII himself seemed to move now in one direction, now in the other. The result was the passionate and widely diverging assessments of his pontificate that persist to this day. There was, however, an altogether different aspect to what happened to the church during the years of Pius XII, and it had nothing to do with decisions or actions of popes, cardinals, bishops, or theologians.

The pontificate extended, we must remember, from the beginning of World War II through the early years of the Cold War. Momentous changes were taking place in the world at large, some of which would have a deep impact on the church and hence on the council. If Vatican II needs to be understood as a repudiation of certain aspects of the nineteenth century and an embracing of certain others, it also must be understood as a response to the immediate and profound changes taking place in the world at mid-century.[91]

The Allied victory, for instance, spelled the end of the repressive, right-wing dictatorships in Germany and Italy and thus provided the condition for the remarkable rise of "Christian Democracy" in those countries, where it would be the dominant political party for decades. In both countries the leading figures and first prime ministers after the war were Catholics—Alcide De Gasperi in Italy and Konrad Adenauer in Germany. In France, where after the war the Republic was even more firmly established than before, the outstanding political figures were Charles de Gaulle and Robert Schuman, both devout Catholics. In France, moreover, Catholics had for decades played a new and brilliant role in literature and the arts—François Mauriac, Georges Bernanos, Paul Claudel, Georges Rouault, and Olivier Messiaen, to name but a few.[92]

On the continent of Europe, therefore, Catholics assumed the leadership in countries where for a century and a half they had been culturally and politically sidelined or had sidelined themselves.[93] They now identified themselves not with monarchy but with the liberty, equality, and fraternity of the democratic ethos. A shift in Catholic political alignment had occurred that would have been unthinkable fifty years earlier. Freedom of speech, freedom of the press, and freedom to practice the religion of one's choice were now accepted without question by Christian Democrats. In this context the right-wing, staunchly Catholic dictatorships under Francisco Franco in Spain and António de Oliveira Salazar in Portugal seemed like embarrassing anachronisms. In 1960, meanwhile, the "Protestant" United States, a country professedly dedicated to "life, liberty, and the pursuit of happiness," elected its first Catholic president, John F. Kennedy. Catholics were "fulfilling" the nineteenth century in ways their ancestors could never have imagined.

The rise of Christian Democracy made unmistakably clear that the old Liberalism was dead, though many of Liberalism's tenets continued in certain circles to be powerfully influential, usually in new guises. World War I had dealt a heavy blow to belief in progress, especially moral progress, which was an essential part of the ideology of Modernity. Moreover, World War II had amply confirmed that, along with undeniable advances in certain areas, the story of the human race could not be told in an unqualifiedly optimistic mode. Thus some of the old bugaboos that had led the papacy into assuming many of its negative positions had simply evaporated.

From 1945 onward, the memories of the war's horrors and in particular the menace posed by the Bomb loomed large in fears for the future and gave impetus to the conviction that peoples had to work together, not simply for the betterment of the world, but to prevent its utter destruction. The establishment of the United Nations at San Francisco in 1945, an institution unwaveringly supported by the Holy See and in effect called for by Pius XII in that important address on Christmas Eve 1944, was a fruit of this consensus. The same consensus gave new impetus to the ecumenical movement. Even though the Catholic Church continued officially to remain aloof from it, in a circumscribed way it condoned or even encouraged Catholic participation.[94] The time had arrived, many people were convinced, to work out old differences through dialogue around the negotiating table.

Despite the impulse to put war and destructive rivalries behind it, the world after 1945 was divided into two great blocks that distrusted each other and threatened world peace. The Iron Curtain had fallen. For Catholicism this meant, among other things, that even the simplest communication with bishops and the faithful in Eastern Europe was difficult and fraught with dangers. The arrest and trial of the primate of Hungary, Cardinal József Mindszenty, in 1948 opened the public's eyes to the brutal attitude of the Communist regime toward the church. The even more brutal suppression of the revolution there by Russian troops in 1956 was just one more confirmation that no reconciliation was possible between the "free world" and "the Soviet bloc."

The strongest Communist parties in the West were in two of the most traditionally Catholic countries—Italy and France. On July 1, 1949, the Holy Office issued a decree excommunicating any Catholic who was a member of the Communist Party and declaring Communism and Catholicism utterly irreconcilable.[95] Meanwhile, Russia and the United States competed in the production of nuclear armaments that threatened the annihilation of the human race. The threat was not something Cassandra dreamed up. As mentioned, a week after the council opened the world waited and watched through the dread of the Cuban Missile Crisis.

The War was over, but even worse seemed imminent. Wars seemed to spring up everywhere. For three years, 1950–1953, war raged in Korea between Communist and non-Communist forces, with the United States deeply involved in support of the latter. Beginning in the mid-1940s Europeans had to withdraw from their overseas possessions, sometimes in the wake of great violence. The death knell was ringing on colonialism, but it sounded amid wars of rebellion against European masters, which were sometimes followed by bloody internal conflicts once the Europeans were gone.

The new nations that resulted resented the earlier efforts to impose Western ways on them, which carried the assumption that those ways were superior to their own. In this situation missionaries found themselves in a crisis situation, viewed sometimes more as agents of a foreign culture than as representatives of a religion that professed universality. They were now bereft of the support the European governments had in one form or another offered. They soon realized that a new era had dawned in which, if Christianity were to survive in those parts, it had to be able to distinguish itself from westernization.

For Catholicism this situation threw glaring light on a specific tradition that could be taken as a symbol of the problem—the Latin liturgy. The language traditionally praised as a guarantor of Catholic unity and a symbol of Catholic universality now seemed in certain locations to be just the opposite. Was it even conceivable that the tradition of Latin liturgy could be changed? In 1962 most bishops who arrived at the council probably thought not. In that regard they were in accord with the Holy Office.

3

The Council Opens

At 8:30 in the gradually clearing morning light of October 11, 1962, the procession began to make its way across the great piazza, now thronged with an applauding, sometimes cheering, crowd.[1] In addition to the tens of thousands gathered in St. Peter's Square, millions more witnessed the grand spectacle on television. The setting itself was magnificent—the piazza and its colonnade, Bernini's masterpiece located in front of a basilica to whose design Bramante, Raphael, and Michelangelo, among others, had contributed. The site, venerated by Christians since at least the second century as the burial place of St. Peter, had been visited by many of the greatest figures in the history of the West—Constantine, Charlemagne, Luther, and countless others of similar significance.

Some 2,500 council fathers, fully vested in flowing white garments with white miters atop their heads, descended the great staircase of the palace next to the church and seemed to flow from it through the piazza into St. Peter's. The Swiss Guards, the Noble Guards, the Palatine Guards, the bishops and patriarchs from the Eastern Catholic churches in their exotic vestments and crowns, and sundry others added color and variety to the scene.

At the very end of the procession, which took more than an hour to complete, came Pope John XXIII, carried on the *sedia gestatoria*, the famous chair borne on the shoulders of attendants. By the time he entered the church, all the others had taken their places. The basilica was filled, not only with the council fathers, the theologians, the non-Catholic observers, and many others who had somehow managed to gain admission, but also with heads of state like Prince Albert of Belgium and President Antonio Segni of Italy. At the altar, over the presumed burial place of St. Peter, crowned by Bernini's magnificent canopy in bronze, the pope got down from the *sedia* and knelt at the altar, where he intoned the hymn *Veni, Creator Spiritus,* "Come, Holy Spirit." The council had begun.

The Opening Days

The most solemn and visually impressive event in the first days of the council was undoubtedly the procession into the basilica on October 11 and the High Mass celebrated immediately after the *Veni, Creator* by Cardinal Eugène Tisserant, dean of the College of Cardinals. But other occurrences were better indicators of how the council would move along its course, something that was altogether uncertain even at this late date. Some, like Cardinal Giovanni Urbani of Venice, anticipated that the bishops had not come merely "to sprinkle holy water" on the status quo, whereas others expected just that.[2] Was the council meant as a celebration of the glories of Catholicism, or was it meant, perhaps along with that, to make some hard decisions, which by definition do not please everybody?

At the end of the Mass Pope John XXIII delivered his opening address to the council, a moment all had been awaiting.[3] He spoke of course in Latin, the official language of the council. *Gaudet Mater Ecclesia* ("Mother church rejoices") were his opening words and hence the name the address bears. We now know that he wrote it entirely on his own, revising it again and again. The words were carefully chosen. Nonetheless, to those untrained in the language of papal discourse, the speech sounded bland and unexceptional. It was delivered, moreover, at the end of a long ceremony that for the active participants had begun hours before. Not all ears were therefore as attentive as they might otherwise have been.

People heard what they wanted to hear. The next day the headline of the *Osservatore Romano* read, "Chief Aim of the Council: To Defend and Promote Doctrine," whereas the headline in *Le Monde,* the influential Paris paper, was "Pope Approves Research Methods in Modern Thought." A proof-texting approach to the document, as with the documents of the council itself, allows both interpretations—and many others besides.

When the text is looked at as a whole, however, and put into the context of papal pronouncements during the long nineteenth century, its force and distinctive characteristics emerge.[4]

To begin with, the pope distanced himself, and therefore the council, from a scolding and suspicious approach to "the world." He expressed the hope that the council would enable the church to "face the future without fear," and he pointedly rejected the voices of those who "in modern times can see nothing but prevarication and ruin . . . [who] say that our era in comparison with the past is getting worse." While the church is aware of problems, it looks with favor on "the marvelous progress of the discoveries of human genius." The world of today is surely too much taken up with politics and economics and thus lacks the time to attend to its spiritual welfare. Such a situation is not right, but we must not forget that the present political order has in many instances created better conditions for "the free action of the church."

How, then, is the church to deal with both what is right and what is wrong in society today? It should do so in a positive way, "making use of the medicine of mercy rather than of severity . . . demonstrating the validity of her teaching rather than by condemnations." He thus raised the crucial question of the council's style of discourse and specified its quality when he said that, while the fundamental teachings of the church must always remain the same, the way they are presented can change. In this instance the style should be "predominantly pastoral in character" because the church, through the council, "desires to show herself to be the loving mother of all, benign, patient, full of mercy and goodness toward the children separated from her." The church can thus be beacon, catalyst, and matrix of unity for the human race.

This great goal, of course, requires the church to remain true to its message. Yet at the same time, "by making appropriate changes and by the wise organization of mutual cooperation, the church will make individuals, families and peoples really turn their minds to heavenly things." Through the council the world expects from the church "a step forward toward doctrinal penetration and a formation of consciences in faithful and perfect conformity to authentic doctrine, which, however, should be studied and expounded through the methods of research and through the literary forms of modern thought."

Although the full import of the pope's address was not grasped by most of those who heard it, it was taken as encouragement by those at the council who were hoping to strike, somehow, a new note. At least the pope had not fallen into what they considered the old ecclesiastical clichés. Especially during the first period of the council, that group repeatedly referred to the address to justify the direction they believed the council should take.

In its understated way the address was in fact remarkable. It said that the council should take a positive approach; it should look forward; it should not be afraid to make changes in the church wherever appropriate; it should not feel constrained to stay within the old methods and forms, as if hermetically sealed off from modern thought; it should look to human unity, which suggested an approach that emphasized commonalities rather than differences; it should encourage cooperation with others; it should see its task as pastoral. The speech also suggested, or could be understood to suggest, that the council take a large view of its task, not limiting its purview simply to members of the Catholic Church. By emphasizing the council's pastoral orientation, moreover, the pope in effect countered those who wanted Vatican II to be "doctrinal," a code word for producing further specifications of church teaching.

"Mother Church Rejoices" was strikingly different from the scolding and grief-stricken tone of the correlative document of Vatican I.[5] John XXIII was fully aware of the import of his words, as he betrayed in a remark afterward to his secretary: "Every now and then [when I was delivering the speech] I glanced at my friend on the right." The "friend on the right" was Cardinal Alfredo Ottaviani, head of the Holy Office.

That night the pope made another appearance at a candlelight ceremony in St. Peter's Square, where he spoke briefly and extemporaneously to the enthusiastic crowd.[6] During the next two days he received in audience several groups. Among them were the observers, who included not only Protestants but, among others, representatives of the Patriarchate of Moscow, the Coptic Patriarchate of Alexandria, the Syrian Patriarchate of Antioch, the Ethiopian Church, the Armenian Catholicate of Cilicia, and the Russian Church in exile. When John spoke to them, in French, he recalled his earlier contacts with various Christian leaders before he became pope: "Never, to my recollection, was there among us any muddling of principles, any disagreement at the level of charity on the joint work that circumstances required of us in aid of the suffering. We did not negotiate, we talked. We did not debate but loved one another."[7]

At a reception the next day, Cardinal Bea addressed the same group as "my dear brothers in Christ." The observers, though wary, were stunned by the warmth of their welcome. Their very presence in the basilica during all the sessions of the council influenced, at least occasionally, the tone of the debates.

But work had to be done. On October 13 the first working session of the council was held. In it the bishops were to elect from their number the members of the ten commissions of the council that would be responsible for the preparation, the presentation, and then the revision of the major documents with which the council had to deal. These ten commissions corresponded one-for-one to the Preparatory Commissions that had been at work since 1960. They were the "committees" of the council, to give them a name from *Robert's Rules of Order,* and they were therefore of crucial importance for the council's functioning.

The bishops were given the names of all bishops present at the council, from which each was to choose 160 (sixteen for each commission). They were also given the names of the members of the corresponding Preparatory Commissions. Since any individual would have known only a tiny percentage of the other bishops present, it would have been easy for them simply to reinstate the bishops of the Preparatory Commissions, and in fact this is probably what was expected to happen. Cardinal Ottaviani had in the meantime circulated a set of names of bishops whom he regarded as appropriate for the different commissions, a move that, however well intentioned, was interpreted by some bishops as manipulation by "the Curia."

After the opening Mass, the session on October 13 got under way with an announcement from the secretary general, Archbishop Felici, that the election would begin immediately. Consternation followed, as bishops tried to fill their ballots with 160 names, while sometimes calling out for advice to one another across the aisles. Cardinal Achille Liénart of Lille, France, rose from the table where the presidents (that is, the panel of ten cardinals chairing the session) sat and asked that the voting be postponed for a few days to allow the bishops a chance to get to know one another and episcopal conferences time to develop their own lists. His intervention was met with prolonged applause. Cardinal Josef Frings of Cologne seconded the motion from the presidents' table. The ten presidents of the council agreed with the proposal, postponed the election until the following Tuesday, and adjourned the session, which had lasted less than an hour.

Liénart's intervention was practical, but it was seen as more than that. It was taken as an indication that the council would run its business in its own way and not meekly assent to what was handed to it. After the adjournment that morning, Cardinal Siri of Genoa went immediately to the Holy Office to meet with Ottaviani and others to try to decide what to do about what he regarded as "a maneuver directed more subconsciously than consciously by a certain antipathy to the Curia." It was an antipathy that arose, he thought, from "the eternal inferiority-complex which the Northerners have in their relations with Rome." He noted in his diary, "The devil has had a hand in this."[8]

In the following days confusion reigned over a number of procedural questions, sparked by the realization that each of the 2,500 or so bishops would produce a list of 160 names, which had to be counted by hand. Did a candidate need to receive a two-third's majority, or a simple majority, or a mere plurality? It gradually began to dawn on the bishops how daunting was the task ahead and how, amid the vision of the great spiritual mission of the council, the physical and moral limitations of the participants and the unwieldy mechanisms of the enterprise would to a great extent determine what could be accomplished.

When some of the procedural questions were finally resolved and the voting on membership in the commissions completed, the results were less dramatic than anticipated. Most of the same names appeared on the new lists of commission membership as on the old, with only sixty-four new persons added.[9] Asia and Africa remained poorly represented. Elected to the Doctrinal Commission, however, were Cardinals König and Léger and Bishop André Charue of Namur, Belgium, who would be leaders in the majority. Moreover, an important point had been made: the council would set its own course, thank you. The announcement also called attention to the role the episcopal conferences might play as centers for consensus building, even though the "Regulations" of the council assigned them no role.

John XXIII had in the meantime added more names to the commissions, as the "Regulations" provided, and in that way he had the opportunity to balance the lists and make sure that no part of the world was excluded from membership in at least one of the commissions. Toward the end of October he further augmented the memberships.[10] In late November of the following year, Paul VI responded to requests to enlarge the commissions even further by asking the fathers to vote for new members.

The Council Opens

He added to the number elected to bring the membership on each commission up to thirty.[11] The result was commissions more responsive to the will of the assembly.

When on October 20 the council held its next session, it was to address the document On the Sacred Liturgy. Before it could move to that matter, however, it discussed, emended, and then approved a "message to the world." The idea for such a message, unprecedented in the history of ecumenical councils, originated especially in the French sector of the council among bishops and theologians like Chenu who feared that the council was in danger of closing itself off from the real issues of the world in which people lived, in danger of losing itself in theological and doctrinal abstractions.[12]

The text was brief. One passage gave voice to the message of mercy, kindness, and human compassion that Pope John hoped the council would express: "We urgently turn our thoughts to the problems by which human beings are afflicted today. Hence, our concern goes out to the lowly, poor, and powerless. Like Christ, we would have pity on the multitude heavily burdened by hunger, misery, and lack of knowledge. . . . As we undertake our work, therefore, we would emphasize whatever concerns the dignity of the human person, whatever contributes to a genuine community of peoples."[13]

The message got minimum coverage in the press and was soon forgotten. But, like the change in voting procedure, it proved an adumbration of the council's future direction. Unlike previous councils, this one would be, or at least hoped to be, as concerned with the world "out there" as it was with its own internal affairs. It was concerned, moreover, not so much as a fault-finder as a compassionate helpmate. It was clear that the world out there needed all the help it could get; indeed, two days later President Kennedy announced the American blockade of Soviet ships heading for Cuba, where Soviet missiles had been photographed within easy reach of the United States. John XXIII was meanwhile at work trying to diffuse the tension, and his efforts may have helped do so.[14]

Within the council the discussion of the text of the message took up the whole session. Felici announced that the next session, the fourth, would be held two days later, on October 22, when the document on the liturgy would be formally presented to the council. The substantive work thus did not begin until eleven days after the opening on October 11. The bishops were getting restless. At this rate, they were already asking, how long would the council last? Many had expected to return home well before Christmas with the council's business finished.

On August 6, 1962, about two months before the council opened, Pope John had promulgated *Ordo Concilii,* the official "Regulations" or procedures according to which the council would conduct its business.[15] Those procedures, drawn up by a subcommittee of the Central Planning Commission and approved by the pope, would determine not only how smoothly and fairly the council would move but to some extent how long it would last from its opening to its closing day. Moreover, by determining how the council did business, the "Regulations" heavily influenced the business itself. In those regards the council was no different from any other meeting, except that the enormous number of participants added complications to an already complicated situation.

During Vatican II both popes revised the "Regulations," yet most of their major features remained stable throughout the council.[16] The most important of them was the unlimited discretionary authority put in the hands of the pope, faithfully reflecting Canon 222 of the code. The "Regulations" themselves were promulgated by a papal act, not by the council, and during the council they were changed by papal act. According to them, the pope appointed the heads of the commissions and could appoint additional members to them; designated who were the theologians, canonists, and others to assist the council; and in general had the council firmly in his hands.

Yet even as the "Regulations" were changed and refined during the council, they still failed to provide procedures indicating how the pope was supposed to make his own views known to the bishops assembled in the basilica. This turned out to be a grave omission. The result was improvisation and communication through various and indirect means. The further result was confusion and misunderstanding and, with Paul VI, seemingly endless need for clarification of what the pope really intended in his many communications. This problem was, moreover, symptomatic of a document that provided in most instances not much more than general guidelines for conducting business. The "Regulations" were incomparably less detailed than, say, *Robert's Rules* and hence more open to challenge and manipulation. Their major—some would say, fatal—failure was in not clearly defining the scope and limits of the authority of the various bodies responsible for different aspects of the council's business. The relationships of those bodies to one another, to the assembly of bishops, and to the pope defy adequate depiction in an organizational chart.

According to the "Regulations," the ten commissions had the task of presenting their texts to the assembly and then emending them in the light of the discussion in the basilica and the written suggestions they received from the bishops. The documents of the council were thus given their form and substance by the commissions. As with any committee, much depended on the leadership given by the chair. Pope John confirmed as heads of the council commissions the same cardinals who had headed the Preparatory Commissions, all except one of whom was head, as mentioned, of the corresponding Congregation of the Curia.

The commissions were: (1) Doctrine (Holy Office); (2) Bishops; (3) Oriental Churches; (4) Sacraments; (5) Discipline of Clergy and Laity; (6) Religious Orders; (7) Missions: (8) Liturgy; (9) Seminaries and Catholic Schools; and (10) Lay Apostolate (the only one that did not correspond to a Congregation of the Curia). On October 22, 1962, Pope John raised the Secretariat for Christian Unity to the status of a commission, thereby increasing the number of commissions to eleven.[17] By delaying this decision until a week after the election of members to the original commissions, the pope, wittingly or unwittingly, ensured that the team Bea had assembled remained intact.

The cardinals heading the commissions had shepherded the documents of the areas assigned to them through the preparatory stage and naturally felt protective of them, reluctant to admit the possibility of radical surgery. Moreover, because of the massive preparations, including the extensive consultations in 1959–1960, they felt, not unreasonably, that the major work of Vatican II had already been done. The council itself would provide a ratification, with some adjustments, of course, of a task already essentially completed.

Sentiments along these lines were reinforced by the role that the prefects of the congregations had in recent decades increasingly played in the ordinary governance of the church as local and provincial synods had, with rare exception, ceased to function. The congregations regulated church life for their respective areas, and their prefects were used to having their word accepted as final. It is understandable, therefore, that the cardinal prefects would have the same attitude toward the council, especially since they had been appointed heads of the commissions by the pope himself and acted as his agents. Moreover, John XXIII had approved the preparatory documents for submission to the council, an approval easily interpreted as imbuing the documents with a certain finality.

No wonder, then, that the heads of the commissions, especially of the Doctrinal Commission, sometimes acted as if they were to give direction to the council rather receive direction from it, an interpretation of their role that the "Regulations" did not seem to disallow. No wonder that Cardinal Liénart's intervention caused consternation in some circles in the Curia and so much upset Cardinal Siri. No wonder that the relationship between the authority of the commissions and the authority of the assembly so profoundly troubled the council well into its second year and to a lesser extent even beyond.

The Two Popes

"The Council" is an abstraction and as such cannot be allowed to obscure the mix of forces and personalities that marked the council. "The Curia" is another, as are "majority" and "minority," to say nothing of terms like "progressives" and "conservatives," which often imply value-judgments. Abstractions are, however, unavoidable and, besides, are valid as indicating consistent or recurring trends.[18] But the council fathers were individuals, each with his own concerns and viewpoints. A bishop might be with the "majority" on one issue and with the "minority" on another. Bea and Ottaviani often disagreed, of course, but Ottaviani did not always agree with Siri; nor, among the theologians of the majority, did Ratzinger always agree with Congar.

A short account of the council like this one cannot possibly represent the nuances of the perspectives at work, but by presenting a few of the great personalities it can give the event a grounding in the human reality that comes under the label Vatican Council II. Among those personalities the two popes were undoubtedly the most important. Once the council got under way, however, it took on a life of its own. No persons or groups could make it come out exactly as they wanted, not even Pope John XXIII or Pope Paul VI.

John convoked the council, gently lent it a certain direction, and made some procedural decisions during its first year that were important for the final outcome.[19] For many people the council was, and still is, "Pope John's council." John was an unlikely pope. Although he was among those considered a viable candidate, a *papabile,* he was not elected until the eleventh ballot—at the age of seventy-six, an advanced age even for a papal conclave. With the exception of Pius X, moreover, the popes of the "nineteenth century" came from noble, aristocratic, or at least well-placed families, whereas Angelo Roncalli was born into a family of peasant origins in the little village of Sotto il Monte, near Bergamo in northern Italy. He remained touchingly devoted to his family until his death and regularly sent handwritten letters to his surviving sister even while he was pope.

His career as a priest carried him to situations and places that gave him a breadth of experience none of his predecessors had. Ordained in Rome in 1904, he had an altogether traditional theological training there. Two years after ordination he began a ten-year stint teaching church history at the diocesan seminary in Bergamo, where he also taught courses in the Fathers of the church.[20]

At this time his interest was piqued by the records of Saint Charles Borromeo's official visit as Metropolitan to the diocese of Bergamo in 1575, which resulted in his editing them in five volumes, the last of which was published in 1957, the year before he was elected pope. It is plausible that Roncalli's growing fascination with Borromeo, who as archbishop of Milan saw his episcopacy as an implementation of Trent and who therefore convoked a number of diocesan and provincial synods in obedience to what the council prescribed in that regard, played a role in John's "inspiration" to convoke the council.[21] At any rate John now had a perspective on the history of the church that was not exclusively Rome-centric.

When World War I broke out in 1914, he served in the Italian army, first as a health worker and then as a chaplain. A few years later Pius XI made him a bishop and sent him as apostolic delegate to Bulgaria, where he remained from 1925 to 1934, and then from 1935 until 1944 he had the same position in Istanbul for Greece and Turkey. For almost twenty years, therefore, he was out of western Europe and living in Orthodox/Islamic countries where Catholics were an almost negligible minority.

In 1944 Pius XII named him nuncio to Paris, the Vatican's most prestigious diplomatic post, at an extremely difficult moment for the church at the close of World War II. He replaced Bishop Valerio Valeri, whose removal General de Gaulle had demanded because of Valeri's compromising relations with the Nazi puppet state in southern France, the hated Vichy regime. A relatively large number of French bishops had tarnished reputations because they were suspected of similar sympathies. De Gaulle,

Catholic though he was, went on the warpath against them. The Interior Ministry drew up a list of twenty-five names, which included, besides Emmanuel Suhard of Paris, two other cardinals. Although Roncalli cannot be given credit for the solution whereby on July 27, 1945, seven prelates quietly left office, he acquitted himself well in this potentially explosive situation. He left Paris in 1953 when Pius XII named him bishop (patriarch) of Venice.

Direct and spontaneous in manner, he was considered naive by his critics. From the beginning of his pontificate, some old hands in the Roman Curia held him in disdain because he was an outsider who, unlike his predecessor, did not know "how things worked." Pius XII had spent his entire career in the direct service of the Holy See. For ten years until his election as pope he had been, as secretary of state, an actual member of the Curia, resident in the Vatican. John's career followed an altogether different trajectory. He came to the center after decades of experience on the periphery, Catholic and non-Catholic.

His stance during the preparation for the council has been described as enigmatic.[22] He followed a hands-off policy toward the work of the commissions and sometimes seemed to support their more conservative tendencies. The Roman Synod held in 1960 at his instigation and under his auspices was thought at the time to provide a dress rehearsal for the council. Lasting only a week, this gathering of Roman clergy ratified the 755 canons prepared for it ahead of time. The canons consisted of regulatory or disciplinary minutiae, some of which carried explicit sanctions for nonobservance.[23] John seemed happy with the results. If the council followed the same pattern, it would be brief, pro forma, and radically old style. *Veterum Sapientia,* the Apostolic Constitution John issued on February 22, 1962, eight months before the council opened, reaffirmed the role of Latin in the church and was interpreted as a discouragement for introduction of the vernacular into the Mass.

Yet his invitation to the other Christian communities in his announcement of the council and the unwavering support he gave to the Secretariat for Christian Unity, which he had himself founded, pointed in the opposite direction. As the council approached, he more and more drew into his confidence the men who would be leaders of the majority—especially Cardinals Bea and Suenens—and he confided to his diary his uneasiness with Cardinal Ottaviani, a powerful leader of the minority.[24] In his opening allocution and especially in his actions from then until his death, he gave signals that, while he intended to let the council act in full freedom, his sentiments lay with the majority. Nonetheless, the council carried him in directions he surely had not anticipated three years earlier.

The fundamental reason for the extraordinary popularity that John won worldwide almost from the moment of his election was the warm humanity that his every word and gesture seemed to communicate. Here was a human being. He smiled, told jokes, was spontaneous in manner and unconcernedly fat. He openly expressed his love for his family. When his spiritual journal was published after his death, it confirmed intuitions of him as somebody who lived out of a deeply felt sense of God's presence and love.[25] No other pope in the history of the church had left behind such a document.

For many Catholics he seemed to be a living image of what they believed or hoped the church to be, as he described it himself in his opening address to the council—"benign, patient, full of mercy and goodness." The personality of John XXIII had as much influence on the council as any words he spoke or interventions he made. When he died of stomach cancer on June 3, 1963, people knew a great world figure had passed, but they also felt that they had, somehow, lost a friend.

Fears and hopes were high, therefore, about the election of his successor. Many Vatican-watchers predicted that Giovanni Battista Montini, archbishop of Milan, would emerge from the conclave as pope.[26] For once the predictions were correct, but it took six ballots in what seems to have been another difficult conclave. Although he and John XXIII enjoyed a close and warm relationship, Montini was as much a contrast to John as John had been to Pius. He came from an old, prosperous, and distinguished family of Brescia, where his father, a lawyer, was active in Catholic circles. As a boy he was somewhat frail and did some of his secondary education at home. Intelligent and devout, he at one point thought of becoming a Benedictine monk but then chose the diocesan priesthood. He did his basic theological studies not in residence at the seminary but as a day student, and he took no part in seminary formation beyond attending the lectures. He was ordained in 1920 at the young age of twenty-two.

He furthered his education in Rome at the Gregorian University and the University of Rome. In 1922 the seminary at Milan granted him almost a pro forma doctorate in canon law, after which he served in the papal nuntiature in Warsaw for about six months, his only protracted stay outside Italy. When he returned to Rome, he almost immediately assumed a

Pope Paul VI with the future Pope John Paul II. Getty Images.

minor post in the Vatican's Secretariat of State, while devoting much of his time to work with Catholic university students in Rome, whom he tried to help in their opposition to the Fascist party. From his family as well as from his experience during these years he harbored a sympathy for the Christian Democratic movement and forged bonds of friendship with the young men who would lead Italy after World War II. In 1933 he entered the service of the Curia full-time in the Secretariat of State, where he remained for twenty-one years until 1954, when Pius XII named him archbishop of Milan. He worked closely with Pius and of course publicly supported his policies.

He smiled, but he did not tell jokes. He was an insider to the Curia, which had both advantages and disadvantages for him as pope. His foundation in theology was Roman and not particularly thorough, yet as a young priest he read broadly in theology. He liked French culture and harbored sympathy for at least some aspects of the "new theology." He did not, however, have a professional's grasp of what was at stake in the theological controversies of the day.

The Council Opens

"Battista," as he was known to his family, was slow to judge or condemn. He considered all the aspects of an issue, reflected, and then, it seems, reflected some more. His critics called him a Hamlet, while others praised his courageous decisiveness.[27] As Paul VI he felt his responsibilities heavily, sometimes giving the impression that the whole burden of the church fell on his shoulders.[28] He intervened often in the council, sending to the commissions his recommendations or orders for the improvement of their texts. His interventions and the way they were made are a crucial part of the story of Vatican II and of the larger problem of the relationship of center to periphery.[29]

By the third period, 1964, Paul's interventions left many, perhaps most, members of the council uncertain as to what he was up to. Was he an unwitting tool in the hands of a numerically insignificant minority? Or was he saving the council from itself? He generally seemed to be behind the orientation the council had taken, but he was given to qualifications, distinctions, refinements, long-winded discourses, and what looked like halfway measures, which generated confusion, misgivings, and even distrust.

How did these two men understand their relationship to the council? Neither ever spelled it out in any systematic way. Nor did either of them take part in the working sessions of the council; nor, with only one exception, were they ever in the basilica during them. They watched the council in the papal apartments on closed-circuit television, listened to it on the radio, or, at least with Paul VI, sometimes simply read the texts of the interventions or a résumé of them.[30]

The character of their interventions in the council provides the best clues for understanding how they saw their role. John intervened in a major way only once—on November 21, 1962, to change a technicality in procedure that would have required the council to continue considering a document that almost two-thirds of the bishops had by public vote judged inadequate. John's was, strictly speaking, a procedural intervention but nonetheless a turning point in the council.

Paul VI intervened often in small matters and great, in matters of substance and procedure. He saw his papal responsibility toward the council as at times requiring him to correct it or, at least, to make sure that the wording of its documents be understood in what he considered the correct way. He was much concerned to rally support for council documents as close to unanimous as possible, and he meant some of his interventions to win over those doubtful about a text or opposed to it.

Had John lived to see the council at the point of definitively approving a document, would he have intervened if he considered it faulty in part? Such an intervention seems out of character and inconsistent with the way he handled himself regarding the council from 1959 until his death. But of course we have no way of knowing. The problem of the relationship of pope to council that goes back at least to the fifteenth century simmered beneath the surface at Vatican II and at times boiled over into full view.

Personalities and Alignments

Besides the two popes, two other figures at the council not only played extremely important roles in Vatican II but also achieved almost emblematic status as embodying two contrasting tendencies—Ottaviani and Bea. Cardinal Alfredo Ottaviani was head of the Supreme Congregation of the Holy Office. During the preparatory stage of the council he was president of the Theological Commission, renamed the Doctrinal Commission once the council got under way.[31] Ottaviani brought to the commission not only his personal gifts and credentials but also his prestige and clout as head of the most powerful body in the Curia—the *Suprema*—which under his leadership had disciplined a number of prominent theologians.

Ottaviani, one of eleven children born into a poor family in the Trastevere sector of Rome, held a doctorate in canon law from the Lateran University (known until 1962 as the Athenaeum S. Apollinaris) and published studies in that field.[32] From 1929 almost until his death he held important positions in the Curia, which from 1935 were exclusively in the Holy Office, of which he was named secretary, or head, in 1959. Intelligent, shrewd, witty, and of unquestioned moral integrity, he continued even as cardinal to maintain an active ministry, especially with the young people of Rome. His academic training inclined him to a metahistorical approach to issues and problems, one of the most telling characteristics setting him and most of the minority off from those whom they opposed. The motto that he chose for his coat of arms as cardinal, *Semper Idem,* "always the same," suggests how he looked at church life and tradition. His long years in the Holy Office and the restricted nature of the circles in which he moved meant he was not used to having his authority challenged.

Other important figures at the council shared Ottaviani's outlook, which was basically that of the popes of the long nineteenth century. Among these figures was Cardinal Ernesto Ruffini, former rector (president) of the Lateran University and since 1946 archbishop of Palermo. He spoke

Cardinal Alfredo Ottaviani. Photograph by Carlo Bavagnoli / Time & Life Pictures / Getty Images.

during the council more often than any other individual. As a young priest he had been one of the first students at the newly established Biblicum, but he later became highly critical of the methods that professors there were increasingly adopting. In addition to several textbooks on Scripture, in 1948 he published a book on evolution in which he affirmed the literal sense of the first chapters of Genesis regarding the creation of the human soul. To substantiate his position, he explicitly cited the decision of the Biblical Commission about the creation stories, issued in 1909 at the height of the Modernist crisis. In 1959, just after the council had been called, the book appeared in English translation.[33]

That same year in an address in Rome, Ruffini suggested that the agenda of the council should be a reaffirmation of "the principal teachings" of the popes from Leo XIII to Pius XII.[34] It is interesting in view of the role he assumed in Vatican II that he had suggested the convocation of a council to both Pius XII and, according to his own testimony, John XXIII on the very day of his election. The council was needed, as he wrote to Ottaviani, to put an end to confusion in doctrine, morality, and biblical interpretation.[35] During Vatican II the insistence of the majority on the pastoral nature of the council was partly to counter the minority's advocacy of this kind of doctrinal council.

Aligned with Ottaviani and Ruffini were others, like Giuseppe Siri, archbishop of Genoa. Siri was austere, authoritarian, sharp in mind and tongue, and impatient with the slow-witted. During World War II his stance against the Fascists and the Nazis was courageous, and at personal risk he sheltered Jews and others the regimes persecuted. A highly respected member of the Italian episcopate, he had been close to Pius XII, who, according to rumor, wanted Siri to be his successor. In that fateful conclave where Roncalli was in fact elected, Siri, only fifty-two, was considered too young. After the long pontificate of Pius, the prospect of an even longer one held little attraction. After the death of Paul VI in 1978, however, Siri came close to being elected, in reaction to the disarray in which many cardinals felt Paul had left the church.[36]

Of similar mind was Michael Browne, an Irishman, former master general of the Dominicans, who was made a cardinal by John XXIII in the spring of 1962, just months before the council opened, and named second-in-charge (vice-president) of the Doctrinal Commission. Another was Archbishop Dino Staffa, secretary for the Congregation for Seminaries and Universities, who became an agitator for the minority. Cardinal Arcadio Larraona, a juridically minded Spaniard, appointed head of the Liturgical Commission just before the council opened, had by the second period assumed such a decisive leadership role as to be dubbed "the soul of the opposition."[37] Cardinal Rufino Santos, archbishop of Manila, was a force within the Doctrinal Commission for traditional approaches to almost every issue. More extreme than any of these was Marcel Lefebvre, archbishop of Dakar and recently elected superior-general of the Holy

Ghost Fathers. After the council he repudiated Vatican II as heretical and led a small but notorious schism.

Members of the minority formed the "International Group of Fathers" *(Coetus Internationalis Patrum)*, whose purpose was to lobby for positions passionately held by the minority.[38] The Group did not really solidify until the second period, when the members rallied in opposition especially to collegiality. From that point on it met regularly. By the beginning of the third period it claimed the patronage of cardinals like Ruffini, Siri, Browne, Santos, and Larraona.

The Group represented the conservative line in all its purity, and its core membership had close ties with right-wing political parties and ideologies. A founder and driving force was Geraldo de Proença Sigaud, archbishop of Diamantina, Brazil. Connected with politically reactionary groups in Brazil and abroad, Sigaud feared anything that might, in his opinion, conceivably spark revolution. Obsessed with fear of Communism, he was even more afraid of subversives inside the church—Christian socialists, Jacques Maritain and his disciples (church-state issue), Teilhard de Chardin and all "evolutionists." Catholics like these, according to him, practiced a "Trojan Horse strategy" that, left unchecked, would destroy the church from within.

Two other leading members of the Group were Lefebvre and Luigi Carli, bishop of Segni. By the third period, Carli emerged as a spokesman for the minority with a stronger profile than Ottaviani. Sigaud, Lefebvre, and Carli were at the heart of an organization that had a central committee of somewhere between five and fifteen (sources differ on the number) and a more general membership of perhaps up to eighty bishops who attended the meetings and subscribed to many, most, or all of the positions the Group fought for during the council.

The Group remained small. On principle it refused to network with the episcopal conferences at the council because it deemed them expressions of collegiality, which it adamantly opposed. Thus it ended up institutionally isolated. Nonetheless, by the end of the council it had on its mailing list about 800 council fathers, who paid much or little attention to the messages, depending on circumstances. The Group acted as a catalyst for the minority and had an impact beyond what its size suggests.

The secretary general, Pericle Felici, was a native of Segni, Carli's diocese. His critics liked to call attention to this fact and draw conclusions about it. As secretary general he held an extremely important and sensitive position. As a young seminarian he came to Rome, where he had all his training in theology and canon law.[39] He had been an assistant to Cardinal Tardini in the antepreparatory stage of the council and won increasing respect and influence from that point forward because of his intelligence, energy, and organizational skills. After the council Paul VI paid high tribute to his talents when he put him in charge of the commission for the revision of the Code of Canon Law.

As Tardini's health declined in 1960, Felici's star rose. Although earlier he had held only minor positions, Pope John appointed him secretary general of the whole preparatory effort. He performed so well that it was an obvious step for John to name him to the same position for the council itself. In the daily functioning of the council, Felici and his team, the General Secretariat, saw to all the physical details, many of which might seem niggling but neglect of which would have created serious disruptions. In that regard he acquitted himself brilliantly. He addressed the assembly several times daily and did so in clear and impeccably correct Latin. He injected humor when he thought it would help coax the assembly into accepting something distasteful.

The failure of the "Regulations" clearly to define the ground rules for the floor of the council meant that it often fell to Felici to try to sort things out, not an enviable task. Under Paul VI he increasingly became the intermediary between the pope and the assembly, delivering to the council messages "from a higher authority." As is now clear, he was sometimes responsible for delivering such messages because others, fearing they would not be well received, refused to do so. He was protective of the authority of his Secretariat, which he saw as the central clearinghouse for council business, and he moved into action against anything he saw as attempts to bypass it.

Not surprisingly, factors like these generated suspicions, or in some cases convictions, that Felici's sympathies lay with the minority and that he used his position to advance that cause.[40] Whatever the justice or injustice of such sentiments, he was as responsible as anybody else for keeping the council functioning as well as it did; indeed, it would be hard to imagine anyone doing it better under the often difficult circumstances.

The conservative bishops of the council relied on theologians to formulate and help back up their positions. These specialists tend not to have a strong profile because their viewpoints were often those expressed in standard seminary textbooks of the time. Important among them, however, was Sebastian Tromp, a Dutch Jesuit, professor at the Gregorian University. Since 1935 he had been an adviser to the Holy Office and was the ghost writer for Pius XII's encyclical *Mystici Corporis.* He also contributed to the writing of both *Mediator Dei,* on the liturgy, and *Humani Generis.* Of wider theological culture, therefore, than many other theologians in the conservative camp, he nonetheless unreservedly threw his weight behind the minority from his important position as Secretary for the Doctrinal Commission, a post to which John XXIII appointed him, and he played the role of a major obstructionist of the turn the council took. At the Gregorian University in Rome on November 25, 1961, a year before the council opened, Tromp delivered an address inaugurating the academic year that was almost a manifesto of the minority's program for Vatican II.[41]

Some of these theologians stood out from the rest owing to public controversy. This was the case, for instance, with Joseph Clifford Fenton, an American diocesan priest and a professor and dean at The Catholic University of America, who in the 1950s was the best-known opponent in the United States of John Courtney Murray's views on religious liberty. A staunch opponent of anything that might even hint of Modernism, he received the prestigious papal medal *Pro Ecclesia et Pontifice* in 1954. A member of both the Preparatory Theological Commission and then the Doctrinal Commission of the council itself, Fenton adamantly defended the "schemas" (drafts) those commissions prepared. On October 13, 1962, two days after the council opened, he wrote in his diary, "I always thought this council was dangerous. It was started for no sufficient reason. There was too much talk about what it was supposed to accomplish. Now I am afraid that real trouble is on the way." Within a month he felt confirmed in his opinion that John XXIII was soft on Communism, "definitely a lefty."[42]

Theologians of this type were strongly represented on the commissions and were thus, along with the bishops on them, responsible for the character of the draft documents first presented to the council. They tended to be influenced by the recent pronouncements of the Holy Office and the encyclical *Humani Generis;* hence, they were suspicious of modern methods of biblical exegesis and intolerant of theological or philosophical systems other than Thomism—as they understood Thomism. They favored a strengthening of the hierarchy's authority and especially the authority of the papacy. They were suspicious of collegiality or, more often, downright hostile toward it. They opposed all "novelty."

This mentality was deeply entrenched in the offices of the Curia, which, despite not having any official role as such in the council, had considerable influence simply by being on the scene, by controlling the presidency of the commissions, and by having close ties with a large number of bishops in the generally conservative Italian, Spanish, and North American hierarchies. As with any bureaucracy, no single mind-set prevailed in the Curia, and even those members who consistently espoused conservative positions often differed among themselves on particulars.[43] Generally speaking, however, the Curia was protective of the center and of its own prerogatives. It was sometimes tenacious in supporting the status quo. Thus "the Curia" became for many bishops and theologians of the majority a shorthand for obstructionism.

No surprise, then, that the Curia began very early to feel itself under threat. Even some conservative bishops had, in the atmosphere of the council, begun to reassess its interventions in the affairs of their dioceses and see them as high-handed. This challenge only increased the persuasion of many in the Vatican offices that they had become the faithful remnant, the true defenders of tradition and interpreters of God's will. By the third period of the council, Yves Congar reported, all that was heard in the corridors of the Curia were bitter complaints that "this accursed council is ruining the church."[44]

During the council the media often pilloried "the conservatives" for obscurantism, intransigence, for being out of touch, and even for dirty tricks. One thing can surely be said in their favor. They saw, or at least more straightforwardly named, the novel character and heavy consequences of some of the council's decisions. The leaders of the majority, on the contrary, generally tried to minimize the novelty of some of their positions by insisting on their continuity with tradition. It is ironic that after Vatican II, conservative voices began insisting on the council's continuity, whereas so-called liberals stressed its novelty.

Cardinal Siri was fundamentally correct in seeing "Transalpines" as leaders in the much-feared novelty. Prominent among them was Cardinal Augustin Bea, who at first glance seems an unlikely candidate to become an emblematic figure for "the progressives."[45] He was seventy-eight years old in 1959, when John XXIII created him a cardinal and appointed him head of the Secretariat for Christian Unity in preparation for the council. He was therefore eighty-one when the council opened. Though of Ger-

Cardinal Augustin Bea with observers/guests. Photograph by David Lees/Time & Life Pictures/Getty Images.

man birth, he was a "Roman" in that he had lived in the city for thirty-five years, served on several Vatican Congregations, including the Holy Office, and from 1945 until 1958 had been the confessor of Pius XII. Bea was anything but a radical.

Yet his background and experience were much broader than those of almost all the "Romans" who did not share his outlook. Even before he entered the Jesuits in 1902 he had studied theology at the University of Freiburg; then, after his ordination ten years later, he studied ancient Near Eastern philology at the University of Berlin in Protestant Prussia. For a short while he served as provincial superior for the Jesuits of Bavaria. In 1924 he began his career of teaching at the Biblicum, where he served as rector (president) for nineteen years, from 1930 to 1949. While rector he obtained from Pope Pius XI in 1935 the unprecedented permission to participate in a congress of Protestant scholars of the Old Testament at Göttingen in Germany. Though cautious, he was fully abreast of the scholarship in his field, which before World War II was dominated by German Protestants. He was thus a logical choice to help draft, with Jacques-Marie Vosté, a Dominican, the encyclical *Divino Afflante Spiritu* in 1943.

In his person he radiated an inner serenity that made him approachable and easy to converse with. It also generated respect for his opinions. This personality trait stood him in good stead when he was called upon to shepherd through the council two of the most difficult texts, strenuously opposed by the minority—on the Jews and on Religious Liberty—and his Secretariat was deeply involved in the formulation of a third difficult schema, On Divine Revelation. Bea was more responsible than probably any other single individual for that triad's finally winning acceptance.

The original purpose of the Secretariat was simply to facilitate contact with other Christian bodies in preparation for the council, and then to ensure a suitable welcome and sojourn in Rome for the "observers" who accepted the invitation. The Secretariat was to be, according to bishops and theologians suspicious of it, merely an information office. Bea and his collaborators, however, had bigger ideas. Almost from the beginning they planned to submit *vota,* or emendations, to the commissions to ensure an ecumenical dimension to the texts. It soon became clear that the commissions, especially the Theological Commission, did not welcome their input.

In the fall of 1961, the Secretariat sent a draft of its document on religious liberty to the Central Preparatory Commission. This led to the most dramatic confrontation between the two viewpoints before the opening of the council. At a meeting of the commission, Cardinal Ottaviani attacked the text as deviating from tradition and urged members not to consider it. The Secretariat, according to him, had no competence to propose a text on church and state, a doctrinal issue that as such belonged exclusively to his Theological Commission. Ottaviani then asserted the sovereign independence of that commission, which meant that it did not have to collaborate with any other bodies. Bea vigorously defended the text and the competence of the Secretariat, but the meeting ended in a stalemate. On October 22, 1962, John XXIII granted to the Secretariat the status of a full commission, thus resolving the procedural issue.[46] With that the Secretariat was on its way to becoming one of the most important entities giving shape to the council.

A skillful member of the Secretariat was the Dutch priest Johannes Willebrands, who since the early 1950s had in Holland been a leader in ecumenism—with the acquiescence of the Holy See.[47] In 1960 John XXIII named him secretary to the Secretariat. Willebrands had written his doctoral dissertation on John Henry Newman, and after World War II he became active in Holland in fostering informal contact between Catholics and other Christian groups. Once appointed to the Secretariat, he was sent by Bea to explain to leaders of those groups, such as the Lutheran World Federation, the outreach that was a goal of the council. When Cardinal Bea died in 1968, Pope Paul VI named Willebrands president of the Secretariat, which had by then been declared a permanent organ of the Roman Curia, and he made him a cardinal.

Outside the Secretariat, important prelates like Cardinal Josef Frings, archbishop of Cologne, Cardinal Achille Liénart, bishop of Lille, Cardinal Julius Döpfner, archbishop of Munich, Cardinal Bernhard Alfrink, archbishop of Utrecht, and, from North America, Cardinal Paul-Émile Léger, archbishop of Montreal, were strong voices for the majority. These men had all been members of the Central Preparatory Commission before the council opened, and they had discovered in one another similar dissatisfactions with the draft texts. They were thereby encouraged to make their views public when the council began.

Among them none was more important that Léon-Joseph Suenens, archbishop of Malines-Brussels, whose forceful yet conciliatory leadership skills put him at the center of many of the council's pivotal hours.[48] Fifty-eight when the council opened, he was as important as Bea as a leader of the majority, and more visible. Pius XII had named him auxiliary bishop of Malines-Brussels in 1945, and John XXIII made him archbishop in 1961 and cardinal in 1962. With doctorates in philosophy and theology from the Gregorian University, Rome, and as former vice-rector of the Catholic University of Louvain, Suenens came to the council with good credentials. A disciple of Lambert Beaudouin, he had become ever more influenced by the newer theological developments, and at the council he had at his disposal a formidable team of Belgian theologians.[49]

In the six months immediately preceding the opening of the council, Suenens established a close relationship with John XXIII that was important in giving shape to the council. His relationship with Paul VI, by contrast, was uneven and not without tense moments. In 1963 Paul appointed him and three other cardinals moderators of the council to chair the sessions in St. Peter's, an obvious sign of esteem. Suenens emerged as the unofficial leader of the foursome. For a year or so the moderators enjoyed

Cardinal Léon-Joseph Suenens. Photograph courtesy of the Cardinal Suenens
Center, John Carroll University.

a good working relationship with the pope, but by the time the council
was coming to a close Suenens believed that their influence with Paul had
almost evanesced.[50]

Cardinal König had an even more impressive academic background
than Suenens. From 1945 until 1952, he taught theology at the Universities
of Vienna and Salzburg and published a three-volume work on compara-
tive religion, *Christus und die Religionen der Erde* (1948). The "Regulations"
allowed bishops to bring personal theologians to the council, but König

was bold in bringing Karl Rahner, who even as the council opened was still under publication restraints imposed by the Holy Office. Rahner, important at the council for many reasons, proposed as early as October 12, 1962, a strategy for the council whose centerpiece was creating new schemas to replace those prepared under Ottaviani.[51]

Rahner was far from the only "silenced" theologian to come to the council and play an important role in it.[52] In fact, the effective rehabilitation of theologians who in the two decades before the council opened had been disciplined by the Holy Office is one of the striking features of the council and another indication that it wanted to effect a change in the status quo. Cardinal Francis Spellman of New York was a conservative churchman, a great friend of Pius XII, and privately critical of John XXIII when the pope announced the council. Yet when he saw during the first period that European prelates were bringing theologians like Rahner to the council, he successfully encouraged Pope John to appoint Murray as an official *peritus*.

Even earlier, in August 1960, John named Henri de Lubac, whose ideas were condemned by *Humani Generis,* as a consultor to Ottaviani's Theological Commission, where he was able to have little influence.[53] Once the council got under way, de Lubac's theological vision was reflected in the form and substance of the key document of the council, *Lumen Gentium.* A dozen years earlier he had been forbidden not only to teach but even to live in a Jesuit house where there were students, lest he corrupt them with his ideas.

Gérard Philips, priest of the diocese of Liège, Belgium, is an example of a distinguished theologian who was more important in the council than Rahner, de Lubac, and many others, but who in the meantime has been almost forgotten. Although he certainly favored and promoted the general orientation of the majority, he tried to play a conciliatory role. Indicative of his success in doing so is that by 1964 he could confide to his diary that he had won the trust of Ottaviani and the good opinion of Fenton and Parente.[54] Not surprisingly, some judged him as clever at synthesis but superficial and too willing to compromise.[55]

Perhaps even more important was the Dominican historian-theologian Yves Congar.[56] He, too, had been caught in the condemnations following *Humani Generis* and in 1954 had been forbidden to teach.[57] As with de Lubac, he was brought to Rome by John XXIII for the preparatory work for the council. Once the council got under way, he became an almost ubiquitously influential *peritus*.[58] He was sought for his opinion on almost every major issue before the assembly. A man of vast erudition with a profound knowledge of Christian history and tradition, he had a breadth of vision that matched the breadth of his learning. His Dominican confrere, Marie-Dominique Chenu, though never named a council *peritus,* was present as theological adviser to Bishop Claude Rolland of Antsirabé, Madagascar, and he played a much more important role than that title to inclusion indicates.[59]

Still another Dominican, the Belgian Edward Schillebeeckx, had learned from his teachers like Chenu to place theology in a historical and human-psychological context. At the time of the council he taught theology at the Catholic University of Nijmegen in Holland. In 1961 the Dutch bishops enlisted him to help them with a pastoral letter to their flocks about their hopes for the council, a document that anticipated many of the positions the council adopted. Like Chenu, he was never named an official *peritus,* but he exercised considerable influence through his contacts with the Belgian and Dutch episcopates, through his lectures in Rome, and in other ways.[60] He was forty-eight when the council opened.

Besides veterans from the theological battles of the 1940s and 1950s, young theologians just beginning their careers played significant roles in shaping Vatican II. Hans Küng was only thirty-five when in 1962 John XXIII named him a *peritus.* Cardinal Frings brought with him Joseph Ratzinger, another thirty-five-year-old.[61] Ratzinger, perhaps the most important of the younger theologians at the council, became a council *peritus* beginning in the second period. He was even more important afterward as head of the Congregation of the Doctrine of the Faith, the old Holy Office under a new name, and eventually as Pope Benedict XVI.

The individuals mentioned were important players in the council. Scores of other bishops and theologians were of course also important, but these were leaders of the two major opposing viewpoints. Council figures as diverse as Siri and Congar both lamented the theological inadequacy of most of the bishops at the council and the disproportionate role they thought theologians played in it.[62] Theologians played a lesser role at Vatican II, however, than they had at the Council of Trent.

The majority had no organization quite like the International Group of Fathers to promote its views, but an informal grouping whose stable nucleus consisted in Cardinals Bea, Frings, König, Liénart, Suenens, and Alfrink came into being early in the council and made possible some concerted action on the council floor. The title of Ralph M. Wiltgen's book *The Rhine Flows into the Tiber* suggests the impact that these "Transalpines" had.[63]

These prelates and others like them spearheaded the reformist impulses in the council. They attracted to their causes bishops from every part of the world, including those, like Cardinal Albert Meyer, archbishop of Chicago, and Cardinal Joseph Elmer Ritter, archbishop of St. Louis, who wanted to distance themselves from the conservative tendencies of the national episcopates to which they belonged. Except for their efforts to promote the declaration On Religious Liberty, the bishops from the United States did not play a particularly notable role in the council. In general, however, they, like so many other episcopates, moved away from more conservative positions as the council wore on.[64]

Wiltgen's title might seem to suggest that all the "Transalpines" influential in the council were Germans or Austrians.[65] The French, however, were at least as important. Given the small size of their country, the impact of the Belgians was extraordinary—with influential theologians like Philips and Schillebeeckx (not to mention others), with the accomplished bishop of Namur, André-Marie Charue, with Émile-Joseph De Smedt, bishop of Bruges, as a heavy-hitting spokesman, with Albert Prignon, rector of the Belgian College in Rome, theologian and close confidant of Suenens, and with Suenens himself at their head. Some commentators joked that the council should be called Louvain I instead of Vatican II.[66] No one paid the Belgians a higher tribute than Congar: "In large measure it was at the Belgian College that the council got its theological shape."[67]

Nor were all the important figures from the other side of the Alps. Cardinal Giacomo Lercaro, the highly regarded archbishop of Bologna, along with his "team" of theologians and auxiliary bishops, was a force to be reckoned with. During the council Carlo Colombo, longtime friend of Giovanni Battista Montini, acted as his unofficial theologian.[68] The council was an international gathering where, despite the overwhelming logistical obstacles, voices were heard from all parts of western Europe—and sometimes even from beyond.

Although, as mentioned, the "Regulations" made no provision for episcopal conferences, national episcopates met during the council with increasing frequency and effectiveness. Until then the Italian episcopate had in its entire history never once met as a group, whereas others, like the American episcopate, got together regularly.[69] At the council the Americans met every week and were for a while dominated by Spellman of New York and James McIntyre of Los Angeles.

Particularly important at the council were the meetings, also weekly, of the French episcopate.[70] Every second week the French opened their meeting to other bishops and experts, for they wanted to foster cooperation, avoid appearing exclusive, and do their part in forestalling the formation of antagonistic groups. They tried to act in concert when they felt that was called for and were behind Liénart's intervention at the beginning of the council asking that the elections to the commissions be postponed.

The African episcopates were particularly well organized, tended to sympathize with the majority, and voted almost unanimously on issues. Although they, like other non-Europeans, had a generally low profile at the council, their coherence made them a strong influence. Even more effective at the council was CELAM, the umbrella group for the twenty-two conferences of the Latin American bishops. The Latin Americans formed CELAM in 1955 and got almost immediate approval from Pius XII. During the council they capitalized on their tradition of working together and had effective leadership from Bishops Helder Pessôa Câmara, auxiliary of Rio de Janeiro and later archbishop of Olinda y Recife, and Manuel Larraín of Talca, Chile, both vice-presidents of CELAM.[71] The bishops from Asia and Oceania lacked the cultural cohesion of the Latin Americans and even of the Africans, all of whom spoke either French or English. They were, consequently, less able to establish a network.

The observers and guests met every Tuesday under the leadership of Willebrands at the Foyer Unitas in the Piazza Navona, next to the church of Sant' Agnese. A few members of the Secretariat staff met with them. The observers had full access to all the documents of the council and were able to make their views on them known to the Secretariat. They made their most important comments, not surprisingly, on the drafts of the document on ecumenism.[72]

Almost inevitably, given the size and complexity of the council, other groupings also developed. In 1963, for instance, a few bishops who were members of religious orders formed "The Bishops' Secretariat" to protect the interests of the orders against what they believed was other bishops' misunderstanding of religious life. They established their office in the headquarters of the Society of Jesus, just outside the piazza of St. Peter's.[73] Another group aimed to turn the attention of the council to the poor and the oppressed and, hence, to try to prevent the council from becoming simply a "sacristy affair." Among its important members were His Beatitude Maximos IV Saigh and Cardinals Pierre-Marie Gerlier of Lyons and Giacomo Lercaro of Bologna. According to the only list that survives, the group had forty-five members, twenty of whom were from Latin America. From North America there were two Canadians. The most powerful spokesmen for the group were Helder Câmara and Georges Mercier, bishop of Lahouat (Sahara de Argelia). The group had no formal organization, yet bishops with these concerns met from time to time during the council and in effect subscribed to the proposition put to them by Gerlier at their first meeting: "The duty of the church in our age is to adapt itself in the most responsive way to the situation created by the suffering of so many human beings. . . . The church must be seen for what it is, the mother of the poor."[74] These bishops were especially concerned with the development of the constitution On the Church in the Modern World.

A more broadly influential group known as the Conference of Delegates (known also as the Inter-Conference, the International Committee, the Conference of the Twenty-Two, and even the Conference of the Twenty-Nine) had a similarly informal beginning. As the council was opening, Cardinal Liénart asked Father Roger Etchegaray, who at the time served as director of the Pastoral Secretariat of the French episcopacy, to try to make contacts with other episcopacies. Etchegaray met with bishops Câmara of Brazil and Larraín of Chile, the vice-presidents of CELAM. Together they conceived the idea of regular meetings of delegates from episcopal conferences. The Conference would be a way of compensating for the difficulty of communication resulting from the almost unmanageable size of the assembly in St. Peter's.

It soon took shape, therefore, as a network to connect bishops from around the world. By the second period of the council, the Conference met every Friday evening for a total of ninety-one sessions during the four years of the council. It created a forum whereby information could be exchanged, especially about what was going on in the meetings of the national episcopates. The delegates carried on their discussions in vernaculars rather than in Latin, and the meetings were held outside Vatican precincts at a large conference center, the Domus Mariae. (The group was sometimes referred to as the Domus Mariae Conference.)

Some twenty-two episcopal conferences or groups of conferences like CELAM began to send delegates to the meetings. Delegates to the Conference reported to it what was going on in their own sector and then reported back to that sector what they had heard at the meeting. With usually only twenty-two delegates present at the meetings, each of whom represented an episcopal conference or grouping of conferences, business could be conducted relatively briskly.

The Conference was important because it let bishops of a reformist bent know even before the formal discussions in St. Peter's that others shared their viewpoint on a particular text. It was just as important in animating the episcopal conferences that took part. Moreover, it gave heart to the bishops from Africa, Asia, and Latin America, who felt marginal because of the leadership played by the Europeans. Many bishops from Africa and to some extent from Asia felt they were still held in tutelage by the Congregation for the Propagation of the Faith. Leaders among the Latin American bishops like Câmara saw the Conference as a vehicle for advancing their concern with poverty and other social issues. The Conference gave these so-called Third World groups of bishops a forum where they could be heard, learn what others were thinking in a less formal atmosphere than the basilica—and make a difference.

The Conference developed into an extraordinarily effective communications network reaching more than two-thirds of the bishops at the council. As things turned out, at least one delegate sat on each of the council's commissions, so that the Conference had direct access to what was happening as the documents were prepared. The Conference was, moreover, an exercise in collegiality as an ongoing process.

That function may have been decisive in the first weeks. The Conference met on the afternoon of November 13, the day before the crucial debate on a schema known as *De Fontibus,* and bishops from around the world found out how widespread dissatisfaction was with the document and how determined some of their colleagues were to reject it outright. The meeting helped rally the forces opposed to *De Fontibus.* Although the Conference, unlike the International Group of Fathers, adopted no group position on issues, by its very dynamism it helped create and sustain the majority.[75]

His Beatitude Maximos IV Saigh led the small, tight-knit group of sixteen bishops and four superiors of religious orders from the Melkite church in the Middle East that, like the Belgians, had an impact on the council well beyond their numbers. In their interventions they forced the council again and again to realize that Catholicism was bigger and more diversified than the bishops of the West seemed to realize. They jolted those bishops out of some assumptions about what the Catholic tradition was. These Melkite bishops, though deeply rooted in their own tradition, also had excellent, Western-style educations and were perfectly fluent in French. They knew the traditions of the Western church, therefore, but they regarded them with a detached and sometimes critical eye.

Latin, they liked to insist, was not the language of the universal church but the language of the Western expression of the church. The Melkite tradition had never lost the collegial style of church governance practiced in the early centuries of the church, and the Melkite bishops saw it as more consonant with the Catholic tradition than its monarchical alternative. Their theological tradition was solidly patristic, never interrupted by the Scholastic phenomenon as happened in the West, and never had to define itself against the Reformation. It was, therefore, in perfect accord with the patristic revival of "la nouvelle théologie" without having to resort to a *ressourcement* in order to be so.

Among these bishops Elias Zoghby, Melkite patriarchal vicar for Egypt, was important, for instance, but none could compare with Maximos— "Patriarch of Antioch and of all the Orient, of Alexandria and Jerusalem," to give him his official title. Eighty-four years old when the council opened, he emerged as one of the most important prelates at it.[76] On ceremonial occasions he wore not the miter of the Western bishops but the crown traditional in his rite. In his interventions he flouted the "Regulations" by speaking French instead of Latin and by addressing "Their Beatitudes," the Eastern patriarchs, before "Their Eminences," the cardinals. He gained attention, but he also won respect and admiration for the substance of his speeches and their straightforward style, which made them among the very few at the council that the bishops anticipated with pleasure and, sometimes, suspense. As early as May 23, 1959, he urged John XXIII to found a new office in the Curia that anticipated what the Secretariat for Christian Unity would become.[77]

Under Maximos's leadership, the Melkites came to the council with clear ideas, some of which were shocking, at least at first, to bishops of the Latin rite. On August 29, 1959, long before the council opened, they sent a joint response to Cardinal Tardini's request for items for the council's agenda. In it they insisted that the first concern of the council was to work for Christian unity, especially with the Orthodox churches. The major obstacle to overcoming the evil of disunity was clear to them: "The principal cause of the evil, we believe, is the tendency of most Latin theologians and canonists to concentrate all the authority Christ granted to his church in the one person of the Sovereign Pontiff and to make him the source of all power and, consequently, to give practically sovereign and completely centralized power to the Roman Curia, which acts in his name. In this perspective it is difficult to see in the apostolic authority of the patriarchs and bishops anything except a pure and simple delegation of the supreme authority of the pope, which he can limit and revoke at will." Canon law itself, they insisted, promoted this tendency. The council must address the evil by defining the true nature of the patriarchs' and bishops' authority.[78]

The vast majority of bishops arrived at the council, however, without perspectives as clear as the Melkites'. They arrived, rather, with a general deference for "what Rome says." They came without much background in the technical and often complex issues they would be called upon to discuss. The process of the council did two things for them. First, through formal and informal contact with their peers, it helped them to discover and express their hopes and beliefs and thus to form partnerships with like-minded bishops. Only in this way did blocs and alignments develop, a few of which I have described.

Second, the process became for them an extended seminar in theology, in which they often heard alternatives to what they had learned in the seminary and until now accepted as beyond question. At the North American College, for instance, where a number of bishops from the United States were housed, at the Biblicum, and at other sites around the city of Rome, theologians delivered lectures on theology and exegesis that drew many bishops.

The learning experience was gradual, of course, but by the middle of the first period it was having a palpable effect, moving more and more council fathers to support positions that just a little while earlier they would have considered daring, if not worse. In any case, the first two weeks made clear to almost everybody that a struggle was emerging between those who expected and hoped that the council would approve what was presented to it (and therefore end in one session) and those who were determined that it do something more.

4

The First Period (1962)

The Lines Are Drawn

AFTER almost two weeks in session, debate finally opened on October 22. By that time bishops had become painfully aware of the problems attendant on a meeting of such size that invited the active participation of all those present. They were also aware of organizational and procedural problems peculiar to this council, two of which were outstanding. The first was the management of the agenda and the moderating of the General Congregations. The "Regulations" stipulated three players in this arena: the Council of Presidents, the Secretariat for Extraordinary Affairs, and the Secretary General, Felici. John XXIII named ten cardinals to the Council of Presidents, whose charge was to direct the council discussions. Of the ten only Tisserant, dean of the College of Cardinals, was from the Curia. They sat at a table just in front of the papal altar and took turns chairing the meetings. From the very beginning, this large and diverse group had difficulty expeditiously handling questions and problems that arose in the course of the sessions.

The Secretariat for Extraordinary Affairs, chaired by Cardinal Amleto Cicognani, secretary of state, was to help the presidents resolve procedural conflicts and function more efficiently. Composed of seven cardinals besides Cicognani, the Secretariat was broadly representative of different viewpoints and hence potentially helpful in finding a middle way amid conflicting pressures. It met outside the sessions of the council, however, and could not act immediately as problems arose from the floor. Cicognani had succeeded Tardini as secretary of state after Tardini's death. By virtue of his office as secretary of state (but not as chair of the council's Secretariat), Cicognani had regular access to the pope and thus could keep the council informed of his views, even though such a function was outside the purview of the "Regulations." Just where the responsibilities of the Secretariat for Extraordinary Affairs ended and those of the presidents began was murky. Into this breach often stepped the secretary general, Felici. His on-the-spot authority in coordinating the day-to-day tasks essential to the council's smooth running, such as the printing and distribution of the documents, was inadvertently enhanced by those blurred lines.[1]

The second problem was the sheer quantity of printed material the bishops were expected to read and digest. They felt inundated. Before arriving in Rome they had received seven schemas, just the beginning of what promised to be a tidal wave. The Preparatory Commissions had produced roughly seventy documents. Although some of these documents were chapters intended for larger texts, they created a first impression of indigestible volume. As the council found its way, most of these documents were put aside or, more generally, incorporated into other schemas. Before that happened, however, the bishops anticipated drowning in them.

The bishops, moreover, had to read the materials they did receive, make decisions about them, and try to keep everything straight in their heads. These documents seemed to be a scattershot collection of materials guided by no discernible orientation except that many aimed at confirming and promoting directions set by the popes of the previous 150 years and at validating theological positions the bishops had learned decades earlier from their seminary textbooks.

Among the seven schemas the bishops received in the fall of 1962, two— On the Sacred Liturgy *(Sacrosanctum Concilium)* and On the Sources of Revelation *(De Fontibus Revelationis)*—turned out to be of the utmost importance. Since the schema on the liturgy was by general consensus assessed as well prepared and had excited less negative commentary beforehand than some of the others, it appeared first on the agenda. Many bishops were wary of liturgical changes, and some harbored suspicions about the orthodoxy of liturgical experts. All of them, however, had experienced some changes and knew that the popes, beginning with the recently canonized (1954) Pius X, had sanctioned and promoted them. In principle, therefore, they could not be altogether opposed to the idea. Just how they would react to the draft was, however, not clear.

The Discussion of the Liturgy

Cardinal Gaetano Cicognani, prefect of the Congregation of Rites and elder brother of the secretary of state, chaired the Preparatory Commission on the liturgy. Annibale Bugnini, a priest who taught at both the Lateran and Urbaniana universities in Rome, served as its secretary, a position of considerable importance. Bugnini was a skilled and respected liturgist who had guided Pius XII in his liturgical changes. He was able to coordinate the efforts of the sixty-five members and consultants who made up the commission to produce, by January 1962, a coherent text that combined a concise statement of principles with concrete recommendations for action. Cicognani, gravely ill at the time and also unsympathetic to aspects of the document, hesitated to sign it. Felici, fearful that Cicognani would die without signing, appealed to Pope John, who appealed to Amleto, who on February 1, 1962, persuaded his still-reluctant brother to affix his signature to the text. *Sacrosanctum* was ready for the council.[2]

Three weeks later, on February 22, the pope appointed Cardinal Larraona as the new prefect of the Congregation of Rites and therefore as head of the Preparatory Commission. As such, he was the successor to Cicognani, who had since died. Larraona aligned himself with some of the most conservative members of the council and became a leader among them.[3] On that same February 22, the Vatican published *Veterum Sapientia,* the Apostolic Constitution that insisted on the intensification of study of Latin in seminaries. As noted, this text might be taken as indirectly confirming the place of Latin in the liturgy.[4] John XXIII not only signed the document but, in an address that day in St. Peter's, singled it out for praise.[5] Where did the pope himself stand on liturgical issues? It was anybody's guess.

As was expected for the head of a Preparatory Commission, Larraona became president of the Liturgical Commission of the council itself. He proved a poor chairman, at least in part because he deliberately tried to obstruct action on a text that displeased him. On October 21, at the first meeting of the commission, moreover, he passed over Bugnini as secretary and replaced him with Ferdinando Antonelli, a priest working in the Curia at the Congregation of Rites. Larraona considered Bugnini too progressive and held him responsible for the disagreeable schema he inherited.

The appointment of Antonelli was all the more surprising because he had played no role in the preparation of the document. Ottaviani, it was rumored, had a hand in his selection. In all the other commissions the secretaries, like the presidents, were retained from the pre-council commissions. Not only was Bugnini not named secretary; he was also almost immediately dismissed from his post as a teacher of liturgy at the Lateran University.[6] Word spread fast. Many at the council construed the incidents as further evidence of machinations by "the Curia" to control the council at any cost, by any means. Ultimately, perhaps to the consternation of those who promoted him, Antonelli turned out to be an evenhanded reporter of what Bugnini bequeathed him.

On October 22, the day after Bugnini's dismissal, Larraona took the floor in St. Peter's to say not much more than that *Sacrosanctum Concilium* would be introduced by Antonelli, who spoke for about twenty minutes. Antonelli began by making two general points.[7] First, just as the Council of Trent and Vatican I had mandated revision and emendation of liturgical texts, experts were now unanimously convinced that, while holding fast to the liturgical tradition of the church, similar changes in texts and rites were needed "to accommodate them to the ethos and needs of our day." The *aggiornamento* theme was clear.

Second, a great pastoral problem had to be addressed. The faithful had become "mute spectators" at Mass instead of active participants in the liturgical action. This development, he said, dated back to the Middle Ages, and recent popes, beginning with Pius X, had taken steps to remedy it. To deal with these issues, Pius XII had established a commission in 1948 that produced a full volume of reflections and recommendations. In 1951 Pius, acting on the recommendations, had restored the Easter Vigil and, in 1955, the liturgy for the entire Sacred Triduum, the last three days of Holy Week. Antonelli, by convincingly arguing that *Sacrosanctum Concilium* was in keeping with recent papal teaching and actions, was able to forestall a problem that would dog other schemas at the council.

He listed five criteria that had guided the Preparatory Commission in drawing up the schema. First, the commission would exercise great care in conserving the liturgical patrimony of the church. Second, it would be guided by a few principles that would undergird a general renewal *(instau-*

The First Period (1962)

ratio) of the liturgy. Third, it would derive its practical and rubrical directives from a doctrinal base. Fourth, it would insist on the necessity of in-
stilling in the clergy a deeper sense of "the liturgical spirit" so that they
could be effective teachers of the faithful. Finally, it would take as its aim
leading the faithful into an ever more active participation in the liturgy.
The document in hand, he reminded his audience, had been approved by
the Central Preparatory Commission and was thus ready for examination
by the council fathers.

Antonelli went on to present the eight chapters of the text, which covered every aspect of liturgical celebration: (1) General Principles; (2) the
Eucharistic Mystery (the Mass); (3) Sacraments and Sacramentals; (4) the
Divine Office (the liturgical hours like Vespers); (5) the Liturgical Year; (6)
Liturgical Furnishings; (7) Sacred Music; and (8) Sacred Art. In presenting
them he underscored how the five criteria were operative throughout the
text. He made no mention of what had been a burning issue in the commission and would be the most time-consuming aspect of the discussion
in St. Peter's, the use of vernacular languages in the Mass.

The text about which he spoke had 105 sections, running without the
notes to about 25 pages of ordinary print. The notes to the text covered a
wide variety of sources but with a generous sprinkling from the encyclical
Mediator Dei. The "Preface" stated that the purpose of the council was to
foster a more vigorous Christian life among the faithful, to promote union
with the "separated brethren" *(fratres separati),* and to call all into the
church. Therefore, the council would make changes in those things subject to change, so as, in this case, to adapt the liturgy better to the conditions of modern life and to foster Christian unity—two themes from
John's opening address, *Gaudet Mater Ecclesia.* It made the important
point that the Eucharistic Liturgy was where the "work of our redemption" especially took place and that it manifested the many aspects of the
"mystery of Christ and the authentic nature of the true church." Thus Antonelli made the crucial connection between liturgy and ecclesiology.

In chapter one the "mystery of Christ" was specified as "the Paschal
Mystery," the mystery that began with Christ's passion but went on to his
resurrection and glorification. With the Paschal Mystery expressed in this
full way as one of its themes, the text subtly shifted a mind-set among
Catholics that since the Middle Ages had located the Redemption almost
exclusively in Christ's suffering and death. The text thereby implicitly promoted a shift in style of spirituality. It once again stated perhaps the obvi-

ous by insisting on the liturgy as nourishment for one's spiritual life. In so doing, however, it affirmed right at the beginning of the council what would become one of its great themes, the call to holiness that God, through the church, addresses to all men and women.

Chapter one was especially important for its insistence on active participation by everyone in the congregation. Such participation was the right and duty of every Christian. It was demanded by the very nature of the liturgy and was conferred upon the faithful by virtue of their baptism. This principle was the most fundamental in the whole schema. It was a counterpoint to the long historical development that bit by bit had located all the action in the priest-celebrant.

The chapter was also important for enunciating other principles. Whatever obscured or distracted from the essential meaning of the liturgical celebrations was to be eliminated. Intelligibility and simplicity were thus to be norms in whatever changes were implemented. Christ was present in the Word of Scripture as well as in the Eucharist, and therefore the significance of that part of the liturgy—the "Liturgy of the Word"—was to be made more effective. This highlighting of "the Word" in *Sacrosanctum* presaged a new centrality of Scripture in Catholic preaching and piety, which would become another major theme of the council. While the essential structure of the Roman Rite was to be maintained, local adaptation, especially in mission territories, was legitimate and encouraged. Greater autonomy was to be granted to bishops in making adaptations appropriate to their cultures, which was a clear call for some decentralization.

About liturgical languages, the chapter said:

> Latin is to be retained in the liturgies of the Western church. Since, however, "in some rites it is clear that the vernacular has proved very useful for the people" [a quotation from *Mediator Dei*], it should be given a wider role in liturgy, especially in readings, announcements, certain prayers, and music. Let it be left to episcopal conferences in different parts of the world, in consultation if need be with bishops of nearby regions speaking the same language, to propose to the Holy See the degree and the modes for admitting vernacular languages into the liturgy.[8]

Whereas the first chapter consisted in principles, only the most important of which I have mentioned here, the others consisted almost entirely in concrete applications or directives. For instance chapter two, on the Eucharist, became specific about the vernacular: "In Mass let a suitable place be made for the vernacular, especially in the readings, in prayers, and in some canticles, in accordance with article 24 of this Constitution." Somewhat ironically, this provision was more conservative than the corresponding directive of the Council of Trent, which had stated simply that "it is wrong to maintain that the mass must everywhere be celebrated in the vernacular."[9] Trent left the question open, but in the violent atmosphere of the day, no change was possible. Vernacular had already come to stand for Protestant.

The next article called for reception of the Eucharist by the faithful on certain occasions under the form of both bread and wine, a change in the medieval tradition of reserving wine for the priest. Trent, again, had left this issue open, but the earlier tradition had been reaffirmed by sixteenth-century popes in the face of the Protestant practice of sharing the cup.[10] Sometimes the directives were generic in the extreme. In chapter three, the schema had only the following to say about the Sacrament of Penance: "Let the rite and formula of the Sacrament of Penance be revised so as more clearly to express the effect of the Sacrament." No matter how generic some of its provisions, the document also laid down a number of specific measures to be adopted in the reform of the liturgy. Despite these prescriptions, the text in some passages pointed in the direction of the non-juridical, Scripture-based, patristic-inspired style the council would eventually adopt as its own. It contained no canons or anathemas.

In his presentation, Antonelli quite properly did not go into detail. When he finished, the president for the day opened the floor for discussion. How would the document be received? The first six speakers that day included some who would turn out to be among the most influential in the whole council. Cardinal Frings of Cologne led off from the presidents' table. His opening words: "The schema before us is like the last will and testament of Pius XII, who, following in the footsteps of Saint Pius X, boldly began a renewal of the sacred liturgy."[11] Frings thus sounded what would become a leitmotif of the majority: the council was carrying forward work that had already begun. His next sentence was equally significant: "The schema is to be commended for its modest and truly pastoral literary style, full of the spirit of Holy Scripture and the Fathers of the Church." He then made four brief suggestions, three of which pertained to use of the vernacular. Within ten minutes of beginning and letting it be known how highly he thought of the draft document, he sat down.

Ruffini spoke next, even more briefly and also from the presidents' table. He criticized the text for being too exclusively focused on the Roman Rite, reminded the fathers that only the Congregation of Rites had authority in matters liturgical, and, more significant, expressed no praise for the document. Then came Lercaro of Bologna. Clear in his approval for the text and insistent on how much it accorded with the tradition of the church, he tried to refute one of the standard criticisms leveled at liturgical reformers: "The changes the document mandates do not grow out of some sterile archeology or out of some insane itching for novelty but out of the requests of pastors and out of pastoral needs—active participation in the liturgy is, according to the memorable words of Pius X, the first and irreplaceable source of the Christian spirit." He concluded: "When taken as a whole and with due allowance for appropriate emendation, I willingly and eagerly in the Lord give my approval to the document."[12]

Then Montini. In substance he approved the text, especially because it rested on the principle of pastoral efficacy. The schema conceded nothing to those who arbitrarily wanted to make changes nor to those who insisted that the rite can in no way be changed, as if the historical form were inseparable from what it signified. Montini called for greater use of the vernacular, but with qualification.[13]

Then came Spellman of New York with one of the longer interventions, in which he managed never to say outright that he liked what he had read. His message was simple: caution. In particular, though the vernacular might be fine in the administration of some of the sacraments, it should not be introduced into the Mass. Later in the course of the debate he was seconded in this opinion by Cardinal McIntyre of Los Angeles: "The sacred Mass should remain as it is."[14] Spellman had meanwhile taken a swipe at professional liturgists by reminding the council fathers that as far as the liturgy was concerned, the perspective of real pastors was often different from that of liturgical scholars.[15]

Döpfner of Munich stated immediately his wholehearted approval of the schema. He registered his disagreement with those who felt that the document should stick to general principles and not descend, as it did in some matters, to specific measures. He probably made this point because he feared what would happen in the Congregation of Rites if the provi-

His Beatitude Maximos IV Saigh. Photograph courtesy of the Melkite Catholic Patriarchate.

sions were left too vague. Then, seemingly in direct response to Spellman, he voiced his support for use of the vernacular even in the Mass.

Meanwhile, outside the precincts of St. Peter's, bishops from the "new churches" began holding press conferences about the liturgy. Bishop Willem van Bekkum of Ruteng, Indonesia, held the first on October 23, followed within a few days by another by Archbishop Eugene D'Souza of Nagpur, India, and then another by Lawrence Nagae of Urawa, Japan.

They all insisted on the urgency in their countries of cultural adaptation, including use of the vernacular. These conferences attracted considerable attention in the media and thus had at least as much impact on the other bishops as if they had been delivered on the council floor.[16]

Back in St. Peter's on October 24, the day after van Bekkum's conference, Maximos IV rose to speak and shook the bishops to attention right off by addressing them in French. His voice was strong, his tone assured. Here was a speaker, the council fathers immediately recognized, with a quite different perspective, a speaker representing a venerable tradition that had not been subject to many of the historical developments that so much conditioned the traditions of the western church.

Maximos praised the document but said he would confine his remarks only to section 24, concerning Latin:

> The almost absolute value assigned to Latin in the liturgy, in teaching, and in the administration of the Latin church strikes us from the Eastern church as strange [*assez anormal*]. Christ after all spoke the language of his contemporaries. . . . [In the East] there has never been a problem about the proper liturgical language. All languages are liturgical, as the Psalmist says, "Praise the Lord, all ye people." . . . The Latin language is dead. But the church is living, and its language, the vehicle of the grace of the Holy Spirit, must also be living because it is intended for us human beings not for angels.

He had two suggestions. First, instead of saying that Latin was to be kept as the language for the liturgy, the text should be emended to say simply that it is "the original and official language of the Roman Rite." Second, instead of saying that the episcopal conferences "propose" to the Holy See whatever use of the vernacular they think appropriate, the text should say that the conferences "decide," subject to the approval of the Holy See.[17] When the session ended, a number of bishops rushed up to Maximos to congratulate him and shake his hand. That very day, Pope John noted in his diary that the Latin issue divided the council into those who had never left their own country "or Italy" and those especially from mission territories.[18]

But Maximos was far from being the last bishop to address *Sacrosanctum*. Discussion of the schema dragged on from October 22 to November 13—three weeks, fifteen sessions, with 328 interventions from the floor and

297 submitted in written form. Although speakers were held to a ten-minute limit, the "Regulations" failed to provide a procedure for closing debate on a topic. Bishops began to fear that the discussion on the liturgy would go on forever. Speaker after speaker repeated the same points. On November 6 Pope John intervened, making an ad hoc change in the "Regulations" to allow the presidents to close discussion if they felt an issue had been adequately addressed. Timely closure was now legal, an important step in moving the agenda along more quickly.

Where did the schema stand when, on November 13, the presidents successfully called for a vote to halt the interventions? It obviously had strong support, perhaps most notably from African and Asian bishops, but it had also received much criticism. Two issues attracted the most attention and generated the most heat. The first was the vernacular. Eighty-one interventions focused on that issue. The second revolved around the competence of local bishops or episcopal conferences to make decisions, and thus concerned the limits of the authority of the Congregation of Rites. Early on, therefore, the crucial issue of center-periphery bounded to the surface. It was well known, moreover, that in the Central Preparatory Commission, when the council was still being planned, resolutions to abolish the Holy Office outright had come to the floor—but had gotten nowhere.

Ottaviani had already come to stand for "the Curia" and to embody everything people disliked about the Holy Office, which was being increasingly criticized. This perception of him was not confined to members of the council. Even for those who followed the council from afar, Ottaviani became almost a household name. Jokes about him circulated broadly and began to appear in newspapers and journals. One morning, supposedly, Ottaviani called a taxi and directed the driver to take him to the council. The driver hit the road for Trent.

As early as October 24 Archbishop Pietro Parente, the assessor (administrative director) of the Holy Office, complained in an angry intervention about criticisms of his Congregation: "We in the Holy Office are martyrs, martyrs." He called on the innovators at the council—*novatores*—to learn a thing or two from the caution with which the Holy See operated and not rush into changes. Although *novatores* could have a less nocuous meaning, in ecclesiastical parlance it was a synonym for heretic, as everybody at the council knew full well.[19]

A few days earlier Ottaviani had criticized *Sacrosanctum* for its literary style. The language was often ambiguous, he said, even in the doctrinal parts. Those parts, furthermore, "invaded" the doctrinal camp and hence needed to be reviewed by theologians, by which he meant his own Doctrinal Commission.[20] His patience was wearing thin. He took the floor again on October 30, opening his intervention with a series of rhetorical questions that made clear how utterly unacceptable he found the schema. Among the questions: "What, now, are we dealing here with a revolution regarding the whole Mass?"[21]

He insisted that the Mass not be changed and that reception of the Eucharist under both forms was a bad idea, as was concelebration, that is, more than one priest officiating at a single Mass. He then hit his adversaries at their most vulnerable point. It was all well and good to quote popes like Pius XII when they agreed with one's position, but what about quoting them when they did not? In 1956, he reminded the council, Pius XII had made it clear to liturgists who had just completed an important meeting at Assisi that Latin was and would remain the language of the Mass.[22]

He was well over the ten-minute limit. Cardinal Alfrink, presiding that day, interrupted the powerful head of the Holy Office to inform him that he had already spoken for the maximum amount of time. This was treatment to which Ottaviani was not accustomed: "I've finished! I've finished! I've finished!" The basilica broke into applause. Ottaviani, insulted and humiliated, boycotted the council for the next two weeks, a dramatic and extraordinarily meaningful gesture from somebody of his stature.

Finally, on November 14 Cardinal Tisserant, the presiding president of the day, put *Sacrosanctum Concilium* to a vote on whether to accept the schema as the base text. Because so many interventions on the document had been critical, this vote, the council's first on a schema, was awaited with considerable tension. A positive vote meant that the document was fundamentally sound, so that after revisions by the Liturgical Commission, it could later in the council be resubmitted for approval of the changes and then for final approval. It also implicitly meant that it need not be submitted to the Doctrinal Commission, as Ottaviani had asked, to have its orthodoxy ensured. The outcome of the voting astounded everybody—a landslide in favor, 2,162 votes, with only 46 opposed. That was a 97 percent approval.

The next year, on December 4, 1963, the council overwhelmingly gave its approval to the revised text of *Sacrosanctum Concilium*, and Paul VI then promulgated it. The final vote was even more of a landslide: 2,147 in favor, 4 against. This was the first document approved by the council and, compared with others, was remarkable for how little it had changed from the original version. Regarding Latin, for instance, the text, though softened slightly, remained substantially the same.[23] Regarding the other hotly debated issue, however, the text in three places affirmed the authority of bishops and bishops' conferences to make decisions in adapting the liturgy to local circumstances. This action effectively nullified Canon 1257 of the Code, which placed all decisions about liturgy exclusively in the Holy See.

By approving *Sacrosanctum,* the council set in motion a programmatic reshaping of virtually every aspect of Roman Catholic liturgy unlike anything that had ever been attempted before. The changes mandated by the Council of Trent, for instance, consisted basically in standardizing traditional texts and paring away some accretions. Worshipers would hardly have recognized the difference. Not true with Vatican II.

The institution that was to guide the reshaping was created almost immediately after *Sacrosanctum* was promulgated. On the morning of January 3, 1964, Cardinal Cicognani summoned Father Bugnini to his office to tell him that Pope Paul VI had created a commission to implement and interpret *Sacrosanctum Concilium* and had named him secretary. The appointment of Bugnini to this crucial post was another example of the remarkable rehabilitations that took place during the council. Moreover, though Cardinal Larraona, still prefect of the Congregation of Rites, was named to the commission, Cardinal Lercaro was to be its president. When the question arose as to where the Consilium, as this body became known, was to meet, Cardinal Cicognani replied tersely, "Wherever you wish, but not at the Congregation of Rites."[24]

The Consilium set about its task. The Mass began to look different. The priest, instead of celebrating Mass with his back to the congregation, from which he was separated by a railing around the sanctuary, now faced the pews. This change signified that the ceremony was an act of worship of a gathered community as well as a sacrifice to God performed in the congregation's name. During the first part of the Mass, the Liturgy of the Word, the celebrant no longer stood at the altar with his back to the people. He now stood in the pulpit facing them, or, if someone else read the Scripture passages, he sat at the side of the altar.

Right after the council Latin was retained in the central Eucharistic prayer, the so-called canon of the Mass, a measure in keeping with *Sacro-sanctum,* but within a few years the Mass in its entirety was being cele-brated in the vernacular worldwide. It had become increasingly obvious that the principles of intelligibility and active participation did not sit well with maintaining for such a meaningful part a language only priests un-derstood. The decree thus contained within itself a dynamism that led to changes that were beyond some of its specific provisions but that were al-most required by its most fundamental principles.

These were only two of the changes implemented through a series of decrees from 1964 until 1975.[25] Were they revolutionary, as Cardinal Otta-viani feared? The answer depends in part on one's definition of revolution, but there can be no doubt that the changes were obvious to even the most casual observer and so considerable that a few Catholics repudiated them as heresy and betrayal.[26] To worship in the vernacular was to worship like Protestants, a complaint heard especially in English-speaking countries. The vast majority of Catholics accepted the changes—enthusiastically, re-luctantly, or somewhere in between, but with full awareness that the Mass, while surely maintaining its basic elements and structure, was to the naked eye and ear different from what it had been before.

Within the council itself the vote that originally approved *Sacrosanc-tum,* on November 14, 1962, had a significance beyond liturgy and wor-ship. It enunciated and gave first voice to at least four principles that would be adopted and developed by other documents and help give Vatican II its final profile. The first is the principle of *aggiornamento,* or adaptation to contemporary circumstances. In fact, however, the provisions and great themes of the text are as much due to the principle of *ressourcement* as to that of *aggiornamento.* The liturgists, that is to say, had returned to the ancient sources in order to find their way. The Mass was thus not so much "modernized" as made to conform more closely to fundamental and tradi-tional principles.

The second is the principle of adaptation to local circumstances: "The church does not wish to impose a rigid uniformity in matters that do not involve the faith or the good of the whole community." Unity, the docu-ment implies, can be maintained within diversity. In stating that "the art of our own times and of every nation and culture shall be given free scope," the council took a step out of its European box.

The third is the principle of episcopal authority and of greater decision-making on the local level. The document is thus consonant with the doctrine of episcopal collegiality. The final principle is the full and active participation of everybody present in the liturgical action. This is a principle of engagement and active responsibility, and by implication it extended beyond liturgy to the church at large, to the church as "the people of God." Liturgy, that is to say, had ecclesiological implications and ramifications.

Was the vote on November 14 a victory for those whom the media were beginning to call "the progressives"? The vote was so close to unanimity that it seemed to be a victory for everybody. Even so, it was by now clear that there were two orientations among the council fathers that seemed destined to clash. Would they? If so, when and over what?

The Turning Point: The Sources of Revelation

On the same day as the vote, Cardinal Ottaviani, absent for two weeks, took the floor to introduce the schema On the Sources of Revelation, prepared by his commission.[27] This document was essentially about the roles in the church of Scripture, Tradition, and "Magisterium" (ecclesiastical, especially papal, teaching authority) and of their relationship to one another. As such, it might seem to be a subject too technical to ignite a conflagration. It became invested, however, with a symbolic importance that was immense. A month had elapsed since the opening of the council, and now the decisive moment for the direction it would take had arrived. As the American Protestant observer Douglas Horton put it in his diary for November 14, "The dam broke."[28]

Ottaviani spoke for only five minutes, less as presenting a text for consideration than as defending it even before discussion began. He was aware, he said, that alternative schemas were circulating, which was contrary to Canon 222 of the Code of Canon Law. Discussion was to take place on this text, no other. The previous day he had informed his commission that since the documents prepared by the Preparatory Commissions had been approved by the pope, they could not be rejected by the council.[29]

Complaints were circulating, he said, that the schema took no account of the new theology, but councils spoke for the ages, not for a particular theological school that tomorrow is forgotten. Remember, moreover, that the commission consisted of bishops and experts from around the world who worked hard to produce the text. He raised the crucial issue of its style, which raised the even more crucial issue of the character of the council:

> You have heard many people speak about the lack of a pastoral tone in this schema. Well, I say that the first and most fundamental pastoral task is to provide correct doctrine. "Teach!" The Lord's greatest commandment is precisely that: "Teach all peoples." Teaching correctly is what is fundamental to being pastoral. Those who are concerned with a pastoral style can later give the church's teaching a fuller pastoral expression. But take notice: councils speak in a style that is orderly, lucid, concise, and not in the style of a sermon or a pastoral letter of some bishop or other, nor even in the style of an encyclical of the Supreme Pontiff. This style of council discourse is sanctioned by its use through the ages.[30]

What was the purpose of the council? The pope had described it as a pastoral undertaking. Ottaviani conceded the point but defined pastoral as essentially clear enunciation of doctrine. That was a limitation his critics were not about to accept. Where Ottaviani and the Doctrinal Commission stood on these points was made even clearer when he turned the microphone over to Father Salvatore Garofalo to make the formal presentation of the schema.

Garofalo opened with the words: "Everybody knows that the principal task of an ecumenical council is to defend and promote Catholic doctrine."[31] In his presentation he never quite let go of that point, coming back to it again and again and quoting *Gaudet Mater Ecclesia* to support it. In that connection he addressed the question of style, more or less repeating what Ottaviani had said but making the additional point that a council could not renounce its duty to condemn errors, no matter what form such condemnations might take. For that reason, he said, the subject treated in the text was of particular importance because ideas were circulating among both theologians and the faithful that were cause for concern. After briefly presenting the outline of the schema, he returned to big themes: the schema was pastoral because it was doctrinal; the schema was ecumenical because it stated clearly for the sake of the separated brethren what the church taught; the style was appropriate because it was perennial.

In a world of
uncertainty, we have
discovered one another.
different, yet alike,
we have the desire
to unite our lives
and continue to
grow together in love
and understanding.

Our thanks to you,
our friends
and loved ones,
for sharing
this special day.
Your presence
makes our joy complete.

Joanna and Vern

August 12, 2006

isted of five chapters.[32] The first was "On the Two
)n," by which was meant Scripture and Tradition.[33]
or point of contention between Catholics and Protes-
insistence on Scripture as the sole basis for Christian
which adduced the Council of Trent as its principal
ined that some truths were found in Scripture; others,
l in Tradition, and these were the truths that the au-
'estament did not set down in writing. It presented
tion as essentially two distinct sources. The chapter
that the task of preserving, defending, and authenti-
e two sources fell exclusively to the ecclesiastical Mag-
'as meant the pope and the Roman Congregations.
ter was "On the Inspiration, Inerrancy, and Literary
Scriptures." Every part of Scripture, down to the last
nspired by God, who as the principal author moved
o write what he intended. That inspiration necessar-
)ture was entirely free from error in both religious
—in qualibet re religiosa vel profana. In that regard, of
des of speaking had to be taken into account—poetry,
so forth.
"On the Old Testament," made only one point: "The
Old Testament and what gives it its momentum is
w Testament, in which its full meaning is made clear."
ne New Testament," condemned the errors that called
torical accuracy of the Gospel accounts of Jesus' words
emned those who called any part of them into ques-
ne "infancy narratives" in Matthew and Luke. It also
rs that attributed Christ's words not to him but to the
to the teaching of the early Christian community.
dealt with practical matters, "On Sacred Scripture in
urch." The Vulgate version (the Latin translation that
as the work of St. Jerome in the fourth century) en-
ity in the church, which had always considered it a
ic bearer of the faith as a version free from all error. Its
Iagisterium was so intimate that it must be considered
part of tradition. The council, of course, also accepted with special veneration the Greek text of the Old Testament known as the Septuagint, which
the Apostles themselves approved. No mention was made of the Bible in

its original languages—the Old Testament in Hebrew and the New Testament in Greek.

The church rejoiced that in our own times the faithful were reading the Bible in vernacular translations and drawing profit from it, but it must also warn them of the danger of misunderstanding the text and of the necessity of following the interpretations provided by the Magisterium. Exegetes currently had at their disposal new information and methods that greatly aided the interpretation of the text, but they were reminded that their interpretations must be in accordance with church teaching.

The authority of the Magisterium was an overriding theme of the whole schema. When Garafalo finished, Liénart took the floor.[34] "It's unacceptable"—*non placet.* That is how he began and that is how he ended. The text must be completely revised—*recogniscatur penitus.* What was wrong with it? First, it misconstrued what the Council of Trent said about the relationship between Scripture and Tradition. Second, it was "frigid" in its language, missing the warmth appropriate to a document about Scripture. Faith was based not on "Scholastic arguments" but on the Word of God. (Scholastic here probably had the double meaning of Neo-Scholastic philosophy/theology and simply academic.)

Then Frings.[35] *Non placet!* The first problem was style. In this document one heard not the voice of the good shepherd but the voice of a professor. Where was the pastoral approach so much desired by Pope John XXIII? In its teaching on the relationship between Scripture and Tradition, moreover, the schema presented not the great tradition of the church but what was found in textbooks from the nineteenth century. The teaching on inerrancy and divine inspiration of the sacred text was far too rigid.

Both Ruffini and Siri pleaded that the text, so carefully prepared, be given a fair hearing and not be rejected out of hand.[36] Siri insisted that the document was needed to reject once again Modernist errors, which despite the condemnation by Pius X still circulated in the church. Cardinal Léger of Montreal asked that the schema be completely revised.[37] As it stood, it was based on fear of error, which gave it a negative tone that would discourage exegetes and be a hindrance to scholarship. Then a *non placet* from Cardinal König of Vienna, who compared it unfavorably to *Divino afflante Spiritu.*[38] Alfrink of Utrecht not only rejected it for many of the same reasons but called for an entirely new schema.[39]

Cardinal Joseph Ritter of Saint Louis, breaking with patterns set by

Cardinals Spellman and McIntyre, similarly rejected it, arguing that the document was filled with pessimism and negativity and that it threw suspicion on the work of Catholic exegetes.[40] (The attacks on professors at the Biblicum, as well as at other Catholic institutions, were of course well known at the council.) Ritter was followed by Bea, former rector of the Biblicum: if we cannot have an entirely new schema, he argued, then this one must be radically—radically indeed—revised. We cannot base what we say simply on fear of error.[41]

This avalanche, while not exactly orchestrated, was also not altogether spontaneous. Theologians had long been at work on the *De Fontibus*. Toward the end of 1961, Cardinal König, a member of the Central Preparatory Commission, had asked Karl Rahner's opinion on the text, to which König of course had access. On January 4 Rahner sent him a severe critique, and as soon as it became clear that the council would examine the schema early on, he prepared a *Disquisitio* on it that began to circulate among the bishops. He explicitly recommended that the council fathers set the schema aside in favor of an entirely new one.

A month or so before the council opened, a group of Dutch-speaking bishops under the leadership of Cardinal Alfrink asked Schillebeeckx to prepare comments on the texts they had received, which included *De Fontibus*. Schillebeeckx's *Animadversiones* (observations), though they did not outright call for a rejection of the prepared texts, were critical of them and, once they were translated into English and Latin, had wide circulation. Meanwhile, in the weeks after the council opened, Rahner and Ratzinger with the blessing of the German bishops composed an alternative text to the official one. This, too, was circulated before November 14. Such an initiative went beyond the provisions of the "Regulations."[42]

On November 9, just days before the schema was presented in St. Peter's, the Secretariat for Christian Unity met under Bea's presidency. The members of the Secretariat were frustrated that before the council they had not been able to get a hearing from Ottaviani on a text dealing with Scripture, which was a subject obviously central to ecumenical dialogue. At this meeting Bea planned the strategy of the Secretariat, which was to insist that the schema betrayed the vision set forth in *Gaudet Mater Ecclesia,* and therefore the purpose for which the council was called; moreover, it took inadequate account of where the issues stood today. Stress was to be laid on the pastoral purpose of the council. Bea was correct in his assessment of John XXIII, who noted in his diary on November 14 that "the schema does not take into account the specific intentions of the Pope in his official discourses."[43]

At a meeting of the Secretariat a week later, on November 16, Bea proposed the idea of a "mixed" commission, that is, a group made up of the members of the Secretariat and the Doctrinal Commission who would work together to produce an acceptable document. In raising such a possibility he was obviously looking to a drastic revision of the schema or a new schema altogether.[44] The Secretariat's opposition to the schema was critically important for the outcome of the debate because it provided an institutional base within the council for all those dissatisfied with *De Fontibus* and with the other texts prepared by the Doctrinal Commission.

As mentioned, on November 13, the day before the debate opened, the Conference of Delegates had met with representatives from a large number of episcopal conferences around the world. What to do about *De Fontibus?* A bishop from each of the conferences presented the view held by his particular conference. Italy refused to give an opinion. (At the meeting of the Italian bishops that same day, Carli of Segni, seeing Modernism in the proposals by Rahner and Schillebeeckx, urged them to vote for the official schema "so as not to leave the council and the church in the hands of the Germans.")[45] A few other representatives reported no consensus. But many of the bishops, representing a wide geographical spectrum, declared their opposition to it—France and Germany, as to be expected, but also Japan, India, the Philippines, Africa, and others. Meanwhile, theologians had for several weeks been conducting their "seminars" on the subject for bishops in various meeting places around Rome during the afternoons and evenings, times when the council was not in session.

Before the bishops set foot in St. Peter's on the morning of November 14, therefore, many of them knew that the schema was in deep trouble. They were fairly well informed about what the problems with *De Fontibus* were, and they were prepared to speak against it. What were those problems? Fundamental was the treatment of Scripture and Tradition in chapter one. The second volume of Hubert Jedin's great history of the Council of Trent, published in 1957, just a few years before Vatican II opened, made clear that subsequent Catholic interpretation of Trent's few words on the subject, used in polemic against Protestants, had gone far beyond what Trent intended to say.[46] Other historical studies had noted that before the sixteenth century, "Scripture alone" was in some form, not quite Luther's, the traditional opinion, held even by Thomas Aquinas.[47] A further problem with the schema was its designation of Scripture and Tradition as *sources* of Revelation, whereas even Trent had made clear that the preaching of Christ and the Apostles was the source, transmitted in two ways—"in written books and in unwritten traditions."[48]

At the very moment of Vatican II, in fact, the whole issue of the relationship among Scripture, Tradition, and Revelation was hotly debated among Catholic theologians, especially in Germany. The schema seemed to be repeating debatable or even incorrect interpretations from the era of the Counter Reformation that had been reinforced and overly simplified in seminary textbooks in the nineteenth and early twentieth centuries. There were a number of objections to the way the draft described the relationship. It seemed to deny, for instance, any intrinsic relationship or reciprocity between the "two sources," as if one did not have to be in some way consonant with the other. Implied in this formulation was a content in Tradition larger, at least potentially, than that of Scripture—a content that could be "developed" almost without limitation, as some theologians feared was happening with dogmas about Mary. Finally, many opponents of the schema objected that it did not adequately underscore the unique role of Scripture in the church, which for them was a goal of Vatican II.

The second problem with the text was its stance regarding modern methods of exegesis. The schema paid lip service to *Divino Afflante Spiritu* but, according to its critics, only grudgingly. The way it spoke of inspiration and inerrancy seemed crude and almost fundamentalist, though that word was never used by its critics at Vatican II. The schema's warnings to exegetes, gentle though they might seem, were taken as indications of a determination to clamp down on them, and then on scholars in general, especially those who took a historical approach to their subject.

The final problem was the language of the schema, the style in which it was written. Style was mentioned by almost all those who spoke against the document and even by many who spoke in favor of it, beginning with Ottaviani and Garofalo. Style? Style was important because it was correctly construed not as a mere ornament of speech but as the expression of values and priorities that were at stake in the council. The style of *De Fontibus* projected attitudes and behavioral patterns that the opponents of the schema wanted to change. A new style of speaking was needed for which the code word was "pastoral." To approve the document in its present form would implicitly mean an approval of Roman theology and what it stood for. The style of the Holy Office in word and deed, as it had historically operated and as Cardinal Ottaviani had imparted it to the Doctrinal Commission, was seen as the foremost expression of what had to go.

Why was the opposition to the schema so fierce? It was not because of any individual point, important though some of those were. It was because of larger issues. Specifically, leaders in the council saw the fate of Vatican II as hanging on the fate of this document. Would the council basically be a ratification of the status quo or would it be something other than that? The vote on *De Fontibus Revelationis* would tell.

The ultimate significance of the debate became increasingly clear with each passing day. By November 19, the eve of the vote on the schema, a sense of impending calamity seized Cardinal Siri. He wrote in his diary: "The situation is serious if the schema fails tomorrow! Lord, help us! Holy Virgin, Saint Joseph, pray for us! You [Mary] can obtain for us the victory, you who alone have overcome all heresies throughout the world."[49]

Unlike the protracted discussion of the schema on the liturgy, the discussion on *De Fontibus* lasted for less than a week, with only 85 speeches from the floor compared with 328 on the liturgy. Most of the speeches were sharply critical of the schema, but no new arguments for or against it were forthcoming. The speeches were more notable for assertions than for arguments developed at any depth.

Two interventions, however, were particularly noteworthy. The first was by Maximos IV Saigh, who found the schema too polemical, too negative, and too repressive—devoid of pastoral and ecumenical sensitivity and filled with formulas from the Counter Reformation and the campaign against Modernism. Most important, he ended by bringing up a sore point that was further exacerbating the animus against the Doctrinal Commission and in particular against Ottaviani. Where, he asked, was the schema on the church? Why had the Doctrinal Commission not released it? That was the schema, he asserted, for which everyone was waiting. Vatican I, with its emphasis on the papacy, gave a partial view of the church, which seemed to reduce the rest of the body—bishops, clergy, and the faithful—to dwarfs drained of life and energy. The task the council faced was to reestablish the proper balance between the prerogatives of the head and those of the rest of the church. The schema on the church would have to be the centerpiece of the council's work, and it would determine how the fathers would deal with all other questions.[50]

The second was the speech by Bishop Émile-Joseph De Smedt of Bruges on November 19, the day before debate ended. He spoke in the name of the Secretariat for Christian Unity, which chose him especially so that he might explain clearly for the council why "ecumenical" did not mean a watering down of the truths of the Catholic faith. An effective and dramatic speaker, he succeeded in relatively few words in clarifying the Secretariat's position on that issue. He spent the first half of his talk insisting on the necessity of a new style of discourse in the church, a style essentially dialogical, which implied a theological method.[51]

He went on. The council had received from the pope the task of furthering ecumenical dialogue. If the council failed in that regard, it would fail in one of the principal reasons it was convoked and snuff out the hopes of all the people who looked to the council for "a step forward." *De Fontibus* may or may not speak clearly, but it was certainly not ecumenical because more was required than lucidity. In its preparation of *De Fontibus* the commission had refused every offer of help from the Secretariat. Now, speaking for the Secretariat, De Smedt had to assert that from the ecumenical viewpoint the document was notably deficient. When he finished, applause broke out.

De Smedt's speech raised the stakes. All at once on the floor of St. Peter's the bishops witnessed the spectacle of an officially constituted body of the council, now enjoying the status of a commission, asserting that it could not accept the work of another. When Bea had spoken on the opening day of the debate, he had spoken in his own name. Now De Smedt spoke in the name of the Secretariat. At this point it became clear that the council had reached a critical point in procedure. What was the point of beginning to discuss particular passages of the document when its very viability was in question?

When the session ended that day, the Council of Presidents met and decided that at the next session they would ask the council whether to continue with *De Fontibus*. If the answer was negative, it was the equivalent of rejection of the schema. The next day, November 20, Felici put the question to the council in the unfortunate form decided upon by the presidents, "Should the discussion be interrupted?" A *yes* vote *(placet)* was thus a vote against the schema, whereas a *no* vote *(non placet)* was a vote in favor of it. Confusion reigned. Felici clarified the meaning of the question. Still confusion. Then Ruffini spoke from the presidents' table to clarify it. Ten minutes later, with bishops still expressing by word and gesture their confusion and frustration, Felici felt constrained to clarify it once again. With this final announcement, it seemed, most of the bishops got it straight—*yes* meant *no,* and *no* meant *yes.*

At the end of the morning Felici announced the results of the vote. Of 2,209 votes cast, 1,368 were for discontinuing debate, 822 for continuing. As a clear victory for opponents of the schema, the vote indicated that a majority was forming in the council that transcended the Transalpines. Powerful though the vote was, however, it fell 105 short of the two-thirds majority that the "Regulations" required for a decision of this kind. Those 105 votes were an almost trifling percentage of the total number of votes cast but sufficient to force the council to continue to deliberate on a measure that a sizeable majority judged unacceptable. That was the frustrating fate the bishops understood to be theirs when they left the basilica on November 20.

The next day the session opened as usual with a Mass. When Mass was over, Cicognani, head of the Secretariat for Extraordinary Affairs, handed Felici a message from John XXIII that he was to read to the council. The message said that the vote of the preceding day was a cause for concern. Although it did not satisfy the technicality of the "Regulations," it indicated that continuing the deliberation might not be the way to reconcile the various opinions that had emerged. "Yielding to the wishes of many," John had decided to refer the document to a "mixed commission" made up of members of both the Doctrinal Commission and the Secretariat for Christian Unity. The task of this new commission would be "to emend the schema, shorten it, and make it more suitable, with an emphasis especially on general principles."[52]

What went on behind the scenes to produce this extraordinary intervention? Rumors spread that Cardinal Bea had gone to the pope, but what seems to have happened is that Cicognani contacted Bea that afternoon. Bea then sent his views through Cicognani to the pope. The solution through a mixed commission bears Bea's imprint. But that evening the Canadian bishops had a previously scheduled audience with the pope. Cardinal Léger took the occasion to ask for a few moments alone with him. Those moments, it seems, were decisive.

Léger had the impression that John XXIII had decided not to intervene, though he confided to Léger that the decision to reject the schema faithfully reflected his own views about it. Léger spoke to the pope "frankly" about the situation. Beyond that, we know nothing except that sometime after the meeting with Léger, with Bea's letter in hand, the pope overcame his hesitation. It would have been a bold move to intervene simply to send the schema back to the Doctrinal Commission, but it was even bolder to put the Secretariat on the same footing with that commission, which was so adamant in insisting on its exclusive right to deal with a doctrinal issue like "the sources of Revelation."

In any case, the decision, totally unexpected, brought a sense of relief to perhaps 90 percent of the council fathers. It brought jubilation to those who led the opposition, but even many of those who had voted in favor of the schema now saw the futility of continuing with it. Would a "mixed commission" work? With Ottaviani and Bea as joint presidents? That remained to be seen. In fact, this schema would have an extraordinarily troubled history for the next three years and not be finally approved as *Dei Verbum,* in a form radically different from the original *De Fontibus,* until November, 18, 1965, just a few weeks before the council ended.

Nonetheless, the intervention was determining for the direction Vatican II would take from that moment forward. It was an intervention that ruled in favor of the prevailing sentiment in St. Peter's. In and of itself, therefore, it was simply a procedural intervention that, while violating the letter of the "Regulations," ruled in favor of what the "Regulations" were meant to accomplish, moving along the business of the council in a fair and orderly way. To that extent it was a neutral decision. Nor did it deal with the substance of the issues under debate.

But by creating a mixed commission, it dealt a heavy blow to the control the Doctrinal Commission was trying to exert, and it was thus a major force in sending the council on a way of its own choosing. In its impact, therefore, the intervention can hardly be called neutral. John did not simply send the draft back to the Doctrinal Commission, which, once he decided to intervene, would have been the obvious thing to do. The importance of the vote of November 20 and of the papal intervention on November 21 can hardly be exaggerated.

Despite the wide variety of viewpoints, priorities, and convictions among the council fathers, two clearly distinct approaches to the council and, more broadly, to the tradition of the church had emerged. Both approaches, however, by now held one conviction in common: something of great significance was afoot in the council. Even outside Vatican II, informed students of what was going on in St. Peter's came to the same conclusion. In *Études,* the distinguished journal published by the French Jesuits, Robert Rouquette commented: "The fate of the council was at stake on Tuesday, November 20. . . . With the vote on November 20 we can consider the era of the Counter Reformation ended and a new era for Christendom, with unforeseeable consequences, begun."[53]

Ending the First Period

Hope of ending the council in one sitting had long since faded, but the vote on November 20 drove the point home. Hardly more than two weeks remained before adjournment on December 8 when the council began deliberating on a new text, On the Mass Media. Although some bishops complained about spending time on what they considered a secondary issue, others were happy for breathing space after the high tension of the previous week. The discussion was perfunctory, generally favorable, and lasted only three days. The assembly approved the schema by an overwhelming majority, sent it back to commission for minor revision, and saw it promulgated the next year, December 4, 1963.

In context the deliberation on the schema was not without irony. At the very time the council was discussing it, the Press Office, which had been set up and put under Felici's supervision to keep the media informed, was in crisis. The official bulletins it issued managed to be at the same time uninformative and blatantly favorable to "the conservatives." Reporters complained, bishops complained. On November 14 the Council of Presidents decided to allow two members of the staff of the Press Office to be present at the General Congregations, which resulted in the bulletins being less one-sided. After a few days, however, the Holy Office threatened to close down the Press Office altogether for having violated the secrecy of the council. The shut-down never happened, surely in part because somebody made clear to the Holy Office that it had no jurisdiction over a body regulated by the council. Matters improved and continued to do so into the next year.[54]

There was no way, of course, to keep secret what was going on at a meeting of well over 2,500 participants—bishops, theologians, observers/guests, and staff persons. While the official bulletins maintained the anonymity of who said what—"some spoke in favor, some against"—names were leaked. Reporters had their moles. Even as the council opened, "Xavier Rynne" began publishing his regular column "Letters from Vatican City" in The New Yorker to give a delicious inside account. The fact

that the author, Francis Xavier Murphy, a priest in good standing, felt constrained to adopt a pseudonym speaks volumes about the intimidation the Holy Office could bring to bear. Irony of ironies, Murphy would next year be appointed a council *peritus* and thus not have to get his information second-hand. The early days had proved beyond all doubt the truth of the old axiom that where everything is a secret, nothing is a secret.

On November 26 discussion opened on a new schema, *De Ecclesiae Unitate* (On the Unity of the Church), which dealt with relations between Eastern Orthodoxy and Roman Catholicism. The text was prepared by the Commission for the Oriental Churches under Cardinal Cicognani without input from either the Theological Commission or the Secretariat for Christian Unity.[55] For the short time the schema was on the floor the seriousness of the subject seemed to escape most of the council fathers, still recovering from the earlier tensions and now anticipating tensions over the schema On the Church, which was next on the agenda.

De Unitate came in for serious criticism from almost every quarter, especially from the Melkite bishops, who felt it very much failed to appreciate their reality in the church and their goals regarding reconciliation with the Orthodox. On November 30, the president called upon the council fathers to approve terminating discussion by simply rising from their chairs. "All rose," say the minutes. The next day, December 1, the chair proposed to the assembly a motion that praised the schema for its good intentions but required that the issues it dealt with be incorporated into other documents of the council. The motion passed with virtual unanimity—2,068 votes in favor, 36 opposed. As it turned out, the Secretariat for Christian Unity incorporated relations with the Orthodox into the decree On Ecumenism.

On that same day Cardinal Ottaviani took the floor to introduce the long-awaited schema On the Church *(De Ecclesia),* which the council fathers to their great annoyance had received only the previous week. By now it was well known that the preparation of this schema had been marked by sharp disagreements between the Theological Commission and the Secretariat for Christian Unity, disagreements that the Central Preparatory Commission did not resolve largely because its own membership reflected the same tensions. This polarization now marked the council itself, and Ottaviani represented in everybody's eyes one of the poles. When he rose to speak, he commanded attention.

In two sentences he told the council fathers of the care with which the

schema had been prepared by a commission of seventy members and approved by the Central Preparatory Commission: "After this long journey the Supreme Pontiff ordered that it be presented to you for your examination." Then he said:

> The concern of those who prepared the schema was that it be as pastoral and biblical as possible, not academic [*scholasticum*], and that it be done in a form comprehensible by everybody. I say this because I expect to hear the usual litany from the fathers of the council—it's academic, it's not ecumenical, it's not pastoral, it's negative, and other things like that.
>
> Further, I'll tell you what I really think. I believe that I and the speaker for the commission are wasting our words because the outcome has already been decided. Those whose constant cry is "Take it away! Take it away! Give us a new schema!" are now ready to open fire. I'll tell you something you may not know: even before this schema was distributed—Listen to me! Listen to me!—even before it was distributed, an alternative schema had already been produced. Yes, even before the merits of this schema have been looked at the jury has rendered its verdict. I have no choice now but to say no more because, as Scripture teaches, when nobody is listening words are a waste of time.[56]

He delivered the talk in what Congar described as a cajoling tone that underneath was "peevish and aggressive."[57] Ottaviani was correct when he said that an alternative schema had been drawn up—by Gérard Philips, who had been a conciliating contributor to Ottaviani's own Preparatory Theological Commission. Philips composed his text at the urging of Suenens, who in turn had been urged by no less a person than Cicognani, the secretary of state and chair of the council's Secretariat for Extraordinary Affairs, to have an alternative text produced.[58] Suenens felt that Philips could provide a middle way that could win the support of both sides and overcome polarization, at least over this issue. Philips indeed tried to conform his text as much as possible to the official one. Meanwhile, as with *De Fontibus,* both Schillebeeckx and Rahner composed and distributed severely critical "observations" on *De Ecclesia.*[59]

After Ottaviani came Bishop Frane Franić of Split-Makaraska, Yugoslavia (Croatia), who made the formal presentation in the name of the

❧ *The First Period (1962)*

Doctrinal Commission. He did little more than list the subjects treated in each of the eleven chapters. The schema was long, eighty-two printed pages, and ranged widely, with chapters on "the nature of the church militant," on church membership, on the episcopacy, on religious orders, on the laity, on the church's Magisterium, on authority and obedience in the church, on church-state relations, and, finally, on ecumenism. Amid these many topics, one preoccupation was notable: obedience to ecclesiastical, especially papal, authority was the remedy for the "crisis of authority" in the world that afflicted even some members of the church.[60]

When the debate opened, there were no salvos like those that greeted *De Fontibus*. Ottaviani had perhaps struck too close to home. Liénart, the first to speak, refrained from a direct attack and, indeed, on the surface could not have been sweeter. The points he made, however, were not congruent with the way the schema developed those same points. Toward the end he "dared" to make some suggestions. He wanted the council fathers to know that he did so "not led by a spirit of contention or opposition but out of love for the truth. 'Friend of Plato, but more a friend of truth.'"[61]

Ruffini was basically pleased with the text.[62] König said kind words but raised a number of issues.[63] Alfrink was next with a few general criticisms but ended by saying, "I should like to request that before the next period of the council the schema be reworked by a mixed commission appointed by His Holiness."[64] Then Cardinal Ritter of St. Louis, who had now displaced Spellman and McIntyre as leader of the American episcopacy, offered a number of criticisms and called for a reworking.[65]

De Smedt did not mince words. He delivered one of the most famous and most quoted speeches of the council when he denounced the schema for its three *isms*—triumphalism, clericalism, and "juridicism" *(triumphalismus, clericalismus, juridismus)*. The document, he asserted, was written in a pompous and romantic style that manifested a "triumphalistic" spirit. The style was out of touch with the reality of the humble people of God. Its clericalism was revealed in the pyramidal structure of the church it presents, with everything flowing from top to bottom. It took little account of the horizontal relationships in the church. The reality of the People of God is more fundamental in the church, he maintained, than hierarchy: "We must beware of falling into . . . some kind of bishop-worship or pope-worship [*episcopolatriam vel papolatriam*]." And, finally, the church is more our mother than a juridical institution.[66]

Congar wrote in his diary for the day that, while he agreed in general with De Smedt's criticism of Roman theology, he found De Smedt's attribution of it to this text excessive.[67] Less dramatic in its delivery but more original in its criticism was the speech three days later, on December 4, by Cardinal Frings, who spoke in the name of the German episcopate. Frings's point was simple and shocking: the schema was not catholic! Catholic meant taking into account the length and breadth of the tradition of the church, Eastern as well as Western, but this schema considered only the past hundred years, as the notes to the text attested. Virtually none of the Greek nor even the Latin Fathers was cited, and the same was true for medieval theologians: "I ask: is this the right way to proceed? Is it scientific, is it universal *(oecumenicus)*, is it catholic—in [the sense of] Greek *Katholon,* which means what embraces the whole and looks to the good of the whole? Thus I ask: is such a way of proceeding genuinely catholic?"[68] Frings here put his finger on the major methodological effort of Vatican II—to rise above "the nineteenth century," and to a large extent the sixteenth century, in order to place the council in an older and larger tradition.

The critics of *De Ecclesia* saw it, therefore, as expressing an inadequate vision of the church because it moved in the tradition of a polemical mentality that took off in the sixteenth century in opposition to Protestantism and intensified, or at least got more authoritatively codified, in the late nineteenth and early twentieth centuries. The 800-page treatise *De Ecclesia Christi* of Cardinal Louis Billot, first published in 1898 and reprinted many times almost to the eve of Vatican II, was an influential text, representative of this approach. Its themes were repeated with more or less the same emphasis in all seminary textbooks on the subject.

These books were preoccupied with the question of authority in the church (who's in charge?); emphasized the monarchical character of papal authority almost to the exclusion of all other authority (power flowed from above); and tended to view the church as a kind of holy counterpart to secular governments—it was, like the state, a "perfect society," having within itself all it needed to function. Moreover, the Roman Catholic Church was the only true church, all others being radically defective by reason either of heresy or of schism and, hence, to be shunned. The language in which these positions were put forward was that of closure, exclusion, and polemics, a language that made the Catholic Church look good by making other Christian communities look bad. The *De Ecclesia* put forth by the Doctrinal Commission, though its language and positions were more temperate than in the textbooks and more temperate than De Smedt's criticism indicated, belonged to this tradition.

Only a few days remained. The document that from the beginning many people believed would be the most important in the council was clearly in trouble. Bishops were anxiously aware, moreover, that they had dealt with only a small percentage of the seventy or so texts prepared for them. Was there any way to escape this avalanche of paper?

Suenens took to the floor. Another critical moment had been reached. The Belgian cardinal provided a program that broke the tension and seemed to provide a way forward.[69] In his speech he claimed to be following a path laid out on September 11 by Pope John XXIII in his radio address about the council to Catholics throughout the world.[70]

Like others, Suenens had been dismayed even before the council opened by the uncoordinated production of documents by the Preparatory Commissions and the unfocused character of the ensemble. In 1962 his lenten letter about the council to his diocese caught John's attention and favor, which resulted in important exchanges between them about the council's shape. In their discussions, Suenens's distinction between the church looking inward *(ad intra)* and looking outward to the world *(ad extra)* was central. The church looked outward to be of help to the world. Also significant, Suenens in his lenten letter expressed the conviction that the council should emphasize, in the tense international situation of the times, what unites Catholics with others, not what separates them.

John asked Suenens to develop a plan that would bring order and focus into the work of the council, which in May Cicognani forwarded to a select group of cardinals. The result was a meeting at the Belgian College in Rome that was attended by Döpfner, Montini, Siri, Liénart, and of course Suenens. At this point it was too late for a massive reorganization of the council's agenda, but Suenens's proposal on December 4 did not come as a surprise to leaders in the council; nor was it unwelcome. Pope John had seen a draft of Suenens's speech before he gave it and had made a few suggestions, which Suenens incorporated.[71] Suenens was speaking for the pope, but the pope had gotten his ideas from Suenens.

When he took the floor on December 4, Suenens asserted that what the council needed was a central theme that would lend it a basic orientation. Let that theme be, as the pope put in on September 11, "the church of Christ, light to the world," *Ecclesia Christi, lumen gentium.* That theme has two parts, the first of which looks to the inner reality of the church and asks the question, "What do you say of yourself?" The second part concerns the relationship of the church to the world outside it, and asks questions about the human person, about social justice, about evangelization of the poor, about world peace. The council will thus proceed by engaging in three dialogues: a dialogue with its own membership, an ecumenical dialogue "with brothers and sisters not now visibly united with it," and a dialogue "with the modern world." He asked that the council adopt that program for its future work. "Let us hope," he concluded," that this plan that I propose open a way for a better hearing of the church and understanding of it by the world today and that Christ be for the men and women of our times ever more the way, the truth, and the light."

Prolonged applause! Everybody seemed to realize how important the intervention was. It did three things. First, it moved the council away from a scattershot approach, from utterly losing its way by focusing on specific issues without regard for more general orientations. Second, it contributed to the growing consensus that the original texts needed more than touching up. In his exchanges with John XXIII, Suenens indicated how important he thought it was to use as much as possible of the work of the Preparatory Commissions. Nonetheless, his plan almost necessarily entailed replacements and some drastic revisions. Finally, it sowed the seeds for a new document utterly unforeseen up to this point, the document most distinctive of the council and the one perhaps most revelatory of the council's meaning, *Gaudium et Spes,* The Church in the Modern World.[72]

The next day Cardinal Montini, who was a participant in the meeting at the Belgian College and who six months later would be Pope Paul VI, stated his agreement with Suenens's plan. In so doing he also said about the *De Ecclesia,* the business on the table, "I cannot remain silent about it. It is inadequate." He called for the schema to be submitted to the proper commissions for revision, one of which was to be the Secretariat for Christian Unity.[73] Montini's support was significant. He was known for caution and moderation, was a leader in the generally conservative Italian episcopate, and was considered *papabile.* His support further ensured for the document what already seemed ensured.

All at once the council seemed to have a center around which the many questions before it could be given cohesion. This was extraordinarily important for differentiating this council from previous councils. Moreover, the prominent place that "dialogue" played in Suenens's address put forth a distinctive mode of speaking and behaving. In calling for dialogue "with the modern world," the speech clearly distanced itself from the berating of the modern world characteristic of the long nineteenth century.

The day after that, December 6, a communication from the pope established a program for work to be done during the intersession, stressing the need to respect the goals of the council while at the same time indicating revision of the schemas. Most important, John announced the formation of a Coordinating Commission with the secretary of state as its president, a body that was now almost universally recognized as urgent. Moreover, its establishment was taken as an indication that a vote on *De Ecclesia* would not be needed, which relieved the council from another formal assault on the Doctrinal Commission.[74] The fathers had delivered seventy-seven speeches on the text, and now it was clear without any formal action being taken that it was going into a big repair shop, where it would be dismantled and whence, everybody expected, it would return looking different.

The first period of the council was over, ending with a sense that, despite all the frustration of the past nine weeks, a way could be found to pull things together. That way entailed at least a thorough reworking of the labors expended by the preparatory commissions. It entailed, it seemed, something bigger than just adjusting some rules or refining some points of doctrine. But just where that way was leading was still not clear when, on December 8, the council adjourned after Mass and an allocution by Pope John XXIII, which was the last time most of the council fathers would ever see or hear him again.

5

The Second Period (1963)

A Majority Prevailing

Aт the close of the first period the bishops left Rome weary. They were, however, pleased at having approved in principle the schemas on the liturgy and on the media. More important, they sensed that something big was afoot. They had flexed their muscles in the rejection of the schema On the Sources of Revelation, which showed that they could be more than a rubber stamp, and they had indirectly done the same for the schema On the Church. They knew the council had taken an unexpected turn. They were surprised and for the most part gratified by the excitement that Vatican II had generated not only in Catholic circles but also in the world at large.

But they were frustrated. They had not finished their business in what many had hoped would be the one and only period of the council. Indeed, they now had no idea how many more such periods would be required, and they felt overwhelmed by the immensity of the tasks stretching before them. They were discouraged, too, by the slow movement of the discussions and by the machinery governing the course of the debates—which were not really debates so much as an ongoing series of speeches that were often repetitious, sometimes banal and off-the-point. About 600 of them, with many more yet to come! Even bishops with a good command of Latin had difficulty understanding it when spoken with a heavy French, German, or Japanese accent, just as the French, Germans, and Japanese had difficulty with an American accent. They were dismayed by what seemed to be power moves behind the scenes. Their frustrations and concerns pointed to problems that continued to trouble the council.

Among those problems were two basic and interrelated issues. The first was Pope John's naming curial cardinals as heads of the Preparatory Commissions, and the second was dealing with the sheer number of documents prepared by those commissions. The new Coordinating Commission, announced on December 6, was to act as a kind of "super commission" *(commissio princeps)*, whose task was to expedite the agenda, resolve conflicts among the heads of the commissions, and see that the documents responded to the aims of the council as laid out by John XXIII on October 11 in his opening allocution.[1] Bishops pinned their hopes for progress on this body, which filled an essential gap in the council's organization. Through the pope's charter it had sufficient authority to make at least some of its decisions stick, and it entered energetically into its task. It was encumbered, of course, by conflicts within its own membership and other problems, but it proved effective, especially during this first intersession.[2]

Cicognani was president. Still the secretary of state, he retained along with that office the presidency of the council's Secretariat for Extraordinary Affairs, and he was, moreover, president of the council's Commission on the Oriental Churches. Four hats, one head! Skillful and practical, he was with this latest appointment even more of a power to be reckoned with in the council. Although he was now in the Curia, he had spent twenty-five years in Washington as Apostolic Delegate and, as mentioned, had urged Suenens to produce an alternative to Ottaviani's *De Ecclesia.* In addition to Cicognani, Pope John named six other members to the Coordinating Commission: Döpfner, Liénart, Spellman, Suenens, Urbani, and Carlo Confalonieri. The last named was, like Cicognani, from the Curia, but he was not aligned with other Curia members like Ottaviani, Larraona, and Browne. Felici, with his under-secretaries, attended the meetings and took part in the deliberations.

By the end of its very first meeting, January 21–27, 1963, the commission produced from the mass of drafts in circulation its own list of seventeen texts. Even though this list would undergo important changes, it remained a touchstone for the agenda of the council from that time forward. With this core group of drafts the commission had effected an important simplification. Moreover, it made individual members of the commission responsible for oversight of each of these schemas, and through them it handed down to the respective commissions directives about the form and substance of the documents they were to revise.

Number seventeen on the new list was entitled "The Presence of the Church in the Modern World," though almost until the end of the council it was generally referred to simply as "Schema 17" or, eventually, "Schema 13."[3] The document was to be elaborated by a mixed commission composed of the Doctrinal Commission and the Commission on the Apostolate of the Laity, and thus it would be under the joint presidencies of Cardinals Ottaviani and Fernando Cento. Cardinal Suenens was to oversee the schema for the Coordinating Commission. Its history through the council was so uncertain that for a while it seemed that it would never make it to the floor. At this early stage it was not much more than a collection of preparatory schemas that dealt with social and moral issues of the day, but it was a step toward fulfilling the second part of what Suenens had called for in his pivotal intervention on December 4, "a dialogue with the modern world."

Number one on the list was the old *De Fontibus,* already partially revised by the mixed commission headed by Ottaviani and Bea. For this group, Liénart was the liaison from the Coordinating Commission. He had led the attack on the original schema but tried to direct the meetings of the mixed commission toward a compromise document acceptable to the council. After nine sessions of the mixed commission, some of them stormy, he got a document, but it was so severely criticized that it could not be put on the agenda for the second period of the council. Only after the document was altogether discarded and a new one composed almost from scratch for the third period would the subject of "the word of God" *(Dei Verbum)* reach the floor of the council.[4]

Number two on the list was *De Ecclesia,* the schema on the church, with Suenens, again, as liaison. When on January 30 Cicognani sent the presidents of commissions directives for the revision of their schema, he asked them to make use as much as possible of materials from the original schema. Nonetheless, the directives for *De Ecclesia* were lengthy and radical. They reduced the number of chapters from eleven to four. They indicated how material treated in the discarded chapters of the original schema could be incorporated into the four new ones, be dealt with in other documents, or simply be "suppressed." While ostensibly a reorganization of the schema, the new chapters pointed to a new document, and they in fact provided the basic outline that *Lumen Gentium* assumed.[5]

The title of the first chapter, "On the Mystery of the Church," was indicative of the depth of the change the directive called for. This replaced "On the Nature of the Church," the first chapter in the original. The new title in and of itself suggested a significant change in perspective, a reaction against the clear and distinct categories of seminary textbooks, but it had more pointed resonances as well. It was no accident that the first chapter of Henri de Lubac's book *The Splendour of the Church,* first published in French in 1954, bore the same title.[6] De Lubac's book, though published after the encyclical *Humani Generis,* still exemplified the broad approach to theological issues that had more recourse to the rhetorical and even poetic language of the Fathers of the Church than to the sharp distinctions of juridical and Neo-Scholastic cultures.[7] That title, surely promoted by Suenens, was a first indication of the rehabilitation of "la nouvelle théologie" and its style of discourse, which would be a hallmark of Vatican II. In the Coordinating Committee Suenens had criticized the original schema precisely because "it uses a literary genre inappropriate for the council."[8]

The directive clearly indicated the principal issue to be treated in the new document: the relationship between Vatican I and Vatican II—more specifically, the relationship between pope and bishops. It focused the issue: "The schema must clarify the sense of 'episcopal collegiality,' whose importance is manifest simply by the fact that bishops are assembled in this very council. This doctrine concerning the episcopal body under and with Peter is of the highest importance for everything the council will determine about episcopal conferences."[9] By insisting that collegiality be "clarified," the directive made clear that the issue could not be sidestepped. Collegiality would become the lightning-rod issue of the council.

On February 21 a special seven-member subcommission of the Doctrinal Commission set about reworking the schema. This was an important turning point because it took the drafting out of the immediate hands of Ottaviani, even though he and the full commission ultimately had to approve the results before sending the text to the floor. Of the seven members, five were from the majority, two from the minority. As important as these five bishops were, just as important were the theologians upon whom they relied, such as Gérard Philips, Karl Rahner, Jean Daniélou, and, eventually, Yves Congar.

Despite the drastic revision called for in the January directive from the Coordinating Committee, Cicognani told the subcommission that "nothing new was to be done," that is, the new schema would have to be based on the old. The subcommission interpreted this advice broadly, deciding early on to use as its base text the one Philips had prepared during the first period.[10] Of the five then nine texts by now in circulation as alternatives to the original *De Ecclesia,* Philips's seemed preferable because it sought a middle path between the old approach and the new. The directive from Cicognani was, however, another instance of the mixed signals that plagued the council.

The subcommission worked quickly and efficiently. At the March 5 meeting of the Doctrinal Commission , it presented the first two chapters of its text. Ottaviani responded by launching a bitter attack on the document. Along with Tromp, he criticized the subcommission for going beyond its mandate by substituting Philips's text for the original. The whole first half of the meeting was taken up by this issue. When it finally became clear that the majority on the commission favored the new text, its enemies—especially Ottaviani, Browne, and Tromp—attacked the text itself, criticizing it as dangerous and relativistic. The second chapter dealt with collegiality, which ignited a battle royal. Within a week, nonetheless, the full commission approved it, a major breakthrough. The other two chapters—on the laity and on members of religious orders—followed in due course. They elicited questions and objections but none as explosive as those for the earlier chapters.[11]

The Coordinating Commission rode herd on the other commissions. By the time the council resumed on September 29 it had accomplished a wonder. It had reduced the number of schema to a manageable size. It had extracted revised texts from almost every commission. Among those texts it had selected five for the agenda that fall: (1) Church; (2) Virgin Mary; (3) Bishops; (4) Lay Apostolate; and (5) Ecumenism. It had made suggestions for revisions to the "Regulations" that would, it was hoped, move the council along more speedily. It had brought representatives of the laity into discussions of the document on the Lay Apostolate and on "Schema 17." The commission achieved this success, moreover, in the difficult circumstances of complicated bureaucracies and in the face of considerable resistance. In a little more than eight months it had made Vatican II a viable assembly and imparted to it the essential shape by which we know it.

A Death, a Conclave, a New Pope

John XXIII died on June 3, 1963. Disturbing rumors about his health were rife as the first period drew to a close, and they caused considerable apprehension, especially among the leaders of the majority. During his final days, passed in agonizing pain, the outpouring of grief and sympathy worldwide for "John, the well beloved" was immense. Nothing like it had ever been seen before at the death of a pope.

John had been alert and active almost to the end. On Holy Thursday, April 11, he published his encyclical *Pacem in Terris* on the problems of world peace, underdeveloped nations, refugees, migrants, and similarly contemporary issues. He had confided the writing to Pietro Pavan, a *peritus* and professor at the Lateran (which shows how misleading generalizations about institutions can be), but the pope, sick though he was, attentively followed the development of the text.

In a break with tradition, John sent his message not only to the usual addressees but to "all men and women of good will." The encyclical was remarkable for its long section on human rights, including freedom of speech and freedom of the press. Unprecedented among them was "the right of being able to worship God in accordance with the right dictates of one's conscience and to profess one's religion both in private and in public." In his radio message in Italian the previous September 11, he had already proclaimed that "fundamental right" in perhaps stronger terms.[12] The encyclical, in calling for the end of the arms race, exhorted Catholics to work with non-Catholics in the cause of peace.[13] Although widely praised, the encyclical also received severe criticism from economically and politically conservative sources. It smacked, they maintained, of Socialism or even Communism.

The previous month, on March 7, John had received in audience Alexis Adzhubei, the editor of *Izvestia,* the notorious Soviet newspaper, and son-in-law of Nikita Khrushchev, the Soviet chairman. The meeting caused a sensation. On that same day the International Balzan Foundation awarded John its prize in recognition of his work for peace. In his acceptance speech he shocked many who looked upon the church as the leader in the campaign against Communism when he said that "on the plane of international competition, whether armed or merely verbal, [the church maintains] an absolute neutrality."[14]

To the dismay of many Italian bishops, moreover, John had from the beginning of his pontificate assumed a hands-off stance regarding Italian politics. When on April 28 the Communist Party made significant gains in the Italian elections at the expense of the Christian Democrats, John's critics blamed him. The critics, especially those in the Curia and the Italian episcopate, thus had another reason to wring their hands over his policies and to hope for better times for Italy and for the church with a new pope.

Eighty cardinals entered the conclave, twenty-nine of them Italians.[15] Given the elaborate mechanisms already in motion, the new pope, no matter who he was, would have no choice but to continue the council. The burning question was not whether the pope would continue Vatican II but what stamp he would put on it. Although the cardinals take a solemn oath not to speak about what happens in a conclave, one way or another information seeps out, and that was certainly true in this case. Cardinal Gustavo Testa, who was given to indiscreet outbursts, said afterward, "Hair-raising things happened at this conclave. I will have to ask the pope's permission to speak about them." He either did not ask or did not receive permission because he said no more. Other indiscretions confirm, however, that the conclave was difficult.

Ottaviani and Siri, who himself received votes, had a candidate in Ildebrando Antoniutti, prefect of the Congregation of Religious, who initially made a decent showing. It soon became clear, however, that neither he nor any other candidate wholly agreeable to the council's minority camp could prevail. As the voting continued, Lercaro and Montini pulled ahead. Montini had spent years in the Curia, had friends there, and, aside from his intervention on December 5, had maintained a low profile during the council. In the cathedral of Milan just before the conclave he delivered a eulogy of John that attracted much notice and was interpreted by some as a statement of his platform, should he be elected.

Working against Montini was his reputation for indecisiveness, which his supporters dismissed as a misleading impression stemming from the long years he spent in the shadow of Pius XII. The cardinals of the majority tended to favor him as the best they could do from among the Italians, but from the beginning he also had the support of the conservative Spellman of New York. Finally, on the sixth ballot, supposedly now backed by both Ottaviani and Cicognani, the conclave elected Giovanni Battista Montini—by a relatively close margin, however, over the minimum needed.

A few days after his election, Paul VI announced that the council would reconvene on September 29.[16] In the three months until that time he was busy with many things but none perhaps more important than refashioning the machinery directing the council. In that regard he made several important decisions, which in a letter dated September 12 he communicated to Cardinal Tisserant.[17] First, he prolonged indefinitely the life of the Coordinating Commission, which had originally been conceived as operating only during the intersession. He confirmed Cicognani both as secretary of state and as the president of this now somewhat expanded commission. The decision to retain the Coordinating Commission made superfluous the Secretariat for Extraordinary Affairs, which had also been under Cicognani, and the pope abolished it.

The Council of Presidents, the ten cardinals who had in turn presided at the General Congregations, had proved cumbersome. Paul's first intention, it seems, was radically to streamline the function by appointing one or maybe two "legates" to chair the council sessions. This intention evolved over the next few months into the creation of four "moderators," who would take turns in the chair, a sort of reduced Council of Presidents. Their remit was, as stated in the revised "Regulations," altogether general: "Four cardinal delegates or moderators, chosen by the Supreme Pontiff, direct the work of the council, succeeding one another in turn in moderating the debates of the General Congregations."[18] None of the moderators was named chairman of this group, so members would somehow have to function as a team. Precisely what "directing the work of the council" entailed was left unspecified.

With the appointment of the moderators, the pope might seem to have retired the Council of Presidents from active service, but he did not do so. He in fact expanded it by three new members and gave it responsibility for ensuring that the "Regulations" were observed and for resolving difficulties that might arise concerning them. Paul meanwhile confirmed Felici as secretary general.

By the time the council reopened, all four moderators found themselves members of the Coordinating Committee, an appointment that facilitated communication and coordination between the two bodies. Three of the moderators were leaders of the majority—Döpfner, Lercaro, and Suenens.

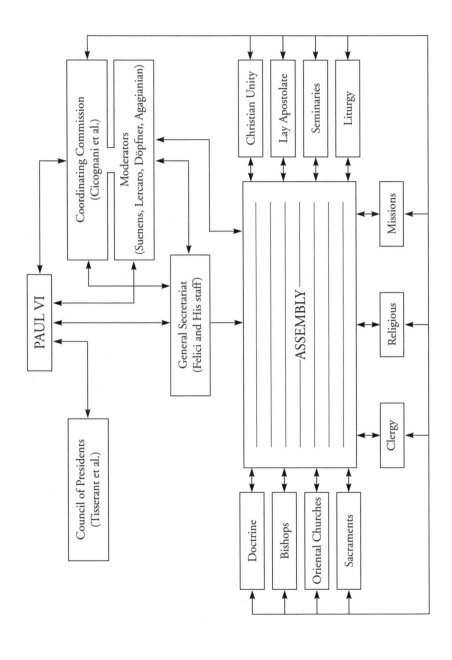

Council Organization. It is impossible to depict adequately the complicated organization of Vatican II, but this chart shows the main lines of communication. The small boxes indicate the ten commissions plus the Secretariat for Christian Unity. They produced the documents discussed by the assembly in St. Peter's. The chart does not take account of the mixed commissions; nor does it indicate other complications, such as the fact that the document On the Mass Media was presented to the assembly under the aegis of the Commission on the Lay Apostolate. During the first intersession (winter, spring, summer 1963), the Coordinating Commission had a determining influence on the commissions, but this gradually diminished as the council wore on. Note that, aside from Paul VI, the persons represented by the boxes were of course also members of the assembly. Paul was a member of the council but not of the assembly, except during the relatively rare Public Sessions.

The fourth, Cardinal Grégoire-Pierre Agagianian, prefect of the Congregation of the Propagation of the Faith and representative of the Curia, was obviously meant as a counterbalance. During the sessions of the council the moderators sometimes took the floor, speaking not ex officio but for themselves, and they did not hesitate to express their views on issues under discussion. Felici believed that such interventions raised questions about their impartiality as chairs of the sessions, and in that regard he was critical of them.[19] But the moderators and other members of the council had, as mentioned, similar questions about Felici's impartiality.

The moderators had weekly meetings with Paul VI. Yet despite requests for clarification, especially by Suenens and Lercaro, they were never able to ascertain how much authority they had or how they related to the pope. Were they the effective leaders of the council and spokespersons for Paul VI? Or were they delegates of the Coordinating Committee, of which they were simple members under the presidency of Cicognani? Or were they to do little more than direct the traffic of the interventions? By the time the council opened they began to act more or less in accord with the first option. For instance, they appointed as their own secretary Giuseppe Dossetti, Lercaro's personal theological adviser. They intended, moreover, to set up their own infrastructure of archives and experts and acted with a degree of independence that was not universally appreciated.[20]

The changes in the "Regulations" were not much of an improvement. Four moderators were certainly better than ten presidents. Other than that, however, the system was at least as clumsy as before and laden with dangerously overlapping responsibilities. As Felici observed in a memorandum at the end of this period, on December 12, 1963: "The existence of a Council of Presidents with a large membership, of four moderators, and of a Coordinating Commission created difficulties in the ongoing process of our work together that probably would not have existed had there been but one responsible body."[21]

Where on the floor of the council did the buck stop? That was the question. The moderators found themselves in a particularly vulnerable position. Were they or was Cicognani (or Felici—or maybe even Tisserant, head of the Council of Presidents) the go-between of pope to council and of council to pope? This indetermination, among others, and the vagueness of the moderators' job description meant, moreover, that Paul VI's door had to be open to both Cicognani and to them, open almost on a daily basis to Felici, and, more broadly, open to appeals from all quarters about any controversial issue or decision. This procedural muddle, never resolved, had grave consequences.

On September 21, a week before the council resumed, Paul VI delivered an address to the Curia. He needed its cooperation "for the ordinary governance of the church" even while the council was in session, of course, and he was fully aware of the bruising the Curia had taken in the first period. The calls for its "reform" threatened to become more insistent when the council reopened in a few days. The Curia abused its authority, its critics maintained, and tried to lord it over the bishops. The behavior of some of its members during the first period seemed to justify the indictment. The animus was widespread, by no means confined to the leaders of the majority.

Paul VI would in any circumstance have wanted to say a word at the beginning of his pontificate to his former colleagues. This would be simple courtesy. But the circumstances under which this meeting with the Curia took place were not ordinary. The pope spoke in Italian for about half an hour to a gathering of some 800 persons, including not only all the heads of the Roman Congregations but all those who worked in them. It also included some of the council fathers who had already returned to Rome. His tone was warm, his words largely comforting. He praised the Curia for its devotion and for the essential service it rendered to the church. He reminded those present of the years he had spent with them, thus identifying himself with them. He elaborated on the glories of Rome, the center.

In the course of this soft-spoken and overtly congratulatory address, he managed to press three delicate points. First, he clearly insinuated that henceforth the Curia would have to accept that residential bishops would have a more active role in the functioning of the Congregations. Second, in a word of "exhortation," he told his audience that he expected them to cooperate with the council. Finally, he explained that it was reasonable for the Curia to undergo some changes in its mode of operation, some "reforms." Times change, he said, and every organization must make adjustments to them.

If these three points aroused apprehension in his listeners, Paul reassured them on the crucial issue. Without explicitly saying so, he communicated that he was removing reform of the Curia from the agenda of the council. "The reforms will be formulated and promulgated," he said, "by the Curia itself."[22] There was nothing to worry about.

On September 29 the council reopened. Unlike the previous year, the council fathers entered the basilica one by one or two by two and took their seats, where they awaited the pope. Paul, preceded by an entourage, walked up the aisle. After the Mass he delivered his address, which lasted over an hour, twice as long as John's opening allocution the year before.[23] His subject was the church. He informed the fathers that he was preparing an encyclical on the subject, but "why communicate in writing what We might communicate to you orally in your presence?" The allocution was meant, therefore, to provide a foretaste of the encyclical, published a year later on August 6 as *Ecclesiam Suam*.

The pope paid homage to Pope John and quoted from *Gaudet Mater Ecclesia*. In particular, he reaffirmed the pastoral nature of the council and the motif of *aggiornamento*. He went on to call for a renewal of the church (which, he noted, does not imply that it had strayed). He asked for forgiveness from the "separated brethren" for any injuries against them and assured them of forgiveness for their offenses. Finally, he declared that the church looks upon the world with kindness and with resolution to be of help in its many needs. It was a dense speech, and not particularly easy to follow; moreover, unlike *Gaudet Mater Ecclesia*, it had no lines that captured attention and invited quotation. Reaction to it was favorable.[24] What Paul underscored and what everybody grasped was that the church was to be the focal point of the deliberations of the council, an echo of the decisive interventions at the end of the first period.

In retrospect, it is easy to see that in the few months since his election Paul VI had already given clues that he would relate to the council differently than had John XXIII. Paul was more vigilant. Although he certainly did not consciously intend it, he sometimes seemed to be setting himself up in competition with the council: he was writing an encyclical on the church at the very time the council was debating the subject, and he reserved to himself, even with a council in session, a matter of great practical and symbolic importance to the council fathers, the reform of the Curia.

Judged by his subsequent actions, Paul played—and, to some extent, saw himself as playing—at least four distinct roles. Sometimes, as when he submitted emendations to the documents that he wanted the commissions to be free to accept or reject, he clearly intended to act simply as a bishop like any other bishop and to be treated as such. But as Supreme Moderator he took on three directive roles: he was the arbiter in procedural disputes, sometimes, as it turned out, in the first instance; he was the promoter of unanimity in the acceptance of the council's decrees (as far as that was in any way possible), lest the council end with a division between winners and losers or, worse still, a schism; finally, he saw himself, in the last instance, as the guardian of orthodoxy at the council. It was not always clear to the assembly in St. Peter's and especially to the commissions which role he was playing at any given moment.

Substance, Procedure, Crisis

On September 30 the council went to work once again. Felici opened the session with the review of the revised "Regulations."[25] The changes included, besides the items already mentioned, provision for the admission to the council of "some distinguished laymen," who were not to speak except by special concession of the pope. They also included a renewed but mitigated emphasis on the confidentiality of the proceedings. Archbishop John Krol of Philadelphia, who summarized Felici's remarks for English-speakers, put the issue this way: "The obligation of secrecy applies in full force to the contents of the schemas that are discussed and to all the discussions and conclusions reached in the sessions of the council commissions. With reference to discussions that take place in these general sessions in this hall, His Holiness commends the observance at all times and in all places of maximum prudence and moderation."[26]

Others summarized the "Regulations" in Spanish, French, German, and Arabic. After this wearisome beginning, Ottaviani then Browne introduced the revised version of the schema on the church. In their low-key presentations the two cardinals did little more than sketch the streamlined form of the document, still substantially the work of Gérard Philips. Thus it had not eleven but only four chapters: (1) the mystery of the church; (2) the hierarchical constitution of the church, and especially the bishops; (3) the people of God, and especially the laity; and (4) the call to holiness. In effect it was a new schema, but Philips incorporated as much as he could of the original *De Ecclesia*.[27] The schema opened with the words that would henceforth designate it, *Lumen Gentium*. In a change from earlier suggestions, however, Christ, not the church, was the "light to the nations"—*Lumen gentium cum sit Christus.*

The most obvious feature of the revised text, aside from its new structure, was that the chapters in the original on ecumenism, evangelization, religious life, and church-state relations had been excised and were now consigned to other commissions. The chapters on the Magisterium and "obedience and authority" in the church had disappeared from the schema and, as it turned out, from the council altogether as topics treated as distinctive units. Of course questions related to them ran through almost all the documents as aspects of the relationship of center to periphery.

These two chapters in particular had evinced the negative and juridical style that De Smedt so heavily criticized the previous year. Characteristic of the vocabulary of the chapter on obedience was the designation of church members as "subjects" *(subditi),* a word that from this time forward vanished completely from the documents of Vatican II. In that regard it is noteworthy that "People of God" became the title for the chapter that substituted for those in the original on church membership and the laity. The strong horizontal line implicit in "People of God," with its stress on the fundamental equality of all members of the church, replaced the strong vertical line of ruler-subject.

An obvious difference between this draft and the original was, with the exception of chapter two on the hierarchy, a style more filled with biblical images and patristic allusions. This feature would intensify in the final version, which almost overflows with images of the church and its members that suggest fecundity, dignity, abundance, charism, goodness, safe haven, welcome, communion, tenderness, and warmth. This style of discourse looked to, suggested, and helped make pervasive the subject of chapter four, the call to holiness.

Perhaps more significant than the chapters that disappeared, therefore, was the new chapter four. Christ, it insisted, calls every Christian to holiness and provides the grace and other means to accomplish it, regardless of one's state in life. Christians fulfill the call through love of God and neighbor in imitation of Christ, an imitation that takes on a rich variety of forms. This first version of the chapter, however, incorporated a great deal of material from the original schema's chapter on religious life. It thus gave considerable attention to the "evangelical counsels" of poverty, chastity, and obedience as practiced in religious orders, which did not fit well with the point the chapter intended to convey. The version approved the following year displaced this emphasis with a broader scope that was clearly indicated in its revised title: "The *Universal* Call to Holiness." Two more chapters were added, one specifically on the laity and another on members of religious orders.

The chapter on holiness encountered no resistance in the council. This indicates not only that it said what everybody thought needed to be said but also, perhaps, that its thematic importance was not fully appreciated. What did the chapter do? It imbued *Lumen Gentium* with its finality by saying explicitly, forcefully, and for the first time ever in a council that holiness is what the church is all about, what human life is all about. By presenting the church as more than a guardian of orthodoxy and an enforcer of good behavior, this crucial document helped move the council beyond the earlier senate-model to a new modality. From this point forward, in fact, the holiness theme began to find a place in the documents of the council by the time they appeared on the floor.

Was the Catholic Church, and that church alone, "the church of Christ"? This issue was addressed in the first chapter. Both the original schema and this one answered the question in the affirmative. But both of them, and the final version as well, indicated in slightly different ways that baptized Christians from other communities are in some way joined to the church. As the original *De Ecclesia* put it, the Holy Spirit operates outside the church "so that our separated brethren are incorporated into it in a way Christ has determined."[28] All three versions of the schema indicate in different ways that even the non-baptized who sincerely follow their consciences are somehow joined to the church and saved. The later versions, however, make the new and important point that many elements of sanctification are available outside the church, and that the Holy Spirit works for the sanctification of all the baptized.[29] Although this can be interpreted as substantially the same teaching as in the Feeney case, it was expressed less grudgingly and with more explicit theological grounding. It focused on the glass as half full rather than as half empty.

As the fathers discussed the document, three points, all in chapter 2, emerged as especially contested. The first was the proposal, not present in the original *De Ecclesia,* to reinstate the diaconate as a permanent office in the church, that is, to ordain men as deacons without the requirement that they then be ordained to the priesthood. Many prelates did not see the necessity or even the advantage of this *ressourcement.* What especially aroused concern, however, was the proposal that this "permanent diaconate" be open to married men. That entailed a significant change in the practice of the Western church, where deacons, even those who in past ages had not later been ordained priests, had been obliged to observe the law of celibacy.

The next two points were closely related to each other and dealt with bishops, whose dignity, prerogatives, and authority were on the way to becoming a central focus of the council. The first was the proposal to resolve a longstanding ambiguity about the ceremony that constituted bishops in their office, which until Vatican II was called their consecration. Was this ceremony a conferral of an ecclesiastical office or dignity, or was it something more? Was it, in fact, like ordination to the priesthood, a sacrament? This issue was raised in the original *De Ecclesia,* which affirmed the sacramentality of the ceremony, as the title to chapter three made clear, "The Episcopacy as the Supreme Grade of the Sacrament of Orders." The new text adopted the same position. Bishops were "ordained."

This rather technical doctrinal issue implicitly raised the delicate question of what authority the sacrament conferred. It thereby raised the more general question, what authority do the bishops, singly and collectively, have in their own right through ordination and not as a concession of the pope? On this question the two texts adopted positions broadly similar but significantly different in nuance.

The texts agreed that the sacrament conferred on bishops the traditional tripartite office of teaching, sanctifying, and governing their flocks. It was over the last of those three—governing—that the difference arose. Thus this difficult topic blended into the final point, episcopal collegiality. The original *De Ecclesia* insisted that, though the sacrament conferred the office *(munus)* of governing, it did not confer the power to exercise it, which bishops received from the Roman Pontiff. Even when bishops gathered in large numbers they made binding decisions not by reason of their own authority but by reason of "participation in the authority of the Roman Pontiff." Those "large numbers" do not seem to mean an ecumenical council; indeed, a few lines later the text spoke of the College of Bishops' exercising "full and supreme power in the universal church" when united with the Roman Pontiff, echoing Canon 228 about ecumenical councils in the Code of Canon Law. But then it went on to qualify that power by stating that it could be exercised only in extraordinary circumstances, only in "devoted subordination to the Vicar on earth of Jesus Christ and only when, how, and in the degree he deems expedient."[30]

The new text was more intent on emphasizing that bishops have inalienable authority by virtue of the sacrament.[31] It carefully stipulated that they cannot exercise that authority without being in communion with the Roman Pontiff. This text agreed with the original that the bishops were "vicars of Christ," and a few lines later added a telling quotation from Leo XIII that they were "not to be thought vicars of the Roman Pontiff. They are called bishops [*antistites,* overseers] because they exercise an authority properly their own and really govern the flocks that are theirs." The text dropped the phrase "by participation in the authority of the Roman Pontiff." The bishops are not, therefore, heads of a branch office of the Vatican.

In speaking of ecumenical councils, the new draft also dropped the qualification of the council's authority—"when, how, and in the degree the Vicar of Christ deems expedient"—though of course affirming "the prerogative of the Roman Pontiff to convoke, preside over, and confirm the council." The bishops' authority, it assured, does not weaken the authority of the Roman Pontiff but, as Vatican I teaches, strengthens it.[32]

In Vatican II, episcopal ordination and collegiality were sometimes treated as if they were distinct issues, but they were in fact intimately related. Moreover, the bishops soon began to see that in dealing with these issues as abstract theological problems they were at the same time answering the question about their own authority in the very council in which they were participating. What authority did the council as council have, and what was the basis for it? The contrast in responses to those questions corresponds to the contrast between Canon 228 of the code, which asserted the older tradition of the supreme authority of councils, and Canon 222, which put full control of councils in the hands of the pope.

Was there a way to reconcile these two traditions? The leaders of the majority thought there was, the minority that there was not—at least not as the majority posed the reconciliation. The new text showed the continuing impact of the original in its repetition in a steady beat of papal prerogatives as defined at Vatican I. The bishops who favored a strong statement on collegiality viewed this repetition of Vatican I as superfluous and even prejudicial, whereas other bishops would have liked it to be the final statement on the hierarchical structure of the church.

On September 30, after the introductory remarks by Ottaviani and Browne, Frings, speaking in the name of sixty-six bishops from the German- and Scandinavian-language groups, opened the discussion. He and those in whose name he spoke liked the schema and believed that, while it was not perfect, it was an adequate base for discussion and emendation. Siri, who followed him, surprised the assembly by also judging the document adequate as a base text. He spiced his brief intervention, however, with a telling and acerbic jab at the document's style: "While we certainly must promote progress in our understanding of truth, it's not progress to say things in a more obscure way."[33]

The next six speakers were also favorably disposed toward the document. Giuseppe Gargitter, bishop of Bolzano-Bressanone, the last to speak that day, proposed that "the People of God," which includes everybody in the church, form a new chapter two, which would then be followed by the chapter on the hierarchy and then a chapter on the laity. Suenens had already proposed putting "People of God" before hierarchy, but Gargitter's intervention was important in moving the council to adopt the idea in the final version. The symbolism of the change was potent: the first reality of the church is horizontal and consists of all the baptized, without distinction of rank. Only then comes the vertical reality, hierarchy.

The following day, October 1, the Chilean archbishop Raul Silva Henríquez, the first to take the floor, reported that the 440 Latin American bishops in whose name he spoke approved the schema. The intervention showed the effectiveness of communication within the large number of national episcopal conferences within CELAM, the umbrella organization of the Latin American conferences. It also helped make obvious that the council had a text it could work with, so that later that morning the moderators put it to a vote. Results: 2,231 affirmative, 43 negative. This was a serene beginning, much different from the radical attacks that *De Fontibus* had met the year before and from the more subdued yet effective rejection of the original *De Ecclesia*.

That same morning, therefore, the council moved to discussion of the introduction and first chapter. Ruffini took the floor. Although he admitted that these parts of the schema had many points "worthy of praise and approval," he then launched into a page-by-page and line-by-line criticism of the text.[34] Two of his criticisms, though buried among the others, were expressions of fundamental problems that the minority had not only with this document but also with the council itself. First, the document stated several times that Christ built his church "on Peter and the apostles," yet "our adorable Savior said to Peter alone, 'You are Peter—*kephas*—and I will build my church on this rock.'" The doctrine of collegiality as the council was proposing it thus had no biblical basis. The verse from Matthew's gospel that Ruffini quoted was emblazoned against gold mosaic in the interior of the dome of St. Peter's, which the council fathers had before their eyes every day.

Second, Ruffini was displeased that the document referred to the church as a sacrament, using a term that Christian catechesis reserves to the seven sacraments "properly so-called." Such usage would cause confusion: "I note, moreover, that George Tyrrell, an apostate priest and virtually the prince of the Modernists, in a heretical fashion often spoke of the church this way."[35] Ruffini gave voice to a specter that haunted the minority: the council was condoning, even adopting, Modernist tenets.

Discussion on the introduction and first chapter lasted for three sessions. The interventions ranged over many topics, with countless suggestions for changes in wording or emphasis. Some issues recurred. Was the church identical with the mystical body of Christ (as Pius XII affirmed in the encyclical *Mystici Corporis*)? If the council is to make a statement on the Virgin Mary, should it be incorporated into this document? What did it mean to say that the episcopacy was the summit of priesthood? What is the relationship of the Catholic Church to other Christian communities and to unbelievers? In that last regard, Bea made a long intervention criticizing the way the document used Scripture, a fault, he maintained, that rendered it useless in dealing with the separated brethren.[36]

Carlos Saboia Bandeira de Mello, bishop of Las Palmas, Canary Islands, obviously displeased not only with the document under discussion but with the whole style the council had adopted, objected to the conciliatory approach toward Protestants in section 9 of the schema, which emphasized what Christians held in common. He hit the nail on the head about a crucially distinctive feature of Vatican II: "It seems to me that in number 9 there is a contradiction between our council and all the other councils. In the others they always anathematized those who did not accept Catholic doctrine, but we do not do that in ours. . . . I want an explanation as to why we are acting so differently."[37]

In his attack on collegiality Ruffini had already touched on an issue that properly belonged in discussion of chapter two. The next day Alfrink raised the same issue by defending the biblical basis for collegiality.[38] Soon thereafter the moderators formally moved discussion to the controversial chapter. Ruffini, the second to speak, shot back at "our beloved Cardinal Alfrink who seemed to be refuting my position" on papal primacy (Alfrink and Ruffini had been students together at the Biblicum!), then raised further objections to collegiality. He passed on to another highly contested proposition, the reinstating of the permanent diaconate. Section 15 of the schema, which dealt with this issue, ended with what seemed to some bishops almost an inflammatory statement: "It will fall to the authorities in the church to decide whether such deacons will be bound or not by the sacred law of celibacy."[39] Celibacy hit the floor of the council.

Cardinal Spellman had just a few minutes earlier made a long intervention on the proposal to reinstate the office. Without raising the celibacy issue, he had stated his opposition to it and pointed out the origin of the idea and the faulty reasoning behind it: "This proposal . . . originates for the most part from Liturgists, who want to reinstate usages of the ancient church without taking account of the real situation today."[40] Then came Ruffini, followed by Cardinal Antonio Bacci, who attacked the proposal and ended with the passionate plea, "With trepidation in my soul I beg you, venerable council fathers, do not inflict a wound on the sacred law of celibacy."[41]

Discussion of chapter two, 360 lines of text, lasted from October 4 until October 15, with 119 interventions on the floor and 56 submitted in writing. The moderators, fully aware that collegiality was the pivotal issue, symptomatic of the orientation toward which the council was heading, let the discussion on chapter two continue for what seemed to some bishops like days on end, with much repetition of the same arguments. Luigi Bettazzi, a young auxiliary bishop from Bologna, delivered one of the cleverest and amusing interventions favoring collegiality. In it he argued that collegiality was based on a longstanding theological and canonical tradition. Collegiality was therefore not a new idea hatched by northern Europeans. *Italian,* not "Transalpine," theologians and canonists were eminent in developing the tradition. If the word *novatores*—innovators or heretics—was to be applied to anybody in this regard, it was to those who opposed the doctrine of collegiality.[42] Bettazzi's intervention signaled, moreover, that the seemingly solid conservative stance of the Italian episcopate on issues before the council was not as solid as it seemed.

On October 10 the moderators had a congenial meeting with Paul VI. They understood from their discussion with the pope that he approved of their asking the assembly to vote on the contested issues in chapter two in a way that would indicate where the bishops stood on them and also be binding on the Doctrinal Commission in its revisions of the chapter. Such a vote went beyond the "Regulations," which provided only for a vote on the chapter as such. The "Regulations," that is to say, did not provide for votes on questions about specific topics within a given chapter.

At the audience on October 10, the precise form the vote might take was not discussed, nor was the process for formulating it, but the advantages, even necessity, of a procedure along this line seems to have been agreed upon. The ongoing debate in St. Peter's seemed to favor a strong statement on collegiality, but there was no way of ascertaining the will of the majority, and thus giving direction to the commission, without some kind of vote.

Moreover, the avalanche (no other word catches the reality) of the oral and written emendations to the text showed no signs of abatement, and, without some guidelines as to how to weigh them, the commission was in danger of being overwhelmed by them. A vote of this kind, however, would challenge the view of those who still saw the commissions as instru-

Three moderators, from left: Cardinals Giacomo Lercaro, Léon-Joseph Suenens, and Grégoire-Pierre Agagianian. Missing is Cardinal Julius Döpfner. Photograph courtesy of the Cardinal Suenens Center, John Carroll University.

ments of papal authority and hence as setting the direction for the council, not vice versa.

The smooth-running audience with Paul VI and this seemingly reasonable procedure set the stage for the most dramatic crisis of the second period.[43] Until the blow struck on October 16, however, all seemed well. After the audience with the pope, the moderators had Dossetti, their secretary, go to work on a draft of questions to be submitted to the assembly when discussion on chapter two concluded. Dossetti, after consultation with Carlo Colombo, adviser to Paul VI on theological issues, had a revised draft ready by October 14, which that day was delivered to Felici to be sent to the printer. A short document, fitting on one side of a page, it opened by explaining that the bishops were being asked to vote so that "there might be some orienting directives for elaborating chapter two of the constitution on the church." Then in four parts it asked a series of eight questions, one of which dealt with episcopal ordination, four with collegiality, and three with the diaconate, which included the explosive issue of celibacy.

Toward the end of the session on October 15, Cardinal Suenens, the moderator for the day, asked the assembly if it was ready to close discussion on chapter two. The vote, overwhelmingly in favor of closure, was greeted with applause. He then said that the next day they would receive a ballot with some questions whose aim was to manifest the mind *(generalis mens)* of the fathers on the most important issues in chapter two and thus provide norms for the Doctrinal Commission in its further elaboration of the schema. The fathers would vote on the questions on the following Thursday, before the chapter as a whole was put to a vote.[44]

Then, as a formal ending to discussion on chapter two, Cardinal Browne, vice president of the Doctrinal Commission and speaking in its name, summarized the commission's task as he understood it, which came down to safeguarding papal primacy. He concluded: "Now that we have heard everything the council fathers have said in these General Congregations, it is evident that our first care in revising chapter two is to make sure that in every single phrase the doctrine of the primacy of jurisdiction of the Roman Pontiff is not only protected but made to shine forth more brightly."[45] The point of chapter two in this interpretation was to enhance papal authority. Browne's intervention underscored the necessity of the vote—others who heard the interventions in St. Peter's would surely have drawn different conclusions from them than did Browne.

The next morning when the bishops entered St. Peter's they did not receive the promised ballots. During the Mass, celebrated in the Coptic rite, Cicognani drew aside Agagianian, the moderator for the day, and engaged him in an animated conversation in full view of some of the bishops. The other moderators soon joined the pair, and the conversation seemed even more heated. Cicognani left them and then came back. He left them again, came back. He left them again and came back. The moderators were visibly agitated.[46]

After the Mass, Cardinal Agagianian announced without explanation that the scheduled vote had been postponed "to another day." What had happened? Word soon spread that Cicognani, acting in the pope's name, had the previous evening ordered the ballots, already printed, to be burned. Bishops were stunned. Conspiracy! Treachery! Such were the words heard inside and outside the assembly.

Somebody had got to Paul VI. The obvious candidates were Felici,

Cicognani, and Ottaviani. Felici at this point saw the moderators as setting themselves up with an authority that went beyond the "Regulations," and he especially resented the increasingly important secretarial role played by Dossetti, who at this point held no official council appointment. He also believed that the most delicate doctrinal point, the precise relationship between papal primacy and collegiality, had not been adequately worked out.[47]

As soon became clear, Ottaviani was furious, at least partly on procedural grounds—why had the moderators not consulted the Doctrinal Commission on these preeminently doctrinal issues? What made them assume that such a vote would bind the Doctrinal Commission, a vote not authorized by the "Regulations"? Cicognani, who as president of the Coordinating Commission had not been consulted by the members of his commission who were the moderators, was surely somehow involved since he gave the orders for the destruction of the ballots.

For the next few days the pope was besieged. To sort out the matter he established an ad hoc commission made up of the Council of Presidents, the Coordinating Commission (to which the moderators belonged), and the General Secretariat. At five in the evening on October 23 this ad hoc commission met under the presidency of Cardinal Tisserant, dean of the College of Cardinals. Tisserant almost immediately made known his sympathy for the moderators. He announced that the Council of the Presidents, of which he was the head, had been favorable to the moderators' plan to submit matters to a vote and that he was ignorant of the reasons that had led to the vote's suspension. He led the ad hoc commission through a highly contentious meeting, at the end of which members agreed to a vote along the lines the moderators had advocated from the beginning.

Within a week the pope favorably reviewed a still further revised ballot. On October 28 Suenens announced to the council fathers that the pope had approved the voting, which would take place two days later. The announcement sparked loud applause. At a meeting of the ad hoc commission the next day, Felici in Ottaviani's name asked for a further postponement of the voting. Six cardinals—Cicognani, Ruffini, Roberti, Siri, Spellman, and Stefan Wyszyński—voted to postpone, all the others to proceed as announced, which is what happened.

The results of the voting on now five questions put to the fathers were dramatic:

1. Should the schema assert that episcopal consecration is the supreme grade of the sacrament of Orders? *2,123 affirmative, 34 negative.*
2. Should the schema assert that every legitimately consecrated bishop in communion with the other bishops and the Roman Pontiff is a member of the Body of Bishops? *2,154 affirmative, 104 negative.*
3. Should the schema assert that the so-called Body or College of Bishops in its evangelizing, sanctifying, and governing task is successor to the original College of the Apostles and, always in communion with the Roman Pontiff, enjoys full and supreme power over the universal church? *2,148 affirmative, 336 negative.*
4. Should the schema assert that the aforementioned power of the College of Bishops, united with their head, belongs to it by divine ordinance [and therefore not by papal delegation]? *2,138 affirmative, 408 negative.*
5. Should the schema assert that it is opportune to consider the reinstatement of the diaconate as a permanent grade of sacred ministry, according to needs in different parts of the church? *2,120 affirmative, 525 negative.*

The votes were another turning point in the council. From the interventions in St. Peter's no one would have predicted such landslides. The results showed beyond question that the assembly had a will of its own and that, despite differences in emphasis and outlook, there was agreement in principle on some critical and controversial issues. Among those issues collegiality was special. The bishops, by their presence at the council and their active participation in it, had actually *experienced* collegiality. It was for them now part of their lived reality. The two weeks that had intervened between October 15 and October 30 gave the bishops time to reflect and to cast an even more considered vote. In principle, collegiality had achieved secure and central status as a way the church operates—or is supposed to operate. The moderators had, moreover, provided an instrument that allowed the assembly to express its will and thus rise above the distracting and seemingly endless flood of emendations in the schema.

Yet there were clouds on the horizon. The vote of October 30 stuck in the craw of the minority. Despite the outcome, the moderators realized that they needed to tread warily. They relieved Dossetti of his role as their secretary. While the vote on the questions indeed gave the Doctrinal Commission guidelines, it did little more than that on the crucial question of the relationship between the papacy and the college of bishops—the subject of question four, on which almost 20 percent of the bishops gave a negative answer. This left plenty of room to maneuver for those who opposed collegiality. The fifth question sidestepped the celibacy issue yet, even so, received a negative vote of almost 25 percent.

Most important, the relationship of the assembly to the commissions was still not resolved, at least not in the minds of certain key individuals. On November 8, a week after the vote, Ottaviani reminded the council fathers that the vote was only "indicative," implying that the commission had the authority to deal with it as it liked. He further reminded them that the commission was the competent body to handle such matters and that *they*, the council fathers, had elected its members to advise the council on matters pertinent to Catholic dogma or faith. Why, he asked, had not the moderators submitted their "points" to the Doctrinal Commission for examination before they went ahead with them on October 14?[48]

Ottaviani's intervention, especially his public scolding of the moderators, angered many bishops to the point of talking, in private, about his removal as president of his commission. Members of the commission itself sent Paul VI a petition to replace Ottaviani, but no action was taken on it.[49] On the morning of October 29, the day before the vote, Ottaviani and Suenens had clashed. "Why are you constantly going to the pope?" Ottaviani demanded to know. "Because you too go to the pope. Furthermore, I am a member of the Council of Presidents, a member of the Coordinating Committee, and I am a Moderator."[50]

Paul never revealed why he stopped the distribution of the ballots. It seems clear that he wanted the vote taken in the first place and was pleased with the results on October 30.[51] His action can perhaps best be explained by saying that, since he realized how significant the vote was and felt there was some justification in the complaints on procedure that reached him, he wanted to be sure the complaints were equitably dealt with so that the results of the voting would be incontestable. Still puzzling, however, is why he took the drastic and dramatic measure of ordering the ballots burned (they could be put under lock and key) and why he did not find a way to communicate his decision to the moderators in a less public, last-minute, and embarrassing way. There is much we do not know. The events that began to unfold on October 15 did increasingly show, however, that the procedural issue under all the procedural issues was the role of the pope himself.

The Council Moves On

Discussion of the schema on the floor of St. Peter's had of course not halted because of the crisis, which was being dealt with, symptomatically, outside the council chamber. On October 16 the fathers took up chapter three of *Lumen Gentium,* entitled "On the People of God and Especially the Laity." The final sentence in the introductory paragraph sounded the basic theme of the chapter: "Pastors were instituted in the church not so that they take upon themselves the whole burden of building up the Mystical Body of Christ but that they might nourish and govern the faithful in a way that would result in everybody cooperating together (each in his own way and order) in accomplishing the common task."[52] The sentence is a succinct expression of one of the leitmotifs of the council, reconciliation between the vertical and the horizontal dimensions in the church. The pastors are in charge, but so as to encourage the active engagement of everybody in the work of the church. "Cooperate" *(cooperentur),* work together—one of the key words in the vocabulary special to Vatican II.

Baptism, the document taught, is the basis for equality in the church, and the sacrament of Orders the basis for the inequality. The tension between equality and inequality recurred in the chapter in various ways, in attempts to balance authority with autonomy, obedience with initiative, discipline with gift or charism. Insistent that in the final analysis the bishops are in charge, the chapter struck an unaccustomed note in ecclesiastical documents by being almost as insistent on initiative "from below." Crucial to that initiative, the text indicated, are the charismatic gifts with which the Spirit blesses the church. The chapter reminded members of the laity of their dignity, called them to share in the work of evangelization, and told them that they sanctify themselves and others even through secular pursuits or occupations *(opera etiam saecularia).* They participate in Christ's priestly, prophetic, and regal mission. The people of Christ as a whole are infallible in their faith when that faith represents a consensus. Such infallibility is a charism that of course includes bishops and the pope but does not rest exclusively in them.

The discussion of chapter three lasted for eight sessions, almost two weeks, with ninety interventions on the floor and thirty-three submitted in writing. There were further calls for this chapter to precede the chapter on the hierarchy. As to be expected, the idea that the laity shared in Christ's priestly mission raised questions, objections, and calls for clarity. To some it seemed like another concession to the Protestant observers, for even the less theologically astute among the bishops knew of Luther's advocacy of "the priesthood of all believers."

Ruffini was, as so often, the first to speak—at great length (surely well over the time limit), with many corrections on the use of biblical citations and, in general, with insistence on the distinction between clergy and laity.[53] A short while later Cardinal Bacci objected to the way the document spoke of the priesthood of the laity and asked that it be emended to specify that this was not priesthood "in the true and proper sense" *(de vero et proprio sacerdotio)*.[54] Others spoke along the same lines, with Siri asking specifically that the praise of the laity be toned down a little. Encouragement is a good thing, he said, but it should not go overboard.[55]

Most interventions on the chapter were favorable, and even those just mentioned were relatively restrained in their criticism. On October 22 Suenens delivered a stirring speech on charisms in the church, asking that the chapter be expanded to deal with them more extensively. The text should make manifest, as did the encyclical *Mystici Corporis,* the intimate connection between the hierarchy—"the administrative apparatus"—and the charismatic gifts of the Spirit. The role of prophets and teachers/theologians needs emphasis and elaboration. Certainly, reverence and obedience are due to pastors, but equal reverence is due to those in the church impelled by the Spirit—and they are often lay people. The cardinal closed by making two recommendations for immediate implementation in the council: increasing the number of lay auditors and seeing to it that this increment included women, "who, lest I am mistaken, make up half of the human race."[56]

On October 25 the council moved to chapter four, the call to sanctity. It was difficult for bishops to disagree with the proposition that holiness is a good thing. Much of the debate centered on a specific aspect of religious orders of men: the exemption of some orders from episcopal jurisdiction in their ministries. The chapter gave considerable attention to this long-standing issue that had been contentious since the thirteenth century and flared up especially at Lateran Council V (1512–1517) and at the Council of Trent (1545–1563). In practice this exemption often meant that, within certain (sometimes considerable) restrictions, priests of these orders could preach, hear confessions, and perform other ministries without being subject to the local bishop. Both Lateran V and Trent tried to eliminate, or at least substantially reduce, such "privileges," but owing to papal protection of the orders they were not able to accomplish much. Vatican II would, along with the new Code of Canon Law, 1983, be more successful.

Discussion on the chapter was interrupted by a solemn commemoration of the election of Pope John and then by an unusual procedure in the council. A nagging and extremely sensitive question during the discussion on the church was whether the separate schema on the Virgin Mary should be incorporated into that document or retain its independent status. Feelings ran high on both sides, with many reasons adduced for and against the alternatives. To incorporate it might be taken as a slight to Mary, while to keep it separate gave her a prominence in the council not accorded the Trinity.

Devotion to the Virgin Mary surged in the long nineteenth century with the apparitions at Lourdes, Fatima, and elsewhere, and especially with the solemn papal definitions of the Immaculate Conception in 1854 and the Assumption in 1950. It was in fact one of the most striking and distinguishing characteristics of Catholic piety that had never been stronger than on the eve of Vatican II. As noted, many bishops and theologians hoped for a further "development" of Marian doctrine in the council. They were thinking of a new definition of, perhaps, her role as co-redeemer with Christ or at least a celebration of her dignity by conferring on her a new title such as "Mother of the Church." Indeed, they saw a further exaltation of Mary's role in the church as the reason for the convocation of the council and a new Marian doctrine as the culmination of its agenda.

Those who were against the separate schema exposed themselves to the suspicion of not being sufficiently "devoted to Our Lady." Their position is best understood in the context of their vision for the council; indeed, many of them saw the council's focus as centering piety on the Bible and the public liturgy of the church rather than on "devotions," including Marian devotional practices, which often seemed to have a life apart from Scripture and liturgy. Including Mary in the document on the church provided, they believed, a theological framework for her cult that otherwise seemed to be lacking.

Henri de Lubac had provided an attractive paradigm for such an inclusion in his book *Splendour of the Church,* the final chapter of which was entitled "The Church and Our Lady." About the time de Lubac's book appeared in the 1950s, the German Jesuit theologian Otto Semmelroth had provided the historical and theological grounding for such an inclusion.[57] Some bishops and theologians in this camp believed, finally, that Marian definitions, a phenomenon of the long nineteenth century, had "developed" enough, at least for the time being, and that they would risk distorting Catholic soteriology if they were expanded. Further promotion of

Mary's prerogatives would, moreover, create another obstacle in the ecumenical movement.

The innocent-sounding question of where to locate a statement on the Blessed Virgin was loaded, therefore, with theological implications and emotional dynamite. Yet the council could not afford to spend days on end debating where to put the statement. Working with the moderators, Paul VI devised the solution by instructing the Doctrinal Commission, which was in charge of both schemas, to chose two of its members, one to present to the council arguments in favor of a separate schema and the other to present arguments in favor of incorporation. The commission chose Cardinal Rufino Santos of Manila to speak for the separate schema, Cardinal Franz König of Vienna to speak for incorporation. The cardinals delivered their talks on October 24.[58] Meanwhile, promoters of the separate schema shifted into high gear, printing and distributing to the council members pamphlets and brochures urging their case.

The voting took place on October 29, the day before the voting on the five questions dealing with collegiality and the diaconate. Given who the two speakers were, some in the council saw the vote as a contest between the minority and the majority and hence an indication of how the vote on the five questions would turn out. The Marian vote was in fact one of the closest in the council, with a margin of only forty votes in favor of incorporation. The close margin left the impression that the council was evenly divided not only on this question but on the larger, ecclesiological questions up for a vote the following day, which clearly turned out not to be the case. As an outcome of the vote on October 29, *Lumen Gentium* now had this further chapter on Mary, drafted principally by Gérard Philips.

On November 5 the council moved to the schema on the bishops, presented by Cardinal Paolo Marella, president of the commission, who was followed by Bishop Luigi Carli, the secretary.[59] Their interventions taken together were longer than the schema itself, a short document of thirty-seven succinct paragraphs. The schema dealt largely with nuts-and-bolts issues—the relationship of bishops to Roman Congregations, the role of coadjutor or auxiliary bishops, the competence and organization of episcopal conferences in different nations and regions, the boundaries of dioceses and parishes, and so forth—but underneath them, of course, lay questions of principle.[60] Carli made it clear in his report, however, that the schema on the church dealt with the doctrinal issues related to bishops, whereas this schema was practical or "pastoral."

Little known at the time was that the Commission on Bishops had not held a single plenary session since the council had disbanded in December 1962, and that neither the schema itself nor Carli's official introductory report on the floor was submitted to the full commission before discussion opened in St. Peter's.[61] This curious failure in procedure, plus the fact that it was Carli who oversaw the revision of the text up to this point, explains why bishops who were members of the commission so frequently took the floor to criticize the schema. Bishop Pablo Correa León of Cútuta, Colombia, one of the first speakers, began by complaining that more than half the members of the commission, of which he was a member, had no role in the elaboration of the schema. He was "even more" dismayed that, contrary to the "Regulations," Carli's report to the council did not reflect the thinking of those members.[62]

The schema received the now-standard criticisms of being too juridical and not sufficiently pastoral in its approach. More pointedly, it took no account of collegiality, and it implied that the rights and privileges the bishops enjoyed for the fulfillment of their office were concessions from the Holy See, not theirs by virtue of their episcopal ordination. Finally, though the first chapter recommended participation by residential bishops in the work of the Roman Congregations, an echo of Paul VI's address to the Curia in September, the wording was vague. On the contrary, the chapter put the Congregations in an unassailable position by identifying their authority with the authority of the pope: "In the exercise of his supreme and full jurisdictional power over the universal church, the Roman Pontiff makes use of the Congregations of the Roman Curia, which thus in his name and with his authority bring his office to fulfillment for the good of all the churches and in service to the same sacred pastors [the bishops]."[63]

As to be expected, Cardinals Ruffini and Browne defended the schema, with the former warning of the danger of national episcopal conferences encroaching on the authority of the Holy See. Browne reasserted the authority of the commissions. It was premature, he said, to expect the schema to deal with collegiality because that doctrine was still under study by the Doctrinal Commission, of which he was vice president: "We must wait, therefore, until the Commission makes its report to the council before this schema deals with anything concerning episcopal collegiality."[64] He had, wittingly or unwittingly, thrown down a challenge.

Somewhat surprisingly, after two days of considerable criticism of the schema, the bishops by a large majority voted to accept it as a base text. The next two days were spent on chapter one, the relationship between

The Second Period (1963)

the Curia and the bishops. Few subjects were of keener interest to the council fathers, and few excited such strong feelings. Every bishop had experience, positive, negative, or both, dealing with the Congregations and felt qualified to expound upon the subject. Fireworks were to be expected.

On November 6, Maximos IV as usual generated excitement.[65] Regarding the problem of the central government of the church, he proposed "a new solution" based on the doctrine of collegiality. The church should be governed by the successors to Peter and the other apostles, not by Peter as surrounded by the members of the Roman clergy, which was fine for the government of the diocese of Rome but not for the government of the universal church. "Roman clergy"? Yes, that's what the cardinals were, as shown by their having a titular church in Rome, especially those who resided in Rome as heads of the Congregations of the Curia (which he called "the court").

Merely making a few residential bishops members of the Roman Congregations, as the schema proposed, was, he said, "a small and timid reform"—*une petite réforme timide*—of the central government of the church. He proposed, instead, a solution that in essence consisted in a relatively small group of bishops who with rotating membership would always be in session in Rome to assist the pope. They would work with the pope in collegial fashion, ever mindful of his special prerogatives. This group, not the Holy Office, would be the *Suprema,* under which the Roman Congregations would function and from which they would take direction.

Maximos had called for an important *structural* change. His proposal, somewhat more complicated than here described, was the first effort at the council to create a practical implementation of collegiality. Thus the issue of how to reduce collegiality to concrete reality got put on the table of the commission. How to make collegiality work in practice? This was a crucial moment in the council.

Two days later Lercaro intervened. He laid down some general principles and agreed that just inserting a few residential bishops into the Congregations did not solve the problem. Something more was required to help the pope in his governance of the church. He went on to say that the problem was too complex to be resolved in a few days on the floor of the council. In fact, the matter should be dropped from the decree. At the end of this period, instead, a special commission of the council should draw up guidelines or "desires" *(vota)* for the pope to move the question along toward a comprehensive resolution.[66]

Lercaro failed to specify who would appoint the new commissions' members, and the "Regulations" did not clearly indicate which body would have the competence to make such appointments. Once again by default, it would seem, the task would land on Paul VI's desk. For whatever reason the commission never came into existence. The idea of a central council superior to the Congregations of the Curia gained momentum in informal discussions from that time forward until, two years later, Paul took matters into his own hands with the creation of the Synod of Bishops.

Lercaro had made an important intervention, but it did not get the attention it deserved because it was sandwiched between two of the most famous speeches of the council. Frings had spoken just before Lercaro. His speech, written in part by Ratzinger, created a sensation. The cardinal began by expressing amazement at Cardinal Browne's intervention. The commissions did not, in his humble opinion, have authority to render judgment on an issue approved after long discussion by the council fathers, as if the commissions had access to a truth hidden from everybody else. They were, rather, instruments of the council, and their job was to carry out the will of the council.

Then he delivered his bombshell, an attack on the whole centralizing tendency in the church but specifically on the Holy Office. Frings noted that in an appendix the schema provided a list of powers that the Holy See might concede to the bishops. That, he said, got things backward. What was needed, rather, was a list of the powers reserved to the Holy See. Frings's proposition was a turnaround of the basic assumption on which the schema was based: the Holy See is the source of all authority in the church.

In another appendix, moreover, the schema provided rules according to which the Congregations should henceforth operate. These rules, Frings insisted, should be moved from the appendix to the main text and be understood to apply to all the Congregations, "even to the Supreme Congregation of the Holy Office, whose procedures in many respects are inappropriate to the times in which we live, harm the church, and are for many a scandal." Applause broke out—*plausus in aula,* as the official record states. Not even by that Congregation, he went on, should anybody be judged and condemned without being heard.[67]

Ottaviani, already scheduled to speak that day, prefaced his prepared remarks with an extemporaneous reply to Frings. He protested to the highest degree the words against the Supreme Congregation of the Holy Office, whose president, he reminded the fathers, was the pope himself. The words sprang from ignorance—lest he give offense by using a stronger expression—yes, from ignorance about how careful the Holy Office was to inquire broadly among experts before the members came to a conclusion and submitted it to the Supreme Pontiff for ratification. He then read the speech he had prepared, in which he reproved the moderators for exceeding their authority and reaffirmed the competence of the Doctrinal Commission to deal, pretty much as it saw fit, with the collegiality issue.

Rumors spread that Ottaviani, Antoniutti, and Siri were demanding a public apology from Frings for his attack on the Curia, threatening that unless it were forthcoming they would leave the council. Meanwhile, rumors spread that the Doctrinal Commission, now supposedly in turmoil, was working to have Ottaviani removed as president. Neither of these took place. What is certain is that the clash between the two cardinals, widely reported in the world press, went beyond the personalities involved and beyond the specific issue of the Holy Office. It dramatized the fundamental issue in the council—*how* the church was to operate in the future: continue its highly centralized mode of operation, with its top-down style of management and apodictic mode of communication, or somehow attenuate them by broader consultation and sharing of responsibility.

On that same November 8, Lercaro in his intervention attempted to lessen the tension that had been building for weeks by showing that the latter approach was compatible with the full exercise of papal authority. A week later, during discussion on the authority of national conferences of bishops on November 13, Carli caused consternation by yet another attack on the legitimacy of the vote on October 30.[68] He said he spoke in the name of thirty fathers "from different nations," which was essentially the *Coetus,* the "International Group of Fathers."

After two more days the discussion on the bishops had run its course. Cardinal Marella thanked the council fathers and assured them that their observations would be taken into account in the revision of the schema. The bishops had addressed a number of particulars, such as retirement and the authority of episcopal conferences. It is curious that amid this general review of the episcopal office no attention was given to the process by which bishops were chosen—a process then, as now, shrouded in secrecy.

About a week later, on November 21, the pope decided to expand all the commissions by five members, four elected by the assembly and one appointed by himself—an effort, it seems, to address the problem of the commissions by giving the assembly a chance to elect members more responsive to its will. Members were thus added but none removed. When, in January 1964, the enlarged Commission on Bishops went to work, it did not revise the original schema but composed a new one.

Ecumenism, Adjournment, and a Surprise Announcement

Time was running out. Final (but not the formal, solemn) votes had been taken on the liturgy schema, which had been overwhelmingly approved, and on the communications schema, approved but with a relatively large number of negative votes on what many considered a lackluster and inadequate document. On November 18 the unprecedented and long-awaited schema On Ecumenism arrived in the hall. The historic importance of the day was widely recognized. Who would have thought even five years earlier that a council of the Roman Catholic Church would address such an issue and, moreover, do so with a fundamentally positive attitude? True, in 1949 the Holy Office had issued an instruction entitled *Ecclesia Catholica* that mitigated the strictures of *Mortalium Animos* and recognized the action of the Holy Spirit in the Ecumenical Movement. In some circles it resulted in greater Catholic interest and engagement, yet before John XXIII's announcement of the council ten years later, nobody could have foreseen how ecumenism would jump to such a central role in the Catholic agenda.[69]

Discussion on the schema consumed the remaining working sessions of this period. The subject, originally a chapter in the first schema on the church drawn up by the Doctrinal Commission, was now firmly in the hands of the Secretariat for Christian Unity. The text consisted of five chapters: (1) "Catholic Principles of Ecumenism"; (2) "The Practice of Ecumenism"; (3) "Christians Separated from the Catholic Church"; (4) "Catholic Attitude toward Non-Christians, Especially the Jews"; and (5) "On Religious Liberty."[70] Chapters four and five already had a troubled history in the council. In what schema should they appear, if they were to appear at all? Arab opposition to a positive statement on the Jews weighed heavily on the council, and many prelates opposed the principle of religious liberty for the same reasons the popes of the nineteenth century had opposed it.

After a short presentation of the subject by Cardinal Cicognani, Bishop Joseph Martin of Rouen introduced the first three chapters with obviously heartfelt emotion that, according to Congar, the bishops found moving. He received a long applause at the end.[71] These chapters underwent considerable rewriting before their final approval the next year in *Unitatis Redintegratio,* but since their style and substance remained the same, it is more economical here to highlight the final version. That document recalled that the restoration of unity among Christians was one of the fundamental concerns of the council, and long sections of the text held up that ideal for admiration. The Holy Spirit dwelling in believers is moving them to work for this great goal by bestowing gifts that urge them toward a confession of one faith, a common celebration of divine worship, and fraternal harmony in the family of God.

To that end, the document laid down some principles to guide Catholics in this endeavor. To begin with, Catholics should remember that "change of heart and holiness of life, along with public and private prayer for the unity of Christians, should be regarded as the heart of the whole ecumenical movement." They should, moreover, acknowledge the faults committed by Catholics in the past that have contributed to the present situation. Let them recognize that "the expression of unity very generally forbids common worship. Grace to be obtained sometimes commends it." Theology should be taught from an ecumenical viewpoint, not polemically, and with awareness that "in Catholic doctrine there exists an order or hierarchy of truths, since they vary in their relation to the foundation of Christian faith." Some teachings, that is to say, are more fundamental than others, as, for instance, are those in the ancient creedal statements of the church. Finally, cooperation among Christians vividly expresses the bond that already exists among them and sets in clear relief the features of Christ the Servant, their master and ideal.

Reasonable though these ideals and principles might seem today, in 1963 they signaled an official turnaround in behavior and the modification of a value system. In that regard, one shift in vocabulary is especially noteworthy. Altogether missing from the text is the call to the other Christian communities "to return," a word prominent in both *Mortalium Animos* and in the much more recent document from the Holy Office, *Ecclesia Catholica*.

It is remarkable that these three chapters made their way through the council as easily as they did. Chapters four and five certainly did not. Bea himself presented chapter four. He informed the fathers that Pope John had specifically instructed the Secretariat to deal with relations with the Jews. The church was born out of Israel, and with Israel it shared and venerated the same sacred text. Why is the church's relationship with the Jews an important issue today? Because of the vicious outburst of anti-Semitism in the modern world that culminated with National Socialism in Germany. It was a German who spoke. At the end the cardinal underscored that this was a religious text and did not touch on "the difficult questions" of the relationship of Arab nations to the state of Israel or to Zionism.[72]

De Smedt presented, at considerable length, the similarly sensitive chapter five. This issue ended up with the Secretariat principally because before the council Protestant groups had made it known that, since certain Latin American governments denied Protestants permission to have their own churches and schools, they considered the council's stance on church-state a litmus test of the sincerity of its ecumenical commitment.[73]

Many bishops requested, De Smedt began, that the council "proclaim" the right of human beings to religious liberty, that is, "the right of human persons to the free exercise of their religion according to the dictates of their consciences." De Smedt took John XXIII's encyclical *Pacem in Terris* as giving the best indication of the tradition of the church in this regard. He then tried to show how the statements of popes beginning with Pius IX needed to be interpreted in the context of their times and how the teaching of religious liberty had been "evolving" or "developing" or even "progressing" in the church until the present moment. His basic message: religious liberty is part of the Catholic tradition; it is not a rupture with the past.[74]

Applause broke out when De Smedt finished speaking, but he had not persuaded everybody. He had a difficult task because under religious liberty lurked a more fundamental issue, a species of "development of doctrine" that seemed to be not a continuation of the immediate past but a deviation from it. Nonetheless, with De Smedt's intervention words like "evolution" and "progress" got a positive meaning and in that form began to take their place in the official vocabulary of the council.

Many bishops now felt that chapters four and five, whatever their merits or demerits, did not quite fit in this schema on ecumenism, whereas the first three chapters formed a cohesive unit. This consideration led to the uncontested procedural decision to vote on those chapters as a unit and, for the moment, leave the other two aside. Bishops could hardly oppose ecumenism in principle since Pope John had made it, in effect, one of the main concerns of the council. Yet many were uneasy, especially those from Latin nations, who feared that it would foster religious indifferentism and weaken the church in the face of Protestant proselytizing. Moreover, the only Protestants the bishops from Latin America knew were aggressive American evangelicals, who would be even more appalled at the prospect of dialogue with Catholics than the bishops were at the prospect of dialogue with them.

What is often forgotten about the document is that the Eastern Ortho-dox, not the churches of the Reformation era, appear as the first object of Catholic ecumenical concern. For that reason Cicognani, as prefect of the Congregation for the Oriental Churches, had introduced the text. In any case, after four days of discussion, these chapters were accepted as a base text, with only eighty-six negative votes cast. The council then moved to individual chapters.

Ruffini spoke against the document as a whole at the beginning of the debate. He did so again, in a more outspoken manner, during discussion on chapter three. He made five points. They are important because, except for the last, they are a neat summary of standard Catholic apologetics found at the time in every seminary textbook: (1) Christ founded only one church, the Roman Catholic. (2) Faults cannot be attributed to the church as such but only to its members. (3) To leave the church because of its sin-ful members is itself a sin. (4) The one true church fervently hopes for the return of the Protestants. (5) Dialogue with non-Catholics is good only if done according to the guidelines the Holy See will publish.[75]

By December 2, however, time had run out, and it had done so before the council could address the more explosive chapters four and five—to the relief of some and the great dismay of others. Bishops from the United States were among those pressing hardest to get religious liberty on the agenda, but they were becoming increasingly aware of the complexity of the issue, of the adamant resistance to it in some quarters, especially in the Doctrinal Commission, and even of the inadequacy of the text pre-sented to them. Murray, now officially functioning as a *peritus*, let the American bishops know how faulty he found the document, which would have many travails to suffer before it reached final and acceptable form. Meanwhile, at the end of the morning of December 2, Cardinal Bea thanked the council for the discussion on the first three chapters, which had safely sailed through the waters of the debate. Although he did not say it, the last two chapters were in limbo.

The final day of the second period, December 4, was the occasion for solemn ratification of the decrees on the liturgy and on the media. At the Public Session in St. Peter's, Paul VI of course presided. At the end of the morning he gave a long address in which he tried to summarize the achievements of the council thus far and lay out tasks or goals for its fu-ture. The two palpable achievements were the two decrees. The tasks and goals as he described them were uncontroversial. He sedulously avoided mention of any of the hot issues that had troubled the period just ended.

Although never saying so expressly, he seemed to suggest that the next period would be the last. This was good news to just about everybody, even though the better-informed bishops thought it optimistic.

But at this point the bishops needed an injection of optimism. The second period had been difficult and frustrating—partly because of organizational problems, inseparable from ideologies, and partly because of the seriousness of the issues, to which many bishops had not given much thought before the council—especially collegiality, ecumenism, and religious liberty. Not only were these issues serious in themselves, but on their resolution turned to a large extent the very character of the council.

At the last moment of the ceremony came an electrifying and totally unexpected announcement. Just as the bishops thought the pope was about to finish his address, he departed from the text earlier distributed to them to reveal that in January he would go on pilgrimage to the Holy Land. After a moment of stunned silence, prolonged applause broke out in the basilica.

With only a few, almost insignificant exceptions, no pope had left Italy except as a prisoner of a foreign power for more than five hundred years. No pope had left Italy even as a prisoner for more than a hundred and fifty years. No pope had left the little precincts of the Vatican since 1870 until, in early October 1962, John XXIII made a pilgrimage to Assisi and Loreto some hundred miles from Rome, to pray for the success of the council. Accustomed as we are today to popes traveling the globe, it is difficult to appreciate how startling and significant Paul's announcement was to those who heard it. The era of "the prisoner of the Vatican" was now really over. The era that ended juridically with the Lateran agreements of 1929, when the papacy gave up all claims to rule the territory of the old Papal States, now ended in high drama on the world stage. Paul was living up to the image of his biblical namesake. He was an apostle on the move.

Reaction to the announcement was enthusiastic. Commentators saw it as a vivid example of *aggiornamento* in action, and thus a strong gesture of support for the direction taken by the council. Once it became known that during the trip the pope would meet with the Greek Orthodox patriarch Athenagoras, the trip seemed to be a ratification of the new ecumenism and a foretaste of full reconciliation among the churches that the council pointed to. Yet some noted that the trip focused attention on the pope and the papal office at the very moment an ecumenical council was in session, and they wondered what, if any, significance should be attached to that aspect of Paul's dramatic gesture.

6

The Third Period (1964)

Triumphs and Tribulations

For three days, from January 4 to January 6, the world witnessed the exciting and unprecedented pilgrimage of Paul VI to the Holy Land.[1] Television audiences across the globe saw him jostled by enthusiastic crowds, maintaining a schedule that could have laid low a younger man. Nothing like these vivid images of a world leader had ever been seen before, and they created a sensation. Not so visible to the public were the pope's eight meetings with Orthodox and Armenian patriarchs, the meetings with representatives of other Christian communities, the warm reception by King Hussein of Jordan, and the polite correctness of the Israeli authorities. Something of great significance was happening.

The high point of the trip was Paul's encounter with Athenagoras, patriarch of Constantinople. Not since the Council of Florence in the mid-fifteenth century had pope and patriarch met and taken steps to end the differences between their two churches. What no one knew at the time was that until just a few days before Paul announced his pilgrimage to the council, he had no plans to meet with any Orthodox leaders. In early December, however, Athenagoras proposed a meeting in Jerusalem of "all the heads of the holy Churches of Christ, of the East and the West." This was like a blessing out of the heavens, and it caused great excitement in Cardinal Bea's Secretariat for Christian Unity. The Secretariat of State had, however, already settled details of the trip and felt that at this late date they could not be changed. It was thus that the patriarch's plan was reduced in scope.

Even so, the meetings between these two Christian leaders on January 5 and 6 were a dramatic moment that captured world attention, and they presaged the declaration of mutual forgiveness they issued two years later at the conclusion of the council. Not in anyone's wildest dreams could such meetings have been imagined even a year earlier, and they gave the council powerful impetus to press forward with the document on ecumenism. Hopes soared. For a few days everything seemed possible.

But in Rome hard work lay ahead, as everybody connected with the council realized. Paul VI had repeatedly indicated that he hoped the third period would be the last. His hope was widely shared across the ideological spectrum. The bishops, especially the leaders among them, were weary, apprehensive about their long absences from their dioceses, concerned about the soaring costs of the council, and eager to reduce the agenda further to manageable tasks. The Coordinating Commission knew that it had to find ways to expedite matters and to bring the council to a close.

Some bishops, however, felt just as strongly that the council should take all the time it needed to do its job right. They feared what might happen if the council fathers had to rush through issues without giving them the consideration they deserved. In any case, for the months between the closing of the second period and the opening of the third, all those involved in the management of the council tried to find means to move it along, even if closure in 1964 turned out not to be feasible.

The most obvious way to speed up the council was to reduce the number of documents. To that end Cardinal Döpfner, probably encouraged by Paul VI, proposed limiting the number of schemas to six—on the church, on bishops, on revelation, on the laity, on ecumenism, and on the effective presence of the church in today's world. The other schemas, such as those on religious life, the missions, and the clergy, would be reduced to skeletal form, sets of propositions that could be voted on without discussion. The "Döpfner Plan," as it came to be called, was adopted and guided revisions during the early months of 1964, but it met resistance once the bishops reassembled and was gradually abandoned.[2]

The commissions, though hampered by the problems endemic to such groups, worked hard. By the middle of the summer, Archbishop Felici was able to send the bishops all the schemas to be treated in the next period,

including those that had already been debated but not yet finally approved. These documents roughly correspond to the sixteen that the council would finally ratify. The very number of texts the bishops received at this time, however, made it seem unlikely that they could dispose of them in just one more period.

Producing the documents had not been easy, and success in coming up with a satisfactory text depended on the convergence of a number of favorable circumstances. The schema on the church, in particular, continued to run into trouble. What was now chapter three, "On the Hierarchical Structure of the Church," was the sticking point because of the doctrine of collegiality. Did that doctrine not entail a change in the teaching of Vatican I on papal primacy, and did it not perforce entail a diminution of papal authority and freedom to act? A small but determined minority gave passionately affirmative answers to these questions and was convinced that ratification of the teaching on collegiality was a betrayal of the tradition of the church. Other bishops, though perhaps not altogether ill disposed toward the doctrine, felt the council was moving too quickly on an idea that had not occurred to them before they arrived in Rome in 1962.

By the middle of May, nonetheless, the whole schema had gone through a final revision, had been approved by the Doctrinal Commission, and was about to be sent to the bishops. But on May 19 Felici informed the commission that the pope was transmitting to it thirteen "suggestions" (suggerimenti) regarding collegiality that he wanted the commission to consider.[3] The pope said he offered these suggestions "in order to prevent as far as possible future erroneous interpretations of the text."[4] This was the first time that either he or his predecessor had taken such an initiative. For that reason it met with concern and, because of the timing, some consternation. The incident adumbrated the extraordinary number of such interventions the pope would make from this point in the council forward— the so-called red pencil of Paul VI.[5]

No one questioned the pope's right to make his position known. What was perturbing was that he had waited until the document was all but signed, sealed, and delivered to offer his suggestions. Were they, in fact, suggestions? Was "suggestion" a diplomatic way of saying something stronger? Felici assured the commission that the pope merely wanted the group to consider his thoughts, as it would those of any other council father, and that he wanted the commission to be completely free regarding them.

The commission, of course, considered them with extreme care, accepted a fair number of them, though sometimes with slight modifications, and sent the pope a detailed report composed by Gérard Philips on what it had done and why. In particular the commission rejected Paul's limitation on collegiality, which he expressed by proposing that the authority of the college of bishops "be exercised according to the prescriptions of the head [the pope]." The commission stuck to its negative and therefore broader formulation of that authority, namely, that it "never be exercised independently of the Roman Pontiff." For Paul's designation of the pope as "head of the church," the commission preferred "visible head" or "supreme pastor," since Christ was the head of the church. In his report to Paul, Philips relayed the commission's hesitation about saying, as Paul wanted, that the pope was "responsible only to the Lord"—*uni Domino devinctus*—because he was "responsible to revelation, to the fundamental structure of the church, to the sacraments, to the definitions of previous councils, etc." This was a gentle correction to a revealing misstep in theology.

In the end, for all the worry the suggestions prompted, they had little impact on the schema. Although at the time the pope seemed to accept with equanimity the commission's actions, some weeks later Felici reported to the Coordinating Commission that Paul still had concerns. At this point, however, the papal concerns regarding collegiality seemed like no more than a small cloud in an otherwise serene sky.

Months later, on the evening of September 13, the day before the council opened, Paul received a long and confidential memorandum undersigned by twenty-five cardinals (sixteen of whom were from the Curia) and by the superiors-general of thirteen religious orders of men. Among the nine non-curial cardinals was McIntyre of Los Angeles. The document warned that the teaching of chapter three, on episcopal consecration and collegiality, posed a mortal danger to the church and undermined its monarchical structure: "The church would be changed from monarchical to 'episcopalian' [*episcopaliana*] and collegial, and would do so, supposedly, by reason of divine ordinance and in virtue of episcopal consecration." The very best that can be said about the chapter, according to the memo, is that it is a novelty—a novelty supported by vague and illogical arguments. The pope had to intervene, as many bishops hoped he would. He should take these two subjects off the agenda of the council, submit them

to a commission of theologians of his own choosing, suspend the council indefinitely after this third period, and then, after hearing the report of the theologians, conclude the council with a fourth and final period at some future date.[6]

The document ended, "Holy Father . . . in this moment of history that we consider heavy with consequences, we place all our confidence in you, who received from our Lord the duty of 'confirming your brothers' [Luke 22.32], the duty you generously accepted saying, 'We will defend holy church from errors of doctrine and morals that inside and outside threaten its integrity and blind us to its beauty.'"[7] The document put the full burden for the council on the pope's shoulders and foresaw catastrophe if he did not take radical action immediately, without recourse to the assembly.

Cardinal Larraona was the chief architect of the memorandum and the person who sought the signatures of the other cardinals. Paul VI soon learned of Larraona's role in the affair and hence addressed to him his uncharacteristically sharp response. The pope was upset at the timing of the letter but also at its substance, built "on debatable arguments." Moreover, he said, if he tried to put into effect the measures the document proposed, the results would be disastrous for the council and therefore for the church.

Paul was not pleased, but he felt the pressure. He received further memoranda for and against the chapter. When the vote on chapter three drew near, he asked Felici whether it might be advisable to postpone it. Felici responded firmly in the negative, arguing that a delay would be counterproductive. He concluded his memorandum on the subject, "In the end it is necessary to have faith in the consciences of the council fathers, in the force of truth, and above all in the help of the Holy Spirit."[8] Paul dropped the idea, but he continued to receive notes and memoranda arguing for and against chapter three. The drama of the chapter was building to a climax.

Just a month earlier, on August 6, Paul had issued his first encyclical, *Ecclesiam Suam,* as promised in his opening address to the council the previous year. In it he sedulously avoided touching on this sensitive issue in any direct way.[9] The expression "people of God" occurs only once in this long document and receives no special emphasis. In section 33 the pope made clear that, while he wanted the council to have "full liberty" in its deliberations, he would at the proper moment and manner express his judgment on them. *Ecclesiam Suam* seems, moreover, to be the first encyclical ever written by a pope himself rather than principally by others to whom he committed the task.

The encyclical had a direct impact on the council in one important regard, the remarkable prominence it gave to dialogue. Paul appropriated the word from Buber, it seems, through the mediation of his friend Jean Guitton, the prominent philosopher-theologian, a French layman. "Dialogue" occurs seventy-seven times, and its meaning and application occupy fully two-thirds of this long document. The encyclical infused the word into the council's vocabulary. In the original version of the document on ecumenism presented to the council the previous year, for instance, the word does not appear a single time. In its revised version, presented after the publication of the encyclical, it becomes one of the text's most characteristic words. Thus it was that "dialogue," so typical of "the spirit" of Vatican II, made its way into the council's vocabulary, where it would have perhaps its most potent effect on the schema On the Church in the Modern World.[10]

Meanwhile, the other schemas had problems of their own. The first three chapters of the decree on ecumenism seemed secure, but the two chapters now detached from it—on the Jews and on religious freedom—were meeting fierce resistance. The original schema on the bishops was completely reworked during this period to make it conform in both subject and style to the results of the debate on *Lumen Gentium,* and the document on revelation underwent a similar transformation even as members of the commission tried to process the 2,481 recommendations extracted from the speeches and written comments of the bishops. The decree on the laity, at one time threatened with reduction to a series of propositions, achieved by dint of extraordinarily hard work its final form, though significant changes would be incorporated into it as a result of debate in St. Peter's.

In June the old schema 17 became schema 13. By that time it already contained the opening words by which it would henceforth be known—*Gaudium et Spes:* "The joy and hope, the grief and anguish of the people of our times." At this point several versions had been produced and circulated, somewhat in competition with one another—a Roman text, a Malines text, and a Zurich text. These were joined by a late-arriving text from the bishops of Poland that Archbishop Karol Wojtyła of Kraków submitted on their behalf. It had some influence on the version that was sent to the council fathers that summer but was not accepted as the base text, as the Poles had hoped.[11] The Church in the Modern World was on its way, which was often more like an obstacle course than a smooth path.

With five new stipulations the "Regulations" were again revised, partly because the procedures still seemed cumbersome and ineffective and partly because they received sharp criticism, especially from Bishop Carli. Indeed, in a pointed memorandum to the pope, Carli again challenged the legitimacy of the vote on October 30 of the previous year. The new stipulation regarding the moderators did not do much more than reword the original: "It falls to the moderators not only to direct the labors of the council but also to regulate the discussion in the General Congregations."[12]

By the opening of the third period, however, the five entities somehow responsible for the council's progress had fallen into routine ways of dealing with one another that worked fairly well except when a crisis arose. The old Council of Presidents still existed, but its function was in practice reduced to ensuring that the "Regulations" were respected—a function that, with one notable exception in this period, it rarely exercised. The Coordinating Committee supervised the revision of the schemas. The commissions, of course, still did the actual revising and thus were crucial for the council's direction, but their membership had been increased so that they were more responsive to the will of the assembly.

The moderators directed the action on the floor. The General Secretariat of the Council under Felici's headship was the liaison among the presidents, the Coordinating Committee, and the moderators and had the more mundane but crucial task of seeing to "housekeeping details" such as printing and distributing the texts, overseeing the voting processes, and keeping track of the schedule of speakers for any given day. Felici also frequently reported to the pope. Things therefore moved more smoothly at the beginning of the third period, but the old unresolved question of where the buck stopped continued to trouble the council. The papal apartments had begun to compete with the floor of St. Peter's as the council's center of gravity.

Meanwhile, on the opening day of the council, the *periti* received a sharp reminder of the limitations of their role. They were to answer questions put to them by bishops but, it seemed, not volunteer their opinions. Moreover, they were not to promote their opinions in any organized and public way through interviews. Finally, they were not to criticize the council to the media or communicate inside information about it. Paul VI, acting at least in part on complaints that the experts were exercising an undue influence on the council, was the ultimate origin of this reminder.[13]

As the council resumed, the world outside it seemed darker than when it had opened two years earlier. The assassination of John F. Kennedy on November 22, 1963, and then the assassination of his presumed assassin projected an image of violence and chaos unfamiliar in the West since the end of World War II. Meanwhile, the situation in Vietnam deteriorated even as the United States became increasingly involved. The decline of Khrushchev's position in the USSR caused fear of an increase in international tension, which Khrushchev had been instrumental in defusing. Algeria was in turmoil as the last French troops departed in the summer of 1964, and France was torn with bitter and menacing disagreements over its withdrawal from the former colony.

Nonetheless, within St. Peter's on September 14, 1964, a cautious optimism prevailed. Some 2,200 council fathers who would be present for this period found their hopes for reconciliation and world peace buoyed by the pope's pilgrimage. They thought it might be possible to wrap up their business in this period, and they felt reassured after Paul's first year as pope that he was solidly behind the direction the council had taken.

The third period opened with a Mass that was a striking innovation—the pope celebrated it at the papal altar with twenty-four others from nineteen different countries. Concelebration, as this practice is known, was something that most people in the basilica had never experienced outside the special circumstance of ordinations to the priesthood. It was in this instance an implementation of a provision of *Sacrosanctum Concilium* promulgated the previous year and a sign that Paul VI took the liturgical reforms seriously and was intent on putting them into action.

Church and Bishops

After the Mass Paul delivered a long address on the church, with a focus on the relationship between the papal and the episcopal offices, which he described as the most serious issue before the council.[14] While conceding to the bishops a role in governing the church, he at the same time insisted on the unique prerogatives of the pope—nothing surprising there. He concentrated on these aspects of the subject and never once described the church as "the people of God." Given the context in which he spoke, his emphasis is understandable, but the omission did not go without comment.

The next day the council went to work on the revised text of *Lumen Gentium*. In his opening words to the fathers, Felici insisted that they were here dealing with a subject of the greatest importance—*maximi momenti*. He exhorted them to pay the closest attention and, as far as possible, to remain in their places. He drove his point home with a bit of humor when he informed them that the coffee bars in St. Peter's would henceforth not open until eleven o'clock: "Before that hour it will do no good to knock on the door because nobody is going to open it."[15]

The first four chapters of the document had been thoroughly debated the previous year. Although chapter four, on the call to holiness, had begot two new chapters—on religious and on the laity—they, too, had in effect been debated and now just needed to be voted on. The only chapters still to be discussed were seven, on the eschatological character of the church, which the commission added in response to oral and written interventions, and then the final chapter, on the Virgin Mary. Once these chapters were presented and discussed, they would be voted on as well.

But what about the troublesome chapter three, on the hierarchical structure of the church? When it was clear to those who subscribed to the September 13 memorandum to Paul VI that their efforts to have collegiality removed from the agenda had failed, they agitated for reopening debate. The pope, the moderators, and the vast majority of bishops opposed this idea, which in any case would have violated the "Regulations" that the minority was so concerned to see observed down to the last jot and tittle. Moreover, the debate the previous year had been long and exhaustive. What new arguments could possibly be adduced on either side?

Nonetheless, a compromise was devised. Before the council fathers voted on chapter three, they would hear three presentations arguing for the text as it stood, and one presentation opposing it. Since the result of the crucial vote on the issue the previous year had been 2,148 in favor of collegiality and only 336 against, the ratio of three speakers to one seemed appropriate, even generous. This measure was conceived as a final concession to the opponents of collegiality. They would have their say on an issue on which almost 90 percent of the council fathers, well over the required two-thirds, had already declared themselves.

On September 15, Cardinal Browne introduced the short and uncontroversial chapter seven, on the church's pilgrim-eschatological character. Twelve speakers followed, all in favor, though of course with qualifications and suggestions. The next day three more spoke in the same vein, and then the council moved quickly to chapter eight, on Mary. In the meantime, however, toward the end of the morning on September 15, Felici announced how the plan for voting on the schema would proceed, subject to the council's approval. For each of chapters one, four, five, and six there would be only one vote, on the chapter as a whole. On chapter two (people of God) there would be four votes on specific sections within the chapter, followed by a vote on the whole. For chapter three, however, there would be, after the four presentations mentioned above, thirty-nine votes on alternative wordings of specific sections, and only then a vote on the chapter as a whole. Chapter three would be scrutinized like no other part of the document. For the proposed changes in wording, the vote was a simple "yes" or "no," but for the chapters as a whole the fathers could also vote "yes, with qualification" *(placet iuxta modum),* which meant that still further emendations to the text could be submitted.

The next day the council voted 2,170 to 32 in favor of the calendar Felici had proposed. That very day, the voting began on chapter one, which passed 2,114 to 11. On subsequent days the votes for chapters two, four, five, and six were similarly favorable. On September 21 the presentations on chapter three took place. Cardinal Frane Franić took the floor to speak against three specific points of the chapter—that the office of bishop was the fullness of priesthood to which the candidate was sacramentally ordained; that the bishops formed a college with responsibility for the whole church; and that the office of permanent deacon be reinstated without imposing the discipline of celibacy. As anticipated, 75 percent of his long intervention dwelt on the second point, collegiality. Then Cardinal König, Archbishop Parente, and Bishop Luis E. Henríquez Jiménez, auxiliary bishop of Caracas, Venezuela, spoke in favor of the chapter.[16] Parente was, as mentioned, assessor of the Holy Office and in the 1940s an outspoken critic of "la nouvelle théologie." For him to speak in favor was a coup for the majority. When the four speakers finished, the calendar for the forty votes on chapter three was announced. It would stretch over eight sessions, from September 21 until the vote on the chapter as a whole was taken on September 30. The process was not to be rushed.

The minority, with Larraona as spokesman, continued to pressure the pope to take action against the chapter. On September 20, the day before the four presentations, Larraona sent a note to Paul warning him of the dire consequences to be expected from the teaching of chapter three. The proponents of that chapter, he said, had spread their novel teaching "by recourse to every conceivable type of propaganda." There was no way, according to him, that the pope could possibly approve of it. By accepting the change the church "would deny her past and the doctrine held up to now; she would accuse herself of having been wrong and of having for centuries acted against the divine law."[17]

Larraona did not let go. The next day, after the presentations, he sent another letter to Paul, praising Franić's "serene" and "limpid" presentation and criticizing the others. He implied that the three bishops who spoke in favor of the chapter had not fairly and fully represented the discussions in the Doctrinal Commission. At the end he notified Paul that a rumor was spreading, presumably concocted by the friends of chapter three, that the pope wanted the council fathers to vote in favor of the chapter and that many of them, "not wanting to displease Your Holiness," were therefore inclined to vote that way.[18] The story about the "rumor" was in essence a preemptive attempt to discount the significance of voting even before it took place.

The voting went forward as scheduled. Once again the results regarding collegiality and the sacramental character of the episcopate were stunningly one sided. Negative votes on the specific sections never exceeded 322 out of an electorate of about 2,245, or 15 percent, much less than the 30 percent the minority was expecting. On these two issues, and most pointedly on collegiality, "the minority" was indeed a minority. Votes against restoring the permanent diaconate were higher, 702, whereas somewhat paradoxically, only 629 voted against ordaining married men, which had seemed to be a more controversial issue. The only amendment the assembly rejected, by a vote of 1,364, was the one providing for ordaining to the diaconate young men who would not be bound to celibacy.

The Doctrinal Commission proposed that the voting on the chapter as a whole be divided into two votes, the first on the sections concerning collegiality and the second on the sections concerning the diaconate. Such a division, the commission maintained, would greatly facilitate its work in dealing with the emendations. Bishop Carli immediately appealed to the moderators, maintaining that such a division was contrary to the "Regulations." He knew, of course, that some bishops would vote against the chapter because it contained the more controversial material on the diaconate. The moderators put the matter to the assembly, which almost unanimously opted for the two-part vote. When the votes were counted, the first section on collegiality received 1,624 affirmative votes, 572 affirmative with qualification, and only 42 negative votes. In this showing the hardcore opponents of the doctrine constituted a statistically insignificant percentage of the council. Somewhat surprisingly, the second section, on the diaconate, received only a slightly larger number of negative votes, fifty-three, and fewer affirmative votes with qualification than had the section on collegiality.

Although the many amendments that had been submitted would have to be considered and another vote on the text taken, followed by the solemn, basically ceremonial vote later before the Public Session, it was now certain that those votes would be resoundingly affirmative. The Doctrinal Commission would have to revise the document in light of amendments, but the hard work had been done. The document had come through the test unchanged in any significant way. It was out of danger, so it seemed, and could now rest easy until the formality of the solemn ratification. This feeling of finality and security was, however, badly misplaced.

The voting process, of course, took only a few minutes of the hours the council fathers spent in St. Peter's every morning. Most of the time was consumed by presentation and discussion of new texts. After debate on the final two chapters of *Lumen Gentium* closed on September 18, the council took up the schema on the bishops, now entitled *Christus Dominus,* Christ the Lord.[19] *Christus Dominus* was much changed from the document the bishops had both approved the previous year and also severely criticized and sent back to the commission for overhaul. Among other changes, the document showed the beginnings of a shift in style.

In anticipation of a positive vote on collegiality and episcopal ordination in *Lumen Gentium,* the document now opened by affirming those teachings. In very general terms, section 5 of chapter one called for a body *(Coetus seu Consilium)* to make collegiality a functioning reality, along the lines proposed by Maximos and others a year earlier. In similarly general terms, it called for a reform of the Curia. The discussion of the schema lasted only four days and ranged over many issues. Carli rose to the floor on the first day to speak against the document produced by the commission of which he was a member. He predictably continued his attack on collegiality.[20]

Somewhat surprisingly, he was the only speaker to focus on that issue, perhaps because the council fathers thought collegiality would be decided a few days later in the voting on chapter three of *Lumen Gentium*. Later in this third period, November 4–7, the assembly voted on *Christus Dominus*. The first two chapters received such a large number of qualified votes that they could not be considered approved and had to be resubmitted to the assembly. Nonetheless, the basic orientation was not in question. A revised and expanded version won final approval the next year.

That final version contained many concrete determinations about diocesan boundaries and similar matters. It recalled the important role that local and provincial councils had played in the history of the church. It proceeded from there strongly to urge the creation of episcopal conferences in regions where they did not yet exist and to commend them where they did.

It also painted a portrait of the ideal bishop, held up for imitation and emulation. It introduced dialogue as an episcopal mode and now spoke of priests as the bishops' collaborators and friends. Through his example as servant leader and through his respect for the needs, charisms, and aspirations of clergy and laity, the bishop worked together with them and inspired and guided them to a deeper spiritual life. In chapter three the decree recommended that bishops establish in their dioceses a council made up of clergy, religious, and laity to review pastoral activities in the diocese and formulate policies concerning them *(practicas expromere conclusiones)*. The bishop was in charge, but for the first time ecclesiastical documents stressed the horizontal dimensions of his relationships to those over whom he presided.

Religious Liberty and the Jews

On September 23, 1964, the highly controversial and further revised declaration On Religious Liberty, now detached from the decree on ecumenism, finally came to the floor.[21] If the declaration had been capable of emotion, it would have shaken with fear and trepidation. Opposition was strong and seemingly more widespread among the bishops than the opposition to collegiality. This was an issue, moreover, that had immediate and profound ramifications for how the church dealt with governments around the world and, most pointedly, for how the church in the future negotiated concordats—if it negotiated them at all. This was not some abstract theological doctrine that had no immediate practical repercussions. On the contrary, it cut right into the heart of an important aspect of the Vatican's diplomacy. It was therefore of vital concern to the Secretariat of State.

For Americans today, the declaration in the final form approved by the council reads almost like a statement of the obvious. Although it frames its principles in Christian terms, for the most part it enunciates their practical ramifications in ways that have generally been operative in the United States since the ratification of the Constitution. For the Catholic Church, however, the document ran counter to theories and practices that not only crystallized in the nineteenth century as a reaction to the "lay state" following the Enlightenment and the French Revolution but also, in a generic way, ran all the way back to the formation of confessional states in both Protestant and Catholic Europe during the Reformation. At that time, according to the formula of the Peace of Augsburg in 1555, the ruler determined the religion of the territory he controlled and was its protector—*cuius regio, eius religio* (whose kingdom, his the religion). These theories and practices in fact got their first expression with Constantine in the fourth century, when, among other things, he convoked the Council of Nicaea and took upon himself the enforcement of its decrees.

In the nineteenth century, the volatile political situation in Catholic countries in Europe and Latin America that followed the stable "marriage of throne and altar" of the previous two centuries led Catholic theologians to come up with a clear formula for church-state relations. The basic premise of the teaching was that only truth has a right to freedom, or, put negatively, as it often was, "error has no rights." In essence the teaching boiled down to the following. First, if the majority of the citizens were Catholics, the state had the duty to profess the Catholic faith and to do all it reasonably could to promote and defend it. This meant that at the same time it was duty-bound to discourage or even suppress other religions, which might include denying their adherents some civil rights. Second, in certain situations, "in order to avoid greater evils," it might be necessary to tolerate other religions and thus allow their free practice. Third, when Catholics are a minority, the state has the duty from natural law to guarantee them full citizenship and free practice of their religion because the state must foster the pursuit of truth, which the Catholic Church possesses.

By the twentieth century this was standard teaching, enshrined in every Catholic textbook on theology and taught in every seminary around the world. It was also the teaching that guided the concordats that the Holy See negotiated, for instance, with the Spanish government under Franco as late as 1953. Not every Catholic was convinced by it, especially after the efflorescence of Christian Democracy at mid-century. In Europe Jacques Maritain espoused a revision of the teaching and caused more worry in the Holy Office than did John Courtney Murray. The teaching did not correspond to the reality of the Western democracies nor to the real beliefs of the Catholic politicians who led them.

Although Catholics in the United States were genuinely shocked when they discovered the church's teaching on the matter, American theologians continued to defend it. The matter came to a crisis point in the 1950s, when Murray began arguing that the teaching needed revision in the light of changed political circumstances. He advocated a form of separation of church and state, much like the situation in the United States. In 1951–1952 he entered into controversy with two professors at The Catholic University of America—Joseph Clifford Fenton and Francis Connell, both of whom were *periti* at the council.[22] Along with Father George Shea from Immaculate Conception Seminary in Darlington, New Jersey, they attacked Murray in the *American Ecclesiastical Review* and agitated with the Holy Office for a condemnation of his views. The *Review,* however, gave Murray space to argue his position.

The matter became public with a speech by Cardinal Ottaviani on March 2, 1953, at the Lateran University in Rome, his alma mater. Although he never mentioned Murray's name, Ottaviani clearly attacked his views.[23] In 1955, under pressure from the Holy Office, Murray's Jesuit superiors told him not to publish further on the matter. That seemed to end the affair, but in 1960 the official teaching was an obstacle raised in John Kennedy's campaign for the presidency. No Catholic, critics claimed, could be president because he would have to obey the church and work for the suppression of all religions except Catholicism.

This was the context in which the American bishops came to Vatican II. Most of them, especially in the light of Kennedy's recent election, had reached the conclusion that the council needed to take action. Once the declaration On Religious Liberty surfaced in the council, the American bishops rushed to support it, to the point that it was in danger of being identified as an "American issue." Murray's appointment as *peritus* gave heart to those who wanted to see the teaching changed. In the same month that Pope John appointed Murray, he published *Pacem in Terris,* in which, as mentioned, he spoke of the human right to worship God "according to the dictates of an upright conscience."[24]

On September 23 Bishop De Smedt once again introduced the matter to the council.[25] The short declaration was now entitled "On Religious Liberty, That Is, on the Right of the Individual and of Communities to Liberty in Religious Matters"—*De libertate religiosa seu de iure personae et communitatum ad libertatem in re religiosa.*[26] Only with the final version did it open with the telling words, "Human dignity"—*Dignitatis Humanae.* De Smedt told the fathers that the Secretariat had revised the original text in accordance with the many suggestions it had received from members of the council. In particular, he pointed out that the new text more clearly expressed the meaning of the term "religious liberty" and the rights that religious bodies possess in civil society, as well as the legitimate limits to expressions of religious liberty; it made more evident that individuals had the obligation to form their consciences by trying to discover what God had revealed and laid down. It also showed why, under the present circumstances, religious liberty was appropriate for the good of society.

De Smedt admitted almost apologetically that the text was still imperfect, but he noted that the commission was eager to revise it further in light of the discussion in St. Peter's. He surely won favor with his innocent-sounding yet barbed protestation, "Our commission is an instrument in the hands of the council." In an almost throwaway line, he tried to anticipate what he knew were the major objections to the declaration: "The documents of the Supreme Pontiffs on this subject deal with the problem under another aspect and in societal conditions different from today's."[27] Cardinal Bea was more straightforward in 1961, when the basic ideas in the declaration were first under discussion: "This is not traditional teaching, but life today is not traditional."[28]

The declaration based its teaching on two fundamental points. First, human beings, created in the image and likeness of God and raised to an even higher dignity by the redemption Christ effected, are called by that very fact to seek and follow the will of God in their lives as that is made manifest to them through their consciences. No government has the right to obstruct that project so long as it does not infringe on the rights of others or hinder the common good. Of course, individuals also have the duty to form their consciences in a responsible way, so as to avoid "subjectivism" and "religious indifferentism." In that regard the church has the duty to proclaim the Gospel and to work to bring people to the fullness of truth.

Second, this idea is based on the church's perennial teaching that the act of faith, to be genuine, must be free and sincere, not coerced. The freedom to follow one's conscience in religious matters is possessed by everybody, Catholic and non-Catholic alike. Governments are forbidden, therefore, to impose civil disabilities on citizens because of their religion and to persecute them for it. The teaching means, moreover, that governments must in this regard honor not only individuals but also the religious organizations or churches in which individuals exercise their freedom. This does not mean that governments should be neutral on the matter or detached from it as if it did not matter; rather, they "should indirectly foster the religious life that, according to the dictates of their consciences, the citizens lead." That last provision, which made it into the final form of the declaration, marks perhaps the most significant difference between the church's declaration and the way separation of church and state has commonly been interpreted in the United States.

As directly and explicitly as any document of Vatican II, *Dignitatis Humanae* engaged all three approaches to the past that were in play with the leaders of the majority. It employed a bold and radical *ressourcement* in that it dug into the tradition for a truth more fundamental than what it wanted to displace, a truth that had been obscured but whose recovery would set the church on a path different from the one it had been treading.[29] It related to *aggiornamento* in that it would bring the church's teaching into line with contemporary political practice and political philosophy. The teaching would be defended in the final text as a "development" or "evolution" *(evolvere intendit)* of recent papal teaching (Pope John's) but could be defended more broadly as a development, an elaboration, or an application of the ancient truth that the act of faith could not and should not be coerced.

When De Smedt sat down, Ruffini took the floor as the first speaker. He offered some points purportedly to improve this "opportune" declaration, but in fact he launched a frontal attack, beginning with the very title, "religious liberty." Since by definition there is only one true religion, it does not admit freedom of choice. True religious liberty cannot be achieved except by embracing the truth, which the Catholic Church possesses. We need to be careful, he said, not to give the impression that in this matter we are saying no more than Article 18 in the "Universal Declaration of Human Rights" adopted by the United Nations on December 10, 1948. If the principles enunciated in the document are always and everywhere to be applied, then the Holy See would have to retract the agreements it entered into with Italy in 1929, with Portugal in 1940, with Spain in 1953, and with the Dominican Republic in 1954.[30]

Cardinal Fernando Quiroga y Palacios, archbishop of Santiago de Compostela, continued the assault. The document seems to have been constructed with an eye to those countries that we call "Protestant," with little attention to those that by long tradition are Catholic. Its language is often obscure and ambiguous, so that, if it were accepted, "unbridled license would follow." It pays little attention to the traditional teaching of the church and moves quickly into "novelty." That's not all: "This concept of liberty is not only extolled with great praise but seems to be proposed as a solemn definition. Thus you could say that Liberalism, so often condemned by the church, is now solemnly approved by Vatican Council II." The doctrine proposed here is not evolution but revolution![31]

In these first two interventions most of the major objections to the declaration came clearly to the fore: it is a change in the church's teaching; it is a change in the church's practice, as made clear in the recent concordats; it fosters subjectivism and religious indifferentism; it opens the door to immorality; it is illogical because it seems to deny that there can be only one religious truth. The only significant addition to the list was raised by Bishop José López Ortiz of Tui Vigo, Spain, on September 24. He simply refused to accept a fundamental assumption of the declaration, that governments were incapable of judging between true and false religions.[32]

Cardinal Ottaviani's intervention was listened to with great attention. For decades he had been a major force in upholding the traditional teaching of the church, and he was known for regarding the concordat of 1953 with Franco's government in Spain as a model of relations between church and state. In his widely disseminated textbook on canon law, he asserted that freedom of conscience was an expression introduced to legitimate religious indifferentism.[33] His speech was firm and clear, as always with him, but not quite so vehement as some expected. He did manage to express more effectively than others a point that was repeatedly made: "I do not understand why a person who errs is worthy of honor. I understand that the person is worthy of consideration, of tolerance, of cordiality, of charity. But I do not understand why worthy of honor."[34]

Cardinal Browne called for a rejection of the document as it stood.[35]

Archbishop Marcel Lefebvre, a leader in the Group and a future schismatic, predicted ruin for the Catholic Church if the declaration were adopted.[36] Others raised the specter of Liberalism and Modernism making their way back into the church even though the popes had roundly and often condemned them.

The document had stout defenders. The American hierarchy, which up to this point had a notably low profile in the council, came out almost in full force. On that first day Cardinal Richard Cushing, archbishop of Boston and personal friend of the Kennedy family, spoke in his booming voice with its heavy (even in Latin) Boston accent "in the name almost of all the bishops of the United States." The declaration, while needing further work, was on the right track and was vitally important for the church in today's world. One aspect in particular was of the highest importance: through this declaration the Catholic Church would show itself to the world as a protagonist for human and civil liberty in religious matters.[37]

Meyer of Chicago almost immediately followed Cushing, and he too spoke "in the name of almost all the bishops of the United States." He gave a number of reasons for the necessity of such a declaration, the first of which was "to show that the Catholic Church promotes religious liberty rather than tries to repress it."[38] Spellman of New York joined in.[39] Ritter of Saint Louis surprised people with his assertion that the arguments in the declaration were "neither simple, nor clear, nor certain," and that they therefore should be dropped. It would be much better, he stated, to shorten the document by eliminating all arguments and limiting it to a simple affirmation and advocacy of religious liberty.[40]

Not only North Americans supported the document. Bishops from behind the Iron Curtain, generally conservative on issues facing the council, gave the document a much-needed boost. They advocated it as a defense against the persecution they were suffering from their governments, though they dared not express that reason so bluntly. Bishop Smiljan Čekada from Skopje in Yugoslavia was the first of them to speak and was one of the strongest and most forthright, noting, for instance, that "no matter what the merits of the philosophical and theological arguments on which the text is based, there can be no doubt that religious liberty is imperatively demanded by the conditions of modern society."[41] Bishop Michal Kłepacz of Lodz spoke in favor of the document for the Polish bishops.[42] The intervention by Archbishop Karol Wojtyła of Kraków was more subtle and philosophical. Although it would have to be counted as favorable to the text, it insisted on the close connection between truth and true liberty and at one point identified liberty with tolerance, just what the declaration was trying not to say.[43]

Cardinal John Heenan of Westminster spoke in support of the declaration in the name of most of the bishops of England, Wales, Scotland, Ireland, Australia, New Zealand, France, and Belgium. Not everybody in the English-speaking world, however, liked the document. Cardinal Norman Gilroy of Sydney, in the name of a number of Australian bishops, submitted in writing a scathing denunciation: "Is it really possible for an ecumenical council to say that any heretic has the right to draw the faithful away from Christ, the Supreme Pastor, and to lead them to pasture in their poisoned fields?"[44]

Gabriel Garrone, archbishop of Toulouse, much respected among his French confreres, made a short but strong speech in favor of the text. He responded to the objection that the church in the past had acted differently from what the declaration proposed. Keep in mind, he said, the historical context and the extent to which the world accepted the principle of *cuius regio, eius religio:* "Moreover, the church, made up of human beings, even in its head, does not hesitate to admit it has erred and to express sorrow for it."[45] Ears were attentive when Carlo Colombo, newly appointed auxiliary bishop of Milan and close friend and colleague of Paul VI, took the floor. Colombo spoke favorably of the text, which was generally (and correctly) taken as a sign that the pope was similarly inclined.[46] In his diary Cardinal Siri noted, in vexation, that Colombo was "entirely on the side of the Transalpines."[47] But Colombo insisted, as did many others, that the text was not ready for a vote.

On September 28 debate ended. It had stretched over four days, with forty-four speeches. The Secretariat for Christian Unity immediately set to work revising the text in light of the spoken and the many written observations that were made on it. Only at this point did Murray begin to participate officially in fashioning the text, in close collaboration with Pietro Pavan, the principal author of Pope John's encyclical *Pacem in Terris.* Although evidence suggested that the text had solid support in the council, its opponents were many, organized, and not inclined to surrender their position. Could the document muster even a two-thirds approval? Such an outcome was far from certain.

Then the council turned its attention to the extremely brief but also highly controversial declaration On the Jews and Non-Christians—*De Ju-*

daeis et de non Christianis.[48] Cardinal Bea had introduced it several days earlier—Bea, not only a German but a Scripture scholar as well. He received thunderous applause as he approached the microphone and similarly thunderous applause afterward when he took his seat. He had become a hero for most of the council fathers, who in this instance were, moreover, at least generally aware of the special difficulties he had had with this document.

Why was the council dealing with the issue at all? It had been absent from the topics submitted by bishops and others before the council opened. It originated with a specific mandate of John XXIII to Bea in September 1960 to facilitate during the preparations for the council a treatment of the relationship of the church to the Jews.[49] John's wartime experiences had made him sensitive to the atrocities of the Holocaust and to the complicity of many Catholics in them. But a specific and immediate stimulus for John's mandate to Bea in September was an audience that he had granted to the Jewish scholar Jules Isaac.[50]

The president of France, Vincent Auriol, had instructed the French ambassador to the Holy See to arrange the audience. In 1947 Isaac had participated in the International Conference at Seelisberg, Switzerland, along with Christians, including Catholics, and other Jews. He had helped draw up a list of recommendations to the churches on how they might remedy their anti-Jewish teachings, the so-called ten points of Seelisberg. In 1959 Isaac himself had published *Jésus et Israël,* in which he showed how ill founded were the slogans that the dispersion of the Jews was a providential punishment for the Crucifixion, that Jewish religion at the time of Christ had degenerated into legalism without a soul, that the Jews had committed deicide, and, most important, that these "facts" justified anti-Semitism.[51]

At the audience Isaac presented the pope with a dossier that included the Seelisberg points and asked him to have the council address them. Other factors, however, were also at work. Earlier in 1960, the rector of the Biblicum, Ernst Vogt, had sent a petition to the Central Preparatory Commission, signed by himself and eighteen members of the faculty, asking that the council address the problem of anti-Semitism. In fact, in addition to Maritain, a few other Catholics, mostly converts from Judaism, had been working for greater understanding between the two faiths.[52] Among them John (Johannes) Marin Oesterreicher, an Austrian Jew converted to Catholicism and ordained a Catholic priest, was particularly important.

He was the founder in 1953 of the Institute of Judeo-Christian Studies at Seton Hall University, South Orange, New Jersey, out of which he edited the Journal *The Bridge* from 1954 until 1970. During the council he was a member of Bea's Secretariat.[53]

By August 1961, well before the council opened, the Secretariat had prepared a brief schema titled "On the Jews." Word leaked out about the document and raised concern in Arab states. But the World Jewish Congress committed a gaffe that caused those states to explode with fury. On June 12, 1962, the Congress, acting on its own initiative, appointed Chaim Wardi, who at the time was living in Israel, as its own "unofficial observer" at the council. Israel's Foreign Ministry and Ministry of Religious Affairs endorsed the appointment. This action tainted the issue with political overtones and suggested to the Arabs that, among other things, the Vatican might be moving toward recognition of Israel. The bishops from the Middle East joined in fierce opposition to the schema because they believed that it would lead to serious difficulties for Christian minorities in that region.

The only observers/guests at the council were of course Christians, and they came by invitation of the Secretariat, not by any self-determination. Thus Wardi never became an observer. But in response to the situation, on June 19, 1962, within five days of Wardi's appointment, Cicognani as head of the Central Preparatory Commission removed the schema from the agenda. His position as secretary of state made him particularly sensitive to the political and diplomatic troubles it would cause in the Middle East. He did not see any good reason that it should be on the agenda in the first place, a sentiment shared by Cardinal Spellman.

In December, after the close of the first period, Bea presented a memorandum to John XXIII stating why the issue had to be treated. Too often Catholic preachers had accused the Jews of deicide and presented them as accursed and rejected by God.[54] The Holocaust showed how important it was to put a stop to depictions that directly or indirectly had promoted such a massive tragedy. The World Council of Churches had recently called upon all the churches associated with it to condemn anti-Semitism. How could the Catholic Church stand aloof from the issue? The memorandum had the desired effect. John agreed to let Bea move ahead.

Although much of the opposition stemmed from what were perceived to be the political ramifications the declaration might have and the difficulties it might raise for Christians in the Middle East, other reasons were also at play. In early 1963, two months after the first period of the council ended, Rolf Hochhuth's play *Der Stellvertreter,* usually translated into English as *The Deputy* but more accurately as *The Vicar [of Christ]*, a rambling and long-winded dramatization of Pope Pius XII's supposed "silence" during the Holocaust, opened in Berlin. The play created a sensation and was soon translated into a number of languages. With equal passion it was denounced as a vilification of a saint and praised as a much-needed exposé. The affair deeply disturbed the Vatican and troubled perhaps nobody more deeply than Paul VI, who had been one of Pius's closest assistants during the war years. The pope worried that the council's declaration might be taken as a validation of Hochhuth's position.

Beyond that specific problem lay the deeper and all too widespread anti-Semitism that based itself on the New Testament, especially on John's gospel with its consistent depiction of "the Jews" as enemies of Christ and, more specifically, on the verse from Matthew's account of Christ's trial, "His blood be upon us and upon our children" (27.25). Were not the Jews of Jesus' time responsible for Christ's death? Was not that responsibility in some sense rightly imputed to the Jews down through the subsequent ages to our own day? How could a document deal with such texts without either denying what the New Testament affirmed or offending the Jews while purportedly extending a hand in friendship? Moreover, were not Catholics to work for the conversion of the Jews, whose religion was incomplete without acknowledgment of the Messiah? Would the document say that the perseverance of the Jews in Judaism is without fault? If so, is that right?[55]

After much discussion and debate, it became clear by the fall of 1963 that the council could not treat the Jews without treating other non-Christian religions, especially Islam, which like Christianity and Judaism descended from the patriarch Abraham.[56] Bishops from the "new churches" of Asia wanted Buddhism and Hinduism included. Thus the document, originally intended as a theological statement on the Jews and in some form a condemnation of anti-Semitism, was eventually expanded into the final version. In September 1964, however, when Bea made his presentation, this short text dealt almost exclusively with the Jews, with just a sentence about the Muslims and a general statement about loving all human beings.

All through the spring and summer of 1964 questions and suggested changes in the draft schema had come pouring into the Secretariat, so that the text was revised again and again in an effort to deal with them. Cicognani and especially Paul VI were deeply involved. It soon became clear that the pope and Bea did not see eye-to-eye on the text, particularly on what was to be said about the crucial issue of deicide, and the document was reworded several times in attempts to reach a compromise. Bea was intent on absolving of the crime not only contemporary Jews but also the Jewish people of Christ's time, as distinct from certain of their leaders. On that issue the pope prevailed in the text Bea presented to the council, which contained only one sentence on the subject: "Let everyone take care not to impute to the Jews of our times what happened during the Passion of Christ."[57]

Bea opened his presentation on September 25, 1964, by recalling that "this Declaration is certainly among the materials that have aroused the greatest public interest." Moreover, many people will judge the council favorably or unfavorably depending on how it deals with the issue.[58] A number of venerable fathers of the council asked that the entire document be removed from the agenda. The Secretariat seriously considered their reasons and finally judged that it was imperative for the council to make a statement. Members of the Coordinating Committee know, Bea said, the effort put into this little document.

He then moved immediately to the question of deicide, which was an implicit plea to change the text the council had before it. While it is true that the leaders of the Sanhedrin headed the campaign leading to Jesus' death, he conceded, they were only a tiny percentage of the Jewish people. We cannot attribute to a whole people what a few leaders perpetrated. And how can we say that even those leaders knowingly committed deicide when Jesus himself asked the Father to "forgive them for they know not what they do"? Surely, even if we should grant—which we do not—that the people of Jesus' time were responsible, there is no way that responsibility can be attributed to later generations.

Toward the end Bea insisted that the declaration "has nothing to do with any political questions," specifically nothing to do with Zionism or with the state of Israel. Yes, it will be possible for people to misinterpret the text and manipulate it for political ends, but we must not for that reason forsake our duty. He ended: "What is at stake here is our responsibility to truth and justice, our duty of gratitude to God, our duty of faithfully and closely imitating Christ the Lord and his apostles Peter and Paul. In setting forth these matters the church and this council absolutely cannot tolerate that any political authority or political considerations intrude."

The discussion opened on September 28 and continued until September 30. Opponents of the schema did not mince words. The most gentle of the negative interventions came from Cardinal Ignace Tappouni, patriarch of Antioch, Syrian rite, who in the name of the other Eastern rite patriarchs simply asserted that the document would cause them grave difficulties in their pastoral activities. The document was "inopportune," and he begged the fathers to remove it from the agenda.[59]

Ruffini, as usual among the first speakers, had the courage to say what others were thinking. He began by stating that the declaration piles up praise of the Jews so high that it sounds like a panegyric. Of course we cannot attribute deicide to the Jews because the word makes no sense—nobody can kill God. Nonetheless, we have a right to expect the Jews to acknowledge that they unjustly condemned Christ to death. We need to pray that God will "remove the veil" from their eyes that prevents them from seeing Christ as the Messiah. That is a sign of our love for them, as is the fact that during the last war we protected them from the Nazis and prevented their deportation. At the end of the war, remember, the chief rabbi of Rome publicly expressed his gratitude for the refuge the Holy See gave to Jews, saving them from certain death.

We do not need exhortations to love the Jews, Ruffini continued. They need exhortations to love us. Everybody is aware that the Jews support and promote the "pernicious sect" called the Masons, which is out to destroy the church and which has often been condemned by the Holy See. As for the Muslims, yes, we should love them, but what about the Buddhists and the Hindus, who do not seem any further from the Christian religion than the disciples of Mohammed? The schema should be revised so that in general terms it says something about the relationship of the church to all non-Christians, especially to those groups with larger membership, but it should do so without singling out any one of them for special mention.[60]

Ruffini laid bare all the major issues. The others who intervened against the schema added little to what he and Tappouni had said. Most speakers, including a number of Americans, spoke in favor, though with different emphases and with many suggestions for improvement. Bea's presentation had its desired effect, however, in that a number of speakers expressed dissatisfaction with the changes that had been introduced into the text from the earlier version, particularly the weaker statement on deicide. By the time the speeches were over and the written comments examined, the Secretariat felt justified in preparing a stronger text, more in accordance with the one it had originally composed.

The bomb did not drop until nine days later.[61] On October 9 the Secretariat held a plenary meeting to examine the work the subcommissions had done on the two declarations. At the meeting Bea read two letters he had just received, signed by Felici. In the first, Felici informed Bea that the pope wanted a new text drafted on religious liberty.[62] The new draft was to be written by some members of the Secretariat along with some members of the Doctrinal Commission—in other words, by a "mixed" subcommittee. Thus not only would the original text be scrapped, but the declaration would be taken out of the exclusive domain of the Secretariat. Felici mentioned, moreover, four persons to be added to the subcommission—Cardinal Browne, Archbishop Marcel Lefebvre, Father Aniceto Fernandez (master general of the Dominican order), and Carlo Colombo. Except for Colombo, they were all publicly and vehemently opposed to the declaration.

In the second letter Felici informed Bea that a joint meeting of the Council of Presidents, the Coordinating Committee, and the moderators had decided, on the basis of a report from Cardinal Cicognani, that the subject of the Jews should not be a separate declaration but should be incorporated into the second chapter of *Lumen Gentium,* where it was already mentioned.[63] Another "mixed" subcommission made up of members of the Secretariat, chosen by Bea, and members of the Doctrinal Commission, chosen by Ottaviani, would compose the new text. Thus this document, too, was removed from the exclusive domain of the Secretariat. In his report Cicognani indicated that the pope wanted a brief reference to the matter included in chapter two of *Lumen Gentium,* on "the people of God."

Almost immediately, word of Felici's two letters reached the media, which exploded with conspiracy theories. Like no other document in the council, the declaration on the Jews became the focus of intense media attention and public scrutiny. Within the council itself, consternation. What had happened? How could actions unilaterally taken that disregarded the normal procedures of the council and that seemed geared to reversing or at least notably qualifying the will of the majority be justified?

At this point it is impossible to fully reconstruct the scenario, but a few things are clear. For sure, the pope had intervened. He had been subjected to terrific pressure from within the council and, on the declaration on the Jews, from outside the council as well, with some of the Arab states threatening to close down their embassies to the Holy See. Felici was the medium through which the pope's message was conveyed. It is now certain that wittingly or unwittingly he did not in every instance accurately represent what the pope seems to have meant. Cicognani, secretary of state and president of the Coordinating Committee, was, as usual, also a key player. But just how to distribute praise or blame among these three and the others who in some way were involved is difficult to ascertain.[64]

Bea moved into action. On October 10 he wrote in Italian directly to the pope.[65] He began by saying that the letter from Felici concerning religious liberty did not reflect Bea's understanding of the pope's mind on the matter as they had discussed it in a private audience on October 5. (Bea included a photocopy of Felici's letter so that the pope could see precisely what it said.) At that meeting Bea and the pope had agreed that after the text was revised by the Secretariat it should be submitted to the Doctrinal Commission to make sure it was orthodox. This procedure was acceptable to both himself and Cardinal Ottaviani and had been followed on other occasions. There had been no talk of a mixed commission. A doubt therefore arose in Bea's mind whether Felici's letter accurately reflected what the pope intended. He detailed for Paul the serious consequences for the council and "for the authority of Your Holiness" if the provisions of Felici's letter were carried out. He asked for a clarification of where the pope stood.

As is clear from the letter, Bea was not opposed in principle to inserting the statement on the Jews into *Lumen Gentium,* and he knew that many members of the council who favored the declaration thought that might be the better course. Yet he feared that such a move implicitly entailed shortening and weakening the text. In the letter, however, Bea dealt mainly with his reservations about relying on mixed commissions, especially if some of the new members were professedly committed to sabotaging the text. A mixed commission was a vote of no-confidence in the Secretariat.

Bea was not the only person to shift into high gear. The next day Paul received a letter signed by thirteen of the leading figures at the council, including Frings, Liénart, Alfrink, König, Döpfner, Meyer, and Ritter. It was short. It was blunt. "With great distress" they had learned that the declaration on religious liberty was to be sent to a new commission, some of whose members opposed the sentiments of the council majority. The signers reminded the pope that in such a serious matter every appearance of violating the procedures and freedom of the council should be avoided. They repeated how distressed and concerned they were. They ended by reminding the pope that, if he really thought it necessary to form a mixed commission, he "in their humble opinion" could do so in the way laid down in the council's procedures, article 58, number 2.[66]

Within a few days the matter was settled by a return to the situation before Bea received the two letters. No one apologized, and no one explicitly disowned anything that had been written, but Bea emerged with his texts firmly in hand. The incident suddenly seemed almost like a bad dream that now was past and had no power to harm. In fact, however, opponents of the two schemas had not laid down their arms.

What was the upshot of it all? The affair was typical of a situation where messages were conveyed by indirection or through third parties, so that for those on the scene it became almost impossible to know how to interpret what was really going on and to whom to address questions or grievances. To the problem of the blurred lines of responsibility that had dogged the council all along was added, therefore, a style of communication that left people wondering who really said what and to whom—and when they said it. The solution was to run to the pope.

Progress on the Agenda

The council, meanwhile, had not been idle. On September 30 it again took up the schema on revelation, first revised by the mixed commission set up by Pope John two years earlier and then further revised by a subcommission of the Doctrinal Commission. This was the first of a series of schemas that the council discussed with relative dispatch in the first three weeks of October. The pope, Felici, and probably the majority of the fathers were pressing hard to have the council end with this period. The Döpfner Plan for the "minor texts" was still being followed and was generally regarded as an efficacious device for accomplishing that goal. In fact, these weeks would see the plan falter and fail, and by that time it had become clear that a fourth period would be needed.

The revised schema on revelation, still without its final title, *Dei Verbum,* followed for the most part the outline of the original document, though the orientations of the first two chapters were significantly different.[67] The original schema at least implicitly viewed revelation as consisting of truths or doctrines, whereas this one, as set forth in the first chapter, emphasized that it was God's self-manifestation, which expressed itself in God's action in history *(gesta)* as well as in pronouncements *(verba).* Revelation took its ultimate form in the very person of Christ. God is the "source" of revelation—God himself, not Scripture or Tradition as such. Although to the uninitiated this might seem like a theological fine point, it was a significant shift away from ahistorical abstractions, as if God had revealed a collection of timeless propositions. It was thus a rejection of an approach that had held sway in Catholic thinking on the subject for centuries and that was enshrined in theological textbooks up to the time the council opened. Unlike the original *De Fontibus,* this text, like the final version, clearly stated that the church's Magisterium is "not above the word of God but acts as its servant."[68]

Not so much this first chapter as the second, which treated the Scripture-Tradition relationship, roused the minority. Even with its rather subtle but new orientation the document could not sidestep the issue, which had been one of the hottest topics in the original discussion in 1962. In that earlier document Tradition had in effect been presented as containing truths that Scripture did not contain; moreover, it acted as the interpretative key for understanding Scripture: though Scripture is inspired, "nonetheless its sense cannot be certainly and fully understood and made clear except by apostolic Tradition."[69] While expressly treating Scripture and Tradition as equals, it implicitly gave Tradition the more privileged role in the church.

The new text took a different approach, which the minority found deeply distressing. The key question for those who opposed the schema was, are there truths in Tradition that are not contained in Scripture? The question thus framed betrays the mentality that chapter one tried to obviate by moving revelation away, in the first instance, from truths/doctrines/propositions. For fathers like Ruffini, Browne, Carli, and others of the minority, the answer to the question was a resounding yes, and for them it was essential that the text proclaim that affirmative loud and clear. They had in mind the Marian dogmas solemnly defined by Pope Pius IX and Pope Pius XII with little or no scriptural warrant. That meant that for the minority this rather abstruse issue of Scripture-Tradition implicated papal authority.

Although the schema sedulously avoided saying what the minority considered essential, neither did it in principle exclude it. For the majority the question was an open one on which it did not want the council to pronounce one way or the other. In the crucial paragraph 8, the schema innovated by presenting Tradition in a more dynamic way, as in a symbiotic relationship to Scripture and as the vital principle in the church of the transmission and interpretation of what God had revealed. In other words, in this approach the key question was not so much what Tradition contained as how it operated. This did not satisfy the minority. As Bishop Franić of Split said in his special intervention, speaking for the minority on the Doctrinal Commission, the fact that Tradition contained truths not in Scripture had been taught in Vatican I and in papal encyclicals as recent as those from Pius XI to Paul VI. If the schema were left in its present form, it might seem that the church had changed its teaching.[70]

The minority had other problems with paragraph 8. For example, it described Tradition as being expressed not only in the church's teaching authority but in the whole being of the church—in its worship and experience of spiritual realities *(ex intima spiritualium rerum experientia)*. To include spiritual experience was not for the minority a harmless instance of the "turn to the subject" but a recrudescence of a central error of the Modernists. Browne, like others smelling Modernism here, warned that this part of the text could be interpreted as a repudiation of Pius X's encyclical *Pascendi.*[71]

Moreover, according to the document, Tradition "progresses" *(proficit)* over time, as understanding increases with reflection and experience. In a less charged atmosphere the minority might not have seen dangers lurking in such ideas, but now it was sensitive to the least nuance. Other objections were raised, some of them betraying a deep suspicion of modern methods of exegesis. How and to what extent was the Bible free from error? For members of the minority the text was not sufficiently strong or clear on this question, and they raised the issue vigorously again in the next period of the council.

But in balance the schema had many more defenders in St. Peter's than detractors. For the ordinary Catholic, chapter six, which encouraged the reading of the Bible for spiritual nourishment, was the most important. This aspect of the text received little comment, probably because in many countries the practice had been growing especially since the publication of *Divino Afflante Spiritu* in 1943. Nonetheless, Bishop Costantino Caminada of Ferentino, Italy, raised the longstanding objection to the practice by warning that without close supervision the laity would be unable to interpret the Bible correctly and would be led into errors. He suggested the alternative of putting together an anthology of carefully selected and carefully explained biblical passages.[72]

When debate ended on October 6, the subcommission of the Doctrinal Commission that had put the text together correctly saw that, despite the objections, it had in substance stood the test and now needed only to be further refined. But as that group went to work, so did opponents of the schema. A few days after the end of the debate, Cardinals Ruffini, Siri, Browne, Larraona, and Ruffino Santos of Manila met to assess the situation and to devise a strategy for the withdrawal of the text.[73] The course of this schema, which to most readers today appears so unthreatening, would continue rough to the end.

At the close of the ninety-fifth General Congregation on October 6, Cardinal Fernando Cento enthusiastically introduced the schema On the Lay Apostolate *(De Apostolatu Laicorum).*[74] He thanked all those who had helped in the composition of the schema, including the laity "of both sexes" from whom the commission had assiduously sought ideas and suggestions. He reminded everybody that John XXIII had established the commission, which was a sign of the hierarchy's esteem for the laity and its role in the church. This schema is of the highest importance *(supremi momenti).* The pastors of the church must have confidence in the laity, and the laity must have confidence in the pastors and respect their authority: "The laity are not simply in the church, but with us they are the church!"[75]

Despite the high importance that Cento assigned the schema, it had at one point been relegated to "mini" status as the Döpfner Plan was worked out. During the months before this period opened, however, it had been saved from that fate, so that a full schema of five chapters was presented to the council. The subject was of great interest to the bishops, as indicated by the large number of requests they sent to the Vatican in the "ante-preparatory" stage of the council asking that the issue be addressed.

By the early years of the twentieth century, an impressive number of lay organizations were flourishing in the church. Especially strong in the United States were the Saint Vincent de Paul Society, the Holy Name Society, the Knights of Columbus, the Catholic Daughters of America, the Sodality of Our Lady, the National Council of Catholic Men, and the National Council of Catholic Women. Similar organizations operated throughout the Catholic world. Of special importance was Catholic Action, vigorously promoted by Pope Pius XI, as "the participation of the laity in the apostolate of the hierarchy."[76] This was the first time, however, that a council had ever taken up such a topic.

The schema affirmed that the laity had an apostolate in the church, which had its sacramental basis in their baptism and confirmation. The laity thus participated in the "royal priesthood of Christ and in his mission." To be truly effective the laity needed training and spiritual formation. They carried out their apostolate individually or by membership in organizations. Their apostolate had two aspects: working to help others for their progress toward God; and working to bring justice and love into their milieus. The final chapter recommended that especially in that second task the laity collaborate with other Christians and with all persons of good will.

Important though the schema was, it was for the most part non-controversial. Cardinal Ritter led off the speeches by praising the text but saying that it was too clerical and juridical. Cardinal Browne came next, approving it but asking for an explicit statement that lay people were obliged to obey their parish priest. Some speakers wanted clearer lines of demarcation between the lay and the clerical apostolate. Eduardo Pironio, auxiliary bishop of La Plata, called for a more biblical and patristic style.[77] And so it went, with many suggestions for improvement or expansion but nothing that challenged the direction the text had taken, which was an implicit commendation for the commission that had composed it. One intervention did raise eyebrows, however. Stjepan Bäuerlein of Srijem (Syrmia), Croatia, defined "the first and principal task" of the lay apostolate as the begetting of children because one reason for the shortage of vocations to the priesthood was the low birthrate in Christian families.[78]

On October 13 the discussion ended with just a few more speeches, followed by the first intervention in the council by a layman. Patrick Keegan, an Englishman and president of the World Federation of Christian Workers, spoke in English. He presented the document as a first step in forging a bond between the hierarchy and the laity in the one mission of the church and in initiating a "family dialogue" between them. Now it was important, he said, to bend every effort to make the laity aware of their responsibilities, especially by bearing witness to the Gospel in their daily lives.[79]

That same day the council then moved to the schema On the Life and Ministry of Priests, the status of which had been drastically reduced according to the Döpfner Plan.[80] When Archbishop François Marty of Rheims introduced it, he mentioned that the commission had been constrained to shorten the text very much, which sounded to some like an implicit plea to return it to its original size.[81] He provided a framework for understanding the tone of the document by saying that the authors of the schema decided to emphasize the positive rather than dwell on the problems and dangers that priests faced today. In the interventions that followed, bishops occasionally mentioned in unspecified ways a crisis in the priesthood. Among the matters that surely concerned the Latin Americans and the Europeans, except for the Spanish and Portuguese, was the significant drop in vocations during the 1950s. The decline was especially sharp in Italy and France.

The document dealt with priests' call to holiness and tried to provide the motivation and means to help them better answer it. In focusing on holiness the declaration reinforced it as an emerging theme of Vatican II. It presented an ideal of the priest as following Christ in a path of poverty, chastity, and obedience that sounded similar to the vows that members of religious orders pronounced. To speak of chastity for priests immediately raised the issue of celibacy, commitment to the unmarried state of life.

In his presentation Marty said: "Since today many confused voices are heard attacking sacred celibacy, it seemed especially opportune expressly to confirm it and to explain its exalted significance in the life and ministry of the priest." Earlier, when the council raised the possibility of a married diaconate, it might seem to have been moving toward a discussion of the celibacy requirement for priests. On the contrary, though bishops raised the issue in private conversations, they were extremely circumspect about saying anything in public. Outside the council, however, the topic was openly discussed and debated in the media, and by the next period it seemed about to burst onto the floor of St. Peter's.[82]

On several points the document, as Marty presented it, indicated somewhat new directions. It called for a "reform," in effect the abrogation, of the benefice system, that is, the system whereby a fixed income was attached to an ecclesiastical office like a bishopric or a pastorate—what the British call "a living." Instead, priests should receive adequate compensation independent of this "feudal" system. Benefices had been on the way out for some time, but the council dealt them the death blow. Even more indicative of the orientation of Vatican II and of the shift in sensibilities it promoted was Marty's description of the way priests should bear themselves in relationship to the laity, "not only as pastors and teachers but also as brothers dealing with brothers."

Cardinal Meyer of Chicago, the first speaker, hit on the problem that most bishops had with the text. It seemed strange, he said, that the bishops and the laity got the full treatment they deserved but that priests were dealt with in such meager measure.[83] He called for a revision that would be more ample in scope and more worthy of the subject. Forty more bishops spoke on the schema with, as usual, a wide range of criticisms and suggestions. It soon became clear that, although there was no consistent criticism of any one aspect of the document, Meyer had made a crucial point and that the text would not pass muster in its present form. On October 15, the day after debate ended, a majority of the bishops voted to send the document back for revision, which was correctly interpreted as a mandate to expand it into a full schema. The vote marked the beginning of the end for the Döpfner Plan.

On October 15 the council took up the schema on the Eastern Catholic churches, *Orientalium Ecclesiarum*.[84] How do these churches, like the Melkite and the Coptic, relate to the universal church? The most fundamental point of the schema was the guarantee that their rites, procedures, and spiritual patrimony were to be respected and protected. The schema also promised that nothing would be asked of "any separated Eastern churches" (Orthodox) that sought reunion beyond what the simple profession of Catholic faith required.

Not surprisingly, the schema elicited comments from many Eastern bishops, with Maximos and Zoghby among them. They used the text to score their consistent and important points: do not identify the Catholic Church with the Latin rite church; do not continue the longstanding and continuing attempts to make the Eastern churches conform to the Latin; respect the patriarchates and remember how they functioned collegially with the bishop of Rome in the past. After two days of discussion this basically satisfactory schema was accepted and, without incident, prepared for final approval by the end of the period.

On October 20 the council was ready for the major and long-awaited schema 13, now called On the Church in the Modern World—*De Ecclesia in Mundo Huius Temporis*.[85] The debate lasted, with a brief interruption, until November 10, dangerously close to November 21, the day Paul VI had set for closing this period. At the beginning of December the pope was leaving Rome to participate in the Eucharistic Congress in Bombay (now Mumbai), the second of his major trips, and he wanted the period concluded before his departure.

The very length of time the council spent on this schema at a juncture when a few confirmed optimists still held on to a dim hope of concluding the council in November signals both its complexity and the importance the bishops attached to it. No council had ever attempted anything like it. It turned attention from what councils had always before been concerned with, internal church affairs, to the world outside. It addressed concrete, contemporary issues and problems, such as world peace and a just socio-economic order. In all its drafts, moreover, it projected an image of the church as a helpmate to all persons of good will, whether Catholic or not, whether Christian or not, and as a beacon of hope for a better world.

Cardinal Cento introduced the text.[86] He was co-chairman with Otta-viani of the mixed commission (Laity and Doctrine) that produced it. In allowing Cento to introduce it, Ottaviani implicitly distanced himself from it (later, in a written communication, he expressed his distaste for it).[87] Cento made a crucial point: dialogue is the preferred mode of opera-tion of the church in relationship to the world, as Paul VI indicated in his encyclical *Ecclesiam Suam.* The commission, he said in conclusion, had labored long and hard, and now it asked for criticism so that it might im-prove the text. Bishop Emilio Guano then made the formal presenta-tion.[88]

Along with an introduction and a conclusion, this draft had four rela-tively short chapters: (1) on the human vocation; (2) on the church in service to God and humankind; (3) on how Christians should conduct themselves in the world in which they lived; and (4) on some special re-sponsibilities of Christians in today's world. The document was unique in that it contained five appendixes *(adnexa),* which developed in more detail some of the issues raised in the main text: (1) on the human person in soci-ety; (2) on marriage and the family; (3) on the promotion of culture; (4) on economic and social issues; and (5) on human solidarity and peace. During the debate bishops asked about the status of these appendixes. Were they simply clarifications? Were they integral to the schema? They received vague, sometimes contradictory answers.

When the document came back to the council in the fourth period, the questions about the appendixes had been resolved by incorporating them into the text simply as "Part Two." The document had by then, of course, undergone other significant revisions. Nonetheless, the great themes that we identify with *Gaudium et Spes* were already present clear and strong in the text presented by Cento and Guano in 1964. Chief among them was human dignity, which was elaborated upon in a number of specific ways that included the dignity of human labor and the dignity of the family.

Running through the text as well were the themes of human solidarity across ethnic, racial, religious, and socioeconomic differences and of the obligation of all peoples to work together for a safer and more just world. The church plays an important and even indispensable role in helping realize such ideals, it said. While remaining true to its mandate to preach the Gospel, the church assumes a servant role vis-à-vis the world. The relationship is reciprocal: the world helps the church in being true to itself—an unprecedented stance for an ecclesiastical document.

The debate opened on a positive note with the two first speakers, Cardinals Liénart and Spellman. The latter was particularly lavish in his praise: "This schema expresses the fundamental hope we have for Vatican II. . . . It should not be weakened."[89] Ruffini was third. While he praised the text as a noble attempt, he offered suggestions for change that would have transformed it. He concluded, indeed, by calling for a "radical revision" *(funditus reficiatur),* but he was one of only a small number of speakers who spoke negatively.[90] It is significant that no one questioned the suitability of some such statement coming from the council.

Nonetheless, many concerns were raised. Several speakers noted that the words "world" and "church" were often used ambiguously and ambivalently, and that their meaning needed to be carefully clarified in each context. Others felt that the text gave too much emphasis to the church's role in human endeavors and not enough to its supernatural mission, which was essentially what the church was about. Some, like Ruffini, felt that the text needed to be based more directly on the papal social encyclicals.

Not until the debate on chapter three, however, was a fundamental concern raised that would assume considerable importance after the council. Cardinal Frings, whose *peritus* was Joseph Ratzinger, was the first to broach it. The schema, according to Frings, relied too exclusively on a theology of the Incarnation and slighted the cross. The mystery of the cross cautions us about the world and impels us "in our following of Christ to a life of sacrifice and of abstinence from worldly goods."[91] On the same day, Archbishop Hermann Volk of Mainz, speaking in the name of seventy fathers, "mostly of the German tongue," made similar points.[92]

At stake here were two broad theological traditions. The so-called Augustinian (or eschatological) tradition, which the Germans wanted to make sure was given its due, was more negative on human capabilities and on the possibility of reconciliation between "nature and grace." Luther, of course, is the best-known and most outspoken proponent of such a "theology of the cross," and at the council observers from that tradition felt the schema did not take enough account of sin.[93] Karl Barth was the theologian who had articulated that theology most effectively in the twentieth century and had influenced especially German-speaking bishops at the council.

The other tradition was more dependent on the theology of the Eastern Fathers of the church and took its Western form most notably in Aquinas. In it the Incarnation was the key mystery, through which all creation was reconciled and raised to a higher dignity than before. Although some German-speaking theologians helped prepare the theological aspects of the text, people thought of it as "French." In its elaboration Rahner had clashed with Congar and Daniélou, and he was, along with Ratzinger, a leader in the German opposition to it. Even some French bishops, however, felt that in its present form the schema did not adequately address the negative aspects of contemporary culture.[94] Two Polish bishops—Kłepacz and Zygfryd Kowalski—painted a dire picture of the decadence and sinful pride of the world.[95]

The fathers listened to more than 150 speeches on the schema. Aside from general issues like the above, the number of specific issues raised and the diversity of the mentalities that raised them make the debate impossible to summarize. Noteworthy, however, was the repeated call for a condemnation of Marxism and the resistance that call met, most surprisingly from some bishops in Communist lands, who feared that it would make their difficult situation even worse. Bishop Gérard Coderre, of Saint-Jean de Québec, speaking in the name of forty bishops, and Bishop Augustin Frotz, auxiliary bishop of Cologne, dedicated their entire interventions to stressing the obligation of the church to promote the position of women in society.[96] Archbishop Joseph Malula, Leopoldville, made the same point and also called for a strong condemnation of racism.[97]

The threat of nuclear warfare weighed heavily on the minds of the bishops. Alfrink criticized the text for being weaker in that regard than John's encyclical *Pacem in Terris,* in which nuclear weapons were absolutely prohibited, so that no war waged with them could be called just. On this issue the council, he said, certainly should not be less straightforward than the pope.[98]

Other bishops spoke in the same vein but none more passionately than Maximos IV Saigh. Addressing the council as usual in French, he began, "Nuclear armament is a threat leading to the total destruction of the planet. This threat increases day by day through the increasing number of countries that possess this infernal machine." The council must be courageous in denouncing the danger before such powerful nations the way John the Baptist was courageous before Herod.[99] Bishop Philip Hannan, then an auxiliary of Washington, defended the weapons on the grounds that with new technology they could be directed to limited targets and, hence, could be reconciled with traditional just-war theory.[100] Archbishop George Beck of Liverpool substantially seconded Hannan.[101] The stand the council would ultimately take on the issue was not clear.

Article 21 of chapter four was titled "The Dignity of Marriage and the Family." It was an explosive subject. The text did three things that roused the ire of council fathers like Ruffini, Ottaviani, and Browne. First, it avoided using the textbook terms "primary" and "secondary" ends of marriage, in which the primary end was the procreation of children and the secondary end was a remedy for concupiscence and the mutual help of the spouses. The document instead spoke at length about the holiness and goodness of the love that bound the spouses; only then did it mention children as the fulfillment of that love. Second, it made the consciences of the spouses the deciding factor for the number of children they should have. Finally, it did not explicitly reaffirm a condemnation of birth control.

Ruffini, Ottaviani, Browne, and a number of others wanted a clear statement reaffirming "the certain teaching" that the primary end of marriage was the procreation of children, and they cited the encyclicals *Arcanum* of Leo XIII, *Casti Connubii* of Pius XI, and the allocutions of Pius XII on the subject.[102] They disliked the emphasis on the consciences of the parents in deciding family size. Beneath the surface of the whole discussion of article 21 seethed the question of birth control, made more urgent by "the pill." The previous year John Rock, a Catholic physician who had participated in the creation of an oral contraceptive, had published his widely reviewed book *The Time Has Come,* in which he advocated a change in approach by the churches, especially the Catholic Church.[103] Later in the year the Belgian theologian Louis Janssens published a long article in which he referred to Rock's book, also arguing that maybe "the time had come."[104]

By now the council knew that a Papal Commission, established by John XXIII in 1963 at the suggestion of Suenens, was studying the problem. Paul had announced it in an address to the cardinals on the previous June 23.[105] Now, between October 23 and 29, council members were three times reminded of the fact—by Archbishop Guano, Cardinal Agagianian, and Archbishop John Deardon of Detroit—and further reminded that birth control as such was not to be debated in the council because it was being studied by the Papal Commission.

There seemed, however, no way to keep the topic entirely off the floor. In discreet and indiscreet ways the bishops kept bringing it up, usually with at least an insinuation that the time had come for a change in the teaching. Thus spoke, for instance, Léger, Alfrink, Joseph Reuss (speaking for 145 fathers "from various countries and parts of the world"), and Rudolf Staverman of Sukarnapura, Indonesia, who expressly argued that marriage had evolved like every historical reality and therefore the church could not just repeat old formulas—the way this schema spoke of marriage was, on the contrary, "healthy and liberating."[106]

Saigh was as usual boldly outspoken and direct. He began, "I call your attention today . . . to birth control." It is a pressing problem that the council must confront. For the faithful it is a sad and agonizing issue, for there is a cleavage between the official teaching of the church and the contrary practice in most families. Moreover, the population explosion in certain parts of the world is condemning hundreds of millions of human beings to misery without hope. The council must find a solution. It must ask whether God really wants this depressing and unnatural impasse: "Let me speak frankly: do not the official positions of the church in this matter require revision in the light of modern research—theological, medical, psychological, sociological?"[107]

It was Suenens's speech, however, that caused a sensation and led Ruffini to write to Cicognani reporting that some fathers were so scandalized by it that they thought he should be removed as a moderator.[108] In 1956, while Suenens was auxiliary bishop of Malines, he had published a small book on the subject for a popular audience defending the standard teaching.[109] Once the council was called, however, he worried that a simplistic reiteration of *Casti Connubii* would carry the day, and at that point he suggested to John XXIII the need for a special study group. The matter had an added urgency in that the United Nations and the World Health Organization had announced the first international conference on world population, scheduled for 1964 in New Delhi.

Two features of Suenens's speech caused the uproar and provoked the ire of Paul VI. First, he more than intimated that a change might be in order.[110] We have learned a few things, he said, since Aristotle and Augustine. He invoked development of doctrine and called attention to the population explosion. He injected a dramatic note into his presentation with the statement, "I plead with you, brothers. We must avoid another 'Galileo case.' One is enough for the church." Second, at the very end he called on Paul VI to make public the names of the members of the Papal Commission. That way, he said, the members will receive the most copious information on the subject, and the whole people of God will be represented. Suenens' words, unfortunately, could sound like a call for a plebiscite. When he finished, applause broke out.

But all was not well. The press played up the speech, noteworthy for coming from a person so eminent in the council. Suenens may have been encouraged to speak by reading Janssens's article, or he may have known that Rock cited him favorably as a distinguished churchman who urged "the need for fertility research.[111] No matter, Paul VI was angry. Visibly upset in a very difficult audience with Suenens shortly afterward, he reproached him for lack of judgment and, without explicitly asking for it, made clear that he expected a retraction.[112] About a week later, on November 7, Suenens said at the end of another speech that he needed to respond "to certain reactions of public opinion." He issued a retraction in the form of a clarification and further affirmed that the decision in the matter rested fully in the hands of the "supreme magisterium."[113]

Paul VI and the Troubled Last Days

On November 6 the council took up the schema on the missions, which had been reduced according to the Döpfner Plan. Once again, though the bishops praised aspects of the text, such as its exhortation to greater adaptation to local cultures and customs and its implied call for less control by the Congregation for the Propagation of the Faith, they overwhelmingly indicated that the subject was too important for such cursory treatment. At the end of three days of discussion, they voted 1,601 to 311 to send it back to the commission for revision and expansion—another blow to the plan.[114]

But a curious incident had occurred. The day before the session in which the schema was to be introduced, Felici announced that the pope would attend that session and speak to the subject. The announcement caught everybody by surprise. No pope had attended a working session of a council since the Fifth Lateran in the early sixteenth century.[115] It is still not clear why Paul decided on such a gesture. To show his interest in the missionary activity of the church, especially in view of his upcoming trip to Bombay? To remind the fathers that he was one of them? To support Cardinal Agagianian, head of the commission that prepared the document?

After he assisted at the Mass celebrated in the Coptic rite, Paul gave a short address commending the schema to the council.[116] The commendation raised further questions. Did he not realize how widespread dissatisfaction with the document was and how likely it was the council would sack it? If not, why not? The outcome was unfortunate. Paul was mortified.[117]

Next the council engaged for two days in a basically positive discussion of the schema on religious orders, which had also been reduced in accordance with the Döpfner Plan to twenty propositions.[118] Many bishops thought the schema was superfluous because religious had a chapter to themselves in *Lumen Gentium,* but since both the bishops and the laity also had such chapters as well as their own schema, they felt they had to go along with the pressure, especially from the superiors-general of the orders, to have a special schema for them.

The schema, while insisting that religious institutes remain faithful to their "purpose, particular spirit, and healthy traditions," called for adaptation to modern conditions, an *aggiornamento.* The aspect of that adaptation that best reveals a basic change in orientation that the council consistently advocated was the schema's injunction that it be done through "the cooperation of all the members of the institute." This adaptation was not to be created unilaterally from on high. Despite the rather relaxed discussion in St. Peter's, the voting—1,155 in favor, 822 opposed—revealed that not all bishops were satisfied that the schema did its job. By the following year it would be significantly revised from this skeletal form into *Perfectae Caritatis.* The final text would emphasize *ressourcement,* return to the original inspiration, as well as *aggiornamento.*

On November 12 the council moved to another relatively short schema, the second that dealt with priests. This time the subject was their training—*De Institutione Sacerdotali.*[119] The very first paragraph stipulated that, while the approval of the Holy See would be necessary, responsibility for designing programs of priestly training was to rest with the local episcopal conferences, a provision that certainly appealed to the bishops. It was also symptomatic of the council's consistent concern for adaptation to local circumstances and for placing more discretion into local hands.

Two other aspects of the document are important. First, it gave overall primacy to the spiritual formation of the seminarians and to helping them answer "the call to holiness." Second, for the seminarians' intellectual training it gave primacy to Scripture, as to the "soul" of theology, a reflection of the conclusions that were emerging from the heated discussions on the schema on revelation. Although the fathers made suggestions and expressed concerns—Ruffini and a few others wanted a clear statement on the preeminent status of Aquinas in the curriculum, as the popes had decreed—the schema received a landslide approval of 2,074 votes to only 41 opposed.[120] Before it was finally approved the following year under the title *Optatam Totius,* it too would undergo elaboration and stylistic recasting.

The third period was rushing to a close, and on the surface all seemed well. The voting on the schemas had moved apace. The tense days of mid-October when Paul VI had intervened on the schema On Religious Liberty and the Jews seemed like an inconsequential blip on the screen. Although a fourth period was now a certainty, it most likely would be short and without major problems. The big battles had been fought and, presumably, won. The vast majority of the bishops had given repeated and unmistakable affirmation to the direction the council had taken on almost every controversial and "progressive" issue. For the last week of the period two schemas that suffered repeated attacks by the minority had survived substantially intact and were again on the agenda—On Religious Liberty and *Lumen Gentium.*

Then a storm of almost hurricane proportions crashed in on a seemingly tranquil sea. Beginning on Monday, November 16, the first day of the last week, a series of events occurred that sent the assembly into the most frustrating few days of the council, so much so that it began to be described as "the black week," *la settimana nera.*[121] Paul VI intervened on three schemas. He (1) postponed the vote on accepting the schema On Religious Liberty as the base text; (2) sent the council a list of nineteen emendations to the decree On Ecumenism that at this stage it had no choice but to accept; and (3) communicated for *Lumen Gentium* a "Preliminary Explanatory Note" *(Nota Explicativa Praevia)* that interpreted the meaning of collegiality in chapter three. Along with the non-controversial decree on the Eastern Catholic churches, *Orientalium Ecclesiarum,* the last two were scheduled for final approval and promulgation at the end of the week, November 21.

As was typical of the council, procedural and substantive issues played themselves out here in ways that were inextricably intertwined. No matter how well meant Paul's actions were, they caused deep distress to the great majority of bishops and, most harmful, fueled suspicion that a small number of council fathers were using him as their tool to attain what they could not obtain through the deliberations in St. Peter's.[122]

The assembly, as mentioned, was to vote on the declaration On Religious Liberty during the week. Votes would be taken on individual chapters according to the formula affirmative, affirmative with reservations, or negative. The schema was being treated, therefore, as an emended text. The problem began on Tuesday and Wednesday, November 17 and 18, when in three separate letters to the Council of Presidents some fathers objected that the document had been so thoroughly reworked that it was in essence a new text and needed to be treated as such.[123] Most of those protesting were from Spanish- or Portuguese-speaking countries, though other names such as Carli's, Ottaviani's, and Lefebvre's were among them. They appealed to the "Regulations," which stipulated that the fathers needed sufficient time to study the texts before voting on them. On November 18 Felici told the assembly what had transpired. He said that the Council of Presidents and the moderators had decided to let the council determine the next day whether or not to proceed to a vote. The council would vote whether or not to vote.

Early the next morning, November 19, Bishop Carli delivered a letter to Cardinal Roberti arguing that such a vote would violate the "Regulations."[124] A short while later Cardinal Tisserant, citing the reasons given in Carli's letter and speaking for the Council of Presidents, abruptly announced that the vote on the schema would be postponed to the next year.[125] Carli had scored a hit and caused the presidents to reconsider.

The announcement shocked the assembly. Not only had the vote on procedure been abrogated, but the schema itself, supposedly ready for voting the next day, was sent off into the yonder and would have to be debated again. The American bishops, as well as many others, were furious and led a petition to Paul that "urgently, most urgently, and with the greatest possible urgency" asked him to reverse the presidents' decision.[126]

When later that morning De Smedt gave his scheduled (and now rather pointless) presentation of the revised declaration, he was repeatedly inter-rupted by sustained applause.[127] When he finished, applause thundered through the basilica. It went on and on as if never to end, the longest such ovation in the four years of the council. It was the only way the bishops could collectively express their anger and frustration.

The pope had had no part in the decision of the presidents. For the next twenty hours he was of course once again under siege—he *had* to reverse the decision; he *had* to sustain it. The next morning, November 20, the last working day of the council, Paul communicated to the assembly that he would uphold the decision of the presidents. This meant that next year the schema would again be introduced and debated. The dismay in the basilica was almost palpable. The decision displeased no bishops more than the Americans. The good news was that Paul promised that the schema would be treated when the council next convened and that it would be dealt with "if possible, before any other."[128] In the glum and heavy atmosphere of this "black Thursday," bishops received Paul's prom-ise with skepticism.

In retrospect, commentators judge Paul's decision positively. The objec-tion raised by those who demanded a delay, no matter what their motiva-tion, was reasonable—the text was markedly different, about twice as long as the original. As early as October 14 Congar had sighted the discrepan-cies between the text debated in September and the one now presented for voting, and in his diary he noted that the discrepancies were so consider-able as to require a new discussion. He blamed two principal redactors of the text, Murray and Pavan, for not foreseeing the problems the revised text would cause.[129] As part of a long memorandum that Felici prepared for Paul VI on November 12, a week before the scheduled vote, he com-municated his own dissatisfaction with how the Secretariat had handled the matter.[130]

Paul was presumed to be favorable to the substance of the decree, as his longstanding sympathies with Maritain's writings on the subject indicated, but he was also known not to be particularly pleased with the text in its mid-November form, an opinion shared by many others who were still prepared to vote for it. Presumably, he did not want later reception of the declaration weakened by questions about the legitimacy of the vote, and in the end his decision resulted in a better text. Paul's basically procedural intervention to settle an issue not of his making happened, unfortunately, amid the fireworks of the most difficult week of the council and was interpreted accordingly.[131] Moreover, the decision pleased the hardcore minority who opposed the declaration, and it gave them another chance to subvert it.

It is more difficult to understand Paul's adamant insistence on acceptance of the nineteen emendations to the text On Ecumenism, a document whose individual chapters had already been approved by the assembly with overwhelming majorities. For instance, chapter two, which received the largest number of negative votes, won a majority of 2,021 to 85.[132] All that remained was the vote on the document as a whole, almost a formality in this case. Felici presented Paul's "kind suggestions authoritatively expressed" *(suggestiones benevolas auctoritative expressas)* to the assembly only on November 19, the next-to-last working day, the day of Tisserant's lightning bolt announcement postponing the vote on religious liberty.[133]

But consternation had reigned behind the scenes for days beforehand. The pope had sent the moderators and the Secretariat for Christian Unity various communications in which he threatened not to promulgate the decree if his emendations were not accepted.[134] The pope had selected the "suggestions" from a longer list that he received from sources that even today have not been definitively identified. What prompted Paul to intervene is not known. It seems clear that he received the text On Ecumenism at a late date owing to an oversight in the Secretariat. But he could hardly have been acting simply out of pique.

The frantic efforts of the Secretariat, whose intermediary to the pope was in this instance Willebrands, finally availed nothing. In the end the pope was adamant. This time the "suggestions" were an order. The problem was not the substance of the changes, which in fact did not alter the text significantly. The Protestant observer Douglas Horton, who presumably would be sensitive to their import, called them "trifling but interesting."[135] The problem was the procedure, an affront to the council by forcing it at the very last minute to ratify changes and have them promulgated in its name without having previously seen or discussed them.[136]

When the final vote was taken on November 20, it was another landslide—2,054 to 64. The number of council fathers voting negatively on the text after Paul's changes had been inserted into it remained roughly the same as before. If Paul VI hoped by his emendations to win over those who fiercely opposed the decree, he failed.

The *Nota Praevia,* that is, the "Preliminary Explanatory Note," to *Lumen Gentium* was an altogether more substantive matter.[137] On Monday, November 16, Felici introduced it to the assembly. It was the norm according to which chapter three was to be interpreted and understood. Although the Note had been distributed to the fathers the previous Saturday with other materials, the announcement dramatized it and was thus the first surprise that kicked off the fateful week. The Note opened by stating that it came from the Doctrinal Commission, but Felici correctly told the assembly that it was "from a higher authority" *(Superiore denique Auctoritate),* which could only mean the pope. Both were correct. The commission composed it, but as ordered to do so by Paul. Gérard Philips was the principal author.[138]

Resentment flared, again—at the last-minute timing, at the impossibility of any public discussion, and especially at the autocratic implications of Felici's announcement of the Note as "from a higher authority." It sounded to some fathers as if the pope were telling the council what the council meant in its own document. And the announcement came at the beginning of the worst week of Vatican II.

Although the Note contained a lot of technical language opaque to all but theologians and canon lawyers on the relationship between the college of bishops and the pope, it was meant in large measure to clarify the meaning of terms, almost as a kind of extended glossary. It began to rise to a higher status, as if it were an intrinsic part of the text. Did the Note, however, simply clarify the meaning of the terms or did it change the meaning of the text? The interpretation of the text that the Note offered now itself had to be interpreted. Philips afterward consistently maintained that the Note did not change the meaning of the document, an opinion shared by most commentators. Shortly after the council Joseph Ratzinger substantially agreed but found this "very intricate text" marked by ambivalence and ambiguities and saw it tipping the balance in favor of the primacy.[139]

But no matter what the intent, could it in fact be seen as interpreting the text in a certain direction?[140] It seems to have done so for the minority. Siri was ecstatic: "Everything is all right! The Holy Spirit has entered the council. . . . The pope has dug in his heels, and only he could have done it."[141] Siguad, a leader of the Group, similarly rejoiced: "The difficulties we had regarding the doctrine of chapter III have been dissipated by the Explanatory Note, and the anxiety of our consciences has now been laid to rest."[142] On the very day of Felici's announcement, Ruffini informed Paul

VI of his pleasure with this "most opportune" Note of *fundamental importance*" (his emphasis) and asked that it be attached to the main text itself.[143]

The Note won the support of the minority for the chapter and for the schema, as shown in the final voting—only 5 negative votes out of 2,156 cast. The price for that virtual unanimity was high. No matter what the pope hoped to accomplish, he in fact gave those who opposed collegiality a tool they could—and would—use to interpret the chapter as a reaffirmation of the status quo. If there was anything about the Note that gave the leaders of the majority pause, it was the ready, even gleeful, support the doctrine of collegiality now received from council fathers who had done everything they could to scuttle it.

The third period ended as scheduled on Saturday, November 21, with a Public Session in the basilica attended by large numbers of dignitaries, special guests, and others. During the session Paul solemnly promulgated three documents—On the Church *(Lumen Gentium)*, On the Oriental Churches *(Orientalium Ecclesiarum)*, and On Ecumenism *(Unitatis Redintegratio)*. The council fathers had a right to be pleased that they now had behind them these three texts plus the two promulgated the previous year—signed, sealed, and delivered to the church. But the surprises of this rocky third period were not over.

In his allocution after the promulgation of the decrees, the pope expressed his special pleasure that the Constitution on the Church was among them. He added: "The most important word to be said about the promulgation [of that decree] is that through it no change is made in traditional teaching."[144] All the fathers present surely subscribed to that statement, but they would just as surely have given it different interpretations.

When a little later the pope spoke of the character of the church as "both monarchical and hierarchical" in a context in which "both primatial and collegial" seemed called for, the fathers' worst fears seemed confirmed.[145] The expression was all the stranger in that *Lumen Gentium* carefully avoided the word "monarchy," though it was used in all theological manuals before the council to describe the structure of the Catholic Church. "Monarch" does not appear a single time in *Lumen Gentium,* nor for that matter a single time in any of the final documents of the council.

A little more than halfway through the long allocution Paul turned to the Virgin Mary and to the last chapter of *Lumen Gentium,* the chapter devoted to her. He said that now was the time to grant what so many of the faithful throughout the world desired, that during the council her maternal role in the lives of the Christian people be announced. Therefore, "for the glory of the Blessed Virgin and for our consolation, we declare her Mother of the Church."[146] There was much applause from the crowd in the church. The pope had just officially conferred upon Mary a new title. He continued speaking of her for the rest of the allocution, thus devoting about 40 percent of the entire speech to Mary, which, even though November 21 was the feast of Mary's Presentation in the Temple, seemed a peculiar emphasis for the occasion. The decree On Ecumenism, for instance, received only passing attention, and the decree On the Oriental Churches none at all.

Council fathers were well aware that the Doctrinal Commission had repeatedly rebuffed attempts to ratify the title Mother of the Church and especially rebuffed attempts to insert it into chapter eight of *Lumen Gentium*.[147] The reasons: the title was not traditional, it would displease Protestants, but, most fundamentally, it seemed to put Mary above the church rather than within it, where she was the preeminent model for Christians. Although Paul's action surely pleased a large number of bishops, even some of those who wanted Mary honored with this title were upset. Once again, at the very end of this difficult week, a surprise had been sprung on them about a document that, after anguished discussion, they considered complete. They heard from the pope, however, that by means of this declaration he had devised for *Lumen Gentium* its "crowning achievement" *(fastigium)*.[148] If so, it was an achievement above and beyond what the council had approved. Philips judged the declaration a deliberate assertion by the pope of his primacy.[149]

That day Paul's face was grim as he was carried out of the basilica through row upon row of bishops, who applauded perfunctorily or, in some cases, not at all.[150] The important decrees on the church and on ecumenism had been approved and promulgated but at a cost. No one doubted that the week had seriously damaged the relationship between the pope and the assembly. Could the loss of trust be repaired? What would the next period be like? Would the end of the council be anything like the end of this third period? Bishops left for home with troubling questions like these on their minds and in their hearts.

published in an Italian journal for the clergy, which he and other members of the International Group circulated widely among the council fathers.[11] He argued that the New Testament and Tradition showed that the Jews bore corporate responsibility for the death of Jesus. Hence the accusation of deicide was correct, and as a description of the guilt of the Jewish people it was as valid as the description of Mary as the Mother of God. Matters were made worse on Passion Sunday, two Sundays before Easter, when Paul VI stated in a sermon in a parish church that the Jewish people not only did not acknowledge Christ when he came but also abused and killed him.[12] Carli seized upon the pope's words with delight and as proof of his position on the matter. The chief rabbi of Rome and the president of the Union of Italian Jewish Communities, for their part, sent telegrams of protest to the Vatican.

Consternation and confusion reigned in the Secretariat over the "deicide" issue. Through the months preceding the opening of the council, members debated whether the word was to be reinserted into the text. In an undeniable indication of the seriousness of the situation, the Secretariat at one point contemplated, on Willebrands's suggestion, recommending that the schema be withdrawn and the whole matter deferred for resolution after the council. Willebrands insisted that if the document was to be removed from the agenda, the Secretariat should do it, to spare the pope further criticism for interfering.

The pope again let the Secretariat know that he wanted denial of the guilt of deicide removed from the text, and that was of course the solution finally settled on. Paul seems to have feared that such a statement might somehow be construed as an implicit denial of the divinity of Christ. (If Mary, as Carli said, is rightly called the "Mother of God," then putting her son to death is rightly called deicide.) It was also among the sticking points for others. How the council might react to the solution, however, remained to be seen.

Carli had emerged as the chief spokesman for the Group. On June 25 he, Marcel Lefebvre, and Geraldo de Proença Sigaud addressed a letter to Paul VI in their own names and in the name of the Group, asking for a change in debate procedures. Cicognani was responsible for forwarding the letter to the pope, which he did, but in a letter dated August 11, a month before the opening of the fourth period, he replied to Carli in the sharpest terms. He told him that the "alliance" *(alleanza)* was highly inappropriate for an ecumenical council and could give rise to others, which would greatly damage the work of Vatican II. It fostered factions and divisions within the council at a time when everybody should strive, as much as possible, to promote unity and serenity of judgment. Cicognani's letter reveals how irksome the maneuvers of the Group had become and how deeply they were resented by the secretary of state, who was also president of the Coordinating Commission.[13]

On the day the council opened, Pope Paul issued the document *Apostolica Sollicitudo,* a *motu proprio* ("on his own initiative") establishing the Synod of Bishops.[14] Although a few people knew the text was in the making, it caught the assembly and even the commission on the bishops by surprise. Article 5 of the revised schema on bishops called for the creation of some such body, which was a response to interventions like those of Maximos and Lercaro two years earlier calling for a central council of bishops as an expression of collegiality with the purpose of helping the pope govern the church. Paul had misgivings about that article and decided to act before it reached the floor.[15] The commission on bishops now had little choice but to incorporate the substance of the pope's intervention into article 5.

The initial response to *Apostolica Sollicitudo* on September 14 was positive. Here was a practical instrument for the bishops' exercise of their collegial responsibility for the church in a body of manageable size. It was also an instrument that would help internationalize the functioning of the Curia and do so with the involvement of the bishops who were out in the trenches. It was an expression of the new role the bishops as a body would play in the governing of the church.

A second look at the document, however, should have given rise to serious misgivings on the part of those who wanted the new body to be an expression of collegiality. Repeatedly stated in this *motu proprio* was that in every particular the Synod was subject "immediately and directly to the power" of the pope. It was strictly an advisory body with no authority beyond what the pope conceded to it.[16] Cardinal Suenens thought at the time that eventually the Synod might issue directives, even to the Curia, but two months later he came to believe that Paul would not make serious use of it.[17]

Whatever the merits of *Apostolica Sollicitudo,* it was an expression of papal primacy, not of collegiality, a word never mentioned in the text. It was a preemptive strike by the center. No syllable in it could give a sleepless moment to Bishop Carli and his colleagues. The body described in

Apostolica Sollicitudo could hardly have been further from what Maximos had proposed the previous year. With one stroke the text cut collegiality off from grounding in the institutional reality of the church.

A Tense Beginning

The bishops awaited the pope's address at the opening of the fourth period with particular concern. Most of them were seeing him for the first time since the painful days of mid-November. Most were aware, moreover, that in his addresses and homilies during the summer he had begun to deplore the "crisis of authority" and the "crisis of obedience" in the church and to lament that "truths that stand outside time because they are divine are being subjected to a historicism that strips them of their content and unchangeable character."[18] Would he take the occasion of his opening address to issue a warning to the council? What would he say about the controversial schemas?

As usual with Paul, the address, couched in an elegant Latin that surely many fathers could not easily follow, was long.[19] Its tone, contrary to what some expected, was altogether positive, an exhortation to charity and union of hearts and minds that abstained from any direct reference to concrete issues in the council. He dedicated the first part to expressing gratitude to God for the great grace of the council, several times repeating what a wonderful event it was—*Grande quiddam hoc est Concilium!* Attentive ears heard something in this address, moreover, that they had not heard on the same occasion a year earlier: "We are one people, the people of God. We are the Catholic Church."[20]

In the last section he spoke fervently of love for the world and of the church's concern for it, surely an implicit commendation of *Gaudium et Spes*. Finally, at the very end, he made two surprise announcements: first, he would create the Synod of Bishops; and second, he would take a trip during this period to the United Nations in New York City, where he would echo the voices of the fathers of the council in proclaiming the message of "concord, justice, fraternal love, and peace among all human beings, who are loved by God and gifted with good will."

The announcements were greeted with applause. Along with the general tenor of the pope's words, they gave the proceedings an upbeat feeling. The address itself seemed to be a vote of confidence in the council, providing the fathers with a badly needed shot of energy and determination to carry on to the end. After the allocution Felici took the floor for his announcements, the most important of which was that the next day debate would begin on the schema On Religious Liberty. Applause again broke out. The pope had kept his promise. The schema had not slipped into the dustbin—nay, it was tops on the agenda.

The following day De Smedt once again introduced the schema, which had been further revised. Nine cardinals spoke that morning, and what they said contained no surprises. The same arguments in favor, the same arguments against. Spellman and Cushing, of course, were in the first camp, Ruffini and Siri in the second. Ruffini made the usual point that liberty could not be dissociated from truth, which the Catholic Church possesses. Otherwise, he said, it degenerates into "madness," to use the word of Gregory XVI. Separation of church and state was clearly condemned by Pius IX in the *Syllabus,* and Pius XII did the same just a dozen years ago in his address on December 6, 1953, to Catholic lawyers.[21] Siri warned that if those at the council made decisions that diminished the authority of the statements on the subject by Leo XIII, Pius XI, and Pius XII, they weakened their own authority.[22]

Even on this first day, however, it became clear that the debate on the schema was not to be simply a replay of the usual majority-minority confrontations. Indeed, for the first time the Spanish bishops emerged from the shadows to take a leadership role in the council—in opposition to the schema. Just as bishops from Canada and especially the United States were enthusiastic in supporting it, the Spaniards with virtual unanimity were determined to do just the opposite. Cardinal Benjamin de Arriba y Castro, archbishop of Tarragona, a major spokesman for the Spaniards, delivered one of the shortest interventions of the council and one of the bluntest. In just a few words he enunciated the core belief of the opponents to the schema: "The fundamental principle in this matter, which must be held without dilution, is this, only the Catholic Church has the right and the duty of preaching the Gospel. Therefore, proselytism of Catholics by non-Catholics is illicit and, insofar as the common good allows, must be impeded not simply by the church but also by the state." He, too, invoked the authority of Pius XII's address to the jurists, and then went on, "Let the council take care not to declare the ruin of the Catholic Church in nations where Catholicism is the only religion practiced."[23]

How widespread among bishops from the Catholic countries was the stance of de Arriba y Castro? We have no way of knowing for sure, but that morning Cardinal Giovanni Urbani, patriarch of Venice, spoke strongly in favor of the schema on behalf of thirty-two Italian bishops. He took the bull by the horns in directly addressing the problem of the pronouncements of "Gregory XVI, Pius IX, Leo XIII, Pius XI, Pius XII, and John XXIII." What was clear, according to Urbani, was a certain "progress" *(progressio)* in those teachings: "The doctrine of civil liberty in religion is rooted in that progress." He ended by admitting that the schema raised issues that rightly caused concern and misgiving, but "the civil right to religious liberty is for certain inscribed in the teaching that the holy church must now and in the future proclaim to the world—not only because it is timely but because it is true."[24] Bishops from the Catholic Mediterranean were not, therefore, united against the schema; nor, certainly, were the Latin Americans.

The schema had other stout defenders, but judging from the interventions of the three days ending on Friday, September 17, opposition seemed menacingly broad and determined. Was it now a contest between bishops from countries where the majority of citizens were non-Catholics and those from countries where Catholics were a majority? To some extent maybe, but that did not quite capture the picture either, as shown by Urbani's intervention and especially by the support the schema received from Catholic Poland. The Group, not at all repentant after Cicognoni's reprimand, was the obvious constant in this mix. Through interventions by Carli, Lefebvre, and others, it continued to do its best to send the schema into oblivion as a betrayal of the tradition of the church and the teachings of the popes.

By that Friday evening, confidence in the viability of the schema had dangerously ebbed even in the Secretariat. No one seriously doubted that it could carry a majority, probably even a two-thirds majority, but Paul VI surely would not promulgate it unless it carried the council more strongly. Moreover, the pope did not want to appear before the United Nations with four, five, six, or seven hundred bishops on record as opposed to religious freedom. The debate in St. Peter's was supposed to conclude on Monday. Should a vote on the schema be risked? The question raged behind the scenes the whole weekend.

Within the Secretariat, Bea remained firm in his belief that, come what may, a vote had to be taken, but others in his entourage vacillated. A weak majority in favor would be the equivalent of the death knell. By Monday the moderators favored postponing the vote by simply sending the schema back to the commission for revision in the light of the interventions and then voting on the revised text later in the period. But Monday morning came, and no announcement was made.

The interventions on Monday, September 20, revived the hopes of the defenders of the schema. Cardinal Joseph Lefebvre, archbishop of Bourges (to be distinguished from Archbishop Marcel Lefebvre), the first to speak, made a powerful impression by his lucid and systematic analysis of the objections of the opposition.[25] As he said, he wanted to allay the fears of those who felt that they could not in good conscience vote for the schema. He reduced the objections to six points, to each of which he replied in a few words: first, the decree would not foster subjectivism and religious indifference; second, it would not mean that the council abdicated the position that the Catholic Church was the only church of Jesus Christ; third, it would not have a bad effect because of the dissemination of error; fourth, it would not diminish missionary spirit; fifth, it does not exalt human beings at God's expense; and sixth, it does not contradict the tradition of the church.

According to reports, Lefebvre calmed the minds of some of the wavering, and the next speaker, Cardinal Stefan Wyszyński, archbishop of Warsaw and primate of Poland, did the same, more from the authority he had as the Catholic champion against the Communist regime than from his eloquence.[26] The fourth speaker that morning, Cardinal Josef Beran, archbishop of Prague, speaking to the council for the first time since his recent release from Communist prison and house arrest, carried even more weight as he put aside abstract reasoning and spoke "from experience."[27] He said that the burning of Jan Hus at the Council of Constance and then the imposition of Catholicism on the population of Bohemia in the seventeenth century had done immeasurable harm to the church. Religion could not be imposed on people. He ended by begging the council to adopt the schema, to which should be added a plea to all governments of the world that deny the free exercise of religion to desist from their ways and free from prison all clergy and laity unjustly held there because of their religious beliefs.

The intervention of Cardinal Agnelo Rossi of São Paolo, who offered suggestions for improvement but spoke in favor of the schema in the name of eighty-two Brazilian bishops, also very much helped the cause.[28] Here was another vote of confidence and from the country with the largest Catholic population in the world. The differences among the council fathers on this issue could not, therefore, be simply divided between those coming from Catholic countries and the rest.

The pendulum had swung strongly in the direction of the schema. Bea urged the moderators to reconsider, and to that effect he also wrote to the pope.[29] Paul responded by informing Felici that he wanted consideration of Bea's request. On that same Monday evening Felici hastily assembled the Council of Presidents, the moderators, and the Coordinating Commission to consider the pope's communication. The result, after what seems to have been a confused discussion, was negative—that is, not to put the schema to a vote. Bea, it seems, again intervened with Paul VI that evening to order a vote, and for sure Ruffini intervened with him for just the opposite. The situation had reached an impasse, and the next day, no matter what, the council had to move on to discussion of the schema On the Church in the Modern World.

The next day the late arrival in the basilica of Agagianian, Tisserant, and Felici, after Mass, did not go unnoticed. At that point, however, no one knew for sure that they were coming from the papal apartments. Business proceeded as usual, with a few remaining speeches on the schema before the council moved on to its next business. At 10:30 Agagianian, the moderator for the day, reminded the fathers that they had already heard sixty-two speeches on the schema. Did they want to terminate discussion? Yes, they did, by a large majority.

With that, De Smedt wound up the proceedings as best he could. Applause. Then Felici, in the name of the moderators, made an electrifying announcement: the fathers were now to vote on the schema. Did it please them to accept this schema as the basis for a definitive version to be presented later? Yes, indeed, it did. The decision to take a vote had been made that morning during a crucial meeting in the papal apartments.

The fathers completed their ballots, and the speeches began on the next schema. Shortly before the session ended, Felici announced the results of the vote: 1,997 in favor, 224 opposed—a majority of almost 90 percent. The schema had not only survived; it had survived splendidly, revealing that the opponents were a much, much smaller number than the interventions in St. Peter's suggested.

The Secretariat went to work once again to revise the schema, harassed all the way through the process by the Group and others who so bitterly opposed it. Time and again, moreover, the opponents of the schema appealed to the pope, who in the hope that the final vote would be virtually unanimous urged the Secretariat to take account of their objections as best it could. The Secretariat tried to comply, but to no avail. When on November 19 the long-awaited final vote was taken, the ranks of the opposition held as solid as ever. The tally was remarkably similar to the vote in September: 249 negative votes out of 2,216 cast, one of the largest negative votes at this stage of its process for any document of the council.

On September 21 Gabriel Garrone, archbishop of Toulouse, introduced the revised and expanded schema On the Church in the Modern World.[30] Discussion would continue through thirteen General Congregations and not end until October 8. The commission feared for the fate of the schema because of its range and its novel character. Moreover, the longest section in Part II dealt with the family, with its two hot points—the ends of marriage and birth control. Add to this the fact that time was exceedingly short for making revisions before the council ended. There was no possibility of bringing it back next year. The positive vote On Religious Liberty gave hope, however, that maybe the schema would make it through the debate without being completely mangled.

The negative attitude of the German bishops was especially worrisome because of the weight their opinions carried. The theologians Karl Rahner and Joseph Ratzinger disliked the text, and in the summer of 1965 both had published articles criticizing it.[31] Cardinal Frings, it was being said, planned to intervene against the schema. On September 17, therefore, a meeting was arranged principally between the French-speakers and the Germans to try to iron out their differences.[32] The Germans felt that the theological foundations of the schema were weak, the tone too optimistic (with more than a touch of Teilhard de Chardin), and the whole enterprise too immature to allow for much more from the council than a letter or message.

Some among them never fully retreated from this position, as their interventions would show, but as the discussion in St. Peter's moved along, the Germans came to support the schema, sometimes reluctantly accepting its approach, sometimes conceding that even an imperfect statement on the subject was better than no statement at all. Working hard on the schema now, moreover, were three high-powered German Jesuit theologians who could be counted on when it came time to deal with the *modi*—Alois Grillmeier, Otto Semmelroth, and Johann Baptist Hirschmann.

On September 22, just a few days after the meeting, Chenu, the highly respected Dominican theologian, gave a lecture in Rome at the Centro di

Documentazione Olandese in which he delivered a passionate defense of the schema, answering especially Rahner's criticisms of it and justifying its theological basis. His speech, widely publicized among the council fathers, surely helped swing opinion in favor of the document.[33] A powerful argument in that direction, moreover, was that it fulfilled in a new and exciting way Pope John's designation of the council's purpose as essentially pastoral. In this schema as in no other, the council turned its attention to the needs and aspirations of the "flock" out there, which in this case extended to all persons of good will.

The debate on the schema as a whole lasted a mere three days. This augured well. In the criticisms there were no surprises. Although Ruffini's negative comments on the text were not dissimilar to the Germans', he expressed them in terms they would probably disavow: "The schema barely touches on the multitude of vices and sins that corrupt large parts of society, especially in nations that glory in their refined culture. Who does not know about the great number of persons from every social class who are consumed by the pursuit of money and are never satisfied with what they get? Likewise, nobody is ignorant that filthy morals contravening the natural law spread more widely every day, with new means of corruption constantly being invented." By new means of corruption he almost surely meant the birth-control pill. Ruffini also objected to the line in the schema that said the church in every age was stained with imperfections. Is this the way, he asked, to present mother church to the world?[34]

Immediately after Ruffini came Siri, who also spoke negatively of the schema.[35] Later in the morning the Brazilian Sigaud, a founder of the International Group, delivered almost a tirade against the document.[36] He challenged the designation constitution, since the document was in no way a "fundamental law" *(lex fundamentalis),* the definition of constitution. The document abandoned the metaphysical principles of Thomism, which are immutable and unassailable, to sink into Nominalism and prepare the way for Marxism. It is imbued with the ideas of Teilhard de Chardin about working for the upbuilding of this world *(constructio mundi),* but this world is passing and destined to be destroyed by fire. The text exhorts Christians to promote scientific and technological advances—well, they have been doing that all along. The advances in those fields came not from Asia and Africa but from Europe and later America—they came from Christians. We are in danger of falling into paganism.

The Germans, more moderate by far, tended to be critical of the sometimes inductive method the schema seemed to favor. Some speakers complained, as before, that the supernatural mission of the church was not given its due measure. Other criticisms were voiced, including the ambiguous way "world" was sometimes used, but they were scattershot amid a general approbation. The question still nagged, however, about what kind of document it was to be, which at this point was already boiling down to a choice between a constitution, which would make it a solemn statement, and a letter or message. Nonetheless, by Friday, September 24, the fathers were ready for discussion of Part I of the text, which had four chapters—the vocation of the human person, the human community, the significance of human activity in the world, and the role of the church in the modern world.

Although Part I met with general approval, bishops raised some of the same objections against it as against the schema as a whole. A big issue was whether or not the text should contain an explicit condemnation of Communism, with some émigré bishops from behind the Iron Curtain pleading for it, whereas some of those still in place showed more caution. As it turned out, the council issued no new condemnation. At the insistence of a petition organized by the International Group, however, it referred to former papal condemnations without mentioning the word. Archbishop Sigaud, disappointed at the solution, observed that there was a big difference between wearing a hat on your head and burying it in your pocket.[37]

It was, however, Part II, which as mentioned roughly corresponded to the original "appendixes," that everybody anticipated. The council took it up on September 29. The first chapter of this part dealt with marriage and the family, on which the debate promised to be as heatedly passionate as ever.

As expected, the ends of marriage, a topic closely tied to the birth-control issue, got the most attention and generated the most heat, but with the same arguments as heard before. Archbishop Zoghby created a minor crisis when he called upon the church to find a way to allow remarriage for an innocent spouse abandoned by the other.[38] The press seized on his speech as advocating divorce.

The next morning, though no announcement was made of it, Charles Journet, the Swiss theologian recently made cardinal by Paul VI, displaced the scheduled first speaker, on orders of the pope.[39] Journet's message was blunt: "The doctrine of the Catholic Church on the indissolubility of sacramental matrimony is the very same doctrine that Jesus Christ revealed to us and that the church has always preserved and proclaimed."[40] A few days later Zoghby got his chance to answer Journet.[41] He professed that he did not attack the indissolubility of marriage but urged the church to consider a dispensation along the lines of the so-called Petrine privilege, which under certain circumstances allows remarriage if the first marriage was between a baptized and a non-baptized person.

The matter went no further. The council concluded its discussion of chapter one of Part II with general approval amid seemingly hundreds of reservations and suggestions on one point or the other. It moved to a favorable discussion of chapter two, on culture, that was somewhat perfunctory except for the striking intervention by the new archbishop of Turin, Michele Pellegrino, former professor of early Christian literature at the University of Turin. He called for two things. First, more explicit recognition that all ecclesiastical disciplines need to be approached from a historical viewpoint. Second, more explicit support in the document and in the practice of the church for freedom of research and expression for clerics and members of religious orders, not simply for the laity, as the text seemed to imply.

In Pellegrino's mind these two points were closely connected. Although he did not make the connection explicit, his denunciation of the punitive excesses during the Modernist crisis provided the link: the fundamental error for which most of the Modernists were punished was their historical approach. Pellegrino brought his argument down from the high heavens when he said: "Let us not think that these and similar punishments [for clerics] are a thing of the distant past. Just a few years ago I met a member of a religious order who was in unwilling 'exile' because of his doctrinal opinions, which today we find in papal and council documents. Everybody knows this is not an isolated case."[42] Congar was almost certainly the exile to whom he referred.[43]

The discussion of chapter three, on economic and social life, elicited the now-familiar criticisms that the treatment was too Western, too optimistic about technological progress, and added nothing to the papal social encyclicals—problems that to some extent could be remedied by the commission when it dealt with the amendments. The fathers moved on, therefore, to chapter five, on political life, which included the controversial issue of nuclear weapons and warfare. All at once, however, television spirited these same fathers out of Rome. They were psychologically now in New York with their eyes fixed on Paul VI during his historic visit there.

War, Peace, and the United Nations

This dramatic occasion once again showed Paul VI at his very best. The trip had immense symbolic value. The pope addressed a completely secular institution. He did so not to proselytize for the Catholic Church but to promote the well-being of the human family. By his very presence at the United Nations on October 4, he gave powerful support to the organization on its twentieth anniversary, just when many had begun to belittle it. He spoke from his heart on a matter of the gravest concern to him as world conditions seemed to be deteriorating, and he thus gave concrete, palpable form to the "Church in the Modern World." People were still not used to popes traveling around the globe, and that fact added greatly to the significance of the occasion and to the breadth of the audience it attracted worldwide through television.

Given the logistics and possible diplomatic pitfalls the trip entailed, the details of it had been relatively easy to arrange. Monsignor Alberto Giovannetti, the emissary of the Vatican at the UN, had approached Secretary General U Thant, who was immediately favorable to the idea, and negotiations began. The snag in protocol as to whether Thant would receive the pope as head of Vatican City or as head of the Catholic Church was speedily resolved when Thant said simply that he would receive him as Paul VI. When President Lyndon Johnson learned that the visit was being planned, he wanted to meet the pope upon his arrival at Kennedy Airport. The Vatican ruled out such a meeting, however, on the grounds that it would give the visit a political appearance. Behind the scenes Giovannetti struggled with Cardinal Spellman over who would manage the visit. In the end they reached a compromise whereby the cardinal would arrange for the strictly Catholic aspects of the trip, such as the papal Mass in Yankee Stadium, and Giovannetti would handle everything else.

The pope was determined to make his address to the United Nations the unquestionable focus of a visit to New York that lasted less than thirty-six hours. The speech—direct, simple, delivered in elegant French, and televised throughout the world—was powerful.[44] Paul introduced himself to his audience as "a man like you, your brother," whose only purpose was "to serve you to the best of Our abilities, with disinterest, humility, and love." He then made his first point: he wanted his presence and message to be "a moral and solemn ratification" of the UN, which he and his immediate predecessors were convinced "represented the road we must travel in the interests of modern civilization and world peace."

The point he drove home throughout the speech was the imperative for nations to cooperate with one another for the common good of humanity. That was the high vocation and mission to which the United Nations was called. No one familiar with the council missed the import of his words when he said: "What you proclaim here is the rights and fundamental duties of human beings—their dignity, their liberty, and above all their religious liberty." Just a few years earlier such a statement from a pope about religious liberty would have been unthinkable. John XXIII had paved the way, but the declaration On Religious Liberty, even though in the council a small but utterly determined minority still sought means to derail it, was already having its impact.

The most moving and emphatic moment of the address came while Paul spoke of the horrors of war and the absolute necessity of world peace. He pleaded, with deep emotion in his voice, "No more war! War never again! It is peace, peace that must guide the destiny of the peoples of the world and of all humanity." These simple words expressed the heart of his message and made a deep impression on all who heard him. It was clear that this plea came from the very depths of his soul.

The highly respected American journalist and political commentator Walter Lippmann astutely analyzed the speech and the occasion:

No one who heard him attentively, or will read him now, can fail to realize that he was speaking a different language from that which is current and conventional. In fact, the pope, who is without pride and has nothing to fear, was thinking what is unthinkable for so many, and he was saying it out loud. His conception of the secular world is quite different from the conception which underlies public discussion—be it in Peking or in Washington. The crucial difference is that in the pope's address the paramount issue is not the Cold War or hostile ideologies. Although religion in general and the Roman Church in particular have been treated as the chief enemies of the communists, the pope said that the pursuit of peace transcends all other duties, and that the paramount crusade of mankind is the crusade against war and for peace. This is a different set of values than are accepted as righteous in the public life of the warring nations. . . .

We shall have heard the pope's message when we have taken those words to heart.[45]

During his few hours in New York, the pope began with a long and enthusiastically cheered ride through the city, paid a visit to Saint Patrick's cathedral, met briefly with President Johnson at the Waldorf-Astoria Hotel, met with the Orthodox, Protestant, and Jewish leaders, and, as mentioned, celebrated an evening Mass for 90,000 in Yankee Stadium. On the return trip to Rome on October 5, his plane touched down at noon at Fiumicino airport. His limousine carried him swiftly to St. Peter's, where the fathers of the council awaited him. After the Council of Presidents and the moderators greeted him at the door, he walked briskly up the aisle to thunderous applause and then made a brief report in Latin.[46]

Again his message was simple and obviously heartfelt as he recalled the kindness with which he had been received and the attentiveness with which he had been heard. But "peace" was the word that recurred again and again in the report. He alerted the council to the significance of what had happened at the UN: "The consequences are grave from Our proclamation of peace. Because through Our mouth We have proclaimed the cause of peace, the Catholic Church is now committed to assuming greater responsibility for promoting the cause of peace."

The next day, October 6, the council took up in earnest and with renewed energy that very issue, chapter five, "On the Community of Peoples and the Promotion of Peace." Did the present situation render obsolete the traditional distinction between just and unjust war? That was the first question asked, and, under the impulse of the pope's address in New York, it moved quickly in the direction of an affirmative answer. In that regard perhaps nobody made a greater impression on the council than Ottaviani, who began his intervention with the blunt assertion, "War must be completely outlawed."[47] He had held and preached that position for his entire public career. When he finished speaking, he was warmly applauded for the first time during the council. Carli, however, held the line, asserting that "even in our atomic age a just war is possible." He then went on to argue that therefore conscientious objection on the part of citizens being recruited for war by their governments was illegitimate.[48]

On the latter issue the consensus seemed to be moving strongly in the other direction, though some Spanish bishops were of the same opinion as Carli. A more pressing issue was the legitimacy of producing and possessing modern weapons as a deterrent to war. The text stated that it was legitimate to possess them, but not everybody agreed. By contrast, the fathers expressed wide support for the establishment of an international body with the authority to oversee the phenomenon and set limits to what nations produced.

On October 8 debate on the schema ended. Much calmer and less contentious than anticipated, it had lasted only two weeks, as the council now marched to a strict calendar. Time was running out fast, and everybody felt the pressure to move things along. The schema, in any case, had passed the test, with its main lines now definitively set. In the name of the commission Archbishop Garrone thanked the fathers for their criticisms and suggestions, which he assured them would be taken into account as the text was revised into its final form.[49]

The ten subcommissions set to work at an almost feverish pace. The sheer coordination of these teams of writers was itself a daunting task. Both Rahner and Ratzinger, the most significant critics, had been added to them.[50] Despite the sometimes contradictory opinions the subcommissions had to reconcile, sorting them out from the 400 closely printed pages containing the texts of the 160 speeches and the proposals submitted in writing, they moved ahead in the revisions remarkably smoothly, with one important and dramatic exception.[51]

The exception was the ends of marriage and birth control. Although the commission was divided on these two issues, the majority prevailed in the final text by refusing to rank the ends of marriage, stating simply that God endowed the married state "with various benefits and with various ends in view." The text began, however, by developing at length the theme of "the intimate partnership of life and the love that constitutes the married state." It insisted on "the equal personal dignity that must be accorded to man and wife in mutual and unreserved affection." "The spouses are effectively led to God and are helped and strengthened in their lofty role as fathers and mothers," for "marriage and married love are by nature ordered to the procreation and education of children." From the viewpoint of traditional Catholic theology the text did several things: it passed over in silence the idea that a purpose of marriage was to provide "an honest remedy" for concupiscence, it refused to rank the purposes, and it newly emphasized love and partnership.

The spouses should welcome children as gifts of God, true, but in some circumstances they might legitimately limit their number. In this regard they should not be capricious but follow their consciences in conformity with the law of God and the teaching of the church. The commission felt that it could not say more on this explosive issue now that Paul had reserved a final determination to himself. On birth control, therefore, the text itself was generic and admitted an interpretation that did not go beyond what theologians were teaching when the council opened. The problem was that everybody knew about the Papal Commission, and many people were drawing the understandable inference that the teaching might be changed. On this issue the final crisis in the council did not break until six weeks later.

The other hot issue—war and armament—went forward in the commission without great drama. The final text admitted the right of nations to defend themselves and even gave a grudging nod to the idea that stockpiling nuclear weapons might under present circumstances act as a deterrent to war. Nonetheless, "The development of armaments by modern science has immeasurably magnified the horrors and wickedness of war," including the crime of "the indiscriminate destruction of whole cities," so that all effort must be expended to outlaw it. To that end an international institution needs to be established with effective power to secure justice for all.

But before such an institution can be successful every effort must be expended to end the abomination of the arms race, which is not only an ineffective way of securing peace but also a deplorable diversion of immense amounts of money from the legitimate purpose of alleviating the miseries that affect large segments of the human race. Nations possessing these weapons run the risk of using them. In the very last week of the council, Philip M. Hannan, newly appointed archbishop of New Orleans, ran a campaign supported by Cardinal Spellman to persuade members of the council to vote against the chapter containing these provisions. In his circular letter Hannan argued, for instance, that possession of nuclear weapons had been beneficial in preserving freedom for a very large portion of the world. The Group threw its support behind the letter. In the end, however, Hannan's efforts against the chapter, widely resented and dangerous to the very viability of *Gaudium et Spes,* came to nought.[52]

The chapter allowed the legitimacy of conscientious objection. It called on wealthy nations to help the poor ones, and it called on Catholics to cooperate with others in international organizations working for peace and justice. As with the section on marriage, the most important aspect of this section was not so much what it said (there was really nothing new here), but how it said it—as a paean to peace and a denunciation of war.

Important though issues like these were, they do not quite capture the religious vision that *Gaudium et Spes* embodied and articulated perhaps better than any of the major documents of Vatican II. Paul VI wanted dialogue to be a major theme of the schema, and he must have been pleased with the degree to which his wish was carried out. The document purports to be about the relationship of the church to "the world." The words that the text uses to express that relationship are words of mutuality, friendship, partnership, cooperation—and dialogue. That is the great theme of *Gaudium et Spes*. The text explicitly addresses "not only the sons and daughters of the church and all who call upon the name of Christ but the whole of humanity as well." *Gaudium et Spes* is an instruction but also an invitation writ large.

In ways great and small, the text says, members of the human family must, by focusing on the good motives and aspirations they share, work together for a more humane world in which the human spirit can reach its full potential. For Christians, "Nothing that is genuinely human fails to find an echo in their hearts."[53] The church's message "is in harmony with the most secret desires of the human heart." With perhaps an allusion to Maritain's *True Humanism, Gaudium et Spes* affirms: "We are witnessing, then, the birth of a new humanism, where men and women are defined before all else by their responsibility to one another at the court of history."

This humanism is, however, a far cry from so-called secular humanism. It is based on a human nature created by God, infused with the Holy Spirit, and destined for God. The text is eloquent, a tribute to that vision of humanity. After speaking of Christians as partners in the Paschal Mystery, configured by the death of Christ but moving forward strengthened by the hope of the resurrection, it goes on to say: "All this holds true not only for Christians but also for all people of good will in whose hearts grace is active invisibly. For, since Christ died for everyone, and since all are in fact called to one and the same destiny, which is divine, we must hold that the Holy Spirit offers to all the possibility of being made partners, in a way known to God, in the Paschal Mystery."

The text praises the dignity of freedom, the dignity of conscience, the dignity of marriage, the dignity of human culture, and, finally, the dignity of the human person—to make dignity a great and pervasive theme of the constitution On the Church in the Modern World. It holds these dignities up for admiration, as is the mode of the epideictic genre, and in so doing it makes use of vocabulary appropriate to the genre. Haubtmann feared that the style *(modus loquendi)* would be attacked in the council because it manifested a crucial commitment to a certain way the church would present itself to the modern world.[54] In adopting a style of speaking, he realized, the council was adopting and promoting a style of being.

For the world to fulfill its promise it needs the church and learns from it. In that regard *Gaudium et Spes* says nothing new or strange. The church needs and learns from the world. That *is* new and strange: "The church is faithful to its traditions and at the same time conscious of its universal mission; it can, then, enter into communion with different forms of culture, thereby enriching both itself and the cultures themselves." That assertion is at the opposite pole from the *Syllabus* of Pope Pius IX.

The document sounds very different from the *Pascendi* of Pope Pius X, not simply because of its positive approach to the world outside the church, but because of its pervasive recognition of the reality and impact of change, as indicated by recourse to words like "development," "progress," and even "evolution." Such words are bolder than *aggiornamento* because they imply a more profound level and pervasiveness of change. They displace the more metaphysical and juridical vocabulary in which ecclesiastical documents traditionally abounded and replace them with words more empirical and historical, as suggested by the frequent call to make decisions in response to "the signs of the times."

Missions, Education, Presbyters, Non-Christian Religions

As the discussion on *Gaudium et Spes* wound down on October 7, Father Johann Schütte, the superior-general of the Fathers of the Divine Word, introduced the schema on the missionary activity of the church, *Ad Gentes Divinitus,* as the document was now called after being rejected by the council a year earlier.[55] Schütte first noted that, in accordance with the wish of the council, the commission had completely rewritten the schema—it was a new text, in which the commission had taken special care to develop the theological foundations of the topic. Now that the era of colonialism and imperialism had come to an end, *aggiornamento* was particularly urgent. Accommodation to local cultures and circumstances was essential. The text, he explained, did not have a separate chapter on that issue because it dealt with it in every chapter.

For the most part the schema was well received, not only because it was such a notable improvement over the original document, but also because weariness and eagerness to move ahead with the agenda mitigated criticism. The future of the Congregation for the Propagation of the Faith (De Propaganda Fide) was a bone of contention behind the scenes, with many bishops agitating for a radical restructuring to make it more collegial in its procedures, more international in its composition, and less prescriptive in its directives.

The debate, begun on October 8, took up only three and a half sessions, an unfortunately meager allotment of time given that about one-third of the bishops came from mission territories and were facing unprecedented difficulties in the new political, economic, and cultural situations in most of their countries. Speaking in the name of the episcopal conferences of Rwanda and Burundi, as well as on behalf of other bishops from East Africa and Nigeria, Michael Ntuyahaga, bishop of Bujumbura, Burundi, pleaded for greater autonomy for the local episcopacy because times had changed: "We live in a transition from missions properly speaking to a time of young churches, which are autonomous and exist in their own right."[56] The strength of the schema was that in fact it tried to capture this reality and deal with it, even though it sometimes expressed it in ambiguous and altogether generic terms.

In calling for explanations of the Christian faith "in terms of the philosophy and wisdom of the people," the text implicitly called for a reordering of the theological enterprise. The result would be "a more profound adaptation [to local cultures] in the whole sphere of Christian life." Here, in almost throw-away lines buried in the text, the council made a statement on perhaps the most profound problem facing the "new churches": how to be Catholic (or Christian) without being unqualifiedly Western. The assembly, in contrast to the previous year, gave the schema an overwhelmingly positive vote, and it then sailed through the final revisions without incident.

During the General Congregations on October 13 and 14, the much-revised declaration On Christian Education *(Gravissimum Educationis)* was put up for vote on the *modi* and on the text as a whole. Although this document never entered center stage at the council, off in the wings it had a tortured history. Even at the last minute, dissatisfaction with the text was widespread and wide-ranging. What was clear was that "education" was understood differently in different cultures. Moreover, the situations of Catholic schools in those cultures varied, with some receiving state-sponsorship and others not. A specific issue that agitated the deliberations of the commission was the role the document should accord Aquinas. The final text, speaking of the "convergence of faith and reason" as a methodological assumption of Catholic teaching, resolved the issue by saying simply, "This method follows the tradition of the doctors of the church and especially St. Thomas Aquinas."

For all the criticism the declaration received, it set out important principles and, in its approach and style, was congruent with the other documents of the council. As it was put to a vote, the commission made clear that, despite various stratagems floating in the assembly to revise it further, this was the final text. At the same time, the commission emphasized, the document did not pretend to be the last word on the subject; indeed, it provided some direction to episcopal conferences and other bodies as they sought to adapt it to their circumstances. In the voting on October 14, the text as a whole received only 183 negative votes out of 1,996 cast.

On October 13, François Marty, archbishop of Rheims, presented the text On the Ministry and Life of Presbyters, another schema rejected the previous year. Two days earlier, however, celibacy, the most explosive issue related to the subject, was authoritatively removed from the agenda by Paul VI.

The matter had come up in an oblique way in 1962 under Pope John XXIII. On June 16 the Central Preparatory Commission discussed a short schema, On Lapsed Priests *(De sacerdotibus lapsis)*. The schema dealt with the question of what to do about priests who had abandoned the priesthood. The assumption of the schema was that in most cases the defection was caused by problems with celibacy. For that reason the schema opened with an uncompromising reaffirmation of the discipline.[57]

The schema, therefore, was not about celibacy as such but about measures to be taken to address a situation that every bishop had to face: priests walking out the door. None of the sixty-eight prelates present at the meeting, which included future leaders of the majority such as Bea, Suenens, Frings, Léger, and others, questioned the validity and appropriateness of the discipline for priests of the Latin rite, but they were looking for ways to ease the ecclesiastical situation of those who had fallen by the wayside. (If the priests had married, for instance, they incurred automatic excommunication.) Should post-factum dispensations from celibacy be granted such men? If so, how and on what grounds was that to be done?

The overwhelming consensus in the commission was that the council should not address the issue, especially since raising it entailed public discussion of complicated canonical procedures. The matter should be left to the discretion of the Holy See. Shortly after John XXIII was informed of the results of this discussion, in a letter to the Central Preparatory Commission he made the consensus binding by taking the matter off the agenda. That was the end of the schema.[58]

In 1962, therefore, as the discussion in the Central Preparatory Commission makes clear, celibacy as such was not in question. But three years later, in 1965, the situation had changed somewhat. Bishops, still a small minority, were talking about the advisability of a modification of the discipline, at least for some regions. When in October the discussion On the Ministry and Life of Priests drew near, some Brazilian bishops hoped to introduce the matter on the floor and wanted to enlist Suenens to help them do so.[59] This was the situation that prompted Paul VI to intervene to withhold celibacy from the agenda. In a letter to Tisserant read to the assembly on October 11, the pope said he had learned that some fathers wanted to raise the issue in the council. He believed such a discussion highly inappropriate, and he further insisted that he intended to safeguard and maintain the ancient discipline of the Latin church in that regard. He did say, however, that if bishops wished, they could send their concerns about the matter to the Council of Presidents, whence they would be transmitted to him.[60] The letter met with applause. The bishops, even most of those who talked about possible change in the discipline, agreed that to open the matter on the floor of St. Peter's would probably generate more heat than light, send the media into a frenzy, and result in inadequate treatment because the time left to the council was so short.

Some bishops believed that, despite Paul's words about his commitment to maintaining the discipline, his invitation to submit observations meant that another body would take up the question behind closed doors. That turned out not to be the case. The schema remained unchanged in this regard, and in his encyclical after the council, *Sacerdotalis Coelibatus,* 1967, the pope carried through on his promise to insist on the discipline for priests of the Latin rite. Somewhat curiously, however, the encyclical provided for the possibility of married ministers from other churches who converted to Catholicism functioning as Catholic priests while remaining with their spouses.[61]

The clergy of the Eastern churches in communion with the Holy See lived under a different discipline, and their bishops tended to take a dim view of the Latin practice. Well before October 11 it became known that Maximos IV intended to deliver a speech on the matter, and he would surely do so in his usual forthright and forceful style. Because of the pope's order, Maximos did not deliver his speech, but along with a covering letter he sent a copy of it to Paul on October 13. The speech was mainly an exposition and justification of the discipline of the Eastern churches. In the letter, however, he minced no words about what he thought of the situation in the Latin church. He agreed that a full public discussion would create scandal rather than anything useful, yet he nonetheless exhorted the pope to create a special commission to study the question. He felt in conscience obliged to tell His Holiness that the problems the Latin church faced in this regard had to be met head-on and not buried as a taboo: "Most Holy Father, this problem exists and is becoming daily more difficult. It cries out for a solution. . . . Your Holiness knows well that repressed truths turn poisonous." Celibacy is a beautiful ideal, he said, but it should not be imposed as an indispensable condition for ordination.[62]

Bea actually raised the subject at some length in his intervention on the schema but did so in criticism of the predominantly Latin or Western orientation of the document, as if the discipline of the Eastern churches was an exception to the rule rather than a legitimate tradition in its own right, a point that Maximos had of course made very strongly.[63] Other speakers, especially from Asia and Africa, also criticized the text for its Western or European perspective.

With celibacy definitively off the agenda, the discussion ranged widely. What became apparent in the course of the five General Congregations the council devoted to the schema was how widely divergent were the circumstances in which priests lived and worked in different parts of the world and how difficult it was to make any generalizations beyond seeming platitudes. Two orientations emerged from the speeches: the first tended to see priests primarily as cultic figures who were empowered to consecrate the eucharistic body of Christ and to forgive sins in God's name, who exercised an almost exclusively top-down authority, and who were under bishops who exercised the same authority in their regard. Priests directed their ministry to the faithful. The other orientation saw priests in a more activist role in society at large, saw them as having a collegial relationship with their bishops and as fostering a similar relationship with those unto whom they ministered. There were almost infinite variations on those orientations. Ruffini, as expected, was a spokesman for the former position, along with Arriba y Castro and others, but not always in ways incompatible with the latter.[64]

Although the schema did not arouse enthusiasm and more than 10,000 suggestions for changes were submitted, on October 16 all but twelve fathers deemed it satisfactory as a basis for further revision. A month later, on November 12, the council approved with similarly overwhelming votes the final text. Surely not without limitations, *Presbyterorum Ordinis* was a considerable achievement. In choosing presbyter over priest *(sacerdos)* to designate the reality, the council engaged in another, specific act of *ressourcement.* "Presbyter" was the older of the two terms. Retrieved from the New Testament and early Christian sources, it suggested a broadening of definition beyond administering the sacraments and offering sacrifice, which is what priest as *sacerdos* implied and which since the Middle Ages had been the standard understanding of it. The presbyter's role was threefold, expressed in a conventional triad: "prophet," that is, proclaimer of the Word of God; "priest," intercessor for and with the community and minister of the sacraments; and "king," leader of the community. In the text, as in others in the council, these three terms underwent important redefinitions, as when "king" was equated with servant.

The document repeatedly insisted that the priest acted in "hierarchical communion with the bishop," and thus emphasized episcopal authority. At the same time, it partially redefined hierarchical here by balancing that authority-relationship with fraternal and collegial qualities. Three aspects of *Presbyterorum Ordinis,* however, are particularly noteworthy. First, the framework for the document's treatment of its subject is ministry—the presbyterate (or priesthood) is about ministry. Ministry, as the word itself denotes, is a form of service that is manifold: the service to Catholics in preaching, administering the sacraments, and leading the community, but also in stretching out a helpful hand to others to work together for the common good. This framing may seem obvious, but it was a very different perspective from what one found in textbooks of the period, where the power to consecrate the bread and wine for the Eucharist and to administer the sacraments received the major, sometimes exclusive, emphasis.

The second aspect was the equal emphasis that the ministry of the Word of God received along with administration of the sacraments and the celebration of Mass. This correlated with the similar enhancement given to "the Word" in the Mass, according to *Sacrosanctum Concilium,* and with the new role in Catholic life for the Bible as laid out in *Dei Verbum.* Before the council, preaching played an important part in Catholic piety—sermons were preached at Sunday Masses and on numerous other occasions such as novenas. What was new here was the theoretical importance with which the text endowed preaching, the intimate relationship it drew between Word and sacrament, and the presupposition running through it that preaching henceforth would for the most part be based more directly on the Bible.

The third aspect was the pervasive insistence on holiness and therefore on the means to aid the spiritual development of the seminarian as well as of the ordained priest. For that reason, the call to holiness, by now a leitmotif of the council, deserves mention. The desired manifestations of holiness that the text singles out are not, for instance, austerity and mortification, though these are certainly not excluded, but "those virtues that are regularly held in high esteem in human relations," such as sincerity, courtesy, and concern for justice.

When discussion on the schema wound up on October 16, it marked the beginning of the end for the council, which took a break for a week and reconvened on Monday, October 25. After the week of the 25th, it took another weeklong break. There were two reasons for this unprecedented change in rhythm. The first became daily more apparent—the fatigue of just about everybody associated with the council. When the vote on the schema on presbyters was taken on October 16, only 1,521 fathers were present in St. Peter's. The low number indicated not only that some bishops had anticipated the break but also that a general weariness gripped the assembly. By this point in the council the fathers had sat through 151 General Congregations and heard well over 2,000 speeches. The grind of the council and its sometimes tense and frustrating situations had taken their toll. During the sessions in St. Peter's bishops were leaving their seats to stroll up and down the side aisles in conversation, to the point that sometimes the collective chatter almost drowned out the voice of the speaker.[65] The recesses were badly needed, but some bishops and *periti* who most needed a rest had to work even harder during them because of the stepped-up intensity of their work in the commissions.

For the commissions, therefore, the respite provided time for revising and polishing the documents to ready them for the next round of votes. That was the second reason for the breaks. The council had debated all sixteen documents, and now all that remained was to vote on the revised drafts of those that had not as yet been fully approved. Such voting had already been going on in small portions for weeks, sharing the time with the speeches on *Gaudium et Spes, Ad Gentes Divinitus,* and *Presbyterorum Ordinis.* The drafts voted on were now ready for promulgation, but other schemas still needed revision, after which amendments proposed by the commissions had to be submitted to the vote of the assembly. The commissions marched to a strict, unrelenting schedule.

Among the documents voted on during these days was the revised text of *Nostra Aetate,* On Non-Christian Religions. This troubled declaration had hit the floor on October 14–15 and, with an ease that no one would have predicted a few months earlier, made its way successfully through the voting on the amendments and chapters. True, the vote on the schema as a whole received 243 negative votes. That was a disturbingly large number, of course, but much lower than anticipated when the document's very viability was in question. What had happened in the meantime?

The Secretariat had moved into action.[66] By agreeing to some changes insisted upon by Maximos, it had won his support, which was crucial. Willebrands, De Smedt, and Pierre Duprey traveled to the Middle East and visited each of the patriarchs, and with that most of the Eastern Catholic bishops came into line. Maximos proposed four changes in the document, which were accepted without a problem. The Secretariat prepared an Arabic translation of the text, which included the relatively long and appreciative section on the Muslims, and this section appeared in the text before the section on Judaism. "Jews" was dropped from the title, so that it was now clear that the declaration was about the relationship of the church to all non-Christian religions.

Then Willebrands and Pierre Duprey personally delivered the translation to the Arab states' embassies in Rome, and the Secretariat made other moves that successfully assured the Arab world that the declaration had no political implications. In this regard, Paul VI's visit to the United Nations was a big help and is part of the essential background for understanding the shift in mood. In the light of these developments the Secretariat of State no longer had reason to resist the declaration.

Back in Rome the Group of International Fathers, the *Coetus,* kept up pressure against the declaration and, as the final vote showed, not without success. Meanwhile, Bea and others who had hoped for an explicit denial of the guilt of deicide had by now resigned themselves to a weaker but still groundbreaking statement, which read: "Although the Jewish authorities with their followers pressed for the death of Jesus, still the things perpetrated during the passion cannot be ascribed indiscriminately to all Jews living at the time nor to the Jews of today. . . . Moreover, the church, which condemns all persecutions against any people . . . deplores feelings of hatred, persecutions, and demonstrations of anti-Semitism directed against the Jews at whatever time and by whomsoever." The document, further, stressed the ties that bound Christians and Jews together in a special way, beginning with their mutual veneration of the Old Testament, the Hebrew Scriptures. Thus did *Nostra Aetate* finally sail into port, a triumph for the Secretariat and for Cardinal Bea in particular.

The Final Weeks

From this point forward the council took on a different character. On October 25 and 26, after the fathers returned from the first recess, they heard the remaining speeches on *Presbyterorum Ordinis,* but after that there was no more public discussion of documents. The sessions in St. Peter's would henceforth be devoted principally to voting. They were interspersed with formal public ceremonies as well as with other sessions that seemed designed to keep the fathers occupied while the commissions worked frantically behind the scenes to complete their revisions.

On October 28 Paul VI presided over a Public Session of the council in which the final, ceremonial vote was taken on five documents: On the Pastoral Office of Bishops *(Christus Dominus),* On the Renewal of Religious Life *(Perfectae Caritatis),* On the Training of Priests *(Optatam Totius),* On Christian Education *(Gravissimum Educationis),* and On the Relation of the Church to Non-Christian Religions *(Nostra Aetate).* During the Mass the pope delivered an address that by reason of its place in the ceremony, its contents, and its relative brevity was a homily, not a programmatic reflection on the documents. He spoke in general terms about the vitality and, indeed, the youth of the church that the council manifested.[67]

After the Mass Felici read the results of the voting, in which 2,322 fathers had taken part. While the first three documents received only one to three negative votes and the fourth, *Gravissimum Educationis,* thirty-five, *Nostra Aetate* received eighty-eight, indicating that the hardcore opposition to the decree had not yielded. The pope then formally promulgated the decrees. That meant that ten of the sixteen documents of Vatican II were now accomplished fact. There was light at the end of this long and exhausting tunnel.

The council spent the next day on the tedious process of voting on the many amendments to the text to be known by its new opening words, *Dei Verbum,* the Word of God. The new title was significant in that it reflected the council's focus on the centrality of the Bible in the theology and devotional life of the church. It was a signal of the rethinking of this important matter that was a pervasive reality in the council.[68]

This was the last vote on that troubled document before the final and almost pro-forma vote at the next Public Session. The very number of amendments to be considered suggests how contentious the basic issues still were. It did not, however, immediately reveal the drama that had been going on behind the scenes almost from the beginning of this final period of the council and that had intensified in the past few weeks.[69]

As mentioned, the text, thoroughly revised by the subcommission of the Doctrinal Commission, had been debated a year earlier and, though heavily criticized, approved as a basis for revision according to the amendments offered by the fathers. Under the leadership of André-Marie Charue, bishop of Namur, Belgium, the subcommission sorted through the suggestions for improvement that poured into it, resulting in a further revised text that the council approved chapter-by-chapter in mid-September. This took place during the debate on religious liberty. Although the schema passed with relatively few negative votes, the large number of "yes, with reservations," *juxta modum,* suggested that trouble lay ahead.

In fact, the hardcore opposition to certain issues treated in the schema, especially the relationship between Scripture and Tradition (section 9 in this text), was ready to exploit every means to bring the key passages around to its way of thinking, and among those means was of course appeal to Paul VI.[70] The text that the subcommission produced expressed the Scripture-Tradition relationship in a manner far too weak to please the minority, which wanted a clear statement that Tradition contained truths not found in Scripture. The minority believed that its position was the authentic interpretation of the two-source teaching attributed to the

Council of Trent. The proponents of the position saw it, therefore, as essential Catholic dogma, and hence they defended it with all their might.

The voting on the schema ended on September 22, after which the subcommittee had to face 1,498 *modi*. These amendments had to be organized, evaluated, condensed, and then put into a form suitable for a yes-no vote. This was a considerable task, but the major problem the subcommission faced was dealing with disagreement within its own membership and from pressures brought to bear on it from the outside, especially from Paul VI. On September 23, the day after the voting ended, Cardinal Ottaviani received from the pope, through Felici, a copy of a letter from Cardinal Siri objecting to the treatment of Tradition. For Siri, as for others who opposed the formulation of the schema, Tradition was in practice scarcely distinct from the Magisterium, especially in its papal form.[71] In the minds of prelates like Siri the problems raised by the definition of Mary's Immaculate Conception by Pius IX and her Assumption by Pius XII lurked in the background of any discussion of what truths Tradition contained or how it operated.

The next day Ottaviani received a second letter through the same route saying that it was the will of "a higher authority" that the subcommission speak more clearly of the "constitutive nature of Tradition as a source of revelation."[72] "Source of revelation" was, as mentioned, an expression that the subcommission had been at pains to avoid.

News of the pope's wishes set off controversy within the subcommission and led to attempts to satisfy Paul VI without committing the document to a position the majority wanted to leave open. These attempts were accompanied by a concern to avoid revealing that the pope had intervened, so as to protect him from the angry reactions his interventions had sparked the previous year. Other commissions similarly withheld from the assembly word about Paul's changes in their texts, and they did so for the same reason.[73] In this instance the subcommission achieved a tentative compromise within its own membership by adding the word "directly" to the statement, "the whole of Catholic doctrine cannot be proved from Scripture alone." Some members of the subcommission believed that this formulation created more problems than it solved.

The full text of *Dei Verbum* had to be approved by the plenary Doctrinal Commission. On September 29 that Commission began examining it, and at its first meeting the addition of "directly" to the text excited heated debate. Rahner vehemently opposed the change, as did the Biblicum in a document presented to the commission. This issue continued to be the center of disagreement during three subsequent meetings of the commission. After seemingly endless debate, confusion, and alternative formulas, on October 4 at the fourth meeting the commission decided to stick with the original statement, that is, without "directly."

A week later Ottaviani, obviously dissatisfied with the solution at which his own commission had arrived, wrote to the pope suggesting the need for another *Nota Praevia*. In passing he provided an insight into how alienated he was from his own commission, whose makeup had substantially changed over the years by the addition of new members, and how helpless he felt to give it the direction he thought best: " [From the way voting goes in the commission] you can see the kind of commission over which I must preside and upon which I cannot impose my own views since I am supported only by a small minority."[74]

Word leaked that Paul VI intended to intervene. A week after Ottaviani's letter, the pope wrote to the commission through Cicognani, asking for clarifications and changes on several points and offering alternative formulas for them.[75] Cardinal Frings had just a few days earlier written him about the uneasiness, confusion, and even resentment caused by papal interventions after commissions had arrived at definitive formulations. The pope replied to Frings in forceful terms defending his actions.[76]

To deal with the pope's letter the Doctrinal Commission held a plenary meeting a few days later, and after considerable discussion and negotiation was finally able to reach agreement in ways it hoped would satisfy the pope, to whom two reports were sent immediately after the meeting ended. For the most contested passage a formula was found that the majority on the commission finally were ready to accept, as was the pope himself: "The church does not draw her certainty for all revealed truths from Scripture alone."[77] In this way the threat of another Note was averted, and thus did this document finally emerge alive from the battlefield.

In his comments to the assembly on the amendments on October 29, the day of the voting, Cardinal Ermenegildo Florit of Florence explained how the sentence should be understood: "Sacred Tradition is not presented as a quantitative supplement to Sacred Scripture, nor is Sacred Scripture presented as codification of all of revelation. It is clear, therefore, that the text of the schema is unchanged in its substance [by this new formulation] but has been perfected in its mode of expression."[78] The votes that day overwhelmingly approved each of the six chapters, with only twenty-seven negative votes for the schema as a whole. The next day Paul VI gave his approval to the printing of the text, which was then readied for distribution to the fathers of the council in anticipation of the ceremonial vote at the next Public Session.

The council then began its second recess, which lasted until November 9. Through the week after the recess the council was occupied in voting on amendments to the documents On the Lay Apostolate *(Apostolicam Actuositatem),* On the Missionary Activity of the Church *(Ad Gentes Divinitus),* On the Ministry and Life of Priests *(Presbyterorum Ordinis),* and On the Church in the Modern World *(Gaudium et Spes).* In this process the only ripple on an otherwise tranquil sea was the arrival on November 6 of twelve *modi* from the pope for the document On the Lay Apostolate. The final copy of the text had already been printed and was ready for distribution. Because of the recess the commission could not meet to deal with the amendments until Monday, November 9, the day before the voting on the text. The *modi* were points of wording and detail, some of which the commission accepted and hastily printed on a supplementary sheet. Without being told, the fathers easily drew the conclusion that these last-minute changes had to originate with Paul VI. Such attempts to shield the pope from criticism thus sometimes backfired and helped fuel rumors.

On that same Monday morning Cardinal Cento introduced for the consideration of the fathers a document on indulgences prepared at the request of Paul VI by the canonists of the Sacred Penitentiary. In the *vota* submitted before the council a number of bishops asked for a review of the subject, which led Paul VI on July 24, 1963, to ask Cento to form a commission for the reform of the system of indulgences, but with the clear understanding that this was a project independent of the agenda of the council. Since time was now available, however, the pope decided to consult the bishops on the matter.

With the Protestant observers present, the subject was touchy. Indulgences had driven Luther to post his "Ninety-Five Theses," the beginning of the Reformation. The Council of Trent in a hasty and somewhat perfunctory decree just before the council ended reaffirmed the legitimacy of indulgences and provided measures to obviate abuses of them. In subsequent centuries the popes, and especially Pius XII, had granted ever more indulgences, with the possibility of gaining large numbers of so-called plenary indulgences in a single day. Some theologians and bishops felt that the matter was again spinning out of control, while others questioned the whole concept, which was, put most simply, that by performing certain good actions individuals could lessen the time in Purgatory for themselves or for others.

The "position paper" prepared by the Cento Commission was delivered to the presidents of the various episcopal conferences on October 15, and two weeks later Felici informed the council fathers that Pope Paul had decided to allow those presidents to make oral reports in St. Peter's on their episcopate's reaction to the document. The reports began on November 10. The result was not happy for those who had prepared the report—or for the pope, who by bringing the document before the council had implicitly manifested support for it. Despite approval from some conferences, such as the Spanish and the Italian, most others were highly critical of the document.

The first prelate to speak, in the name of the Melkite episcopate, was the intrepid Maximos IV Saigh, and he fired off the most radical criticism.[79] By categorically denying that there was any connection between the intercession of the church and the partial or full remission of any temporal punishment resulting from sin, the concept on which the practice rested, he torpedoed the basis for it. Moreover, he challenged the assumption of a continuity between the practice of the early church and the medieval doctrine and practice of indulgences: "There is no indication that in the primitive and universal tradition of the church indulgences were known and practiced as they were in the Western Middle Ages. More specifically, during at least the eleven centuries when the Eastern and Western churches were united there is no evidence of indulgences in the modern sense of the term. . . . The theological arguments that try to justify the late introduction of indulgences into the West constitute, in our opinion, a collection of deductions in which every conclusion goes beyond the evidence." The solution, unless the church decides to abolish indulgences altogether, is to institute a thorough reform of both practice and theology as they pertain to the matter, which the present document does not do.

The interventions the next day from Alfrink speaking for the Dutch episcopate, König for the Austrian, and Döpfner for the German did not help matters.[80] The last two, especially, made a strong impression. Döpfner did not go so far as to call for the abolition of indulgences, but he severely criticized the theology that underlay the document, the misleading way it handled the history of indulgences, and the changes in practice, all too minimal, that it advocated. He was the last to speak that day. As it turned out, he was the last to speak altogether, even though only eleven episcopates had made their reports.

The next day had been scheduled exclusively for voting on amendments to *Presbyterorum Ordinis,* but the fathers assumed that on the following day, November 13, the reports on indulgences would continue. At the beginning of the session, however, Felici unexpectedly announced that because of time constraints there would be no more reports in St. Peter's. Was that really the reason? The bishops who had not had a chance to speak, Felici added, should hand in written reports to his Secretariat.[81]

In the written reports the episcopal conferences of Belgium, England and Wales, Scandinavia, Haiti, Brazil, Chile, Congo, Rwanda, Burundi, Dahomey, Japan, and Laos expressed dissatisfaction with the document prepared by the Penitentiary, and the last three called for the abolition of indulgences.[82] Two years later, on January 1, 1967, Paul VI would issue an Apostolic Constitution on the matter, *Indulgentiarum Doctrina,* which consisted in a modest revision of the original text along with a list of twenty-one norms related to practice.[83] He answered the problem of discontinuity between the earlier and the medieval teaching/practice by appealing to development or "progress" *(profectus)* of doctrine: the Holy Spirit is the agent through which "not change [*permutatio*] but progress in practice and in the very doctrine of the church is made, so that from the basic truths of revelation are brought forth new and good things for the help of the faithful and the whole church." Therefore, the church today, he continued, invites the faithful to make use of indulgences.

November 18 was devoted to another Public Session, in which the final, quasi-ceremonial vote was taken on *Dei Verbum* (2,344 in favor, 6 opposed) and on *Apostolicam Actuositatem* (2,305 in favor, 2 opposed). The pope solemnly promulgated the schemas and then delivered his allocution.[84] After reminding everyone that only twenty days remained for the council, he asked those present to turn their eyes to the future, that is, to the implementation of the measures the council had enacted. He described the steps he himself had taken or intended to take: he had set up three new bodies responsible for aspects of that implementation (for the liturgy, for the revision of Canon Law, and for the communication media) and three Secretariats (for Christian unity, for non-Christian religions, and for non-believers); he intended to hold the first Synod of Bishops in 1967; he had already begun plans for some changes in the Roman Curia and, indeed, very shortly would issue norms that henceforth would govern the principal Congregation (here designated as *prima,* not *suprema*), the Holy Office.

Paul's words about the Curia substantially repeated what he had said two years earlier. In that regard the most telling sentence was: "There are no serious reasons for changing its structure." By this point in the council Paul had decided that the Vatican Congregations would be responsible in the post-council period for the implementation of the council's decrees, except in those instances just mentioned in which he had made other provisions. In one of the moderators' regular audiences with Paul in mid-October, Suenens had told the pope that bishops feared the consequences after the council of an unreformed Curia, especially if the major personnel remained the same. Paul interrupted him, defended the Curia, said no major changes were needed, and indicated that he did not intend to change any of the cardinal presidents of the Congregations.[85]

In this same address on November 18, he warned against exaggerated interpretations of what the council had enacted and against interpretations that twisted Pope John's *aggiornamento* (here, *accommodatio*) to a "relativism . . . Henceforth it will mean for us an enlightened grasp of the intentions of the council and a faithful implementation of its directives. . . . The time for debate is over." As Paul liked to do, he ended the allocution with three unanticipated announcements. First, to promote spiritual renewal he had initiated the beatification process for his two immediate predecessors, Pius XII and John XXIII. This decision put a definitive end to the movement that took off right after John's death for the council to canonize him by acclamation, and it paired John (and the post-council period) with a pope with whom he was often contrasted. Second, as a way of perpetuating the memory of the council, he would construct a new church in Rome dedicated to Mary, Mother of the Church. Finally, as part of the spiritual celebration of the council, he proclaimed a special Jubilee that would last from December 8, the last day of the council, until Pentecost.

It was an informative address, though curious in that he said not a word about the two documents he promulgated. The terms in which the reform of the Curia was described confirmed that nothing radical was to be expected. Calling attention once again to Mary as Mother of the Church and announcing his decision to initiate the process of beatification for the two popes highlighted the general program of the address, which was the responsibility and, implicitly, the prerogatives of the papacy, with little attention to the episcopacy in a council at which collegiality was a central and defining issue.

Nonetheless, the ceremony signified and celebrated accomplishment. For almost all persons connected with the council, this was a great day. And it made clear that the end was nigh. The battles had been fought, and now the task, it seemed, was simply to tidy up and to formalize what remained of the work of the past four years—or, better, the past six years, from 1959 until 1965. Such an optimistic assessment proved once again, however, to be off the mark. During the final stage of preparation of *Gaudium et Spes,* which took place during the council recess, November 20–30, trouble erupted.

Within two days after the Public Session on November 18, the subcommission dealing with the section on marriage and the family under Archbishop John Dearden of Detroit had completed its revision, for which it had consulted the Papal Commission on birth control. It was then that individuals, especially the Italian Franciscan Ermenegildo Lio, a *consultor* to the Holy Office, and the American Jesuit John Ford, a member of the Papal Commission, began to exert direct and indirect pressure on the pope to take action to change the text to make it clearly forbid the use of contraceptives; otherwise, they argued, Paul would be seen as calling into question the teaching of previous popes. To leave the text as it was would suggest that a change in teaching was possible. Colombo, Paul's theologian, had similar views.[86]

Paul intervened.[87] On Wednesday, November 24, Ottaviani, a president of the mixed commission responsible for *Gaudium et Spes,* received a letter from Cicognani written in apodictic style indicating changes that the pope insisted be made in the text. Among them was an open and clear rejection of contraceptives. In that regard the text had to make explicit reference to the encyclical *Casti Connubii.* The letter sent the commission into shock, as it tried to deal with a situation that had become all too familiar. Somebody, moreover, leaked word of the papal intervention to the press, which caused further disarray and desperation.

The basic problems were the same: How could the council make a pronouncement on an issue that the pope had removed from its competence? How could it make a pronouncement on an issue it had not discussed? How could it make a pronouncement when another body appointed by the pope himself was examining the matter? How could the subcommission at this last minute present for a final vote a text in which such a radical change had been made? Why did the letter come only at this late date, this last minute? If the council made a statement, would that not render the Papal Commission superfluous?

As with similar interventions, complicated and almost frantic negotiations surged and ebbed behind the scenes for the next few days.[88] The uproar in the world press added further pressure. On November 25, at a long and dramatic meeting of the full mixed commission, opinions clashed, with some members convinced that the papal *modi* were commands that had to be followed and with others insisting, rather contrary to the evidence, that they could be treated like the *modi* of any other member of the council. That afternoon Cicognani, Tisserant, Felici, and a few others met with Paul VI, who continued to insist that, though he would accept alternative wordings, he would not accept anything that changed his basic points. If others had their consciences, Felici reported Paul as saying, he had his.

Then, as had happened before, on the next day, November 26, Cicognani sent a letter stating that the *modi* were "counsels" [*consigli*] of the pope and that they should be treated like the *modi* of any other bishop. What had happened? Not known. The commission, in any case, swiftly decided to take the pope at his word. Although it made some modifications in the text, it did not explicitly condemn the use of so-called artificial means of birth control. It stated, instead, that Catholics were forbidden to use methods that the church had condemned, to which was attached a footnote referring to *Casti Connubii* and two other papal documents, as well as a reference to Paul VI's address to the cardinals on June 23, 1964, in which he had announced the existence of the Papal Commission and stated that the matter needed thorough investigation.[89]

Ottaviani, obviously displeased, informed the pope of what had transpired. On November 28 Paul wrote on Ottaviani's report that he accepted what the commission had decided, and thus did this last crisis, nine days before the council ended, find its resolution. In the final vote on this chapter in *Gaudium et Spes* only 155 negative votes were cast. The issue, of course, did not die. The Papal Commission continued to function for another year and a half, with the majority of the members providing the pope at the end with a report favoring a change in the church's position. Finally, as is well known, on July 25, 1968, Paul VI with his encyclical *Humanae Vitae* settled the matter in favor of the teaching of Pius XI and Pius XII.

The council resumed on November 30 and in two days completed its voting on the four documents still awaiting promulgation. There was no session on December 3, and the sessions on December 4 and Monday, December 6, finished up the few remaining odds and ends of business. The working sessions of the council were over. The formal ceremonies marking the end had already begun. On the afternoon of December 4, Paul VI presided at an ecumenical prayer service for the benefit of more than a hundred non-Catholic observers and guests at the basilica of St. Paul's Outside the Walls, the place where in 1959 Pope John announced his intention to call a council. Just four years earlier such an ecumenical event was utterly inconceivable and, even at the time, not well received by all the bishops in the council. Afterward in the adjoining Benedictine monastery Cardinal Bea presented each of the observers to Pope Paul, who gave them a small bronze bell adorned with emblems of the four Evangelists and the monogram of Christ.

Although there was still some business to conduct on December 6, the formalities of closure, relatively modest at this point, got under way in the basilica.[90] Felici announced to the fathers that Paul VI was giving each of them a gold ring as an expression of his good will toward them, which was accompanied by his apostolic blessing. He then promulgated Paul's bull announcing the Jubilee, which included a plenary indulgence to all the faithful who fulfilled the usual conditions.[91] The mayor of the city of Rome had had a silver medal struck for the council fathers, and this highly personalized gift—engraved on each medal was the name of the father for whom it was intended—was distributed during the session.[92] Cardinal Suenens concluded the morning with a speech to express the four moderators' gratitude to all those who had worked so hard to move the council forward. He overlooked nobody, from God, the pope, and the Council of Presidents down to ushers and musicians.[93]

Suenens's thank-you concluded the session in St. Peter's that day, but outside another event took place that related directly to the concerns of the council. The *Osservatore Romano* published *Integrae Servandae,* the document Paul VI had promised on the reform of the Supreme Congregation of the Holy Office, henceforth to be known as the Congregation for the Doctrine of the Faith.[94] The juridical form of *Integrae Servandae* was another *moto proprio.*

The mandate for the Congregation for the Doctrine of the Faith was essentially the same as before: "to protect the teaching on faith and morals throughout the entire Catholic world." New was the inclusion of the more positive task of "investigating new teachings and new opinions . . . and promoting studies of such matters and scholarly meetings." The faith of the church will be better served "by an institution for the promotion of good doctrine" than by one whose function is exclusively negative. The document also spelled out certain procedures meant to ensure that those accused of deviating from the faith or received teachings had an opportunity to defend themselves once their opinions had been found wanting.

The next day, December 7, the solemnities moved into high gear at another Public Session, with the pope present in the basilica, filled to overflowing with dignitaries and others who were fortunate enough to get a ticket allowing them entrance. After a few preliminaries and the final voting on the four documents still requiring promulgation, one of the most moving and dramatic moments of the whole council took place. Bishop Willebrands went to the pulpit and read in French the "Joint Declaration" of Paul VI and Patriarch Athanagoras regretting the excommunications of the Greeks by the Latins and the Latins by the Greeks in 1054, acknowledging the responsibility of both sides for the tragedy, and promising to work toward a full communion between the two churches. This was the fruit of the meeting of the two leaders in the Holy Land two years earlier. At the same time a similar reading took place in the patriarch's basilica in Istanbul. After Willebrands read the text, he exchanged an embrace of peace with Meliton, the Orthodox Metropolitan of Heliopolis, which elicited enthusiastic applause in the basilica.

Mass then began, during which Paul VI gave a long address, officially a "homily," in elegant and difficult Latin. In it he concentrated on "the religious significance of the council" and what it meant for the church and the world.[95] He emphasized, to a somewhat surprising degree, the aberrations and sinfulness of the times. For this situation the church, remaining true to her "patrimony of doctrine and precepts," was the remedy. Like the Good Shepherd, he said, the council adopted a loving attitude toward the world. Perhaps most striking in the talk was the unidirectional relationship that the pope depicted between church and world, bypassing the reciprocity that was notable in *Gaudium et Spes*.

After Mass Felici read the results of the voting that had taken place earlier: On Religious Liberty *(Dignitatis Humanae)*, 2,308 in favor, 70 opposed; On the Missionary Activity of the Church *(Ad Gentes Divinitus)*, 2,394 in favor, 5 opposed; On the Ministry and Life of Priests *(Presbytero-*

rum Ordinis), 2,390 in favor, 4 opposed; On the Church in the Modern World *(Gaudium et Spes)*, 2,309 in favor, 75 opposed. Token opposition to two of the documents contrasts with noticeably more opposition to the other two, which nonetheless was proportionately minuscule. After Felici announced the results, the pope officially promulgated these last four decrees of the council. The final event of the session was the reading by Cardinal Bea of Paul VI's Apostolic Letter formally lifting from the Latin side the excommunication of the Greeks of 1054. With hymns and the final blessing by the pope, the ceremony ended.

Beginning at 9 the next morning, December 8, a crowd estimated at 300,000 gathered in St. Peter's Square and along the via della Conciliazione for the final ceremony, which was also transmitted worldwide on television. Shortly after 10, with all the church bells in the city of Rome ringing, the council fathers began their long procession out of the "bronze doorway" of the papal palace to assume their places in the piazza. Paul VI followed, carried on the *sedia gestatoria*. Upon arrival at the altar in the square, he immediately began the Mass. After the singing of the gospel of the day, the feast of the Immaculate Conception of Mary, he delivered a relatively brief homily in Italian, which was mostly a greeting and word of friendship to those present in the square, by now filled to overflowing, to those who followed the ceremony on radio or television, and finally to all humanity.[96] He said he could address all humanity because for the church "no one is a stranger, no one is excluded, no one is distant." He singled out for special greeting the bishops whose governments would not allow them to come to the council, particularly those held in prison. Toward the end he turned to the topic of Mary, praising her as model and inspiration.

After the Mass the pope blessed the cornerstone of the new church in Rome dedicated to Mary, Mother of the Church, and then read in French a short word of farewell, which was also an introduction to a series of rather lengthy messages from the council, all in French, to different categories of persons—heads of governments, intellectuals and scientists, artists, women, workers, the poor and sick, youth.[97] Jacques Maritain may well have been their author, or one of their authors, but they originated almost certainly in the Secretariat of State at the pope's instigation. Ironically, therefore, these messages from the council were neither constructed nor reviewed by it. Each was read by a cardinal assisted by other cardinals, who saw them for the first time only the previous afternoon.[98]

The entire ceremony closed with Archbishop Felici's reading of the pope's Apostolic Letter, *In Spiritu Sancto,* declaring the council concluded and enjoining that "everything the council decreed be religiously and devoutly observed by all the faithful."[99] Paul VI then imparted the final blessing and dismissal, "In the name of our Lord Jesus Christ, go in peace." To which the vast crowd responded, "Thanks be to God!"—*Deo gratias!*—and then broke into applause and cheers.

Conclusion

WHEN the council opened on October 11, 1962, no one knew what to expect. Reliable indicators, such as the Roman Synod of 1960 and the draft documents drawn up by the Preparatory Commissions, pointed to a modest or even regressive outcome. While some quarters entertained hope that the council would validate the findings of recent biblical, patristic, and liturgical research and take account of significant philosophical shifts, they also feared that it might, instead, reaffirm positions codified in seminary textbooks that by and large ignored such scholarship. There were, of course, contrary indicators, not the least being Pope John's invitation to "the separated brethren" to attend the council.

As young men, the bishops coming to the council had been indoctrinated by the textbooks. Why, then, would they not go along with what was presented to them by the commissions, which enjoyed the added authority of being headed by cardinals of the Roman Congregations? Nobody expected that almost as soon as the council opened two groups of leaders, both relatively small, would emerge from among those thousands of bishops, and that the rest of the bishops would have to judge between the two sides not only on a number of specific issues but also on a general orientation of the council. The conflict between the two parties that soon broke out constituted the drama of the council. Had the conflict been foretold, few would have wagered that an overwhelming majority of bishops, hovering between 85 and 90 percent, would so early on, so consistently, and so insistently side with "the Transalpines."

Yet they did. This convergence meant that the council moved in a direction that no one could have predicted. In some instances, true, the council did little more than confirm and validate realities already in place or in process. When *Apostolicam Actuositatem,* On the Apostolate of the Laity, encouraged lay people to take an active role in the work of the church, it built on a momentum already under way. When *Dei Verbum,* On Divine Revelation, encouraged Catholics to read the Bible for their spiritual profit, it lent support to a practice that had been growing among them for at least twenty years, since *Divino Afflante Spiritu.* When *Unitatis Redintegratio,* On Ecumenism, allowed that under certain circumstances it was not only permissible but commendable to worship with those of other faiths, it sustained the judgment of many Catholics, especially those who had spouses, parents, or friends from those faiths, that the commendation was overdue. When in *Gaudium et Spes,* On the Church in the Modern World, the council fathers encouraged Catholics (and others) to take an active part in efforts for peace and international cooperation, some surely had in mind individuals like Robert Schuman, twice premier in postwar France and known as "the Father of Europe" because of the foundation he laid for the European Union. Schuman died in 1963 after leading such an exemplary life that he is now being considered for beatification.

The council was thus in keeping not only with the central tenets of Christian faith and the practices of the Catholic tradition but also with movements and aspirations of more recent vintage. It both fulfilled and rejected the long nineteenth century. Hauntingly present in St. Peter's were de Maistre, de Lamennais, Pius IX, and Pius X. Present as well were Guéranger, Beauduin, Migne, Mersch, and Lagrange. Alongside them were Möhler, Newman, and Teilhard de Chardin. In a dark corner skulked Darwin, Marx, and Freud. Not to be forgotten in a brighter corner were folks like Maréchal and Buber. The ghosts of Mussolini and Hitler found entrance. Pope Pius XI was present in the basilica, but Pius XII stepped into the spotlight at almost every crucial juncture. This list is far from complete.

The conflicts in the council, so bitterly and doggedly fought, unmistakably show that some basic values were at stake. Since the leading protagonists on both sides of the debate were for the most part the same no matter what the issue under discussion, there had to be fundamental, across-the-board issues in play to account for the polarity. As the bishops debated a specific issue, whether they were aware of it or not, they wrestled with the issue's more profound implications.

Commentaries on the council have obscured rather than clarified the difference between the two parties by describing the contest as pitting liberals or progressives on the one side against conservatives or reactionaries on the other. I have preferred the terms "majority" and "minority" because they are less prejudicial and are directly verifiable. Nonetheless, the bishops of the minority emerged as conservative in the conventional sense of defending positions current at the time, and for that reason (and for lack of a better one) I sometimes use the term for them.

Were the bishops who were leading the majority progressive? They were certainly more in touch with current philosophical and theological developments than were their counterparts in the minority, and they made use of theologians who were partly responsible for those developments. On that level, therefore, this partisanship of theirs was an aspect of *aggiornamento* and was progressive in that sense. These bishops were in general more open to updating and willing to apply it more broadly than those of the minority. In that regard, too, they could be called progressive.

For the most part, however, they argued that their positions were more conservative than those of the conservatives because they were retrievals of traditions fundamental and ancient. His Beatitude Maximos IV Saigh articulated this basic premise more clearly than any other figure at the council. He was the most daringly progressive because he was the most radically conservative. His interventions consistently invoked ancient traditions of the church to challenge the status quo, and he thus opened up for the council fathers a new breadth in the choices they had to make.

But the Western bishops leading the majority also came to the council with a sense of breadth and malleability. They had imbibed it from theologians aware of the limitations of the textbooks and engaged in a battle to correct them. That was the strength of such bishops and theologians. To some extent it was also their weakness. They assumed an easier translation of ideas from the scholars' study to the social reality of the church than proved to be the case. They were, moreover, not untouched by elitism and sometimes played fast with the historical record. They were dismissive of the law of unintended consequences, as when bishops from lands where Catholicism was the established religion warned of the dangers of Protestant proselytism when the church was no longer protected by the state.

The leaders of the minority worked within a narrower theological and cultural horizon. For their contemporaries they fit the stereotype of the proponents of "Roman theology," a theology heavily conditioned by canon law, indifferent to the problems raised by historical methods, and often hermeneutically naive. They had been schooled to disdain modern approaches to theology as passing novelties or, still influenced by *Pascendi* and *Lamentabili,* to attack them as dangerously subversive. They were the ultimate Ultramontanists. Of them the majority asked a great deal. By trying to convince them to go along with this or that position, the majority essentially asked them to adopt a new mind-set and a new value system and to affirm assumptions they feared and abhorred.

The leaders of the minority conveyed in word and deed an entitlement that irked and sometimes enraged the majority. It fueled the antagonism that the assembly sometimes directed toward them, as when the bishops applauded or withheld applause at the wrong times. Insofar as they were part of the Curia, they made use of organizational machinery and a network of communication to advance or defend their causes, which further fueled resentment and suspicions of conspiracy. They were, however, more keenly aware than their opponents of possible negative consequences of decisions the council might make, almost to the point of wanting no changes except a further tightening of the screws.

Mediating between the two parties were the two popes. John by temperament, choice, and even spiritual conviction was a non-interventionist. Before the council he gave a free hand to the Holy Office, as when, right under his nose, it suspended Stanislas Lyonnet and Maximilian Zerwick, teachers at the Biblicum. He let the Roman Synod follow its own path and allowed the Preparatory Commissions to do their work as best they saw fit. While the council was in session, he maintained a hands-off policy. Although he stepped in once to resolve a major crisis, he did not intervene so as to cause a crisis. In creating the Coordinating Commission after the first period, he fully empowered it to give shape to the sprawling agenda and to cut the mountain of documentation down to manageable size.

His successor was of a different, more worrisome temperament. Paul VI came into office with a council already steaming ahead—or, in the eyes of the minority, careening out of control in the wrong direction. Paul made dramatic moves, as with his spectacular pilgrimages to the Holy Land and India and his visit to the United Nations, yet he gave the impression of an essentially shy person acting on the world stage. As a young man he had a virtually private theological education, improved upon when he moved to Rome as a young priest, but it was essentially parochial. He spent his middle years in the Curia.

He was well read in contemporary theology and a personal friend of the philosopher Jacques Maritain and the lay theologian Jean Guitton. He was sympathetic to French thought and culture, secular and sacred. This intelligent and spiritually sensitive man thus acquired more confidence in his theological skills than his training warranted. He pored over council documents with a meticulous "red pencil" in hand, and he edited them as they were in the making, a papal action unprecedented in the annals of ecumenical councils. He firmly kept four issues off the agenda—priestly celibacy, birth control, reform of the Curia, and the mechanism to implement collegiality at the center.

He had a complex relationship to the assembly in St. Peter's. He sometimes acted as a council father like any other, sometimes as a promoter of the council's direction, sometimes as a brake to it, sometimes as an agent to promote consensus, sometimes as the arbiter of procedural conflicts for which he was occasionally responsible, sometimes as interpreter to the council of its meaning, sometimes as monitor of its orthodoxy, and sometimes as rival to its authority. Three factors contributed to creating this situation: first, the carte blanche of the pope as Supreme Moderator, which stemmed directly from his primacy; second, the procedural muddle of the "Regulations" and the blurred determinations of who was responsible for what on the council floor: and, finally, Paul's personality, convictions, and scruples.

Conflicts of personalities and ideologies created the drama of Vatican II. The procedural muddle catalyzed it. A child could draw the organizational chart for the council of Trent. The "Congregation of Theologians" at Trent prepared documents they then submitted to the bishops for discussion in commissions and eventually in General Congregations, where the big debates and determining votes took place. Three or four papal legates presided with authority to make on-the-spot decisions. The pope held trump cards but, hundreds of miles away in Rome, could not influence the day-to-day course of the council. The organizational chart of Trent was thus simple and straightforward. The organizational chart of Vatican II was so complex as to defy a depiction that captures all the currents and countercurrents. The complexity originated with John XXIII. Paul VI did not create but inherited it. For whatever reason, he did nothing to make it less complex.

As it turned out, this biggest meeting in the history of the world was much more than a four-year-long celebration of the glories and perennial faith of Catholicism. It was much more than the "Roman circus" skeptics predicted beforehand. Something happened. The council addressed and changed principles and practices of worship, building on initiatives of previous decades but doing so in an incomparably more comprehensive and systemic way. It agreed with the Council of Trent that the Mass was rightly described as a sacrifice united with the sacrifice of Christ on the cross, but Vatican II went further by explicitly including the Resurrection in it, as the fullness of the "Paschal Mystery." It gave new emphasis to the Mass as a replication of the sacred banquet that was the Last Supper. It enhanced the part of the Mass known as the Liturgy of the Word. It encouraged styles of piety centered on the Mass, the Liturgical Hours, and the Bible rather than on devotional practices like novenas that had proliferated in Catholicism since the Middle Ages.

Vatican II highlighted the importance of baptism as the foundation of the Christian life and as the entrance into the body of the church. It thereby validated a less restrictive understanding of membership in the Catholic Church, for the church to some degree includes all the baptized. At the same time the council took pains not to exclude from salvation even the unbaptized.

It affirmed that what had been revealed to the human race from above was not doctrines as such but the very person of God, especially as the divinity was manifested in the person of Christ. Without explicitly affiliating itself with any specific school of Christology, the council consistently presented Christ as servant and liberator. He was celebrated as friend of all people, especially the poor and victims of war and injustice.

In one of its rare negative statements, the council denounced the arms race and registered skepticism that stockpiling weapons was a deterrent to war—indeed, it "serves only to aggravate the problem." This was in keeping with the concern the council more generally manifested for "the world," a concern unprecedented in the history of councils. For instance, Vatican II addressed the pastoral constitution On the Church in the Modern World not to church members but to all persons of good will. It committed the church to spare no effort in working for the complete outlawing of war, and to that end it supported and promoted every international organization, including, of course, the United Nations, designed to further humanitarian goals.

It made its own the right of people to free assembly and association. By affirming that it was consonant with human nature for citizens to play an active role in the political community and to exercise the right to vote, it distanced itself from forms of government in which that role and right could not be exercised. In the economic sphere it insisted that every effort be made to eliminate economic inequalities that worked against the creation of a just society.

Now, in a silent rejection of earlier positions, it fully embraced the right of individuals not only to inquire freely in matters of religion but also to practice the religion of their choice without intimidation or coercion from civil authorities. In that regard the council affirmed that in the last analysis the moral norm that everybody is obliged to obey is their own conscience, which is not a vague feeling of right and wrong but a moral judgment. It insisted, therefore, on the duty to form one's moral "judgments in the light of truth, to direct one's activities with a sense of responsibility, and to strive for what is true and just in willing cooperation with others." In forming those moral judgments, individuals must give proper consideration to the teachings of the church.

The council gave new prominence to marriage as a loving partnership in which couples are led to God as they share in the joys and sorrows of life. Children, it said, are the supreme gift of marriage and contribute to the good of the parents themselves. Nonetheless, for appropriate reasons parents may limit the number of children they have, provided they do so using moral means. Governments have the right and duty to foster family life and to safeguard the rights of parents to educate their children.

In different ways the council affirmed the dignity of the lay state, as when, with new forthrightness, it reminded the laity and others of the "priesthood of all believers," when it reminded them that they possess charisms and special gifts of the Spirit, and when it reminded them that they were called to lead a holy life. It explicitly affirmed that the body of the faithful cannot err in matters of faith when a consensus prevails in it. It enthusiastically encouraged lay participation in the mission of the church, especially in what it called "the temporal order," that is, out in the marketplace of daily life. If lay persons remain in communion with ecclesiastical

Conclusion

authority, they have the right to establish different kinds of associations to advance the work of the church and the common good.

The council sought to underscore the authority of bishops while at the same time making its exercise less authoritarian; it sought to do the same for priests and to indicate ways to better their relationship both to their bishop and to their flocks. For bishops, priests, and everybody in authority, it proposed and tried to make appealing the ideal of the servant-leader. It reaffirmed a place for Aquinas in the curriculum of seminaries but laid down a program in which Scripture would hold a newly central role because it was "the soul of all theology." It confirmed the utility and legitimacy of using modern methods in the study of the Bible. It recommended that seminarians, especially those in the "new churches," study in close contact with the way of life of their own people. For all seminaries it above all insisted that greater attention be given to the spiritual development of the students.

It condemned anti-Semitism and deplored displays of it "at any time and from whatever source." It similarly condemned all forms of discrimination and harassment "on the basis of race, color, condition in life, or religion." It called upon Catholics to participate in the ecumenical movement and to cooperate with persons of other faiths (or of no faith) in all enterprises geared to the common good. It allowed Catholics under certain circumstances to participate in worship services with members of other religions. It supplied the impetus for later official dialogues of the Catholic Church with other churches.

Vatican II was unprecedented in the history of councils for the notice it took of changes in society at large and for its refusal to see them in globally negative terms as devolutions from an older and happier era, despite the fact that the council met just shortly after the bloodiest half-century in the history of the human race. It recognized that a profound shift in human awareness was taking place in the substitution of a dynamic and more evolutionary concept of nature for a static one. Furthermore, it recognized that this changing situation raised new problems that the church and society at large had to face. The church, it made clear, is *in* the modern world—not above it, not below it, not for it, not against it. Therefore, like everybody else *in* the world, the church must assume its share of responsibility for the well-being of the world, not simply denounce what it finds wrong.

Those are some of the up-front issues with which the council dealt, some of the stances it took, some of the decisions it made. Although few, if any, of them were altogether new for the church, taken in the aggregate they indicate a generalized change from what prevailed just a few years earlier and, in many instances, from what had prevailed for centuries. They surpass in that regard what the majority at the beginning of Vatican II had any right to hope for, yet they fall short of the much higher expectations they entertained once the council got under way.

There were deeper issues. Among the changes in "the world" that the council had to take account of, perhaps none had more profound implications for the future than the end of colonialism and the growth of "the new churches" in Africa and Asia. In those parts of the world the church had a Western face. Running through the council was a recurring, though badly understated, preoccupation with this issue and with what it now meant to be a "world-church," to use Karl Rahner's term. As any serious thinker at the council realized, the problem was very complex. The council faced it by laying out general norms and ideals.

For the new churches it recommended adaptation to local cultures, including philosophical and theological adaptation. It also recommended that Catholic missionaries seek ways of cooperating with missionaries of other faiths and of fostering harmonious relations with them. It asserted that art from every race and country be given scope in the liturgy of the church. More generally, it made clear that the church was sympathetic to the way of life of different peoples and races and was ready to appropriate non-superstitious aspects of different cultural traditions. Though obvious-sounding, these provisions were portentous. Where would they lead?

This issue, crucially important in its own right, is also an aspect of the three issues-under-the-issues. It is, for instance, a radical *aggiornamento,* a call for taking account of a significant change in something that happened, seemingly overnight, in society at large. It implies and almost demands greater autonomy of the periphery not only in decision-making but also in the process of adaptation, which can be effectively done only by those on the scene. If the adaptation to local culture is carried through, even on a superficial level, it implies new relational models, models surely different from the legislative and judicial traditions of the West.

Thus we come back to the three across-the-board issues. At the council the leading protagonists on both sides came to Vatican II with different

Conclusion

theological and cultural sensitivities and with different expectations or hopes for the outcome. They clashed over specific issues, underneath which lay the three more general and fundamental ones. The first was how the church would deal with change. By its own definition the Christian church is a conservative society whose essential mission is to pass on by word and deed a message received long ago. If it adulterates the message or loses sight of it, it has lost its soul, its reason for existence. Yet the church has in one form or another recognized that the message is not an abstraction above and beyond the human beings who first received it or the human beings who have interpreted and passed it on through the centuries. Thus the message entered the historical process, and thus it to some extent became subject to change. By definition a transcendent message, it also by definition is meant for men and women of all times and cultures and so must be made meaningful for them.

That is in the simplest terms the agreed-upon framework in which the issue played itself out in various ways over the course of the four periods between 1962 and 1965. The issue did not become acute for Christians until the long nineteenth century, when historical methods transformed all branches of sacred learning and made scholars keenly aware of the many discrepancies in the Christian tradition between past and present. By the time the council opened, a number of Catholic scholars, largely from northern Europe, had been deeply affected by this development, whereas others, largely from southern Europe, had been less influenced by it and even resisted it. The latter were nonetheless aware that the doctrines of the Immaculate Conception of Mary and her Assumption, for instance, could not be found in explicit or at least literal terms in early Christian writings. Change was, therefore, also an issue for them.

It was almost inevitable that the issue would emerge at the council. Pope John essentially put it on the agenda by describing the council's purpose in part as an updating, an *aggiornamento,* and by saying in his opening address that, though the message of the church is the same, the way it is presented may need to be changed. All the council fathers could agree with those words, but the leaders of the future majority took them as an encouragement for their enterprise.

Aggiornamento, development, *ressourcement*—those were the three categories the council wrestled with, often unwittingly, in this first of the three issues-under-the-issues. They are synonyms for change and in the council often euphemisms for it. They can be taken as synonyms—and euphemisms—for reform. Vatican II thus falls under the rubric of a reform council.

Of the three categories, development (and its close equivalents like evolution and progress) was the least threatening because it inserted change into an unfolding continuity. Yet even amid this continuity change was at its core. The word "change" stuck in the throats of bishops at the council, and it stuck in the throat of Paul VI. Nonetheless, the council frequently employed change-implied words and did so to such a degree that they became part of its most characteristic vocabulary. They suggested that even the final documents of the council were not final in the sense of establishing an end-point beyond which there would be no further movement.

Taken together, *aggiornamento,* development, and *ressourcement* plunge us into the dynamics of the council. Updating as such was not a problem to either party. It became a problem only in terms of its limits (how far could it legitimately go?) and its pastoral appropriateness (would it accomplish what it promised?). Often in the council, therefore, updating was implicitly or explicitly invoked for a change without dissenting voices being raised. In the decree On the Life and Ministry of Priests, nobody objected to the abolition of the benefice system for clerical recompense. Times had changed. Should the council change just-war teaching because of changed times? Here the bishops differed sharply among themselves, with Ottaviani categorically in favor of radical *aggiornamento* and many "Transalpines" opposed to it or waffling. What is peculiar to Vatican II, however, is the scope given to updating and the admission of it as a broad principle rather than as a rare exception.

During the council bishops and theologians sometimes invoked "development" to cover almost any kind of change, but it specifically meant, as mentioned, an unfolding of something already present implicitly or in germ. As with updating, both parties recognized and embraced development as a legitimate and necessary category. The minority objected to development only when invoked, as in the declaration On Religious Liberty, to justify a change that seemed not to further but to contradict the direction in which church teaching had been heading. In this case, in fact, *ressourcement* better captured the process being used.

Ressourcement, though a neologism, expressed a recurring pattern in Western cultural and ecclesiastical life from the eleventh century forward, as is suggested by its near-synonym, renaissance. It advocated skipping over what was currently in place to retrieve from the past something more appropriate or more authentic. The impulse to return to the sources drove much of the historical research in sacred subjects during the long nineteenth century. The conviction that the past held information and norms applicable to the present imbued the historical quest with its energy. From the middle of the nineteenth century forward the phenomenon, certainly not new, became widespread in Catholicism.

The three ways of dealing with change all played roles in Vatican II, where sometimes two (or all three) were in play at once, as is explicit in the decree On Religious Life, *Perfectae Caritatis:* "The up-to-date renewal of religious life comprises a constant return both to the sources of Christian life and to the primitive inspiration of the institutes and their adaptation to the changed conditions of our times."

Of the three categories, *ressourcement* was the most traditional yet potentially the most radical. It was also the most pervasive at the council. It undergirded the constitution On the Sacred Liturgy. The fundamental principle of the liturgical reform was the participation of the whole assembly in the sacred action, a principle derived from ancient liturgical practice. Restoring the dignity of the first part of the Mass, the Liturgy of the Word, was similarly derived. And so forth. The application of such principles to the present, the *aggiornamento,* was a consequence, not the starting point.

Other examples abound. The decree On Ecumenism begins with hope for the "restoration" of Christian unity that prevailed before the Reformation. In the contested passages of the constitution On Divine Revelation, *Dei Verbum,* over the Scripture/Tradition relationship, the majority wanted to recapture modes of thinking that predated the sixteenth-century controversies. When further on the document encouraged the reading of Scripture as the primary source of Christian piety, it wanted to overcome Catholic suspicions of the practice generated in that same era. In the declaration On Religious Liberty, it retrieved and refashioned for its purpose the old teachings on the free character of the act of faith and on the primacy of conscience in moral decision-making.

With chapter three of the constitution On the Church, *Lumen Gentium,* a special case, the rest of the constitution tried to reproduce ways of thinking and talking about the church that prevailed before the burgeoning of the discipline of canon law and the creation of the Scholastic method in the High Middle Ages and, as well, before the polemics on the nature of the church during the Reformation era. In so doing it substituted the more rhetorical and poetic language of the theologians of the first millennium for the more juridical, political, and agonistic language that bit by bit had taken over ecclesiological discourse.

No instance of *ressourcement* was more central to the drama of Vatican II and to its aspirations than collegiality. Proponents of collegiality at the council saw it as a recovery of an aspect of church life increasingly sidelined in the West since the eleventh century. It had been virtually pushed off the ecclesiastical map by the ways the definition of papal primacy of Vatican I had been interpreted and implemented. Yet, though the church had never officially defined collegiality as part of its constitution, for centuries it had taken it for granted as its normal mode of operation. The church of the first millennium functioned collegially, as no one at the council proclaimed more effectively than Maximos, and in local councils and other ways the collegial mode continued to function even in the West well into the modern period.

Collegiality brings us to the heart of the second issue-under-the-issues, the relationship between center and periphery. Yet it is impossible adequately to speak of collegiality without at the same time speaking of *ressourcement*. To speak of it, moreover, is implicitly to raise the third issue-under-the-issues, the style in which the church operates. Collegiality tellingly manifests the intimate relationship among the three issues-under-the-issues.

Collegiality's claim to legitimacy at Vatican II surely did not surface independently of political developments in the postwar years. Christian Democracy in its parliamentary forms flourished, with the blessings of both Pius XII and John XXIII. Both these popes spoke eloquently about how participation in the political process accorded with human dignity. Collegiality had much better claims for consideration at Vatican II than being a species of *aggiornamento* in tune with the politics of the contemporary West, but it nonetheless enjoyed an affinity with "the signs of the times."

Ressourcement and development locked horns over collegiality and did battle over it. In the West, papal primacy "developed" incrementally in a steady and almost continuous line up until the long nineteenth century, when it accelerated at (for the church) almost breathtaking speed—papal definitions of the Immaculate Conception and the Assumption, the growth and increasing authority exercised by the Roman Congregations, the devolution of the appointment of bishops almost exclusively into the hands of the pope, and, of course, in 1870 the definitions of papal primacy and infallibility.

By contrast, collegiality had not "developed" in the West through the centuries. It had gradually atrophied. Popes paid lip service to the idea even in the long nineteenth century, when they addressed their encyclicals to their "venerable brothers," the bishops, and diocesan and provincial synods were occasionally held. The atrophying process had set in, however, long before. Now a process of *ressourcement* had retrieved it. Its proponents placed it side by side with papal primacy as defined by Vatican I and packaged the two of them as compatible, as to a large extent they had been in a much earlier era. In their view collegiality was, indeed, an enhancement of papal primacy and an aid to its proper functioning.

The minority did not buy it. This kind of a *ressourcement,* despite all the fine words of the majority, seemed to them to limit the solemn definitions of Vatican I and to threaten the way the church operated in the center. Collegiality was unworkable, unacceptable, dangerous, and perhaps even heretical. It was "a novelty." To them it smacked of Conciliarism, which popes had solemnly condemned. It smacked of Gallicanism, which popes had also solemnly condemned. The minority bishops opposed collegiality (as they understood the majority to describe it) most pointedly, however, because it was incompatible with papal primacy. Since they often seemed to understand primacy in Bismarck's terms as an absolute monarchy possessing all authority in the church, which it doled out or recalled at will, primacy and collegiality were by definition irreconcilable. The minority opposed collegiality, therefore, on sincerely held theological and logical grounds, yet it is no accident that some leaders among them were from the Curia or associated with it. They worked in and for the center.

The majority at the council certainly did not press for a statement on collegiality merely to make a theological point. They brought it to the fore, like other *ressourcements,* because it had practical ramifications. The bishops who promoted the doctrine and fought for it so passionately wanted to redress what they saw as the imbalance between the authority exercised especially by the Roman Congregations and their own authority as heads of "local churches." Collegiality was the supreme instance in the council of the effort to moderate the centralizing tendencies of the ecclesiastical institution, of the effort to give those from the periphery a more authoritative voice not only back home but also in the center.

Although the statements in various documents insisting on the authority of episcopal conferences to regulate affairs on the local or regional level validated an institution already functioning in many parts of the church, they reasserted and tried to strengthen the autonomy of such groups. This was another effort to counter centripetal forces. The decree On the Pastoral Office of Bishops in the Church quite properly contains the longest statement on the authority inherent in the conferences, but it received similar affirmation in other documents. The constitution On the Sacred Liturgy, for example, stated that, while oversight of the liturgy belongs in the last instance to the Holy See, it belongs in the first instance to episcopal conferences in various parts of the world, a provision especially welcome to the "new churches."

Making the same centrifugal point in different terms, the constitution On the Church notes that bishops "are not to be regarded as vicars of the Roman Pontiff, for they exercise the power they possess in their own right." The bishops are not branch managers of local offices of the Holy See. Their exercise of power out of authority intrinsic to their office was a corollary to the doctrine of episcopal ordination. That corollary explains in large part why the minority was so fiercely opposed to the doctrine.

The documents tend, however, to be soft-spoken on the center-periphery relationship. They qualify the authority of episcopal conferences with references to the authority of the Holy See. In the council the relationship between bishops and the Curia is developed only once, in a short paragraph in the decree On the Pastoral Office of Bishops in the Church. The passage gives no hint at the intensity of the bishops' feelings on this topic and is a good example of how deceptive the placid surface of the documents can be. It is not the documents, therefore, that reveal how hot the issue was but the narrative of the battles for control of the council itself.

In that regard Cardinal Ottaviani's stance regarding the prerogatives of his Doctrinal Commission, which he regarded as operating with papal mandate and hence not responsible to the debates on the floor, is the most striking example early on in the council of precisely what galvanized his opponents and what they wanted to change. Collegiality was not, however, only a teaching geared to modifying the church's central operating mechanisms. It grounded a wider and broader goal of the council that radiated out from it.

Collegiality was symptomatic of a more general trend to promote collegial relationships throughout the church, as for instance the decrees

On Bishops and On the Life and Ministry of Priests indicated by calling for the creation by bishops of diocesan councils or senates in which the priests would cooperate in the government of the diocese. While the documents insisted that the relationship between the bishop and his priests is hierarchical, the priests are, still, consistently described as his collaborators. The bishop should regard them as "brothers and friends." Pius X forbade priests to meet together except with the bishop's explicit and rarely given permission, whereas the decree On the Life and Ministry of Priests encouraged precisely the opposite. This decree as well as the decree On the Apostolate of the Laity encouraged the participation of the laity, along with priests and religious, in councils of various kinds on the parish, diocesan, and national levels.

The center-periphery issue thus blends into the style issue, though the latter is much broader. With what style does the church communicate and operate? How does it present itself, and how does it "do business?" What is its personality? The style of the documents of Vatican II is what at first glance as well as most profoundly sets it apart from all other councils. During the council bishops, following the orientation from John XXIII, consistently and repeatedly described the council as pastoral in nature, and they sought a style for the documents to conform to it. The leaders of the majority came to the council with a clear idea that the style was to be biblical and patristic, and by the second period they had won their point.

To describe the style simply as "pastoral," however, is to miss this important specificity and thereby to miss the profound implications of the genre and vocabulary the council most characteristically used to convey its message. The adoption of the new style, which was really an old style, was the most far-reaching of the many *ressourcements* in which the council engaged. At the same time it was a repudiation of other styles and of the model derived in the early Christian centuries from political institutions of the Roman Empire.

A style choice is an identity choice, a personality choice, a choice in this instance about the kind of institution the council wanted the church to be. The fathers chose to praise the positive aspects of Catholicism and establish the church's identity on that basis rather than by making Catholicism look good by making others look bad. In this way and in others the style shift expressed and promoted a shift in values and priorities. The shift in style as proposed in Vatican II thus entailed changing behavioral patterns, but the change in those patterns, as in the adoption of dialogue as a preferred mode of discourse, was not a technique or a strategy but an outward expression of the adoption of an inner pattern of values. Style, sometimes misunderstood as merely an ornament of speech, an outer garment adorning a thought, is really the ultimate expression of meaning. The "what" of speech and the "how" of speech are inseparable.

The first element in the style shift was the substitution of a rhetorical form for the judicial and legislative forms that had characterized previous councils. In this new style canons, anathemas, and verdicts of guilty-as-charged found no place. The Roman Synod of 1960, the "dress rehearsal" for Vatican II, issued 755 canons. The council, which ended just five years later, issued not a single one.

The documents of the council, of course, contain provisions for the implementation of its decisions and are concrete in detailing the hoped-for outcomes. The constitution On the Sacred Liturgy, for instance, lays down clear norms for liturgical revisions. But in general the final documents are more intent on winning inner assent to truths and values and on raising appreciation for them. To a large extent they engage in a rhetoric of praise and congratulation.

The vocabulary employed by the form is the key to unlocking what is at stake. Although it becomes more pronounced in the documents approved at later stages in the council, it is, under the circumstances, remarkably consistent throughout. Although the words can be divided into categories like horizontal-words, equality-words, reciprocity-words, interiority-words, change-words, empowerment-words, and others, they evince an emotional kinship among themselves and, along with the literary genre in which they are encased, imbue Vatican II with a literary unity unique among councils. In this way they express an overall orientation and a coherence in values and outlook that markedly contrast with those of previous councils and, indeed, with most official ecclesiastical documents up to that point. Vatican II, a language-event.

Among the words are brothers/sisters, friendship, cooperation, collaboration, partnership, freedom, dialogue, pilgrim, servant ("king"), development, evolution, charism, dignity, holiness, conscience, collegiality, people of God, priesthood of all believers. Liberty, equality, and fraternity as well as other formerly unwelcome guests knocked at the door and gained entrance to the feast. A simple pairing of the models implied by this vocabulary with the models it replaced or balanced conveys the import of this third issue-under-the-issues. It suggests, indeed, that at stake were almost two different visions of Catholicism: from commands to invitations, from laws to ideals, from definition to mystery, from threats to persuasion, from coercion to conscience, from monologue to dialogue, from ruling to serving, from withdrawn to integrated, from vertical to horizontal, from exclusion to inclusion, from hostility to friendship, from rivalry to partnership, from suspicion to trust, from static to ongoing, from passive acceptance to active engagement, from fault-finding to appreciation, from prescriptive to principled, from behavior modification to inner appropriation.

The values that these words express are anything but new to the Christian tradition. They are as common in Christian discourse, or more common, than their opposite numbers. But they are not common in councils, especially as framed in an epideictic or panegyric genre. Vatican II did not invent the words or imply that they were not already operative in the church. Yet, taken as a whole, they convey the sweep of a newly and forcefully specified style of the church that the Second Vatican Council held up for contemplation, admiration, and actualization.

In promoting those values the council did not deny the validity of the contrasting values. No institution can, for instance, be simply open-ended. Sooner or later decision is required. No institution can be all-inclusive. Most especially, if Vatican II is innovative for the pervasive emphasis it placed on horizontal relationships, it is also noteworthy for its correlative insistence on the vertical. That this insistence on the vertical sometimes seems obsessive was a result of the relentless drumbeat of the minority, but the majority never intended to deny or undermine the principle of hierarchical structure. It was seeking not displacement but modulation and balance.

Despite the way leaders at the council sometimes expressed themselves, they fully realized that Vatican II as a self-proclaimed pastoral council was for that reason also a teaching council. Vatican II taught many things, but few more important than the style of relationships that was to prevail in the church. Its style of discourse was the medium that conveyed the message. It did not, therefore, "define" the teaching but taught it on almost every page through the form and vocabulary it adopted. In so doing it issued an implicit call for a change in style—a style less autocratic and more collaborative, a style willing to seek out and listen to different viewpoints and to take them into account, a style eager to find common ground with "the other," a style open and above board, a style less unilateral in its decision-making, a style committed to fair play and to working with persons and institutions outside the Catholic community, a style that assumes innocence until guilt is proven, a style that eschews secret oaths, anonymous denunciations, and inquisitorial tactics. The majority believed that Pope John XXIII pointed to something along that line when in his opening allocution to the council on October 11, 1962, he said that the church should act by "making use of the medicine of mercy rather than severity . . . and by showing herself to be the loving mother of all, benign, patient, full of mercy and goodness."

The style is thus values-expressive. In passage after passage values appreciative of "the other," for instance, mark the discourse of the council, as when the declaration On Non-Christian Religions, *Nostra Aetate,* speaks of Hinduism and Buddhism: "The Catholic Church rejects nothing of what is true and holy in these religions. She has a high regard for the manner of life and conduct, the precepts and doctrines that, although differing in many ways from her own, nevertheless often reflect the ray of the truth that enlightens all human beings."

The familiar passage on conscience in the constitution On the Church in the Modern World takes us into another aspect of the style shift, which emphasizes obedience not to external authority but to a higher norm:

> Deep within their consciences men and women discover a law that they have not laid upon themselves but which they must obey. Its voice, ever calling them to love and to do what is good and to avoid what is evil, tells them inwardly at the right moment: do this, shun that. For they have in their hearts a law inscribed by God. Their dignity lies in observing this law, and by it they will be judged. . . . By conscience that law is made known in a wonderful way that is fulfilled in love for God and for one's neighbor. Through loyalty to conscience Christians are joined to others in the search for truth and for the right solution to so many moral problems that arise both in the lives of individuals and in social relationships.

Consonant with obeying the dictates of one's conscience is the political freedom that allows one to do so. Thus such freedom enters into the vocabulary of Vatican II as a good to be cherished and secured, as the opening words of the declaration On Religious Liberty, *Dignitatis Humanae,* enjoin:

> The dignity of the human person is a concern of which people of our time are becoming increasingly more aware. In growing numbers people demand that they should enjoy the use of their own responsible judgment and freedom and decide on their actions on grounds of duty and conscience, without external pressure or coercion. They also urge that bounds be set to government by law, so that the limits of reasonable freedom should not be too tightly drawn for persons or for social groups. This demand in human society for freedom is chiefly concerned with the values of the human spirit, above all with the free and public practice of religion.

Not alienation from others but a search for communion with them, a quest for mutual understanding, and the prospect of working together for the common good—all great themes of the council—are powerfully suggested by the opening words of the constitution On the Church in the Modern World, *Gaudium et Spes:* "The joy and hope, the grief and anguish of the men and women of our times, especially those who are poor or afflicted in any way, are the joy and hope, the grief and affliction of the followers of Christ as well. Nothing that is genuinely human fails to find an echo in their hearts."

Although passages like these can be found in other documents of the council, the sentiments expressed in them are found most typically in three of the most hotly contested texts—*Nostra Aetate, Dignitatis Humanae,* and *Gaudium et Spes.* As objected to by the minority, they thus bring us back to the center-periphery issue. Insofar as the style, genre, and sentiments are reminiscent of biblical and patristic sources, they bring us back to *ressourcement.* Again, the three issues-under-the-issues are three different ways of looking at Vatican II that reveal the remarkable coherence of the council's final product—the sixteen official constitutions, decrees, and declarations—despite the compromises, ambiguities, misleading euphemisms, stylistic infelicities, and the hundreds of specific issues that abound in them and sometimes look like clutter.

Therefore, though the documents have many and obvious weaknesses, in their most characteristic expression they pertain to a literary genre and evince a sometimes inelegant literary unity. Unlike the texts of previous councils, to say nothing of the Roman Synod of 1960, the documents of Vatican II are not a grab-bag of ordinances. They implicitly cross-reference one another. They are coherent with one another and play off one another.

Each of them echoes, specifies, qualifies, or enlarges on themes, values, and principles found in other documents. In this way, through this intertextual process, an implicit but nonetheless powerful and pervasive paradigm, different from what previously prevailed, was in the making. Recognition of the intertextual character of the sixteen documents is therefore the first step in uncovering the paradigm and therefore an essential step in constructing a hermeneutic for interpreting the council.

For the first time in history, a council would take care self-consciously to infuse its documents with vocabulary and themes that cut across them all. In that sense Vatican II conveyed a "spirit." When properly examined, "the letter" (form and vocabulary) reveals "the spirit." In revealing the spirit it reveals not a momentary effervescence but a consistent and verifiable reorientation. And for understanding the biggest meeting in the history of the world nothing, of course, is more important than grasping that reorientation.

Among the recurring themes of the council expressive of its spirit, the call to holiness is particularly pervasive and particularly important. It is a theme that the new genre and vocabulary allowed to surface, just as the more juridical vocabulary of previous councils had inhibited it. It is the theme that to a large extent imbued the council with its finality. If the call to holiness is what the church is about, as the constitution On the Church indicates, then it is not surprising that that is what the council to a large extent was about. Behind the many *ressourcements* of the long nineteenth century lay the persuasion that the past held treasures useful for the present, not so much as knowledge for its own sake but as guides to deeper and more authentic Christian living. While those *ressourcements* strove to be academically rigorous, their energy derived from the belief that they had pastoral implications, that they were helpful to the human spirit. The call to holiness did not appear out of nowhere.

In its general orientation, as articulated especially in its most characteristic vocabulary, the council devised a profile of the ideal Christian. That ideal, drawn in greatest length in *Gaudium et Spes,* is more incarnational than eschatological, closer to Thomas Aquinas than to Karl Barth, more reminiscent of the Fathers of the Eastern Church than of Augustine—

more inclined to reconciliation with human culture than to alienation from it, more inclined to see goodness than sin, more inclined to speaking words of friendship and encouragement than of indictment. The style choice fostered a theological choice.

The result was a message that was traditional while at the same time radical, prophetic while at the same time soft-spoken. In a world increasingly wracked with discord, hatred, war, and threats of war, the result was a message that was counter-cultural while at the same time responsive to the deepest human yearnings. Peace on earth. Good will to men.

The council was about much more, then, than a handful of superficial adjustments of the Catholic Church to the modern world, about much more than changes in liturgical forms, and certainly about much more than the power plays of prominent churchmen. No later than the middle of the second period of the council, 1963, the majority aimed high at what it hoped to accomplish. The council was to be something more than an inconsequential blip on the ecclesiastical radar screen. Whether the centuries to come will judge it in expansive terms is, however, far from clear today.

On the final outcome of the council the minority left more than a set of fingerprints, which means that it left its mark on the three issues-under-the-issues. On the center-periphery issue the minority never really lost control. It was in that regard so successful that with the aid of Paul VI the center not only held firm and steady but, as the decades subsequent to the council have irrefutably demonstrated, emerged even stronger. From the outset the contest was unequal. The council was held in the center, named for the center, operated to a large extent with the equipment of the center, and was destined to be interpreted and implemented by the center. The creation of the Synod of Bishops severed collegiality, the doctrine empowering the periphery, from institutional grounding. The "Preliminary Explanatory Note," whatever its correct interpretation, certainly did not strengthen the statement on collegiality in chapter three in the constitution On the Church. Collegiality, the linchpin in the center-periphery relationship promoted by the majority, ended up an abstract teaching without point of entry into the social reality of the church. It ended up an ideal, no match for the deeply entrenched system.

The three issues are interdependent. As one goes, so go the others. The crisis in the council and afterward over a possible weakening of the center's teaching on birth control graphically displayed that interconnectedness.

The crisis engaged how the church deals with the past, in this instance with past papal pronouncements. It therefore immediately implicated the authority of the center, which almost predetermined the style of finding a solution to the problem. Even before the council ended in 1965, there was a discrepancy between what the bishops hoped they had accomplished and what had happened. The majority was consistently frustrated in its efforts to make its will felt through the establishment of real structural changes. It sometimes seemed to think that winning the affirmation of certain principles in the face of opposition to them would ensure their implementation.

By their very nature the three issues do not in practice admit final and absolute resolution. Attempting such a resolution would in the long run spell disaster. Nations are among the many social entities that must deal with these issues, and their histories illustrate how the pendulum swings back and forth over time—a stricter or looser construction of the nation's constitution, greater or lesser attention to regional needs and demands, a more militant or more cordial international stance. But does the same rule apply for the large, complex, long-lived, and international institution that is the Catholic Church? That is the big question that only the future can answer.

It is, in any case, to this level of generalization that my presentation of the Second Vatican Council has brought us. Although I have reduced the narrative to its bare bones and have simplified the issues to make them correspond to the narrative's pace, what nevertheless must now be clear is the council's massive complexity and therefore the complexity of saying anything valid about it that does not die the death of a thousand qualifications.

Yet as this book has shown, it is possible to move beyond specific issues, to move beyond proof-texting techniques that lift sentences or paragraphs out of context, to move beyond loaded labels like conservative/reactionary and progressive/liberal, which are the ways the council has until now consistently been approached and interpreted. I have tried to show that it is possible to move beyond those approaches to arrive at generalizations about the council grounded in its narrative contexts and in the vast expanse of the documentation it has left behind. In order to arrive at such generalizations, I devised out of the same narrative and documentation some categories of analysis and interpretation, a hermeneutic, and much of the burden of the book has been to validate those categories.

That is the scope and burden of this book. I hope that it has rendered persuasive both the generalizations and the categories through which I arrived at them. I hope, more fundamentally, that the accomplishment of the book has been to render a little clearer what happened—and what did not happen—at the Second Vatican Council.

Chronology of Vatican II

1958–1960

October 9, 1958	Pius XII dies
October 28, 1958	John XXIII elected
January 25, 1959	John announces the council
May 17, 1959	John establishes Ante-Preparatory Commission under Cardinal Domenico Tardini
June 5, 1960	John establishes the Preparatory Commissions, *Superno Dei Nutu*

1962

October 11	Council opens. John's allocution *Gaudet Mater Ecclesia*
October 13	Elections to council commissions postponed to allow for consultation within episcopal conferences
October 22	John raises Secretariat for Christian Unity to status of commission
November 14	Draft of constitution On the Sacred Liturgy approved
November 20–21	Draft of schema On Sources of Revelation rejected and mixed commission established
December 4	Cardinal Suenens's intervention: church looking inward and looking outward to be the focal point of council

December 6	John announces creation of Coordinating Commission
December 8	First period ends

1963

March	John establishes the Papal Commission on Birth Control
April 11	John XXIII's encyclical *Pacem in Terris* published
June 3	John XXIII dies
June 21	Pope Paul VI elected
September 21	Paul addresses Curia and announces its future reform
September 29	Second period opens. Revised "Regulations" establishing four moderators to guide General Congregations
October 16	Crisis over legitimacy of previously scheduled vote on crucial aspects of schema On the Church
October 30	Crisis resolved, but legitimacy of vote continues to be challenged
November 18	Schema On Ecumenism (including Jews and Religious Liberty) introduced
December 4	Second period ends. Paul announces pilgrimage to Holy Land. On the Divine Liturgy, On Mass Communication promulgated

1964

January 4–6	Paul VI in Holy Land. Meetings with Patriarch Athenagoras
May 19	Felici informs Doctrinal Commission of thirteen "suggestions" from Paul VI, the first of such interventions by the pope
June 23	Paul announces to cardinals the existence of the Papal Commission on Birth Control
September 13	Paul receives letter signed by twenty-five cardinals (and others) warning him of the dangers of collegiality
September 14	Third period opens
September 21	Four presentations on chapter three (collegiality, etc.) of constitution On the Church
September 23	Debate opens on declaration On Religious Liberty
September 28	Debate opens on declaration On the Jews and Non-Christian Religions (introduced by Bea three days earlier)
September 30	Chapter three of On the Church approved overwhelmingly. Revised schema On Divine Revelation introduced
October 9	Secretariat for Christian Unity startled by new procedures for dealing with the two controversial schema. Crisis resolved a few days later.

October 20	Schema On the Church in the Modern World introduced
October 23	First of three announcements that council was not to treat birth control
November 6	Paul VI appears at the General Congregation to speak in favor of the schema On Missionary Activity
November 16–20	Troubled last week: (1) Preliminary Note for chapter three of On the Church; (2) last-minute papal amendments to On Ecumenism; (3) postponement of vote On Religious Liberty
November 21	Third period ends. Paul announces Mary as Mother of the Church. On the Church, On the Catholic Eastern Churches, On Ecumenism promulgated
December 2–5	Paul VI in India for Eucharistic Congress

1965

September 14	Fourth period opens. Paul announces forthcoming visit to UN. With *Apostolica Sollicitudo* Paul VI establishes the Synod of Bishops
September 21	Declaration On Religious Liberty approved
October 4	Paul addresses UN, celebrates Mass in Yankee Stadium
October 11	Paul forbids discussion of celibacy
October 14–15	Declaration on Non-Christian Religions approved
October 28	Public Session. On Pastoral Office of Bishops, On Renewal of Religious Life, On Christian Education, On Training of Priests, On Non-Christian Religions promulgated
November 18	Public Session. On Divine Revelation, On Apostolate of Laity promulgated
November 24	Paul VI insists that subcommission on family for schema On the Church in the Modern World explicitly condemn birth control
December 4	Paul VI leads a service with observers/guests at St. Paul's Outside the Walls
December 7	Ceremonies in St. Peter's in which the excommunications of 1054 between Latins and Greeks are lifted. Promulgation of On Religious Liberty, On Missionary Activity, On Ministry and Life of Priests, On the Church in the Modern World
December 8	Solemn closing of the council in the piazza of St. Peter's

 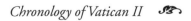

Council Participants
Frequently Mentioned

Agagianian, Grégoire-Pierre (1895–1971), cardinal, prefect of the Congregation for the Propagation of the Faith *(De Propaganda Fide);* member of the Central Preparatory Commission; during the council a moderator and president of the Commission on Missions.

Alfrink, Jan Bernard (1900–1987), cardinal-archbishop of Utrecht, member of the Central Preparatory Commission, member of the Council of Presidents; a leader of the majority.

Arriba y Castro, Benjamin de (1886–1973), cardinal-archbishop of Tarragona (Spain), important spokesman for the Spanish bishops.

Bea, Augustin (1881–1968), cardinal, German Jesuit, former rector of the Biblicum (1930–1949), member of Central Preparatory Commission and president of the Secretariat for Christian Unity; an important leader of the majority.

Benedict XVI, Pope. See Ratzinger, Joseph.

Browne, Michael (1887–1971), cardinal, Irish Dominican, former rector of the Angelicum (Dominican theological school in Rome) and then Master General of the Dominicans (1955–1962), member of the Preparatory Commission on Bishops, vice president of the Doctrinal Commission; a leader of the minority.

Bugnini, Annibale (1912–1982), Italian liturgist, professor at the Lateran University, secretary of the Preparatory Commission on the Liturgy, council *peritus*, in 1964 named secretary of the *Consilium* to apply *Sacrosanctum Concilium*.

Carli, Luigi (1914–1986), bishop of Segni (Italy), member of the Commission on Bishops, a leader of the minority and member of the Group of International Fathers, the *Coetus*, for which he became a major spokesman.

Cento, Fernando (1883–1973), cardinal, former nuncio to Belgium (1946–1953), member of the Central Preparatory Commission, president of the Commission on the Apostolate of the Laity and, with Cardinal Ottaviani, of the mixed commission (Doctrine and Laity) for *Gaudium et Spes*.

Charue, André-Marie (1898–1977), bishop of Namur (Belgium), in October 1962 elected to the Doctrinal Commission, of which he became a vice president in late 1963.

Chenu, Marie-Dominique (1895–1990), French Dominican, theologian/historian specializing in medieval Scholasticism, professor at Le Saulchoir, the Dominican House of Studies, a founder of "la nouvelle théologie," during the council theological adviser of Bishop Claude Rolland of Antsirabé, Madagascar, his former student.

Cicognani, Amleto Giovanni (1883–1973), Italian cardinal, apostolic delegate to the United States for twenty-five years (1933–1958), secretary of state (1961–1969), prefect of the Congregation for the Oriental Churches, member of the Central Preparatory Commission, president of the Preparatory Commission on the Oriental Churches, president of the council's Commission on the Oriental Churches, president of the Coordinating Commission (brother of Cardinal Gaetano Cicognani, president of the Preparatory Commission on the Liturgy, who died in 1962).

Colombo, Carlo (1909–1991), priest from Milan, theological advisor to Paul VI, consultant for Preparatory Theological Commission, made auxiliary bishop of Milan in 1964 (not to be confused with Cardinal Giovanni Colombo, who succeeded Montini as archbishop of Milan).

Congar, Yves-Marie (1904–1995), French Dominican, professor of theology at Le Saulchoir, author of many influential books before the council, censured after the encyclical *Humani Generis*, consultant for the Preparatory Theological Commission, council *peritus* serving on several commissions, made cardinal in 1994, the year before his death.

Daniélou, Jean (1905–1974), French Jesuit theologian, early promoter of "la nouvelle théologie," founder with Henri de Lubac of the important series of texts entitled *Sources Chrétiennes*, dean of the Theological Faculty of the Institut Catholique de Paris from 1963 to 1969, council *peritus*, made cardinal in 1969.

Dearden, John F. (1907–1988), archbishop of Detroit, head of the subcommission on the controversial section, marriage, in the constitution On the Church in the Modern World, created cardinal by Paul VI in 1969.

De Smedt, Émile-Joseph (1909–1995), bishop of Bruges, vice president of the Secretariat for Christian Unity, important spokesman in the council for the Secretariat, especially for the declaration On Religious Liberty.

Döpfner, Julius (1913–1976), cardinal-archbishop of Munich, member of the Central Preparatory Commission, member of the Coordinating Commission, moderator, author of an early 1964 plan to reduce the number and size of the schemas.

Dossetti, Giuseppe (1913–1996), priest of the diocese of Bologna (ordained only in 1959), formerly vice secretary of the Italian Christian Democratic party, personal theological adviser of Cardinal Lercaro, for a short time in 1963 informal secretary to the four moderators, named council *peritus* for the last two periods, founder of the Istituto per le scienze religiose, Bologna, which under the directorship of the late Giuseppe Alberigo has since the council produced and published many important studies on Vatican II.

Etchegaray, Roger (1922–), French Basque priest, director of the pastoral Secretariat of the French Episcopal Conference, council *peritus* for last two periods, instrumental in the founding, early in the council, of the Conference of Delegates ("Conference of the Twenty-Two," or Domus Mariae Group), later cardinal-archbishop of Marseille.

Felici, Pericle (1911–1982), Italian canonist, made titular archbishop of Samosata in 1960, secretary of the Central Preparatory Commission, secretary of the Council, made cardinal in 1967.

Fenton, Joseph Clifford (1906–1969), American theologian at the Catholic University of America, editor of the *American Ecclesiastical Review,* adversary of John Courtney Murray, consultant for the Preparatory Theological Commission, council *peritus,* as was his colleague from the Catholic University, Francis Connell, who was also an adversary of Murray.

Florit, Ermenegildo (1901–1985), professor of Scripture at the Lateran University, then archbishop of Florence, member of the Preparatory Commission for Bishops and then of the Doctrinal Commission, made cardinal in 1965.

Franić, Frane (1912–2007), bishop of Split-Makaraska (Yugoslavia [Croatia]), member of the Preparatory Theological Commission and of the Doctrinal Commission, occasional spokesman for the minority.

Frings, Joseph (1887–1978), from 1942 archbishop of Cologne, member of the Central Preparatory Commission, member of the Council of Presidents, almost blind by the time the council opened, brought with him as personal advisor Joseph Ratzinger.

Frings was a powerful spokesman for the majority. His best-known intervention was his criticism of the Holy Office on November 8, 1963.

Guitton, Jean (1901–1999), French Catholic layman, philosopher/theologian, elected to the prestigious Académie Française in 1961, friend of Paul VI; named lay auditor by John XXIII during the first period, a year before others were appointed by Paul VI.

Haubtmann, Pierre (1912–1971), priest of the diocese of Grenoble (France), *peritus* beginning in 1963, in charge of the final writing of *Gaudium et Spes* and coordinator of the ten subcommissions working on it, aided in this task by the Jesuits Roberto Tucci and Johann Baptist Hirschmann and by canon Charles Moeller of Louvain.

John Paul II, Pope. See Wojtyła, Karol.

König, Franz (1905–2004), cardinal-archbishop of Vienna, member of Central Preparatory Commission, elected to Doctrinal Commission in October 1962, an important supporter of *Nostra Aetate,* named Karl Rahner his personal theologian for the council.

Larraona, Arcadio (1887–1973), Spanish cardinal, member of the Central Preparatory Commission, after the death of Cardinal Gaetano Cicognani in 1962 named prefect of the Congregation of Rites and president of the Liturgical Commission; a leader of the minority.

Lefebvre, Marcel (1905–1991), missionary in Africa, archbishop of Dakar (Senegal), in 1962 elected superior-general of the Holy Ghost Fathers, member of the Central Preparatory Commission, founding member of the Group/*Coetus* and hardcore member of the minority, notorious after the council for repudiating it and being excommunicated in 1988 for illicitly ordaining four bishops for his schismatic group (he is to be distinguished from Joseph Lefebvre, cardinal-archbishop of Bourges.)

Léger, Paul-Émile (1904–1991), cardinal-archbishop of Montreal, member of the Central Preparatory Commission, elected to the Doctrinal Commission in October 1962; a leader of the majority.

Lercaro, Giacomo (1891–1976), cardinal-archbishop of Bologna, thought to be *papabile* after the death of John XXIII, member of the Liturgical Commission, active in the "Church of the Poor" group, a moderator and member of the Coordinating Commission.

Liénart, Achille (1884–1973), cardinal-archbishop of Lille (France), president of French Episcopal Conference, member of the Central Preparatory Commission, member of the Council of Presidents and of the Coordinating Commission; important spokesman for the majority.

Lubac, Henri de (1896–1991), French Jesuit theologian, seriously wounded at the battle of Verdun in World War I and a member of the Resistance to the Nazis during World War II, a leading figure of "la nouvelle théologie," founder with Jean Daniélou of the important series of texts *Sources Chrétiennes,* censured after the encyclical *Humani Generis,* named an adviser to the Preparatory Theological Commission and then council *peritus,* made a cardinal in 1983.

Maritain, Jacques (1883–1973), French layman, philosopher, convert to Catholicism, well known on both sides of the Atlantic, not an official council participant in any capacity, but longtime friend of Paul VI whose influence was felt during the council in a number of ways.

Maximos IV Saigh (1878–1967), Melkite patriarch of Antioch (Syria) and leader of the Melkite bishops at the council, member of the Central Preparatory Commission, member of the Commission on the Oriental Churches, noted at the council for his outspoken comments, which he always delivered in French.

McIntyre, James Francis (1886–1979), cardinal-archbishop of Los Angeles, member of the Central Preparatory Commission, member of Commission on Bishops; though much in sympathy with the minority he intervened relatively infrequently during the council.

Meyer, Albert (1903–1965), cardinal-archbishop of Chicago, member of the Central Preparatory Commission, member of the Secretariat for Extraordinary Affairs and then of the Council of Presidents, generally favorable to the positions of the majority; with a doctorate in Sacred Scripture from the Biblicum, considered the intellectual among the American bishops.

Montini, Giovanni Battista (1897–1978), cardinal-archbishop of Milan, member of Central Preparatory Commission, elected pope as Paul VI in 1963.

Murray, John Courtney (1904–1967), American Jesuit theologian, expert on church-state relations, forbidden to write on the subject in 1955, named council *peritus* in 1963, influential in the writing of *Dignitatis Humanae.*

Ottaviani, Alfredo (1890–1979), Italian cardinal, secretary (head) of the Holy Office from 1959, member of the Central Preparatory Commission, president of the Preparatory Theological Commission and of the Doctrinal Commission; generally seen as the leading figure of the minority especially in the early phases of the council.

Parente, Pietro (1891–1986), assessor (secretary) of the Holy Office, severe critic of "la nouvelle théologie" in 1940s–1950s and possible author of or contributor to *Humani Generis,* member of the Central Preparatory Commission and of the Doctrinal Commission, important as a minority person favoring episcopal collegiality.

Pavan, Pietro (1903–1994), professor at the Lateran University, principal collaborator with John XXIII on the encyclical *Pacem in Terris,* consultant for the Central Preparatory Commission, council *peritus,* important for his work with Murray in the composition of *Dignitatis Humanae.*

Philips, Gérard (1899–1972), priest of the diocese of Liège (Belgium), theologian and professor at Louvain, consultant of the Preparatory Theological Commission, council *peritus,* one of most important theologians at the council, in particular for his work on *Lumen Gentium* and on the *Nota Explicativa Praevia* for it.

Prignon, Albert (1919–2000), rector of the Belgian College in Rome, confidant of Cardinal Suenens, and council *peritus* beginning in May 1963; his diary (fourth period only) is especially valuable for its account of his almost daily conversations with Suenens *(Journal conciliaire).*

Quiroga y Palacios, Fernando (1900–1971), cardinal-archbishop of Compostela (Spain), member of Central Preparatory Commission, member of Commission on the Oriental Churches.

Rahner, Karl (1904–1983), German Jesuit theologian, under suspicion before the council but named by John XXIII as consultant to the Preparatory Commission on the Sacraments, personal theologian of Cardinal König of Vienna, then named council *peritus.*

Ratzinger, Joseph (1927–), German theologian, professor at Bonn and then Münster, personal theologian of Cardinal Frings of Cologne and then council *peritus* beginning in 1963, among the more important of the younger theologians at the council, carrying considerable weight with the German bishops. Later cardinal and pope, Benedict XVI.

Ritter, Joseph Elmer (1892–1967), cardinal-archbishop of St. Louis, member of the Central Preparatory Commission, vice president of the Commission on Clerical Discipline; emerged as an American spokesman for the majority.

Roncalli, Angelo Giuseppe (1881–1963), elected pope in 1958 as John XXIII.

Ruffini, Ernesto (1888–1968), cardinal-archbishop of Palermo, member of the Central Preparatory Commission, member of the Council of Presidents; a notably frequent and strong spokesman for the minority.

Schillebeeckx, Edward (1914–), Belgian Dominican theologian, student of M.-D. Chenu at Le Saulchoir, at the time of the council, professor at the Catholic University in Nijmegen, the Netherlands, theological adviser to Cardinal Alfrink, never named a *peritus* but exercised influence through his relationships with the Dutch and Belgian episcopates and in other ways.

Sigaud, Geraldo Proença de (1909–1999), bishop of Diamantina (Brazil), a member of the Society of the Divine Word, a founder of the Group of International Fathers *(Coetus)* and a spokesman for its positions.

Siri, Giuseppe (1906–1989), cardinal-archbishop of Genoa, member of the Central Preparatory Commission, member of the Council of Presidents, highly respected in the Italian episcopate to the point of being considered *papabile;* a spokesman for the minority.

Spellman, Francis (1889–1967), cardinal-archbishop of New York, fervent supporter of the Vietnam War, a member of the Central Preparatory Commission, member of the Council of Presidents and of the Coordinating Commission, sided with the minority on many issues and at first tended to dominate the American episcopate.

Suenens, Léon-Joseph (1904–1996), cardinal-archbishop of Malines-Brussels, member of the Central Preparatory Commission and of the Coordinating Commission, a moderator, one of the most influential members of the council, a leader of the majority, proposed plan for the scope of the council in a crucial intervention on December 4, 1962.

Tisserant, Eugène (1884–1972), French cardinal, dean of the College of Cardinals, Archivist and Librarian of the Holy Roman Church, among the most learned of the entire episcopate (elected to the Académie Française in 1961), member of the Central Preparatory Commission, head of the Council of Presidents.

Tromp, Sebastian (1889–1975), Dutch Jesuit, professor at the Gregorian University in Rome, principal collaborator with Pius XII on the encyclical *Mystici Corporis,* secretary of the Preparatory Theological Commission and then of the Doctrinal Commission, council *peritus,* closely allied with Cardinal Ottaviani.

Urbani, Giovanni (1900–1968), cardinal-patriarch of Venice (successor there of John XXIII), member of the Coordinating Commission, occasional spokesman for Italian moderates.

Willebrands, Johannes (1909–2006), priest of the diocese of Haarlem (the Netherlands), active in ecumenical endeavors before the council, secretary of the Secretariat for Christian Unity, council *peritus* until made titular bishop in 1964, crucially important member of the Secretariat, made a cardinal in 1969.

Wojtyła, Karol (1920–2005), bishop (then archbishop, 1963) of Kraków, despite his youth a leader among the Polish bishops at the council, chief architect of a Polish alternative schema for On the Church in the Modern World, cardinal in 1967 and in 1978 pope, John Paul II.

Wyszyński, Stefan (1901–1981), primate of Poland, archbishop of Warsaw and

Gniezno, imprisoned and then placed under house arrest by the Communist government, 1953–1956, member of the Central Preparatory Commission, of the Secretariat for Extraordinary Affairs and then of the expanded Council of Presidents.

Zoghby, Elias (1912–2008), Melkite patriarchal vicar for Egypt (the See of Alexandria, Cairo, and the Sudan), imprisoned in 1954 by the Nasser regime because of his opposition to restrictions placed on Christians and kidnapped in 1982 by pro-Iranian terrorists; during the council made eleven interventions generally along the line set by Maximos IV.

Abbreviations

AAS	*Acta Apostolicae Sedis: Commentarium officiale* Vatican City: Typis Polyglottis Vaticanis, 1909–.
ADA	*Acta et Documenta Concilio Oecumenico Vaticano II Apparando. Series prima (Antepraeparatoria).* 12 vols, plus index and appendixes. Vatican City: Typis Polyglottis Vaticanis, 1960–1961.
ADP	*Acta et Documenta Concilio Oecumenico Vaticano II Apparando. Series secunda (Praeparatoria).* 7 vols. Vatican City: Typis Polyglottis Vaticanis, 1964–1969.
Alberigo/Komonchak, *History*	Giuseppe Alberigo and Joseph Komonchak, eds., *History of Vatican II,* 5 vols. Maryknoll, NY: Orbis, 1995–2006.
AS	*Acta Synodalia Sacrosancti Concilii Vaticani II.* 32 vols. Vatican City: Typis Polyglottis Vaticanis, 1970–1999.
Burigana, *Bibbia nel concilio*	Riccardo Burigana, *La Bibbia nel concilio: La redazione della costituzione "Dei verbum" del Vaticano II.* Bologna: Il Mulino, 1998.
Caprile, *Cronache*	Giovanni Caprile, ed., *Il Concilio Vaticano II: Cronache del Concilio Vaticano II.* 5 vols. in 6. Rome: Edizioni "La Civiltà Cattolica," 1966–1969.
Carlen, *Encyclicals*	Claudia Carlen, ed., *The Papal Encyclicals.* 5 vols. Wilmington, NC: McGrath Publishing Company, 1981.
Congar, *Mon journal*	Yves Congar, *Mon journal du concile,* ed. Eric Mahieu. 2 vols. Paris: Éditions du Cerf, 2002.
Deuxième concile	*Le deuxième concile du Vatican (1959–1965): Actes du colloque.* Rome: École française de Rome, 1989.

Doré, *Volti di fine concilio* Joseph Doré and Alberto Melloni, eds., *Volti di fine concilio: Studi di storia e teologia sulla conclusione del Vaticano II.* Bologna: Il Mulino, 2000.

Faggioli, *Vescovo e concilio* Massimo Faggioli, *Il vescovo e il concilio: Modello episcopale e aggiornamento al Vaticano II.* Bologna: Il Mulino, 2005.

Fattori, *Evento e decisioni* Maria Teresa Fattori and Alberto Melloni, eds., *L'evento e le decisioni: Studi sulle dinamiche del concilio Vaticano II.* Bologna: Il Mulino, 1997.

Fesquet, *Drama* Henri Fesquet, *The Drama of Vatican II: The Ecumenical Council, June 1962–December 1965,* trans. Bernard Murchland. New York: Random House, 1967.

Grootaers, *Actes et Acteurs* Jan Grootaers, *Actes et Acteurs à Vatican II.* Leuven: Leuven University Press, 1998.

Herders Kommentar *Herders theologischer Kommentar zum zweiten Vatikanischen Konzil,* ed. Peter Hünermann and Bernd Jochen Hilberath. 5. vols. Freiburg im Br.: Herder, 2004–2006.

John XXIII, *Pater amabilis* Angelo Giuseppe Roncalli–Giovanni XXIII, *Pater amabilis: Agende del pontefice, 1958–1963,* ed. Mauro Velati, Edizione nazionale dei diari di Angelo Giuseppe Roncalli–Giovanni XXIII, 7. Bologna: Istituto per le scienze religiose, 2007.

Lamberigts, *Commissions conciliaires* M. Lamberigts, Cl. Soetens, and J. Grootaers, eds. *Les Commissions conciliaires à Vatican II.* Leuven: Bibliotheek van de Faculteit Godgeleerdheid, 1996.

Melloni, *Cristianesimo nella storia* Alberto Meloni et al., eds., *Cristianesimo nella storia: Saggi in onore di Giuseppe Alberigo.* Bologna: Il Mulino, 1996.

Nolan, *Privileged Moment* Ann Michel Nolan, *A Privileged Moment: Dialogue in the Language of the Second Vatican Council, 1962–1965.* Bern: Peter Lang, 2006.

Paolo VI e l'ecumenismo *Paolo VI e l'ecumenismo: Colloquio internazionale di studio.* Brescia: Istituto Paolo VI, 2001.

Paolo VI, problemi ecclesiologici *Paolo VI e i problemi ecclesiologici al Concilio: Colloquio internazionale di studio.* Rome and Brescia: Edizioni Studium and Istituto Paolo VI, 1989.

Paul VI, *Insegnamenti* *Insegnamenti di Paolo VI.* 17 vols. Vatican City: Libreria Editrice Vaticana, 1965–1979.

Philips, *Carnets conciliaires* Gérard Philips, *Carnets conciliaires de Mgr. Gérard Philips, secrétaire adjoint de la commission doctrinale: Texte néerlandais avec traduction française et commentaires,* ed. and trans. K. Schelkens. Leuven: Peeters, 2006.

Prignon, *Journal conciliaire* Albert Prignon, *Journal conciliaire de la 4e Session,* ed. L. Declerck and A. Haquin. Louvain-la-Neuve: Publications de la Faculté de Théologie, 2003.

Rynne, *Vatican II*   Xavier Rynne, *Vatican Council II*. Maryknoll, NY: Orbis,
                               1999.

Tanner, *Decrees*   Norman Tanner, ed., *Decrees of the Ecumenical Councils*. 2 vols.
                               Washington, DC: Georgetown University Press, 1990.

Turbanti, *Mondo moderno*   Giovanni Turbanti, *Un concilio per il mondo moderno: La
                               redazione della costituzione pastorale "Gaudium et spes" del
                               Vaticano II*. Bologna: Il Mulino, 2000.

Vorgrimler, *Commentary*   Herbert Vorgrimler, ed., *Commentary on the Documents of
                               Vatican II*. 5 vols. New York: Herder and Herder,
                               1967–1969.

Wiltgen, *Rhine into Tiber*   Ralph M. Wiltgen, *The Rhine Flows into the Tiber: The
                               Unknown Council*. New York: Hawthorn Books, 1967.

Notes

Introduction

1. See, e.g., Jared Wicks, "New Light on Vatican Council II," *Catholic Historical Review*, 92 (2006), 609–628. For ongoing reviews of recent literature on the council, see the articles by Gilles Routhier in *Laval théologique et philosophique* beginning in 1997; and the similar ones by Massimo Faggioli in *Cristianesimo nella Storia* beginning in 2003.

2. The pope, the first of the signatories, signed the documents "Paul, bishop of the Catholic Church." He was followed by the rest of the council fathers, beginning with the cardinal dean, Eugène Tisserant. The signatures were preceded by the formula of promulgation: "The fathers of the holy council approved each and every item that is laid down in this decree. And in the Holy Spirit We together with those revered fathers, through the apostolic authority handed on to Us by Christ, approve, decree, and establish them, and for the greater glory of God we order that what the council determined be promulgated."

3. "The Final Report: Synod of Bishops," *Origins*, 15 (Dec. 19, 1985), 444–450, at 445–446.

4. The standard English-language commentary is still Herbert Vorgrimler, ed., *Commentary on the Documents of Vatican II*, 5 vols. (New York: Herder and Herder, 1967–1969). Helpful and reader-friendly is Adrian Hastings, ed., *A Concise Guide to the Documents of the Second Vatican Council*, 2 vols. (London: Darton, Longman and Todd, 1968–1969). The most recent comprehensive treatment is Peter Hünermann and Bernd Jochen Hilberath, eds., *Herders theologischer Kommentar zum Zweiten Vatikanischen Konzil*, 5 vols. (Freiburg: Herder, 2004–2006).

5. See, e.g., Joseph A. Komonchak, "The Council of Trent at the Second Vatican Council," in *From Trent to Vatican II: Historical and Theological Investigations,* ed. Raymond F. Bulman and Frederick J. Parrella (New York: Oxford University Press, 2006), pp. 61–80. See also Giuseppe Alberigo, "From the Council of Trent to 'Tridentinism,'" ibid., pp. 19–37; and John W. O'Malley, "Trent and Vatican II: Two Styles of Church," ibid., pp. 301–320.

6. See, e.g., Stephen Schloesser, "Against Forgetting: Memory, History, Vatican II," *Theological Studies,* 67 (2006), 275–319.

7. See Antonio Acerbi, "Il magistero di Giovanni XXIII e la svolta conciliare," in *Giovanni XXIII e il Vaticano II: Atti degli Incontri svoltisi presso il Seminario vescovile di Bergamo 1998–2001,* ed. Gianni Carzaniga (Cinisello Balsamo: San Paolo, 2003), pp. 51–71, which suggests approaches to the council similar to mine.

8. John Courtney Murray, "This Matter of Religious Freedom," *America,* 112 (Jan. 9, 1965), 40–43, at 43.

9. See Gilles Routhier, *Vatican II: Herméneutique et réception* (Quebec: Fides, 2006), pp. 171–211.

10. See, e.g., John W. O'Malley, "Vatican II: Did Anything Happen?" *Theological Studies,* 67 (2006), 3–33.

11. For an incisive review of the solutions theologians have advanced for the hermeneutical problems of Vatican II, see Routhier, *Vatican II: Herméneutique,* pp. 361–400. See also Ormond Rush, *Still Interpreting Vatican II: Some Hermeneutical Principles* (New York: Paulist Press, 2004); Joseph A. Komonchak, "Benedict XVI and the Interpretation of Vatican II," *Cristianesimo nella Storia,* 28 (2007), 323–337; Peter Hünermann, "Der 'Text': Eine Ergänzung zur Hermeneutik des II. Vatikanischen Konzils," ibid., 339–358; Christoph Théobald, "Enjeux herméneutiques des débats sur l'histoire du concile Vatican II," ibid., 359–380; Giuseppe Ruggieri, "Recezione e interpretazioni del Vaticano II: Le ragioni di un dibattito," ibid., 381–406.

12. Karl Rahner, "Towards a Fundamental Theological Interpretation of Vatican II," *Theological Studies,* 40 (1979), 716–727.

13. See, e.g., Henri Teissier, "Vatican II et le tiers monde," in *Deuxième concile,* pp. 755–767.

1. Big Perspectives on a Big Meeting

1. See John XXIII, *Pater amabilis,* pp. 23–24, entry for January 15. See also p. 25, entry for January 20.

2. See Caprile, *Cronache,* 1/1:3–29 and 5:681–701; and François-Charles Uginet, "Les projets de concile général sous Pie XI et Pie XII," in *Deuxième concile,* pp. 65–78.

3. See Caprile, *Cronache,* 1/1:39–45 and 5:703–705.

4. ADA I, 3–6, at 6.

5. See John XXIII, *Pater amabilis,* p. 25.

6. Ibid., pp. 23–24.

7. For the invitations that Pius IX sent to the Orthodox and "to Protestants and other non-Catholics" in 1868, on the eve of Vatican I, see Wiltgen, *Rhine into Tiber,* pp. 119–120.

8. For detailed accounts of preparations for the council, see the first volume of Alberigo/Komonchak, *History,* and the first volume (in two parts) of Caprile, *Cronache.*

9. See Carlo Felice Casula, "Il cardinale Domenico Tardini," in *Deuxième concile,* pp. 208–227; and Vincenzo Carbone, "Il cardinale Domenico Tardini e la preparazione del Concilio Vaticano II," *Rivista di Storia della Chiesa in Italia,* 45 (1991), 42–88, at 53–54.

10. ADA II/1, x–xi.

11. For a detailed analysis of the responses, see Étienne Fouilloux, "The Antepreparatory Phase: The Slow Emergence from Inertia (January 1959–October 1962)," in Alberigo/Komonchak, *History,* 1:55–166 at 97–135.

12. See, e.g., M. Lamberigts and Cl. Soetens, eds., *À la veille du concile Vatican II: Vota et réactions en Europe et dans le Catholicisme oriental* (Leuven: Factulteit der Godgeleerdheid, 1992), as well as the contributions dealing with the French, Italian, British, American, and Polish hierarchies in *Deuxième concile,* pp. 101–177.

13. See, e.g., ADA II/4, 268–269; II/5, 325–327, 387–388, 543–544.

14. AS I/1, 27–39, 82–89; and Caprile, *Cronache,* 1/1:209–217, 2:56–60. For a more available list of the commissions and their heads, see Nolan, *Privileged Moment,* pp. 58–59.

15. See, e.g., Massimo Faggioli and Giovanni Turbanti, *Il concilio inedito: Fonti del Vaticano II* (Bologna: Il Mulino, 2001).

16. See Klaus Wittstadt, "On the Eve of the Second Vatican Council (July 1–October 10, 1962)," in Alberigo/Komonchak, *History,* 1:493; but also Hilari Raguer, "An Initial Profile of the Assembly," in ibid., 2:172, for some discrepancy in the numbers. For a handy breakdown, see Caprile, *Cronache,* 5:552–557.

17. For a complete listing of the official *periti,* see the *Indices* (published in 1980) to volumes I–IV of AS, pp. 937–949. Volumes V and VI of AS were published later.

18. Douglas Horton, *Vatican Diary 1962: A Protestant Observes the First Session of Vatican Council II* (Philadelphia: United Church Press, 1964), p. 43. On the outfitting of the basilica, see Wittstadt, "Eve of the Council," pp. 479–492.

19. See Wittstadt, "Eve of the Council," pp. 497–499.

20. Tanner, *Decrees,* 2:820–1135.

21. See, e.g., Jan van Laarhoven, "The Ecumenical Councils in Balance: A Quantitative Overview," in Peter Huizing and Knut Wolf, eds., *The Ecumenical Council—Its Significance in the Constitution of the Church,* Concilium, no. 167 (New York: The Seabury Press, 1983), pp. 50–60. There are three recent general histories: Giuseppe Alberigo, ed., *Storia dei concili ecumenici* (Brescia: Queriniana, 1990); Roger Aubert et

al., *Storia dei concilii* (Cinisello Balsamo: San Paolo, 1995); and Klaus Schatz, *Algemeine Konzilien: Brennpunkte der Kirchengeschichte* (Paderborn: Schöningh, 1997). A handy sketch in English is Norman P. Tanner, *The Councils of the Church: A Short History* (New York: Crossroad, 2001). Still useful is Hubert Jedin, *Ecumenical Councils of the Catholic Church: An Historical Outline* (New York: Herder and Herder, 1960).

22. See, e.g., Giuseppe Ruggieri, "I sinodi tra storia e teologia," *Cristianesimo nella Storia,* 27 (2006), 365–392.

23. See Nelson H. Minnich, "The Voice of Theologians in General Councils from Pisa to Trent," *Theological Studies,* 59 (1998), 420–421; and, more broadly, Minnich, "The Role of Schools of Theology in the Councils of the Late Medieval and Renaissance Periods: Konstanz to Lateran V," in *I Padri e le scuole teologiche nei concilii,* ed. Johannes Grohe et al. (Vatican City: Libreria Editrice Vaticana, 2006), pp. 59–95.

24. See, e.g., Leo Donald Davis, *The First Seven Ecumenical Councils (325–787): Their History and Theology* (1983; reprinted., Collegeville, MN: The Liturgical Press, 1990).

25. See, e.g., Fergus Millar, *The Emperor in the Roman World (31 B.C.–A.D. 337)* (Ithaca: Cornell University Press, 1977), pp. 590–607. Although it deals principally with the early empire, see also Richard J. A. Talbert, *The Senate of Imperial Rome* (Princeton: Princeton University Press, 1984), especially pp. 431–487.

26. See Klaus Schatz, *Vaticanum I, 1869–1870,* 3 vols. (Paderborn: Ferdinand Schöningh, 1992–1994), 1:121–126.

27. See Carmel McEnroy, *Guests in Their Own House: The Women of Vatican II* (New York: Crossroad, 1996).

28. See, e.g., Klaus Schatz, *Papal Primacy: From Its Origins to the Present,* trans. John A. Otto and Linda M. Maloney (Collegeville, MN: The Liturgical Press, 1996); and Hermann J. Pottmeyer, *Towards a Papacy in Communion: Perspectives from Vatican Councils I and II,* trans. Matthew J. O'Connell (New York: Crossroad, 1998).

29. See, e.g., Herman Josef Sieben, "On the Relations between Councils and Pope up to the Middle of the Fifth Century," in Huizing and Wolf, *Ecumenical Council,* pp. 19–24.

30. The still classic study of the origins of this teaching is Brian Tierney, *Foundations of the Conciliar Theory: The Contribution of the Medieval Canonists from Gratian to the Great Schism* (Cambridge: Cambridge University Press, 1955).

31. For an account of these events and analysis, see Giuseppe Alberigo, *Chiesa conciliare: Identità e significato del conciliarismo* (Brescia: Paideia Editrice, 1981).

32. See Francis Oakley, *The Conciliarist Tradition: Constitutionalism in the Catholic Church, 1300–1870* (Oxford: Oxford University Press, 2003).

33. Hubert Jedin's account of the popes from Martin V to Clement VII in this regard is still the most accessible: *A History of the Council of Trent,* trans. Ernest Graf, 2 vols. in English (London: Thomas Nelson and Sons, 1957–1961), 1:5–75, 220–244;

original German, *Geschichte des Konzils von Trient,* 4 vols. in 5 (Freiburg i/Br.: Herder, 1948–1975).

34. See Hubert Jedin, *Crisis and Closure of the Council of Trent: A Retrospective View from the Second Vatican Council,* trans. N. D. Smith (London: Sheed and Ward, 1967); and John W. O'Malley, "The Council of Trent: Myths, Misunderstandings, and Misinformation," in *Spirit, Style, Story: Essays Honoring John W. Padberg, S.J.,* ed. Thomas M. Lucas (Chicago: Loyola Press, 2002), pp. 205–226.

35. *Codex iuris canonici* (Vatican City: Vatican Press, 1958).

36. Council and synod are, in technical parlance, synonyms. The volumes of the official documentation for Vatican II, for instance, are entitled *Acta synodalia.* Sometimes in practice, however, "council" is reserved for the twenty-one ecumenical councils (or synods!). For a synoptic view of the local and provincial councils/synods, see Hermann Josef Sieben, *Die Partikularsynode* (Frankfurt a/M: Josef Knecht, 1990); and note the attention Brian E. Daley gives them, "Christian Councils," in *The Encyclopedia of Religion,* ed. Mircea Eliade. 16 vols. (New York: Macmillan, 1987), 4:125–132. See also Jakub T. Sawicki, *Bibliographia synodorum particularium* (Vatican City: S. Congregatio de Seminariis et Studiorum Universitatibus, 1967); and the pertinent articles and reviews in the *Annuarium Historiae Conciliorum.* The series of monographs under the general editorship of Walter Brandmüller entitled simply *Konziliengeschichte* provides a plethora of examples of such councils. On collegiality itself, see the still useful collection of studies, *La collégialité épiscopale: Histoire et théologie* (Paris: Cerf, 1965).

37. See Ruggieri, "Sinodi," pp. 385–387.

38. See Brian E. Daley, "Structures of Charity: Bishops' Gatherings and the See of Rome in the Early Church," in *Episcopal Conferences: Historical, Canonical, and Theological Studies,* ed. Thomas J. Reese (Washington, D.C.: Georgetown University Press, 1989), pp. 25–58, at 28; Joseph Anton Fischer and Adolf Lumpe, *Die Synoden von den Anfängen bis zum Vorabend des Nicaenums* (Paderborn: Ferdinand Schöningh, 1997); and Paolo Bernadini, "Sinodalità e concili africani del terzo secolo: Vent'anni di studi," in *Synod and Synodality: Theology, History, Canon Law and Ecumenism in New Contact,* ed. Alberto Melloni and Silvia Scatena (Münster: Lit Verlag, 2005), pp. 115–142.

39. See José Orlandis and Domingo Ramos-Lisson, *Die Synoden auf der Iberischen Halbinsel bis zum Einbruch des Islam (711)* (Paderborn: Ferdinand Schöningh, 1981).

40. Of course there were exceptions, such as the Plenary Council of Sicily convoked in 1952 by Cardinal Ernesto Ruffini. See Angelo Romano, *Ernesto Ruffini: Cardinale arcivescovo di Palermo (1946–1967)* (Caltanissetta-Rome: Salvatore Sciascia Editore, 2002), pp. 238–256.

41. See Sieben, *Partikularsynode,* p. 21: "die Konzilien sind Teil des kirchlichen Alltags. Sie sind alles andere als aussergewöhnliche Ereignisse."

42. See André Birmelé, "Le Concile Vatican II vu par les observateurs des autres

traditions chrétiennes," in Dorè, *Volti di fine concilio*, pp. 225–264; Thomas F. Stransky, "Paul VI and the Delegated Observers/Guests to Vatican Council II," in *Paolo VI e l'ecumenismo*, pp. 118–158; Mauro Velati, "Gli osservatori del Consiglio ecumenico delle chiese al Vaticano II," in Fattori, *Evento e decisioni*, pp. 189–257. For a personal recollection, see Max Thurian, "Paul VI et les observateurs au Concile Vatican II," in *Paolo VI, problemi ecclesiologici*, pp. 249–258. "Observers" were those delegated by some body outside the council to represent it. "Guests" were those invited by the Secretariat. Different sources give different numbers depending on whether they counted the Guests. In the actual practice of the council the distinction was for the most part purely formal.

43. See, e.g., the twelve contributions describing press coverage in twelve countries in *Paolo VI, problemi ecclesiologici*, pp. 431–559. For the press in the United States, see Gerald Fogarty, "American Journals and Paul VI at Vatican II," ibid., pp. 547–59.

44. Fesquet, *Drama*.

45. See, e.g., Gigliola Fragnito, *La Bibbia al rogo: La censura ecclesiastica e i volgarizzamenti della Scrittura, 1471–1605* (Bologna: Il Mulino, 1997).

46. Marie-Dominique Chenu, *Une École de théologie: Le Saulchoir* (Paris: Cerf, 1985), p. 132. The volume contains four studies by other scholars relating to Chenu's piece on Saulchoir, first published in 1937 and in 1942 placed on the Index of Forbidden Books; see Jean-Pierre Torrell, "Paul VI e l'ecclésiologie de 'Lumen Gentium': Thèmes choisis," in *Paolo VI, problemi ecclesiologici*, pp. 144–186 at 173; and especially Étienne Fouilloux, "Autour d'une mise à l'Index," in *Marie-Dominique Chenu: Moyen-Âge et modernité* (Paris: Le Centre d'Études du Saulchoir, 1997), pp. 25–56.

47. See Bernard J. F. Lonergan, "The Transition from a Classicist World-View to Historical Mindedness," in a volume of his studies, *A Second Collection: Papers*, ed. William F. J. Ryan and Bernard J. Tyrrell (Toronto: University of Toronto Press, 1996; orig. publ. 1974), pp. 1–9.

48. R. G. Collingwood, *The Idea of History* (New York: Galaxy, 1956), pp. 42–45.

49. AS I/1, 166–175, at 168 and 171. See John W. O'Malley, "Reform, Historical Consciousness, and Vatican II's Aggiornamento," *Theological Studies*, 32 (1971), 573–601.

50. Tanner, *Decrees*, 1:257.

51. Jacques Maritain, *Antimoderne* (Paris: Éditions de la Revue des jeunes, 1922). See Stephen Schloesser, *Jazz Age Catholicism: Mystic Modernism in Postwar Paris, 1919–1933* (Toronto: University of Toronto Press, 2005), pp. 160–170, at 163.

52. John Courtney Murray, "This Matter of Religious Freedom," *America* (Jan. 9, 1965), p. 43 (his emphasis).

53. See Yves M.-J. Congar, *Vraie et fausse réforme dans l'Église* (Paris: Cerf, 1950), pp. 43, n. 35, 601–603, 623. I am indebted to Professor Christopher J. Ruddy for this reference.

54. See Brian E. Daley, "The *Nouvelle Théologie* and the Patristic Revival: Sources,

Symbols and the Science of Theology," *International Journal of Systematic Theology*, 7 (2005), 362–382.

55. See John W. O'Malley, "Erasmus and Vatican II: Interpreting the Council," in Melloni, *Cristianesimo nella storia*, pp. 195–211; and O'Malley, "Introduction" to volume 66 of *The Collected Works of Erasmus* (Toronto: University of Toronto Press, 1988), pp. ix–li, especially pp. xv–xxx.

56. Pius XII, *Humani Generis*, in Carlen, *Encyclicals*, 4:175–183 at 177 and 178–179.

57. See, e.g., Thomas O'Meara, "Raid on the Dominicans: The Repression of 1954," *America* (Feb. 5, 1994), 8–16.

58. See John W. O'Malley, "Developments, Reforms, and Two Great Reformations: Towards a Historical Assessment of Vatican II," *Theological Studies*, 44 (1983), 373–406, at 92–97.

59. See John W. O'Malley, "Vatican II: Did Anything Happen?" *Theological Studies*, 67 (2006), 3–33.

60. See Emmanuel Lanne, "L'origine des synodes," in his *Tradition et communion des Églises: Recueil d'études* (Leuven: Leuven University Press, 1997), pp. 199–217; and Philip R. Amidon, "The Procedure of St. Cyprian's Synods," *Vigiliae Christianae*, 37 (1983), 328–339. Francis Dvornik has been criticized for overstating the identification between the procedures of the Senate and those of the councils and synods in his "Emperors, Popes and General Councils," in *Dumbarton Oaks Papers* (Cambridge, MA: Harvard University Press, 1951), 6:3–23; and in his *Early Christian and Byzantine Political Philosophy: Origins and Background* (Washington: The Dumbarton Oaks Center for Byzantine Studies, 1966). For a detailed treatment of pre-Nicaean councils, see Fischer and Lumpe, *Synoden von den Anfängen*. On a related issue, see Ralph E. Person, *The Mode of Theological Decision Making at the Early Ecumenical Councils: An Inquiry into the Function of Scripture and Tradition at the Councils of Nicaea and Ephesus* (Basel: Friedrich Reinhardt Kommissionsverlag, 1978).

61. See O'Malley, "Vatican II: Did Anything Happen?" and, by way of contrast, Hermann Josef Sieben, *Katholische Konzilienidee im 19. und 20. Jahrhundert* (Paderborn: Ferdinand Schöningh, 1993), where this shift is noted in only the most oblique way.

62. Tanner, *Decrees*, 1:99.

63. Ibid., 2:735.

64. Ibid., 1:597.

65. Ibid., 1:411.

66. See, e.g., George A. Kennedy, *Classical Rhetoric and Its Christian and Secular Tradition from Ancient to Modern Times* (Chapel Hill: University of North Carolina Press, 1980); and his *Greek Rhetoric under Christian Emperors* (Princeton: Princeton University Press, 1983).

67. See John W. O'Malley, *Four Cultures of the West* (Cambridge, MA: Harvard University Press, 2004), especially chapters 2 and 3, pp. 77–177. For a case study of the

transforming impact of the genre, see my *Praise and Blame in Renaissance Rome: Rhetoric, Doctrine, and Reform in the Sacred Orators of the Papal Court, c.1450–1521* (Durham: Duke University Press, 1979), especially pp. 36–76. For a more technical discussion of the issues involved, see Heidi Byrnes, "The Dialogism of Meaning, the Discursive Embeddedness of Knowledge, the Colloquy of Being," in *Hermeneutic Philosophy of Science, Van Gogh's Eyes, and God: Essays in Honor of Patrick A. Heelan, S.J.*, ed. Babette E. Babich (Dordrecht/Boston/London: Kluwer, 2002), pp. 411–422.

68. See Garry Wills, *Lincoln at Gettysburg: The Words That Remade America* (New York: Simon and Schuster, 1992).

69. On soft and hard rhetoric, see O'Malley, "Developments, Reforms," pp. 97–102, 111–114.

70. *Gaudium et Spes,* no. 16.

71. See, e.g., Hubert Jedin and Giuseppe Alberigo, *La figura ideale del vescovo secondo la Riforma cattolica,* trans. from the German, E. Durini and G. Colombi, 2nd ed. (Brescia: Morcelliana, 1985).

2. The Long Nineteenth Century

1. For general background, see Hermann J. Pottmeyer, *Towards a Papacy in Communion: Perspectives from Vatican Councils I and II,* trans. Matthew J. O'Connell (New York: Crossroad, 1998); Owen Chadwick, *A History of the Popes, 1830–1914* (Oxford: Oxford University Press, 1998); Nicholas Atkin and Frank Tallett, *Priests, Prelates and People: A History of European Catholicism since 1750* (Oxford: Oxford University Press, 2003); and Christopher Clark and Wolfram Kaiser, eds., *Culture Wars: Secular-Catholic Conflict in Nineteenth-Century Europe* (Cambridge: Cambridge University Press, 2003).

2. See, e.g., Nigel Aston, *Religion and Revolution in France, 1780–1804* (Washington: The Catholic University of America Press, 2000).

3. Note the title of the book by Clark and Kaiser, *Culture Wars.* See, moreover, Philippe Boutry, "L'Église et la civilisation moderne de Pie IX à Pie X," in *Deuxième concile,* pp. 47–63; and Bernard Laurent, "Catholicism and Liberalism: Two Ideologies in Confrontation," *Theological Studies,* 68 (2007), 808–838.

4. The genres of papal documents and their various titles are extremely complex, and almost every generalization of them needs considerable qualification. See, e.g., Claudia Carlen, ed., *Papal Pronouncements: A Guide, 1740–1978,* 2 vols. (Ann Arbor, MI: The Pierian Press, 1990), 1:xi–xiv; and J. Michael Miller, ed., *The Encyclicals of John Paul II* (Huntington, IN: Our Sunday Visitor, 1996), pp. 9–23.

5. *Discorsi et radiomessaggi di Sua Santità Pio XII,* 20 vols. plus index (Vatican City: Tipografia Poliglotta Vaticana, c. 1940–1959).

6. On the general subject, see Francis A. Sullivan, *Magisterium: Teaching Authority in the Catholic Church* (New York: Paulist, 1983), especially pp. 62–78.

7. Gregory XVI, *Mirari Vos,* in Carlen, *Encyclicals,* 1:235–241, sections quoted 2, 7, 10, 11, 14, 17, 20. For the occasion of the encyclical, see Chadwick, *Popes,* pp. 12–31.

8. *Syllabus Pii IX,* in Henricus Denzinger and Adolfus Schönmetzer, ed., *Enchiridion Symbolorum, Definitiorum et Declarationum de Rebus Fidei et Morum,* 33rd ed. (Rome: Herder, 1965), p. 584: "Romanus Pontifex potest ac debet cum progressu, cum liberalismo, et cum recenti civilitate sese reconciliare et componere." See Philippe Boutry, "l'Église et la civilisation moderne de Pie IX à Pie X," in *Deuxième concile,* pp. 47–63.

9. See, e.g., Philip C. Rule, *Coleridge and Newman: The Centrality of Conscience* (New York: Fordham University Press, 2004).

10. On de Maistre and his contemporaries, see Francis Oakley, *The Conciliarist Tradition: Constitutionalism in the Catholic Church, 1300–1870* (Oxford: Oxford University Press, 2003), pp. 182–216.

11. Pope Gregory XVI, *Il trionfo della Santa Sede e della Chiesa: Contro gli assalti dei novatori combattuti e respinti colle stesse loro armi* (Venice: G. Battaggia, 1832). See Pottmeyer, *Papacy in Communion,* pp. 51–61.

12. See, e.g., Jeffrey von Arx, ed., *Varieties of Ultramontanism* (Washington: The Catholic University of America Press, 1998); and Gisela Fleckenstein and Joachim Schmiedl, eds., *Ultramontanus: Tendenzen der Forschung* (Paderborn: Bonifatius, 2005), especially pp. 7–19 on historiography and on definitions of the term.

13. Tanner, *Decrees,* 2:814–215. See Richard P. McBrien, *The Church: The Evolution of Catholicism* (New York: HarperCollins, 2008), pp. 107–121.

14. See David I. Kertzer, *Prisoner of the Vatican: The Popes' Secret Plot to Capture Rome from the New Italian State* (Boston and New York: Houghton Mifflin, 2004), especially pp. 207–285.

15. See Leo XIII, *Aeterni Patris,* in Carlen, *Encyclicals,* 2:17–27. See also James Hennesey, "Leo XIII's Thomistic Revival: A Political and Theological Event," *Journal of Religion,* 58, Supplement (1978), S185–S197.

16. Leo XIII, *Aeterni Patris,* in Carlen, *Encyclicals,* 2:24, 23, 25.

17. See Gerald A. McCool, *Catholic Theology in the Nineteenth Century: The Quest for a Unitary Method* (New York: The Seabury Press, 1977); McCool, *The Neo-Thomists* (Milwaukee: Marquette University Press, 1994); Serge-Thomas Bonino, ed., *Saint Thomas au XXe siècle: Colloque du centenaire de la "Revue thomiste" (1893–1992)* (Paris: Éditions Saint-Paul, 1994); Henri Donneaud, "Le renouveau thomiste sous Léon XIII: Critique historiographique," in *Marie-Dominique Chenu: Moyen-Âge et modernité* (Paris: Le Centre d'Études du Saulchoir, 1997), pp. 85–119; and Ruedi Imbach, "L'étude historique de saint Thomas et les thomismes," ibid., pp. 121–130.

18. See Jared Wicks, "Manualistic Theology," in René Latourelle and Rino Fisichella, eds., *Dictionary of Fundamental Theology* (New York: Crossroad, 1990), pp. 1102–1105.

19. Leo XIII, *Diuturnum,* in Carlen, *Encyclicals,* 2:53.

20. Leo XIII, *Au Milieu des Sollicitudes,* in Carlen, *Encyclicals,* 2:277–283.

21. Leo XIII, *Graves de Communi Re,* in Carlen, *Encyclicals,* 2:479–486.

22. Pius X, *Vehementer Nos,* in Carlen, *Encyclicals,* 3:45–51, especially p. 46, and *Iamdudum,* ibid., 127–130.

23. Pius X, *Vehementer Nos,* in Carlen, *Encyclicals,* 3:47, 48.

24. Giorgio Feliciani, "The Process of Codification," in Peter Huizing and Knut Wolf, *The Ecumenical Council—Its Significance in the Constitution of the Church,* Concilium, no. 167 (New York: The Seabury Press, 1983), pp. 37–41, at 40.

25. See John W. O'Malley, *Trent and All That: Renaming Catholicism in the Early Modern Era* (Cambridge, MA: Harvard University Press, 2000), especially pp. 1–15.

26. Chadwick, *Popes,* p. 252.

27. "Responsa ad epistolam circularem cancellarii Bismarck," in Denzinger, *Enchiridion,* pp. 603–607. The final sentence, p. 607: "Hinsichtlich der Regierungshandlungen des Papstes ist dadurch nicht das Mindeste geändert worden."

28. On the history of modern biblical criticism, see, e.g., Alexa Suetzer and John S. Kselman, "Modern Old Testament Criticism," in *The New Jerome Biblical Commentary,* ed. Raymond E. Brown et al. (Englewood Cliffs, NJ: Prentice Hall, 1990), pp. 1113–1129; and John S. Kselman and Ronald D. Witherup, "Modern New Testament Criticism," ibid., 1130–1145. More pertinent to this book is François Laplanche, *La crise de l'origine: La science catholique des Évangiles et l'histoire au XXe siècle* (Paris: Albin Michel, 2006).

29. On Lagrange and, more broadly, on l'École, see Jerome Murphy-O'Connor, *The École Biblique and the New Testament: A Century of Scholarship (1890–1990)* (Göttingen: Vanderhoeck and Ruprecht, 1990); and Jean-Luc Vesco, ed., *L'Ancien Testament: Cent ans d'exégèse à l'École biblique* (Paris: J. Gabalda, 1990). I am grateful to Daniel J. Harrington for these references.

30. For the pertinent responses, see Dean P. Bechard, ed. and trans., *The Scripture Documents: An Anthology of Official Catholic Teachings* (Collegeville, MN: The Liturgical Press, 2002), especially pp. 187–206.

31. The classic though now dated study of the phenomenon is Émile Poulat, *Histoire, dogme et critique dans la crise moderniste* (Paris: Casterman, 1962). See now, e.g., Bernard M. G. Reardon, ed. *Roman Catholic Modernism* (London: Adam and Charles Black, 1970); Marvin R. O'Connell, *Critics on Trial: An Introduction to the Catholic Modernist Crisis* (Washington, DC: The Catholic University of America Press, 1994); Pierre Colin, *L'audace et le soupçon: La crise moderniste dans le catholicisme français, 1893–1914* (Paris: Desclée de Brouwer, 1997); and C. J. T. Talar, "'The Synthesis of All Heresies'—100 Years On," *Theological Studies,* 68 (2007), 491–514.

32. "Decretum S. Officii *Lamentabili,*" in Denzinger, *Enchiridion,* pp. 669–674.

33. Pius X, *Pascendi Dominici Gregis,* in Carlen, *Encyclicals,* 3:71–98.

34. See Atkin and Tallett, *Priests, Prelates,* p. 163.

35. On Benigni, see Chadwick, *Popes,* pp. 356–358; *Dizionario biografico degli ital-*

iani (Rome: Istituto della Enciclopedia Italiana, 1960–), 8:506–508; and especially Émile Poulat, *Intégrisme et Catholicisme intégral: Un réseau secret international anti-moderniste, La "Sapinière" (1909–1921)* (Tournai: Casterman, 1969).

36. On the conservative and Ultramontane stance of the Jesuits, see Giacomo Martina, *Storia della Compagnia di Gesù in Italia (1814–1983)* (Brescia: Morcelliana, 2003), especially pp. 209–227.

37. For the most comprehensive overview of Christian liturgy in its many manifestations, see Geoffrey Wainwright and Karen B. Westerfield Tucker, eds., *The Oxford History of Christian Worship* (New York: Oxford University Press, 2006). Nineteenth- and twentieth-century developments within Roman Catholicism are covered by André Haquin, "The Liturgical Movement and Catholic Ritual Revision," ibid., pp. 696–720.

38. See Thomas F. O'Meara, "The Origins of the Liturgical Movement and German Romanticism," *Worship,* 59 (1985), 326–342; and R. W. Franklin, "Response: Humanism and Transcendence in the Nineteenth-Century Liturgical Movement," ibid., pp. 342–353.

39. See Maria Paiano, *Liturgia e società: Percorsi del movimento liturgico di fronte ai processi di secolarizzazione* (Rome: Edizioni Storia e Letteratura, 2000).

40. *Acta Pontificia* 1 (1903), pp. 308–314, at 309.

41. See the commentary by Reiner Kaczynski on *Sacrosanctum Concilium,* in *Herders Kommentar,* 2:1–227, at 15–21. More generally on Tübingen, see the lucid summary by Donald Dietrich and Michael J. Himes, "Introduction," in *The Legacy of the Tübingen School: The Relevance of Nineteenth-Century Theology for the Twenty-First Century,* eds. Donald Dietrich and Michael J. Himes (New York: Crossroad, 1997), pp. 11–19. See also Michael J. Himes, *Ongoing Incarnation: Johann Adam Möhler and the Beginnings of Modern Ecclesiology* (New York: Crossroad, 1997).

42. See, e.g., Keith F. Pecklers, *The Unread Vision: The Liturgical Movement in the United States of America, 1926–1955* (Collegeville, MN: The Liturgical Press, 1998), pp. 9–16.

43. See, e.g., Pecklers, *Unread Vision,* pp. 1–79, at 50–51.

44. Pietro Parente, "Nuove tendenze teologiche," *L'Osservatore Romano* (February 9–10, 1942), which was republished (unsigned) in Latin in *Periodica,* 31 (1942), 184–188.

45. Jean Daniélou, "Les orientations présentes de la pensée religieuse," *Études,* 79 (April–May 1946), pp. 5–21. I am indebted to Professor Christopher J. Ruddy for this reference.

46. Jean Daniélou, *Bible et liturgie* (Paris: Cerf, 1951); English translation, *The Bible and the Liturgy* (Notre Dame, IN: Notre Dame University Press, 1956).

47. Henri de Lubac, *Catholicism: Christ and the Common Destiny of Man,* trans. Lancelot C. Sheppard and Elizabeth Englund (San Francisco: Ignatius, 1988), p. 35; original French, *Catholicisme: Les aspects sociaux du dogme* (Paris: Cerf, 1947).

48. See Jared Wicks, "Six Texts by Professor Joseph Ratzinger as *Peritus* before and during Vatican Council II," forthcoming, *Gregorianum,* 89 (2008).

49. See Rino Fisichella's entry, "Newman, John Henry," in Latourelle and Fisichella, *Fundamental Theology,* pp. 734–738.

50. The title in the first edition was simply *De sacra traditione contra novam haeresim evolutionismi* (Rome: Typographia Iuvenum Opificum a S. Iosepho, 1904), but in subsequent editions *immutabilitas* was added. As in a number of other instances, I am indebted to Jared Wicks for calling my attention to this book. Billot was created cardinal in 1911 by Pius X, but he agreed to renounce the dignity later because of his connections with the rabidly reactionary *Action Française* condemned by Pius XI.

51. Josef Andreas Jungmann, *Die lateinischen Bussriten in ihrer geschichtlichen Entwicklung* (Innsbruck: Rauch, 1932). Jungmann insisted, however, that it was the same sacrament "that had been dispensed in the church since her founding," p. 238.

52. Josef Andreas Jungmann, *Missarum Solemnia: Eine genetische Erklärung der römischen Messe* (Vienna: Herder, 1948); first English edition, *The Mass of the Roman Rite: Its Origins and Development (Missarum Solemnia),* trans. Francis A. Brunner (New York: Benzinger, c. 1951–1955).

53. Brian Tierney, *Foundations of the Conciliar Theory: The Contribution of the Medieval Canonists from Gratian to the Great Schism* (Cambridge: Cambridge University Press, 1955). See Tierney's new "Introduction" to the reprint (Leiden: E. J. Brill, 1998) and his "Afterword: Reflections on a Half Century of Conciliar Studies," in *The Church, the Councils and Reform: The Legacy of the Fifteenth Century,* ed. Gerald Christianson, Thomas M. Izbicki, and Christopher M. Bellitto (Washington, D.C.: The Catholic University of America Press, 2008), pp. 313–327.

54. Yves M.-J. Congar, *Vraie et fausse réforme dans l'Église* (Paris: Cerf, 1950).

55. On Gilson, see now Francesca Aran Murphy, *Art and Intellect in the Philosophy of Étienne Gilson* (Columbia: University of Missouri Press, 2004).

56. In May 1959, Gilson and de Lubac were together attending lectures at a conference at the Sorbonne. During a break in the courtyard after one lecture, Gilson expressed himself on the subject, as de Lubac recalled years later, *Letters of Étienne Gilson to Henri de Lubac: Annotated by Father de Lubac,* trans. Mary Emily Hamilton (San Francisco: Ignatius Press, 1988), p. 11.

57. Jacques Maritain, *Antimoderne* (Paris: Éditions de la Revue des jeunes, 1922). See Stephen Schloesser, *Jazz Age Catholicism: Mystic Modernism in Postwar Paris, 1919–1933* (Toronto: University of Toronto Press, 2005), pp. 162–170. The most recent biography is Jean-Luc Barré, *Jacques and Raïssa Maritain: Beggars for Heaven,* trans. Bernard E. Doering (Notre Dame, IN: University of Notre Dame Press, 2005).

58. Jacques Maritain, *Humanisme intégral: Problèmes temporels et spirituels d'une nouvelle chrétienté* (Paris: Fernand Aubier, 1936); English translation, *True Humanism,* trans. M. R. Adamson (London: Geoffrey Bles, the Centenary Press, 1938).

59. See, e.g., Jacques Maritain, *Antisemitism* (London: Geoffrey Bles, the Centenary Press, 1939), a lecture given in Paris in 1938 and later that year in New York under the auspices of the National Conference of Jews and Christians.

60. See Michael R. Marrus, "The Ambassador and the Pope: Pius XII, Jacques Maritain and the Jews," *Commonweal*, 131, 18 (October 22, 2004), 14–19.

61. Martin Buber, "What is Man?" in *Between Man and Man*, trans. Ronald Gregor Smith (London: Routledge and Kegan Paul, 1947), pp. 118–208, at 129. For an extended treatment of Buber in relation to Vatican II, see Nolan, *Privileged Moment*, pp. 156–176.

62. Martin Buber, "Dialogue," in *Between Man and Man*, pp. 1–39, at 7.

63. Hans Urs von Balthasar, *Martin Buber and Christianity: A Dialogue between Israel and the Church* (London: Harvel Press, 1960), p. 9; original German, *Einsame Zweisprache: Martin Buber und das Christentum* (Cologne: Jacob Hegner, 1958).

64. Pius XI, *Mortalium Animos*, in Carlen, *Encyclicals*, 3:313–319.

65. See, e.g., Heribert Jone, *Moral Theology*, trans. Urban Adelman, 18th ed. (Westminster, MD: Newman, 1963), p. 70.

66. Pius XI, *Casti Connubii*, in Carlen, *Encyclicals*, 3:391–414, especially 399–400.

67. See, e.g., Leslie Woodcock Tentler, *Catholics and Contraception: An American History* (Ithaca: Cornell University Press, 2004).

68. See, e.g., Andrea Riccardi, *Il potere del papa da Pio XII a Paolo VI* (Rome and Bari: Laterza, 1988), especially pp. 3–153.

69. AAS 37 (1945), pp. 10–22.

70. Pius XII, *Divino Afflante Spiritu*, in Carlen, *Encyclicals*, 4:65–79.

71. See Joseph A. Fitzmyer, "A Recent Roman Scriptural Controversy," *Theological Studies*, 22 (1961), 420–444.

72. As quoted in Fesquet, *Drama*, p. 416.

73. Émile Mersch, *Le corps mystique du Christ: Études de théologie historiques*, 2 vols., 2nd ed. (Paris: Desclée de Brouwer, 1936); English, *The Whole Christ: The Historical Development of the Doctrine of the Mystical Body in Scripture and Tradition*, trans. John R. Kelly (Milwaukee: Bruce, c. 1938). Also important was Mersch's *La théologie du corps mystique*, 2 vols. (Paris: Desclée de Brouwer, 1944); English, *The Theology of the Mysical Body*, trans. Cyril Vollert (St. Louis: Herder, 1951).

74. Pius XII, *Mystici Corporis*, in Carlen, *Encyclicals*, 4:37–63.

75. See, e.g., George B. Pepper, *The Boston Heresy Case in View of the Secularization of Religion: A Case Study in the Sociology of Religion* (Lewiston, NY: Mellen, 1988), pp. 1–61; and especially Patrick Carey, "Avery Dulles, St. Benedict's Center, and No Salvation Outside the Church, 1940–53," *Catholic Historical Review*, 93 (2007), 553–575.

76. Pius XII, *Mediator Dei*, in Carlen, *Encyclicals*, 4:119–154, especially 128–131.

77. Pius XII, *Mediator Dei*, in Carlen, *Encyclicals*, 4:130 (nos. 59–60). See also p. 128 (49).

78. See Annibale Bugnini, *The Reform of the Liturgy, 1948–1975,* trans. Matthew J. O'Connell (Collegeville, MN: The Liturgical Press, 1990), pp. 5–10.

79. As early as September 17, 1946, however, Pius warned the Jesuits gathered in Rome for the Twenty-ninth General Congregation of the Society of Jesus about the dangers of the "nova theologia," i.e., "la nouvelle théologie." *Acta Romana Societatis Iesu,* 11 (1946), 58.

80. Reginald Garrigou-Lagrange, "La nouvelle théologie où va-t-elle?" *Angelicum,* 23 (1946), 126–145. See Étienne Fouilloux, "Dialogue théologique? (1946–1948)," in *Thomas au XXe siècle,* pp. 153–195; and R. Guelluy, "Les antécédents de l'encyclique "Humani generis" dans les sanctions romaines de 1942: Chenu, Charlier, Draguet," *Revue d'Histoire Ecclésiastique,* 81 (1986), 421–497.

81. Pius XII, *Humani Generis,* in Carlen, *Encyclicals,* 4:175–184, especially p. 177.

82. See, e.g., Giuseppe Alberigo et al., *Une école de théologie: Le Saulchoir* (Paris: Cerf, 1985); Yves Congar, *Journal d'un théologien (1946–1956),* ed. Étienne Fouilloux (Paris: Cerf, 2001), pp. 232–272; and Thomas O'Meara, "'Raid on the Dominicans': The Repression of 1954," *America* (February 5, 1994), pp. 8–16. See more broadly Étienne Fouilloux, *Une Église en quête de liberté: La pensée catholique française entre modernisme et Vatican II* (Parise: Desclée de Brouwer, 1998).

83. AAS, 30 (1952), 542–546.

84. See Peter Godman, "Graham Greene's Vatican Dossier," *Atlantic Monthly,* no. 288 (July–August 2001), pp. 84–88.

85. See Joseph A. Komonchak, "The Silencing of John Courtney Murray," in Melloni, *Cristianesimo,* pp. 657–702.

86. AAS, 54 (1962), 526. The bibliography on Teilhard is large. For a survey and assessment, see Thomas M. King, "The Milieux Teilhard Left Behind," *America* (March 30, 1985), 249–253. See also Claude Cuénot, *Teilhard: A Biographical Study,* trans. Vincent Colimore (Baltimore: Helicon, 1965).

87. Quoted in O'Meara, "'Raid,'" p. 14.

88. Roger Aubert, *La théologie catholique au milieu du XXe siècle* (Tournai: Casterman, 1954).

89. See Wicks, "Manualistic Theology"; McBrien, *Church,* pp. 142–147; and Étienne Fouilloux, "Les théologiens romains à la veille de Vatican II," in *Histoire et théologie: Actes de la Journée d'études de l'Association française d'histoire religieuse contemporaine* (Paris: Beauchesne, 1994), pp. 137–160. After the first period of the council, Gérard Philips described the two tendencies in an article much quoted at the time, "Deux tendances dans la théologie contemporaine," *Nouvelle Revue Théologique,* 85 (1963), 225–238. In that regard, see Étienne Fouilloux, "Du rôle des théologiens au début de Vatican II," in Melloni, *Cristianesimo nella storia,* pp. 279–311.

90. Paul VI, *Insegnamenti,* 1:270–272, at 272: ". . . che la sua [the Lateran's] affermazione nel concerto dei grandi, celebri e benemeriti istituti romani di alta cultura ecclesiastica sia quella della sincera riconoscenza, della fraterna collaborazione, della

leale emulazione, della mutua riverenza e dell'amica concordia, non mai d'una gelosa concorrenza, o d'una fastidiosa polemica; non mai!" The pope concluded his talk with these words, which gave them special emphasis.

91. See Stephen Schloesser, "Against Forgetting: Memory, History, Vatican II," *Theological Studies,* 67 (2006), 275–319.

92. See, e.g., Schloesser, *Jazz Age Catholicism.*

93. For a study of the genesis of this political development from the French Revolution forward, see Jay P. Corrin, *Catholic Intellectuals and the Challenge of Democracy* (Notre Dame, IN: University of Notre Dame Press, 2002).

94. See, e.g., the important Instruction of the Holy Office, *Ecclesia Catholica,* December 20, 1949, AAS 42 (1950), 142–147. See also Étienne Fouilloux, *Les catholiques et l'unité chrétienne du XIXe au XXe siècle: Itinéraires européens d'expression française* (Paris: Le Centurion, 1982); and Jerome-Michael Vereb, *"Because He Was a German": Cardinal Bea and the Origins of Roman Catholic Engagement in the Ecumenical Movement* (Grand Rapids, MI: W. B. Eerdmans, 2006), pp. 11–120.

95. AAS 41 (1949), p. 334.

3. The Council Opens

1. For descriptions of the opening days, see Rynne, *Vatican II,* pp. 45–56; Caprile, *Cronache,* 2:1–40; and Andrea Riccardi, "The Tumultuous Opening Days of the Council," in Alberigo/Komonchak, *History,* 2:10–232.

2. As quoted in Riccardi, "Opening Days," in Alberigo/Komonchak, *History,* 2:65.

3. AS I/1, 166–175. English translation in Floyd Anderson, ed., *Council Daybook, Vatican II: Sessions 1–4,* 3 vols. (Washington, DC: National Catholic Welfare Conference, 1965–1966), 1:25–29.

4. The most detailed analysis is by Giuseppe Alberigo and Alberto Melloni, "L'allocuzione *Gaudet Mater Ecclesia* di Giovanni XXIII (11 ottobre 1962): Sinossi critica dell'allocuzione," in *Fede, tradizione, profezia: Studi su Giovanni XXIII* (Brescia: Paideia, 1984), pp. 223–283.

5. See Tanner, *Decrees,* 2:804–805, commented on by Jared Wicks, "New Light on Vatican Council II," *Catholic Historical Review,* 92 (2006), 609–628, at 621.

6. AS I/1, 202–203.

7. AS I/1, 196–198. For a list of the observers, see ibid., 192–196.

8. As quoted in Riccardi, "Opening Days," in Alberigo/Komonchak, *History,* 2:29 and note 12.

9. For the membership list of the commissions, see AS I/1, 83–89.

10. For a listing of the new members, see AS I/1, 559–562.

11. For the new members, see AS II/6, 306–307, and III/1, 17–20.

12. See Turbanti, *Mondo moderno,* pp. 119–135.

13. AS I/1, 230–232.

14. On John's role in trying to ease the crisis, see Riccardi, "Opening Days," in Alberigo/Komonchak, *History,* 2:94–104.

15. ADP I, 306–325. See, e.g., Philippe Levillain, *La méchanique politique de Vatican II: La majorité et l'unanimité dans un concile* (Paris: Beauchesne, 1975).

16. Levillain, *Méchanique politique,* p. 444, describes the revisions as done with "une empirisme néfaste."

17. AS I/1, 78. Although the announcement was made on October 22, the document signed by Cicognani was dated October 19.

18. See, e.g., the informative four categories of bishops devised by Melissa J. Wilde, *Vatican II: A Sociological Analysis of Religious Change* (Princeton: Princeton University Press, 2007), especially pp. 6, 32–56.

19. On John XXIII and the council, see, e.g., Grootaers, *Actes et Acteurs,* pp. 3–30. See also Peter Hebblethwaite, *Pope John XXIII: Shepherd of the Modern World* (Garden City, NY: Doubleday, 1985); Giuseppe Alberigo, *Papa Giovanni (1881–1963)* (Bologna: Edizioni Dehoniane, 2000); and Mario Benigni and Goffredo Zanchi, *John XXIII: The Official Biography,* trans. Elvira Di Fabio (Boston: Pauline Books and Media, 2001), original Italian, 2000. For an almost daily chronicle from John's own hand, see now *Edizione nazionale dei diari di Angelo Giuseppe Roncalli–Giovanni XXIII,* 5 vols. to date (Bologna: Istituto per le scienze religiose, 1987–). An interesting, wide-ranging reflection on John and the council is Antonio Acerbi, "Il magistero di Giovanni XXIII e la svolta conciliare," in *Giovanni XXIII e il Vaticano II: Atti degli Incontri svoltisi presso il Seminario vescovile di Bergamo 1998–2001,* ed. Gianni Carzaniga (Cinisello Balsamo: San Paolo, 2003), pp. 51–71. More broadly on John XXIII, see Enzo Bianchi et al., *Un cristiano sul trono di Pietro: Studi storici su Giovanni XXIII* (Gorle: Servitium, 2003); and Bruno Bertoli, ed., *Il patriarca Roncalli e le sue fonti: Biblia, padri della chiesa, storia* (Venice: Studium Cattolico Veneziano, 2002).

20. On his love for the Fathers, see Gianni Bernardi, "Familiarità con i Padri della Chiesa," in *Il patriarca Roncalli,* ed. Bertoli, pp. 99–128.

21. See, e.g, Alberto Melloni, "History, Pastorate, and Theology: The Impact of Carlo Borromeo upon A. G. Roncalli/Pope John XXIII," in *San Carlo Borromeo: Catholic Reform and Ecclesiastical Politics in the Second Half of the Sixteenth Century,* ed. John M. Headley and John B. Tomaro (Washington: The Folger Shakespeare Library, 1988), pp. 277–299. The documents in question: *Gli atti della visita apostolica di S. Carlo Borromeo a Bergamo (1575),* 5 vols. (Florence: Olschki, 1936–1957). On his interest in history more broadly, see Bruno Bertoli, "Il 'gusto per la storia,'" in *Il patriarca Roncalli,* ed. Bertoli, pp. 129–183.

22. For a review and analysis of his actions during the preparatory phase, see Joseph A. Komonchak, "The Struggle for the Council during the Preparation of Vatican II (1960–1962)," in Alberigo/Komonchak, *History,* 1:167–356, at 350–356.

23. See *Prima Romana Synodus, A.D. MDCCCCLX* (Vatican City: Typis Polyglottis Vaticanis, 1960).

24. See John XXIII, *Pater amabilis,* pp. 469, 490, 491, 511, 513.

25. John XXIII, *Journal of a Soul: Pope John XXIII,* trans. Dorothy White (New York: Image Books/Doubleday, c. 1980). The revised, critical edition is the first volume (2003) of the *Edizione nazionale dei diari.*

26. On Paul VI and the council, see, e.g., Grootaers, *Actes et Acteurs,* pp. 31–92. See also Peter Hebblethwaite, *Paul VI: The First Modern Pope* (New York: Paulist Press, 1993).

27. On the range of judgments about him, see, e.g., Philippe Levillain, "L'opinion publique et Paul VI pendant la seconde et la troisième période de Vatican II," *Paolo VI, problemi ecclesiologici,* pp. 274–285; and Franco Molinari, "Il carattere di Paolo VI e una interpretazione," ibid., pp. 424–425.

28. See, e.g., Prignon, *Journal conciliaire,* p. 174.

29. See Jan Grootaers, "Le crayon rouge de Paul VI: Les interventions du pape dans le travail des commissions conciliaires," in Lamberigts, *Commissions conciliaires,* pp. 317–351.

30. See John XXIII, *Pater amabilis,* p. 446; and Prignon, *Journal conciliaire,* 92.

31. See Francesco Leoni, *Il cardinale Alfredo Ottaviani, carabiniere della Chiesa* (Rome: Apes, 2002); as well as Andrea Riccardi, *Il potere del papa da Pio XII a Paolo VI* (Rome and Bari: Laterza, 1988), pp. 62–79.

32. Ottaviani's best-known work, frequently republished, was *Institutiones iuris publici ecclesiastici,* 2 vols. (Rome: Athenaeum pontificii seminarii romani ad S. Apollinaris [later Lateran University], 1926).

33. Ernesto Ruffini, *La teoria dell'evoluzione secondo la scienza e la fede* (Rome: Orbis Catholicus, 1948), p. 188; English, *The Theory of Evolution Judged by Reason and Faith,* trans. Francis O'Hanlon (New York: J. F. Wagner, 1959), p. 147.

34. On Ruffini and the council, see especially F. M. Stabile, "Il Cardinale Ruffini e il Vaticano II," *Cristianesimo nella Storia,* 11 (1990), 83–176, which contains ninety-two previously unpublished letters by Ruffini; and Angelo Romano, *Ernesto Ruffini: Cardinale arcivescovo di Palermo (1946–1967)* (Caltanissetta-Rome: Salvatore Sciascia Editore, 2002).

35. See Romano, *Ruffini,* pp. 489, n. 2, and 490.

36. See Benny Lai, *Il papa non eletto: Giuseppe Siri, cardinale della Santa Romana Chiesa* (Rome: Laterza, 1993), especially pp. 262–281.

37. The description is Prignon's, *Journal conciliaire,* p. 146.

38. See Wilde, *Vatican II: Sociological Analysis,* pp. 69–81; Hilari Raguer, "An Initial Profile of the Assembly," in Alberigo/Komonchak, *History,* 2:195–200; and especially Luc Perrin, "Il 'Coetus Internationalis Patrum' e la minoranza conciliare," in Fattori, *Evento e decisioni,* pp. 173–187.

39. See the analysis and reminiscence of Vincenzo Fagiolo, "Paolo VI e il Segretario Generale del Concilio Ecumenico Vaticano II," in *Paolo VI, problemi ecclesiologici,* pp. 213–224.

40. See Grootaers, *Actes et Acteurs,* pp. 301–313.

41. Sebastian Tromp, "De futuro Concilio Vaticano II," *Gregorianum,* 43 (1962), 5–11.

42. As quoted in Gerald P. Fogarty, "The Council Gets Under Way," in Alberigo/Komonchak, *History,* 2:92; and Giuseppe Ruggieri, "Beyond an Ecclesiology of Polemics: The Debate on the Church," ibid., p. 348.

43. See Andrea Riccardi, "Preparare il concilio: Papa e Curia alla vigilia del Vaticano II," *Deuxième concile,* pp. 181–205.

44. Congar, *Mon journal,* 2:177.

45. See, e.g., Grootaers, *Actes et Acteurs,* pp. 277–286; Stjepan Schmidt, *Augustin Bea: The Cardinal of Unity,* trans. Leslie Wearne (New Rochelle, NY: New City Press, 1992); and Jerome-Michael Vereb, *"Because He Was a German": Cardinal Bea and the Origins of Roman Catholic Engagement in the Ecumenical Movement* (Grand Rapids, MI: W. B. Eerdmans, 2006).

46. On the early history and development of the Secretariat, see Mauro Velati, "Le Secrétariat pour l'Unité des Chrétiens et l'origine du décret sur l'Oecuménisme (1962–1963)," in Lamberigts, *Commissions conciliaires,* pp. 181–203; and, for a fuller picture of the situation, see Lamberigts, *Una difficile transizione: Il cattolicesimo tra unionismo ed ecumenismo (1952–1964)* (Bologna: Il Mulino, 1996).

47. See, e.g., Grootaers, *Actes et Acteurs,* pp. 501–521; and also Velati, *Difficile transizione,* passim.

48. See Grootaers, *Actes et Acteurs,* pp. 314–325, and his entry for Suenens in *Nouvelle Biographie Nationale* [Belgium], 6:329–334; and especially Leo Declerck and Toon Osaer, "Les relations entre le cardinal Montini/Paul VI (1897–1978) et le cardinal Suenens (1904–1996) pendant le Concile Vatican II," *Notiziario,* 51 (2006), 49–76.

49. See, e.g., Philips, *Carnets conciliaires,* pp. 106, 124, 130, 140.

50. See, e.g., Prignon, *Journal conciliaire,* pp. 250–251.

51. See Fogarty, "Council Under Way," in Alberigo/Komonchak, *History,* 2:79–84. See also, e.g., Cardinal Franz König, *Open to God, Open to the World* (London: Burns and Oates, 2005).

52. See, e.g., Jared Wicks, "I teologi al Vaticano II: Momenti e modalità del loro contributo al Concilio," *Humanitas,* 59 (2004), 1012–1038. See J. A. Di Noia, "Karl Rahner," in *The Modern Theologians: An Introduction to Christian Theology in the Twentieth Century,* ed. David F. Ford (Oxford: Basil Blackwell, 1997), pp. 118–133.

53. See, e.g., Fergus Kerr, "French Theology: Yves Congar and Henri de Lubac," in Ford, *Modern Theologians,* pp. 105–117.

54. For the remark about Ottaviani, see Philips, *Carnets conciliaires,* p. 121. On Philips, see Grootaers, *Actes et Acteurs,* pp. 382–419; and Philips, *Primauté et collégial-*

ité: Le dossier de Gérard Philips sur la Nota Explicative Praevia (Lumen gentium, Chap. III) (Leuven: Leuven University Press, 1986). See also L. Declerck and W. Verschooten, *Inventaire des papiers conciliaires de monsigneur Gérard Philips, secretaire adjoint de la Commission Doctrinale* (Leuven: Peeters, 2001), especially pp. xxiii–xxxviii.

55. See Hans Küng, *My Struggle for Freedom: Memoirs,* trans. John Bowden (Grand Rapids, MI: W. B. Eerdmans, 2003), pp. 349–351.

56. See, e.g., Kerr, "French Theology," in Ford, *Modern Theologians,* pp. 105–117; Gabriel Flynn, ed., *Yves Congar: Theologian of the Church* (Grand Rapids: MI: W. B. Eerdmans, 2005); and especially Congar's diaries, *Journal d'un théologien, 1946–1956,* ed. Étienne Fouilloux (Paris: Cerf, 2002), and *Mon journal du concile,* ed. Éric Mahieu, 2 vols. (Paris: Cerf, 2002).

57. For an account of his travails with the Roman and Dominican authorities, see Congar, *Journal d'un théologien.*

58. See Étienne Fouilloux, "Comment devient-on expert à Vatican II? Le cas du Pére Yves Congar," in *Deuxième concile,* pp. 307–331; and Jared Wicks, "Yves Congar's Doctrinal Service of the People of God," *Gregorianum,* 84 (2003), 499–550.

59. See *Marie-Dominique Chenu: Moyen-Âge e modernité* (Paris: Le Centre d'Études du Saulchoir, 1997).

60. Robert J. Schreiter, "Edward Schillebeecks," in Ford, *Modern Theologians,* pp. 152–161; and Philip Kennedy, *Schillebeeckx* (Collegeville, MN: The Liturgical Press, 1993), especially pp. 13–30. On Alfrink, see Grootaers, *Actes et Acteurs,* pp. 522–543.

61. On Frings (and Ratzinger) see Dieter Froitzheim, *Kardinal Frings: Leben und Werk* (Cologne: Wienand, 1979); and now Norbert Trippen, *Josef Kardinal Frings (1887–1978),* 2 vols. (Paderborn: Ferdinand Schöningh, 2003–2005). The bibliography on Ratzinger is large. Particularly pertinent for the council is Jared Wicks, "Six Texts by Prof. Joseph Ratzinger as *Peritus* before and during Vatican Council II," forthcoming, *Gregorianum,* 89 (2008); and Wicks's Yamauchi lecture, "Prof. Ratzinger at Vatican II: A Chapter in the Life of Pope Benedict XVI" (New Orleans: Loyola University, c. 2006).

62. See, e.g., Agostino Marchetto, *Il Concilio Ecumenico Vaticano II: Contrappunto per la sua storia* (Vatican City: Libreria Editrice Vaticana, 2005), pp. 296, 321, 328.

63. Wiltgen, *Rhine into Tiber.* Wiltgen, who developed close ties with members of the Group and others who opposed the dominance of what Wiltgen calls "the European alliance" (France, Belgium, Germany, Austria), wrote his book on the council to represent their viewpoint.

64. See, e.g., Vincent A. Yzermans, ed., *American Participation in the Second Vatican Council* (New York: Sheed and Ward, 1967).

65. See Klaus Wittstadt and W. Verschooten, eds., *Der Beitrag der deutschsprachigen und osteuropäischen Länder zum Zweiten Vatikanischen Konzil* (Leuven: Biblioteek van de Faculteit Godgeleerdheid, 1996).

66. See, e.g., Grootaers, *Actes et Acteurs,* pp. 340–484; Claude Soetens, ed., *Vatican*

II et la Belgique (Ottignies: Éditions Quorum, 1996); and Leo Declerck, "Le rôle joué par les évêques et periti belges au Concile Vatican II: Deux exemples," *Ephemerides Theologicae Lovanienses,* 76 (2000), 445–464.

67. Congar, *Mon journal,* 2:72, "Le concile, pour sa partie théologique, s'est fait en grande part au Collège Belge." This entry in the diary is largely a eulogy of Prignon, for whom Congar had the highest respect.

68. See, e.g., Grootaers, *Actes et Acteurs,* pp. 287–300.

69. On the Italians at the council, see Giuseppe Battelli, "Alcune considerazioni introduttive per uno studio sui vescovi italiani al concilio Vaticano II," in *Deuxième concile,* pp. 267–279.

70. On the French at the council, see Alain Michel, "L'épiscopat français au deuxième concile du Vatican," in *Deuxième concile,* pp. 281–296.

71. See the reflections by Marcos G. McGrath, bishop of Panama, who was an important council participant, "La creazione della coscienza di un popolo latinoamericano: Il CELAM ed il concilio Vaticano II," in Fattori, *Evento e decisioni,* 135–142.

72. See Thomas F. Stransky, "Paul VI and the Delegated Observers/Guests to Vatican Council II," in *Paolo VI e l'ecumenismo,* pp. 118–158, especially at 128–130; and Mauro Velati, "Gli osservatori del Consiglio ecumenico delle chiese al Vaticano II," in Fattori, *Evento e decisioni,* pp. 189–257.

73. See Wiltgen, *Rhine into Tiber,* pp. 107–109.

74. As quoted in Raguer, "Initial Profile," in Alberigo/Komonchak, *History,* 2:200–203, at 202. See Denis Pelletier, "Une marginalité engagée: Le groupe 'Jésus, l'Église et les pauvres," in Lamberigts, *Commissions conciliaires,* pp. 63–89; and now Helder Câmara, *Lettres conciliaires 1962–1965,* trans. José de Broucker, 2 vols. (Paris: Cerf, 2007).

75. See Grootaers, *Actes et Acteurs,* pp. 133–165; Grootaers, "Une forme de concertation épiscopale au Concile Vatican II: La 'Conférence des Vingt-deux' (1962–1963)," *Revue d'Histoire Ecclesiastique,* 91 (1996), 66–112, with documents; and Pierre C. Noël, "Gli incontri delle conferenze episcopali durante il concilio: Il 'gruppo della Domus Mariae,'" in Fattori, *Evento e decisioni,* pp. 95–133. For a measurement of the effectiveness of the conference, see Wilde, *Vatican II: Sociological Analysis,* especially pp. 63–70.

76. See, e.g., *L'Église grecque Melkite au Concile: Discours et notes de Patriarche Maximos IV et des Prélates de son Église au Concile oecuménique Vatican II* (Beirut: Dar al-Kalima, 1967); and Gaby Hachem, "Primauté et oecuménisme chez Melkites catholiques à Vatican II," *Revue d'Histoire Ecclésiastique,* 93 (1998), 398–441.

77. See Vereb, *"Because He Was a German,"* pp. 11–23.

78. *L'Église grecque,* pp. 5–8, at 6.

4. The First Period (1962)

1. See, e.g., his own comments in that regard, AS VI/2, 554.

2. For the role of Felici, the pope, and Amleto Cicognani, see Wiltgen, *Rhine into*

Tiber, pp. 140–141. The commentary on *Sacrosanctum concilium* by Josef Andreas Jungmann, a *peritus* on the commission, in Vorgrimler, *Commentary,* 1:1–87, is lucid, thorough, and, though somewhat dated, still among the best. The corresponding commentary by Reiner Kaczynski in *Herders Kommentar,* 2:1–227, takes account of more recent scholarship on the council and provides a bibliography (pp. 211–227) that is up-to-date, though it pays little attention to scholarship in languages other than German. A valuable feature of this commentary is a series of interspersed listings in chronological order of different postconciliar reforms, e.g., of the liturgical books.

3. See Maria Paiano, "Les travaux de la Commission Liturgique conciliare," in Lamberigts, *Commissions conciliaires,* pp. 1–26 at 6–7.

4. AAS, 54 (1962), 129–135.

5. AAS, 54 (1962), 173–175.

6. See Paiano, "Commission Liturgique," p. 7; and Annibale Bugnini, *The Reform of the Liturgy, 1948–1975,* trans. Matthew J. O'Connell (Collegeville, MN: Liturgical Press, 1990), pp. 14–38, especially p. 30, n. 4.

7. AS I/1, 304–308.

8. AS I/1, 272.

9. See John W. O'Malley, "Trent and Vernacular Liturgy," *America* (January 29, 2007), pp. 16–19; and Gerard S. Sloyan, "The Latin of the Roman Rite: Before Trent and after Vatican II," in *From Trent to Vatican II: Historical and Theological Investigations,* ed. Raymond F. Bulman and Frederick J. Parrella (New York: Oxford University Press, 2006), pp. 103–116.

10. See O'Malley, "Trent and Liturgy."

11. AS I/1, 309–310.

12. AS I/1, 311–313, especially 313.

13. AS I/1, 313–316.

14. AS I/1, 369–371, at 371.

15. AS I/1, 316–319, at 316–317.

16. See Wiltgen, *Rhine into Tiber,* pp. 35–37. Wiltgen arranged these conferences.

17. AS I/1, 377–379, at 377–378.

18. See John XXIII, *Pater amabilis,* p. 446. See also ibid., p. 448, entry for October 27.

19. AS I/l, 423–427, at 425.

20. AS I/1, 349–351.

21. AS I/1, 18–21, especially 18: "Nunc, num revolutio quaedam fieri vult de tota missa?"

22. See AAS, 48 (1956), 711–725, at 724: ". . . que l'Église a de graves motifs de maintenir fermement dans le rite latin l'obligation inconditionée pour le prêtre célébrant d'employer la langue latin . . ."

23. Original text, n. 24: "Latinae linguae usus in Liturgia occidentali servetur." Final text, n. 36: "Linguae latinae usus, salvo particulari iure, in ritibus latinis servetur."

Further on in n. 36 provision is made for "more ample" use of the vernacular, even in Mass.

24. See Bugnini, *Reform,* pp. 49–59.

25. For the documents, with commentary, see Bugnini, *Reform.*

26. For responses to some critics of the reforms, see, e.g., John F. Baldovin, "Klaus Gamber and the Post-Vatican II Reform of the Liturgy," *Studia Liturgica,* 33 (2003), 223–239; and Baldovin, "Cardinal Ratzinger as Liturgical Critic," in *Studia Liturgica Diversa: Essays in Honor of Paul F. Bradshaw,* ed. Maxwell Johnson and L. Edward Phillips (Portland: Pastoral Press, 2004), pp. 211–227.

27. For the history of the text and full commentary, see Burigana, *Bibbia nel concilio,* and for the "shipwreck" of *De Fontibus,* pp. 105–169. The commentary on the text that developed into *Dei Verbum* in Vorgrimler, *Commentary,* 3:155–272, is especially interesting for having been authored in large part by Joseph Ratzinger. The corresponding commentary by Helmut Hoping in *Herders Kommentar,* 3:697–831, provides an international bibliography, pp. 820–831, an excellent sketch of theological developments up to the time of the council, pp. 701–716, and an analysis of Ratzinger's position, pp. 709–711. See also Ronald D. Witherup, *Scripture: Dei Verbum* (New York: Paulist Press, 2006).

28. Douglas Horton, *Vatican Diary 1962: A Protestant Observes the First Session of Vatican Council II* (Philadelphia: United Church Press, 1964), p. 111.

29. See Riccardo Burigana, "La Commissione 'De Divina Revelatione,'" in Lamberigts, *Commissions conciliaires,* pp. 27–61, at 29.

30. AS I/3, 27–28.

31. AS I/3, 28–32.

32. AS I/3, 14–26.

33. I use upper case for Tradition in this context, where it has a precise and technical meaning.

34. AS I/3, 32–34.

35. AS I/3, 34–36.

36. AS I/3, 37–39.

37. AS I/3, 41–42.

38. AS I/3, 42–43.

39. AS I/3, 43–45.

40. AS I/3, 47–48.

41. AS I/3, 48–51.

42. See Burigana, *Bibbia nel concilio,* pp. 108–128; and Helmut Hoping's commentary on *Dei Verbum* in *Herders Kommentar,* 3:699–831, at 722–725.

43. John XXIII, *Pater amabilis,* p. 454, ". . . la stesura della proposta non tenne conto delle precise intenzioni del Papa nei suoi discorsi ufficiali." See Giuseppe Ruggieri, "The First Doctrinal Clash," in Alberigo/Komonchak, *History,* 2:241–243, 256.

44. See Burigana, "La Commissione," p. 32.

45. As quoted in Ruggieri, "Doctrinal Clash," p. 249.

46. Hubert Jedin, *A History of the Council of Trent,* trans. Ernest Graf (London: Thomas Nelson, 1961), 2:52–98.

47. See Aquinas, *Summa Theologiae,* I.l, especially article 8 ad secundum.

48. Tanner, *Decrees,* 2:663.

49. As quoted in Ruggieri, "Doctrinal Clash," p. 256.

50. AS I/3, 53–54.

51. AS I/3, 184–187.

52. AS I/3, 259.

53. Robert Rouquette, "Bilan du concile," *Études* (January 1963), pp. 94–111, especially at 95, 104.

54. See Grootaers, *Actes et Acteurs,* pp. 166–182; and Hilari Raguer, "An Initial Profile of the Assembly," in Alberigo/Komonchak, *History,* 2:221–232.

55. On the history of this text, see Mauro Velati, "Le Secrétariat pour l'Unité des Chrétiens et l'origine du décret sur l'Oecuménisme (1962–1963)," in Lamberigts, *Commissions conciliaires,* pp. 181–203.

56. AS I/4, 121.

57. Congar, *Mon journal,* 1:282. For three contrasting evaluations of Ottaviani's tone, see Rynne, *Vatican II,* p. 110; Fesquet, *Drama,* p. 88; and Giuseppe Ruggieri, "Beyond an Ecclesiology of Polemics: The Debate on the Church," in Alberigo/Komonchak, *History,* 2:329.

58. See Philips, *Carnets conciliaires,* pp. 83 and 157–158, n. 16.

59. See Ruggieri, "Ecclesiology of Polemics," pp. 305–317.

60. AS I/4, 122–125. For a detailed analysis of this text, see Antonio Acerbi, *Due ecclesiologie: Ecclesiologia giuridica ed ecclesiologia di comunione nella "Lumen Gentium"* (Bologna: Edizioni Dehoniane, 1975), pp. 107–149. For a concise history and analysis of the text (and others related to it) through to final approval, see Richard Gaillardetz, *The Church in the Making: Lumen Gentium, Christus Dominus, Orientalium Ecclesiarum* (New York: Paulist Press, 2006).

61. AS I/4, 126–127.

62. AS I/4, 127–129.

63. AS I/4, 132–134.

64. AS I/4, 134–136.

65. AS I/4, 136–138.

66. AS I/4, 142–144.

67. Congar, *Mon journal,* 1:285.

68. AS I/4, 218–220.

69. AS I/4, 222–227.

70. For John's address and its use of the inward/outward distinction, see ADP I/1, 348–355, at 350.

71. See Turbanti, *Mondo moderno,* pp. 104–110. See also Prignon, *Journal concili-*

aire, pp. 262–263; and especially Suenens' own account, which includes some of the pertinent documents leading up to the intervention, "Aux origines du Concile Vatican II," *Nouvelle Revue Théologique,* 107 (1985), 3–21.

72. On the evolution of the idea of such a schema, see Turbanti, *Mondo moderno,* pp. 170–198.

73. AS I/4, 291–294.

74. AS V/1, 34–35. See also ibid., 35–37.

5. The Second Period (1963)

1. AS V/1, 33–36.

2. For a detailed description of the work of this Coordinating Commission and the other commissions during the intersession, see Jan Grootaers, "The Drama Continues between the Acts: The 'Second Preparation' and Its Opponents," in Alberigo/Komonchak, *History,* 2:365–495.

3. On the complicated history of the development of this text, see Turbanti, *Mondo moderno,* pp. 181 ff., or his summary, "La commissione mista per lo schema XVII–XIII," in Lamberigts, *Commissions conciliaires,* pp. 217–250.

4. For a detailed account of these difficult months of the schema, see Burigana, *Bibbia nel concilio,* 171–253.

5. See AS V/1, 185–188.

6. Henri de Lubac, *The Splendour of the Church,* trans. Michael Mason (New York: Sheed and Ward, 1956), pp. 4–5; French original, *Méditation sur l'Église* (Paris: Aubier, 1954).

7. See Charles Pietri, "L'ecclésiologie patristique et *Lumen gentium,*" in *Deuxième concile,* pp. 511–537.

8. AS V/1, 159: "Adhibetur genus litterarium concilio non conveniens."

9. AS V/1, 186.

10. See Giuseppe Alberigo and Franca Magistretti, *Synopsis Historica Constitutionis Dogmaticae Lumen Gentium* (Bologna: Istituto per le scienze religiose, 1975). This volume is indispensable for following the genesis of the text almost word for word from the original *De Ecclesia* to the promulgated document. It also contains other documents pertinent to the text, such as the four major rewrites besides Philips's that were in circulation (German, Italian, French, and Chilean) and from which the revisors tried to draw as much as they could (pp. 381–428). Jared Wicks called my attention to this important book.

11. See Grootaers, "The Drama Continues," in Alberigo/Komonchak, *History,* 2:391–412, especially 402–403; and the direct account of the meeting from Philips's own notes in Philips, *Carnets conciliaires,* pp. 97–98.

12. See ADP I, 348–355, at 352.

13. See Carlen, *Encyclicals,* 5:107–129.

14. AAS 55 (1963), 238–240, at 239. See also ibid., 448–458.

15. For the conclave, see Peter Hebblethwaite, *Paul VI: The First Modern Pope* (New York: Paulist Press, 1993), pp. 318–332.

16. See AAS 55 (1963), 581; as well as the somewhat wide-ranging article by Giacomo Martina, "Paolo VI e la ripresa del Concilio," in *Paolo VI, problemi ecclesiologici,* pp. 19–55.

17. AS II/1, 9–13.

18. AS II/1, 24.

19. AS VI/2, 553.

20. See Felici's comment, AS VI/2, 552–553.

21. AS VI/2, 552. This memorandum of Felici reflecting on the second period is a judicious review of what went wrong in the procedures and needed correction.

22. AS II/1, 49–56, especially 54: "Saranno dalla Curia stessa formulate e promulgate."

23. AS II/1, 183–200.

24. Congar, for instance, described it as "très vigoureux, très structuré, qui donne des directives précises pour le travail du concile," *Mon journal,* 1:404.

25. AS II/1, 21–46.

26. AS II/1, 211.

27. AS II/1, 215–281. The original *De Ecclesia* is found ibid., I/4, 12–91. See the commentary on *Lumen Gentium* by Gérard Philips, Karl Rahner, et al. in Vorgrimler, *Commentary,* 1:105–305; and by Peter Hünermann in *Herders Kommentar,* 2:263–582, with bibliography 565–582. See Richard P. McBrien's recent, lucid analysis: *The Church: The Evolution of Catholicism* (New York: HarperCollins, 2008), pp. 162–192.

28. AS I/4, 19: ". . . ut fratres separati, modo a Christo statuto, eidem [ecclesiae] incorporentur."

29. AS II/1, 221, with commentary on 231. On the vexed question of the precise meaning in no. 8 of the final text of the expression "the church of Christ subsists in the Catholic Church," see Francis A. Sullivan, "The Significance of the Vatican II Declaration that the Church of Christ 'Subsists in' the Roman Catholic Church," in René Latourelle, ed., *Vatican II: Assessments and Perspectives, Twenty-Five Years After (1962–1987),* 3 vols. (New York: Paulist, 1989), 2:272–287; Francis A. Sullivan, "A Response to Karl Becker, S.J., on the Meaning of *Subsistit in,*" *Theological Studies,* 67 (2006), 395–409; Sullivan, "The Meaning of *Subsistit in* as Explained by the Congregation for the Doctrine of the Faith," ibid., 69 (2008), 116–124; and Jared Wicks, "Questions and Answers on the New *Responses* of the Congregation for the Doctrine of the Faith," *Ecumenical Trends,* 36/7 (2007), 1–7, 16–17. See also the explanations by Alois Grillmeier in Vorgrimler, *Commentary,* 1:149–151; and by Peter Hünermann, with reference to the Declaration of the Congregation for the Doctrine of the Faith, August 6, 2000, in *Herders Kommentar,* 2:366–367.

30. AS I/4, 26–27.

31. See Ladislas Orsy's review of Massimo Faggioli's study, *Vescovo e concilio,* in *Theological Studies,* 68 (2007), 460–461.

32. AS II/1, 233–234, 236, 239–240. That bishops are not vicars of the pope is a quotation from *Satis cognitum,* encyclical of Leo XIII, June 29, 1896.

33. AS II/1, 347: "Cum progressum cognitionis veritatis promovere recte debemus, progressus non esset si aliqua dicerentur minori claritate quam antea."

34. AS II/1, 391–394.

35. AS II/1, 391. The idea of the church as sacrament, consonant with the recovery of patristic sources, was much in circulation in the 1950s. See, e.g., Otto Semmelroth, *Die Kirche as Ursakrament* (Frankfurt a/M: J. Knecht, 1953).

36. AS II/2, 20–32.

37. AS II/2, 114.

38. AS II/1, 428–430.

39. AS II/1: 235: "Quo in casu ad praepositos ecclesiae spectat decernere utrum tales diaconi sacra caelibatus lege adstringantur necne."

40. AS II/2, 83.

41. AS II/2, 88.

42. AS II/2, 484–487.

43. The fullest account is Alberto Melloni, "Procedure e coscienza conciliare al Vaticano II. I 5 voti del 30 ottobre 1963," in Melloni, *Cristianesimo nella storia,* pp. 313–396. See also Melloni's account, shorter but less clear, "The Beginning of the Second Period: The Great Debate on the Church," in Alberigo/Komonchak, *History,* 3:70–91.

44. AS II/2, 597.

45. AS II/2, 601: "Attentis omnibus quae a venerabilibus Patribus in congregatione generali dicta sunt, erit evidenter nostra attenta cura in revisione cap. II, ut ita caveatur de omnibus phrasibus quae in eo inveniuntur, ut doctrina de primatu iurisdictionis Romani Pontificis non solum servetur sed ut semper magis fulgeat."

46. See Congar's description of the scene, *Mon journal,* 1:475–476 and 482.

47. See his "commentary" on the subject, October 17, 1963, AS VI/2, 373–374, which he gave to Paul VI and Cicognani.

48. See AS II/4, 624–625.

49. See Melloni, "Procedure," p. 385.

50. As quoted in Melloni, "Beginning of the Second Period," in Alberigo/Komonchak, *History,* 3:99.

51. See Melloni, "Procedure," pp. 383–384.

52. AS II/1, 256–257: "Pastores scilicet instituti sunt, non ut totum onus aedificandi Mystici Christi Corporis in se suscipiant, sed ut fideles ita pascant et regant, ut cuncti suo modo et in suo ordine ad commune opus explendum cooperentur."

53. AS II/2, 627–632.

54. AS II/2, 637–638.

55. AS II/3, 278–279.

56. AS II/3, 175–178.

57. Otto Semmelroth, *Urbild der Kirche: Organischer Aufbau des Mariengeheimnisses* (Würzburg: Echter Verlag, 1954); English, *Mary: Archetype of the Church*, trans. Maria von Eroes and John Devlin (New York: Sheed, c. 1963).

58. AS II/3, 338–342, 342–345.

59. AS II/4, 435–445. For the development of the schema, see Klaus Mörsdorf in Vorgrimler, *Commentary*, 2:165–300; Guido Bausenhart in *Herders Kommentar*, 3:225–313, with bibliography, 304–313; and especially Faggioli, *Vescovo e concilio*.

60. AS II/4, 364–392.

61. See Faggioli, *Vescovo e concilio*, pp. 135–172.

62. AS II/4, 462.

63. AS II/4, 366: "In exercenda sua in universam ecclesiam suprema ac plena iurisdictionis potestate, Romanus Pontifex sacris utitur Romanae Curiae Dicasteriis, quae proinde nomine et auctoritate illius munus suum explent in bonum omnium ecclesiarum et in servitium eorumdem sacrorum pastorum."

64. AS II/4, 476–478, 486.

65. AS II/4, 516–519.

66. AS II/4, 619–621.

67. AS II/4, 616: ". . . cuius modus procedendi in multis non iam congruit nostris temporibus et ecclesiae detrimento et multis scandalo est." On Ratzinger's part in the composition, the most accessible account is in Jared Wicks's Yamauchi lecture, "Prof. Ratzinger at Vatican II: A Chapter in the Life of Pope Benedict XVI" (New Orleans: Loyola University, c. 2006), p. 12, where he says, "Actually Cardinal Frings added on his own seven lines of sharper criticism beyond Joseph Ratzinger's draft. They concerned the right of persons accused of doctrinal error to be presumed innocent and to make a defense against the accusation." For more detail, along with texts, see Norbert Trippen, *Josef Kardinal Frings (1887–1978)*, 2 vols. (Paderborn: Ferdinand Schöningh, 2003–2005), 2:383–388.

68. AS II/5, 72–75.

69. *Ecclesia Catholica*, Instruction of the Holy Office dated December 20, 1949, AAS, 42 (1950), 142–147. For a full account of the developments in the decade before the council, see Mauro Velati, *Una difficile transizione: Il cattolicesimo tra unionismo ed ecumenismo (1952–1964)* (Bologna: Il Mulino, 1996). See also the studies in the volume *Paolo VI e l'ecumenismo*.

70. AS II/5, 412–441. For commentary, see Werner Becker in Vorgrimler, *Commentary*, 2:1–164; and Bernd Jochen Hilberath in *Herders Kommentar*, 3:69–223, with bibliography, 217–223. See also Edward Idris Cardinal Cassidy, *Ecumenism and Interreligious Dialogue: Unitatis redintegratio, Nostra aetate* (New York: Paulist Press, 2005).

71. Congar, *Mon journal*, 1:539; AS II/5, 472–479.

72. AS II/5, 481–485.

73. See Thomas F. Stransky, "Paul VI and the Delegated Observers/Guests to Vatican Council II," in *Paolo VI e l'ecumenismo,* pp. 118–158, at 126–128.

74. AS II/5, 485–495.

75. AS II/6, 339–340.

6. The Third Period (1964)

1. On the trip, see Rynne, *Vatican II,* pp. 266–273; and Claude Soetens, "The Ecumenical Commitment of the Catholic Church," in Alberigo/Komonchak, *History,* 3:339–345; and Giuseppe Alberigo, "Conclusion: The New Shape of the Council," ibid., 506–507.

2. See Grootaers, *Actes et Acteurs,* pp. 185–222.

3. See Jan Grootaers, *Primauté et collégialité: Le dossier de Gérard Philips sur la Nota Explicativa Praevia (Lumen gentium, Chap. III)* (Leuven: Leuven University Press, 1986), pp. 30–31, 125–139, where the pertinent documents are provided.

4. AS V/2, 507–509, at 508.

5. See Jan Grootaers, "Le crayon rouge de Paul VI: Les interventions du pape dans le travail des commissions conciliaires," in Lamberigts, *Commissions conciliaires,* pp. 316–351.

6. The full text can be found in *Paolo VI, problemi ecclesiologici,* pp. 595–604. In this same dossier are contained all the crucial memoranda and other documents leading up to the "Nota praevia" on chapter three, edited by Giovanni Caprile, pp. 587–697.

7. *Paolo VI, problemi ecclesiologici,* p. 601.

8. In ibid., pp. 617–619, at 619.

9. Carlen, *Encyclicals,* 5:135–160.

10. See Nolan, *Privileged Moment,* pp. 163–176 and passim.

11. On the Polish text as well as a Spanish and a French text, see Turbanti, *Mondo moderno,* pp. 458–469.

12. AS III/1, 14–15.

13. AS III/1, 24, 156–157; V/2, 95; VI/3, 33.

14. AS III/1, 140–151.

15. AS III/1, 157: "Inutile est pulsare ad ianuam; nemo aperiet." See Matthew, 25:10–13.

16. AS III/2, 193–218.

17. The letter is printed in *Paolo VI, problemi ecclesiologici,* pp. 619–621.

18. For the letter, see ibid., pp. 622–623.

19. AS III/2, 22–44. On the genesis and development of the document, see, as mentioned, especially Faggioli, *Vescovo e concilio.*

20. AS III/2, 72–74.

21. See Pietro Pavan, in Vorgrimler, *Commentary,* 4:49–86; Roman A. Siebenrock,

in *Herders Kommentar,* 4:125–218, with bibliography, 208–218; and especially Silvia Scatena, *La fatica della libertà: L'elaborazione della dichiarazione Dignitatis humanae sulla libertà religiosa del Vaticano II* (Bologna: Il Mulino, 2003), especially pp. 201–324.

22. The literature on Murray is extensive. See, e.g., Joseph A. Komonchak, "The Silencing of John Courtney Murray," in Melloni, *Cristianesimo nella storia,* pp. 657–702; and Dominique Gonnet, "L'apport de John Courtney Murray au schéma sur la liberté religieuse," in Lamberigts, *Commissions conciliaires,* pp. 205–215, as well as his book on the subject, *La liberté religieuse à Vatican II: La contribution de John Courtney Murray, S.J.* (Paris: Cerf, 1994).

23. Alfredo Ottaviani, *Doveri dello stato cattolico verso la religione* (Rome: Pontificio Ateneo Lateranense, 1953), pp. 9–10. On December 6 of the same year, Pius XII delivered an address to Italian jurists that seemed to reiterate the traditional teaching, "Ci riesce," *Discorsi e radiomessaggi di Sua Santità Pio XII* (Vatican City: Typografia Poliglotta Vaticana, n.d.), 15:483–492, at 486–489.

24. Carlen, *Encyclicals,* 5:107–129, at 108 (no. 14).

25. AS III/2, 348–353.

26. AS III/2, 317–327.

27. AS III/2, 348: "Textus Summorum Pontificum de hac re sub alio aspectu et in aliis conditionibus socialibus problema attingunt."

28. Quoted in Giovanni Miccoli, "Two Sensitive Issues: Religious Freedom and the Jews," in Alberigo/Komonchak, *History,* 4:100.

29. For a study that carefully documents the rupture between papal teaching in the nineteenth century and *Dignitatis Humanae,* see Bernard Lucien, *Grégoire XVI, Pie IX et Vatican II: Études sur la liberté religieuse dans la doctrine catholique* (Tours: Éditions Forts dans la Foi, 1990).

30. AS III/2, 354–356.

31. AS III/2, 357–359.

32. AS III/2, 483–485.

33. See Ottaviani, *Doveri,* and especially *Institutiones juris publici ecclesiastici,* 2nd ed., 2 vols. (Vatican City: Typis Polyglottis Vaticanis, 1936), 2:57.

34. AS III/2, 375–378.

35. AS III/2, 470–471.

36. AS III/2, 490–492.

37. AS III/2, 361–362.

38. AS III/2, 366–368.

39. AS III/2, 613–614, written intervention.

40. AS III/2, 368–369.

41. AS III/2, 378–381.

42. AS III/2, 503–505.

43. AS III/2, 530–532.

44. AS III/2, 611–612.

45. AS III/2, 533–535.

46. AS III/2, 554–557. On Paul VI's support for the text, see Grootaers, *Actes et Acteurs,* pp. 59–92.

47. As quoted by Miccoli, "Sensitive Issues," in Alberigo/Komonchak, *History,* 4:131.

48. AS III/2, 327–329.

49. For the pre-history and history of the text, see John M. Oesterreicher, in Vorgrimler, *Commentary,* 3:1–154. See also Roman A. Siebenrock, *Herders Kommentar,* 3:591–693, with bibliography, 678–923.

50. See the document, "La reception de Jules Isaac par Jean XXIII," June 13, 1960, *Documentation Catholique,* 65 (1968), 2015–2016.

51. English translation as *Jesus and Israel,* trans. Sally Gran (New York: Holt, Rinehart and Winston, 1971). More pointed is Isaac's book *The Teaching of Contempt: Christian Roots of Anti-Semitism,* trans. Helen Weaver (New York: Holt, Rinehart and Winston, 1964); French original, 1962.

52. See Dorothee Recker, *Die Wegbereiter der Judenerklärung des Zweiten Vatikanischen Konzils: Johannes XXIII, Kardinal Bea und Prälat Oesterreicher—eine Darstellung ihrer theologischen Entwicklung* (Paderborn: Bonifatius, 2007); and John Connelly, "Catholic Racism and Its Opponents," *Journal of Modern History,* 79 (2007), 813–847.

53. On Oesterreicher, see Recker, *Die Wegbereiter,* pp. 310–399.

54. Accounts of Catholic anti-Semitism now abound. See, e.g., Michael Phayer, *The Catholic Church and the Holocaust, 1930–1965* (Bloomington, IN: Indiana University Press, 2000); David I. Kertzer, *The Popes against the Jews: The Vatican's Role in the Rise of Modern Anti-Semitism* (New York: Vintage Books, 2001); and, more wide-ranging, Kenneth Stow, *Jewish Dogs: An Image and Its Interpretation* (Stanford: Stanford University Press, 2006).

55. See Oesterreicher, in Vorgrimler, *Commentary,* 3:1–17.

56. See Wiltgen, *Rhine into Tiber,* pp. 73–78.

57. AS III/2, 328: "Caveant praeterea ne Iudaeis nostrorum temporum quae in Passione Christi perpetrata sunt imputentur."

58. AS III/2, 558–564.

59. AS III/2, 582.

60. AS III/2, 585–587.

61. See Miccoli, "Sensitive Issues," in Alberigo/Komonchak, *History,* 4: 166–193.

62. AS V/2, 773.

63. AS V/2, 764–765.

64. See Grootaers, "Crayon rouge," in Lamberigts, *Commissions Conciliaires,* p. 322.

65. AS V/2, 778–779.

66. AS VI/3, 440–441.

67. AS III/3, 782–791. For the original text, see ibid., I/3, 14–26. See Joseph Ratzinger et al., in Vorgrimler, *Commentary,* 3:155–272; Helmut Hoping, in *Herders Kommentar,* 3:695–831, bibliography, 820–831; and especially Burigana, *Bibbia nel concilio.*

68. It is instructive to put the three versions treating this matter side-by-side.

1. Original text, 1962, AS I/3, 16: "Ut autem ambo [Scripture and Tradition] fontes revelationis concorditer et efficacius ad salutem hominum concurrerent, providus Dominus eos tanquam unum fidei depositum custodiendum et tuendum authenticeque interpretandum tradidit non singulis fidelibus, utcumque eruditis, sed soli vivo Ecclesiae Magisterio. Magisterii Ecclesiae ergo est, utpote proximae et universalis credendi normae, non modo iudicare, adhibitis quae divina Providentia suppeditat auxiliis in iis, quae, sive directe sive indirecte, ad fidem et mores spectant, de sensu et interpretatione cum Scripturae Sacrae tum documentorum et monumentorum quibus temporis decursu Traditio consignata est et manifestata, sed ea quoque illustrare et enucleare quae in utroque fonte obscure vel implicite continentur."

2. Text from 1963 never put on agenda, AS III/3, 784–785: "At S. Scriptura ac S. Traditio, uti sacrum verbi Dei depositum, non singulis hominibus, sed vivo et infallibili Ecclesiae Magisterio concreditum est; quod quidem Magisterium non supra verbum Dei est, sed eidem ministrat, quatenus illud, ex divino mandato et Spiritu Sancto assistente, tuetur et authentice interpretatur, illustrando et etiam enucleando quae in una vel altera Depositi parte implicite et obscure continentur. Exinde regula fidei proxima quidem est Ecclesiae Magisterium, remota vero Sacrum Depositum. Patet igitur S. Scripturam, S. Traditionem ac Ecclesiae Magisterium, iuxta sapientissimum Dei consilium, ita inter se internecti et consociari, ut unum sine aliis consistere non possit. Tria simul ad animarum salutem suo modo efficaciter conferunt; sensu quoque fidelium subordinate concurrente."

3. Final version, *Dei verbum* (10), 1965, AS IV/6, 601: "Sacra Traditio et Sacra Scriptura unum verbi Dei sacrum depositum constitutunt Ecclesiae commissum, cui inhaerens tota plebs sancta Pastoribus suis adunata in doctrina Apostolorum et communione, fractione panis et orationibus iugiter perseverat, ita ut in tradita fide tenenda, exercenda profitendaque singularis fiat Antistitum et fidelium conspiratio.

Munus autem authentice interpretandi verbum Dei scriptum vel traditum soli vivo Ecclesiae Magisterio concreditum est, cuius auctoritas in nomine Iesu Christi exercetur. Quod quidem Magisterium non supra verbum Dei est, sed eidem ministrat, docens nonnisi quod traditum est, quatenus illud, ex divino mandato et Spiritu sancto assistente, pie audit, sancte custodit et fideliter exponit, ac ea omnia ex hoc uno fidei deposito haurit quae tamquam divinitus revelata credenda proponit. Patet igitur Sacram Traditionem, Sacram Scripturam et Ecclesiae Magisterium, iuxta sapientissimum Dei consilium, ita inter se connecti et consociari, ut unum sine aliis non consistat, omniaque simul, singula suo modo sub actione unius Spiritus sancti, ad animarum salutem conferant."

69. AS I/3, 16.

70. AS III/3, 124–129.

71. AS III/3, 187–188, at 188.

72. AS III/3, 336–337.

73. See Hanjo Sauer, "The Doctrinal and the Pastoral: The Text on Divine Revelation," in Alberigo/Komonchak, *History*, 4:230.

74. AS III/3, 418–421. The text is to be found ibid., 368–390. See Ferdinand Klostermann, in Vorgrimler, *Commentary*, 3:273–404; and Guido Bausenhart, in *Herders Kommentar*, 4:1–123, bibliography, 110–123.

75. AS III/3, 421: "Laici, denique, non solum in Ecclesia, sed nobiscum Ecclesia sunt."

76. See, e.g., Bernard Minvielle, *L'apostolat des laïcs à la veille du Concile (1949–1959): Histoire des congrès mondiaux de 1951 et 1957* (Fribourg: Éditions Universitaires, 2001).

77. AS III/4, 149–151.

78. AS III/4, 187.

79. AS III/4, 220–222.

80. AS III/4, 225–240. See Joseph Lécuyer et al., in Vorgrimler, *Commentary*, 4:183–297; and Ottmar Fuchs and Peter Hünermann, in *Herders Kommentar*, 4:337–580, bibliography, 570–580.

81. AS III/4, 241–243.

82. On the issue, see John W. O'Malley, "Celibacy: Decisive Moments in Its History," in *Sexuality and the U.S. Catholic Church: Crisis and Renewal*, ed. Lisa Cahill et al. (New York: Crossroad, 2006), pp. 94–106; and for full detail, Georg Denzler, *Das Papstum und der Amtszölibat*, 2 vols. (Stuttgart: Anton Hiersemann, 1973–1976), especially 2:325–370.

83. AS III/4, 244–246.

84. AS III/4, 485–497. See Johannes M. Hoeck, in Vorgrimler, *Commentary*, 1:307–331; and Bernd Jochen Hilberath, in *Herders Kommentar*, 3:1–68, bibliography, 67–68.

85. AS III/5, 116–142, 147–201. The basic study is Turbanti, *Mondo moderno*. See also the multi-authored commentary that takes up the entire fifth volume of Vorgrimler, *Commentary*, with an excursus on the encyclical *Humanae Vitae* by Leonard M. Weber, pp. 397–402. See also Hans-Joachim Sander, in *Herders Kommentar*, 4:581–886, bibliography, 870–886; and, for a brief, accessible analysis, Norman Tanner, *The Church and the World: Gaudium et Spes, Inter Mirifica* (New York: Paulist Press, 2005).

86. AS III/5, 201–203.

87. See AS III/5, 425–428.

88. AS III/5, 203–214.

89. AS III/5, 217–219.

90. AS III/5, 220–223.

91. AS III/5, 562–563.

92. AS III/5, 586–588.

93. See Norman Tanner, "The Church in the World *(Ecclesia ad extra),*" in Alberigo/Komonchak, *History,* 4:273–274.

94. AS III/6, 259–261 (Charles de Provenchères, Aix en Provence).

95. AS III/5, 550–552, 580–583.

96. AS III/5, 728–730; AS III/6, 42–44.

97. AS III/5, 737–739.

98. AS III/6, 459–461.

99. AS III/7, 50–51.

100. AS III/7, 54–56.

101. AS III/7, 59–61.

102. AS III/6, 52–54, 85–86, 86–88.

103. John Rock, *The Time Has Come: A Catholic Doctor's Proposals to End the Battle over Birth Control* (New York: Alfred A. Knopf, 1963).

104. Louis Janssens, "Morale conjugale et progestogènes," *Ephemerides Theologicae Lovanienses,* 39 (1963), 787–826.

105. AAS 56 (1964), 581–589, at 588–589. For the history of the Papal Birth Control Commission, see Robert McClory, *Turning Point: The Inside Story of the Papal Birth Control Commission, and How Humanae Vitae Changed the Life of Patty Crowley and the Future of the Church* (New York: Crossroad, 1995). For a study of American Catholic attitudes, opinions, and practices from the late nineteenth century until the publication of *Humanae Vitae* in 1968, see Leslie Woodcock Tentler, *Catholics and Contraception: An American History* (Ithaca, NY: Cornell University Press, 2004).

106. AS III/6, 71–73.

107. AS III/6, 59–62.

108. See F. M. Stabile, "Il Cardinale Ruffini e il Vaticano II: Le lettere di un 'intransigente,'" *Cristianesimo nella Storia,* 11 (1990), 83–176, at 137–138.

109. L.-J. Suenens, *Love and Control: The Contemporary Problem,* trans. George J. Robinson (Westminster, MD: Newman Press, 1961).

110. AS III/6, 57–59.

111. Rock, *Time Has Come,* pp. 155–156.

112. See Leo Declerck and Toon Osaer, "Les relations entre le cardinal Montini/ Paul VI (1897–1978) et le cardinal Suenens (1904–1996) pendant le Concile Vatican II," *Notiziario,* 51 (2006), 49–77.

113. AS III/6, 379–381, at 381. See McClory, *Turning Point,* pp. 58–62.

114. AS III/6, 327–332. On the difficult history of the schema, see E. Louchez, "La Commission De Missionibus," in Lamberigts, *Commissions conciliaires,* pp. 251–277.

See also Suso Brechter, in Vorgrimler, *Commentary,* 4:87–181; and Peter Hünermann, in *Herders Kommentar,* 4:219–336, bibliography, 330–336.

115. See Nelson H. Minnich, "Julius II and Leo X as Presidents of the Fifth Lateran Council (1512–1517)," in *La papauté à la Renaissance,* ed. Florence Alazard and Frank La Brasca (Paris: Honoré Champion Éditeur, 2007), pp. 153–166.

116. AS III/6, 324–325. On the pope's intervention, see Louchez, "De Missionibus," pp. 267–268.

117. That is what Philips told Congar. See Congar, *Mon journal,* 2:278.

118. AS III/7, 143–157. See Friedrich Wulf, in Vorgrimler, *Commentary,* 2:301–370; and Joachim Schmiedle, in *Herders Kommentar,* 3:491–550, bibliography, 549–550.

119. AS III/7, 539–551. See Josef Neuner, in Vorgrimler, *Commentary,* 2:371–404; and Ottmar Fuchs and Peter Hünermann, in *Herders Kommentar,* 3:315–489, bibliography, 482–489. I have not been able to consult Alois Greiler, *Das Konzil und die Seminare: Die Ausbildung der Priester in der Dynamik des Zweiten Vatikanums* (Leuven: Peeters, 2003).

120. AS III/7, 706 (Ruffini); ibid., 718–720 (Staffa); III/8, 14–16 (Caggiano); ibid., 17–18 (Bacci).

121. For a detailed narration and analysis, see Luis Antonio G. Tagle, "The 'Black Week' of Vatican II (November 14–21, 1964)," in Alberigo/Komonchak, *History,* 4:387–452.

122. Prignon, e.g., speaks of the minority using "a kind of blackmail" on the pope, "une sorte de chantage," *Journal conciliaire,* p. 78.

123. AS V/3, 79–82.

124. See Wiltgen, *Rhine into Tiber,* pp. 234–238.

125. AS III/8, 415.

126. AS V/3, 89–91, ". . . instanter, instantius, instantissime. . . ."

127. AS III/8, 449–456.

128. AS III/8, 554–555.

129. Congar, *Mon journal,* 2:202: "On m'a donné à lire le texte actuel du schéma *De libertate.* Il ne reste à peu près rien de l'ancien texte. Dans ces conditions, il foudra une discussion nouvelle. Je trouve qu'il y a, dans cette démarche, une certaine légèreté. Les rédacteurs (surtout Pavan et Murray) ne se doutent pas des difficultés que leur texte soulèvera. La partie biblique est médiocre. On n'a pas assumé les objections de Broglie [Guy de Broglie-Revel]. Bref, je ne trouve pas cela vraiment satisfaisant." Jared Wicks called my attention to this passage. See Wicks, "New Light on Vatican Council II," *Catholic Historical Review,* 92 (2006), 609–628, at 626, n.43, and 627.

130. AS VI/3, 509, in a memorandum dated November 12 and corrected in accordance with observations of Paul VI, "Note sull'origine e sull' evoluzione degli schemi in esame al concilio."

131. See Grootaers, "Crayon rouge," in Lamberigts, *Commissions conciliaires,* p. 322.

132. On Paul and ecumenism, see the contributions in *Paolo VI e l'ecumenismo.*

133. AS III/8, 422–423.

134. See, e.g., AS V/3, 68, 71–72.

135. Douglas Horton, *Vatican Diary 1964: A Protestant Observes the Third Session of Vatican Council II* (Philadelphia: United Church Press, 1965), p. 179.

136. See Pierre Duprey, "Paul VI et le decret sur l'Oecuménisme," in *Paolo VI, problemi ecclesiologici*, pp. 225–248. For a list of the emendations and commentary, see Werner Becker, in Vorgrimler, *Commentary*, 2:1–163, at 159–164.

137. AS III/8, 10–13.

138. For Philips's own account of his role and what transpired, see his *Carnets conciliaires*, pp. 134–141.

139. See Joseph Ratzinger, *Theological Highlights of Vatican II*, trans. Henry Traub et al. (New York: Paulist Press, 1966), pp. 114–116. I am indebted to Jared Wicks for calling my attention to this passage.

140. See Grootaers, *Primauté et collégialité: Le dossier Philips;* and Giovanni Caprile, "Contributo alla storia della 'Nota Explicativa Praevia,'" in *Paolo VI, problemi ecclesiologici*, pp. 589–687. For a lucid account of these interventions and arguments insisting that the Note did not affect the teaching of chapter three, see Claude Troisfontaines, "À propos de quelques interventions de Paul VI dans l'élaboration de 'Lumen Gentium,'" in ibid., pp. 97–143. See also the incisive article by Jean-Pierre Torrell, "Paul VI et l'ecclésiologie de 'Lumen Gentium': Thèmes choisis," ibid., 144–186, in which Torrell makes the point that Paul would not have given ear to the minority if their claims did not find some resonance with his own feelings. See also Vincenzo Carbone, "L'azione direttiva di Paolo VI nei periodi II e III del Concilio Ecumenico Vaticano Secondo," ibid., 58–95, at 83–89; and the comments by Joseph Ratzinger, "Announcements and Prefatory Notes of Explanation," in Vorgrimler, *Commentary*, 1:297–305. In his diary for November 18, 1964, the Protestant observer Douglas Horton said, "I read the note over later in the day to make sure nothing of collegiality had been given away in it and decided that it was one of those devices sometimes used in committee to save face but change nothing," *Vatican Diary 1964*, p. 163.

141. As quoted in Benny Lai, *Il Papa non eletto: Giuseppe Siri cardinale della Santa Romana Chiesa* (Bari: Laterza, 1993), p. 402.

142. As quoted in Rynne, *Vatican II*, p. 413, in note marked *.

143. AS V/3, 73.

144. AS III/8, 909–918, at 911.

145. AS III/8, 913.

146. AS III/8, 916.

147. For a chronicle of the events leading up to the declaration and a defense of the pope's action, see Carbone, "L'azione direttiva," in *Paolo VI, problemi ecclesiologici*, pp. 91–95. For a lengthy analysis, see René Laurentin, "La proclamation de Marie 'Mater ecclesiae' par Paul VI: *Extra concilium* mais *in concilio* (21 novembre 1964),"

ibid., pp. 310–375. When Congar informed Philips on November 19 of what the pope intended to do, Philips replied, "That does not surprise me. The pope is authoritarian. He is absolutely determined to affirm his superiority over the council. . . . He wants to have an occasion to make clear his personal magisterium. We [in the Doctrinal Commission?] tried to resist him as much as we could." Congar, *Mon journal,* 2:278.

148. AS III/8, 917.

149. Philips, *Carnets conciliaires,* p. 141.

150. That is how Rynne describes the scene, *Vatican II,* p. 426.

7. The Fourth Period (1965)

1. See the account in Peter Hebblethwaite, *Paul VI: The First Modern Pope* (New York: Paulist Press, 1993), pp. 408–414.

2. Paul VI, *Insegnamenti,* 2:687, original in English.

3. Paul VI, *Insegnamenti,* 2:716, original in English.

4. Giovanni Caprile, "Contributo alla storia della 'Nota Explicativa Praevia,'" in *Paolo VI, problemi ecclesiologici,* pp. 589–687, at 589. The Holy See sent documentation to the journal to help it fulfill the pope's wish, which is published here. It includes correspondence from September to November 1964 between the pope and Larraona, Ruffini, Ottaviani, Carli, and others, and it gives a vivid picture of the pressure being brought to bear on Paul VI.

5. The article is reprinted in Caprile, "Contributo," in *Paolo VI, problemi ecclesiologici,* pp. 681–697.

6. For a detailed narrative and analysis of these months and the fate of the schemas, see Riccardo Burigana and Giovanni Turbanti, "The Intersession: Preparing the Conclusion of the Council," in Alberigo/Komonchak, *History,* 4:505–615.

7. See, e.g., Congar, *Mon journal,* 2:316–318.

8. See Turbanti, *Mondo moderno,* pp. 479–493.

9. See, e.g., Giovanni Turbanti, "La commissione mista per lo schema XVII–XIII," in Lamberigts, *Commissions conciliaires,* pp. 217–250 at 244–245.

10. AS III/8, 637–648.

11. Luigi Carli, "La questione giudaica davanti al Concilio Vaticano II," *Palestra del Clero,* 44 (1965), 185–203; and Carli, "È possibile discutere serenamente della questione giudaica?" ibid., 465–476.

12. The offensive words, as given in the printed text, Paul VI, *Insegnamenti,* 3:1209: "Narra [the gospel passage], infatti, lo scontro fra Gesù e il popolo ebraico. Quel popolo, predestinato a ricevere il Messia, che Lo aspettava da migliaia di anni ed era completamente assorto in questa speranza e in questa certezza, al momento giusto, quando, cioè, il Cristo viene, parla e si manifesta, non solo non lo riconosce, ma lo combatte, lo calunnia et ingiuria; e, infine, lo ucciderà." They are quoted by Carli, "È possibile," p. 471.

13. The documents are printed in Caprile, *Cronache,* 5:53–54.

14. AAS 57 (1965), 775–780.

15. See Grootaers, *Actes et Acteurs,* pp. 444–446, 450; and Faggioli, *Vescovo e concilio,* pp. 403–417. The Conference of Delegates on October 23, 1964, had drawn up some principles; see Pierre C. Noël, "Gli incontri delle conferenze episcopali durante il concilio: Il gruppo della Domus Mariae," in Fattori, *Evento e decisioni,* 95–133, at 122–123.

16. AAS 57 (1965), 776, "Nostrae potestati directe atque immediate subiectum"; ibid., "consilia dandi."

17. See Prignon, *Journal conciliaire,* pp. 62, 250–251.

18. See, e.g., *Insegnamenti,* 3:1008.

19. AS IV/1, 125–135.

20. AS IV/1, 129: "Unus populus sumus, videlicet populus Dei. Nos efficimus Ecclesiam Catholicam."

21. AS IV/1, 204–207. For Pius XII's address, see AAS 45 (1953), 794–802.

22. AS IV/1, 207–209.

23. AS IV/1, 209–210.

24. AS IV/1, 211–215.

25. AS IV/1, 384–386.

26. AS IV/1, 387–390.

27. AS IV/1, 393–394.

28. AS IV/1, 399–403.

29. AS V/3, 357, 365.

30. AS IV/1, 553–558.

31. See Karl Rahner, "Über den Dialog in der pluralistischen Gesellschaft," *Stimmen der Zeit,* 176 (August 1965), 321–330; and Josef Ratzinger, "Angesichts der Welt von heute: Überlegungen zur Konfrontation mit der Kirche in Schema XIII," *Wort und Wahrheit,* 20 (August–September 1965), 493–504.

32. See Joseph A. Komonchak, "Augustine, Aquinas or the Gospel *sine glossa?* Divisions over *Gaudium et spes,*" in *Unfinished Journey: The Church Forty Years after Vatican II, Essays for John Wilkins,* ed. Austen Ivereigh (New York: Continuum, 2003), pp. 102–118; and a longer version, "Le valutazioni sulla *Gaudium et spes:* Chenu, Dossetti, Ratzinger," in Doré, *Volti di fine concilio,* pp. 115–153.

33. See Turbanti, *Mondo moderno,* pp. 643–651; and Turbanti, "Il ruolo del P. D. Chenu nell'elaborazione della costituzione *Gaudium et Spes,*" in *Marie-Dominique Chenu: Moyen-Âge et modernité* (Paris: Le Centre d'études du Saulchoir, 1997), pp. 173–212.

34. AS IV/2, 21–23.

35. AS IV/2, 24–25.

36. AS IV/2, 47–50.

37. *Gaudium et Spes,* number 21, note 16; Tanner, *Decrees,* 2:1080. See Wiltgen, *Rhine into Tiber,* pp. 272–278.

38. AS IV/3, 45–48.

39. See Prignon, *Journal conciliaire,* p. 141; and Gilles Routhier, "Finishing the Work Begun: The Trying Experience of the Fourth Period," in Alberigo/Komonchak, *History,* 5:159, n. 440.

40. AS IV/3, 58–59.

41. AS IV/3, 257–258.

42. AS IV/3, 135–137.

43. In his diary for October 1, 1965, Congar, who was not in St. Peter's that day, says about Pellegrino: "Il a revendiqué la liberté de recherche dans l'Église et a parlé d'un religieux naguère envoyé en exil et qu'on cite maintenant au concile. . . . On me dit qu'il s'agit de moi. C'est possible. J'ai rencontré Pellegrino à Strasbourg." Congar, *Mon journal,* 2:415. See also Prignon, *Journal conciliaire,* p. 75, who notes that Pellegrino's appointment to Turin was opposed by the Curia.

44. AS IV/1, 28–36, in original French. For an English translation, see Fesquet, *Drama,* 662–670.

45. As quoted in Rynne, *Vatican II,* pp. 499–500.

46. AS IV/1, 36–38.

47. AS IV/3, 642–643.

48. AS IV/3, 657–660.

49. AS IV/3, 735–738.

50. For a list of the subcommissions and their members as of this date, see Turbanti, *Mondo moderno,* pp. 632–634.

51. See Peter Hünermann, "The Final Weeks of the Council," in Alberigo/Komonchak, *History,* 5:386–427.

52. See ibid., pp. 419–421; and especially Wiltgen, *Rhine into Tiber,* pp. 278–282. For the texts in their Italian version, see Caprile, *Cronache,* 5:493–498.

53. This seems to be an allusion to the Roman writer Terence, *Heautontimorumenos,* I.l.25: "Homo sum, humani nihil a me alienum puto." The council text: ". . . nihilque vere humanum invenitur quod in corde eorum non resonet."

54. See Turbanti, *Mondo moderno,* pp. 636–638.

55. AS IV/3, 699–707. For the text of the decree, see ibid., 663–692. For a history of the text in English, see James B. Anderson, *A Vatican II Pneumatology of the Paschal Mystery: The Historical-Doctrinal Genesis of Ad Gentes I, 2–5* (Rome: Editrice Pontificia Università Gregoriana, 1988), especially pp. 1–209.

56. AS IV/4, 196–198, at 198.

57. ADP II/4, 403–412 (text); 412–433 (comments and votes).

58. See the important comments by Felici, in Caprile, *Cronache,* 5:706–709, which contains the substance of Felici's *Il Vaticano II e il celibato sacerdotale* (Vatican City: Tipografia Poliglotta Vaticana, 1969).

59. See Prignon, *Journal conciliaire,* pp. 149–150.

60. AS IV/1, 40, with Tisserant's reply, 41. See Mauro Velati, "Completing the Conciliar Agenda," in Alberigo/Komonchak, *History,* 5:194–195, 231–237; and for gen-

eral background John W. O'Malley, "Celibacy: Decisive Moments in Its History," in *Sexuality and the U.S. Catholic Church: Crisis and Renewal*, ed. Lisa Sowle Cahill et al. (New York: Crossroad, 2006), pp. 94–106. For John XXIII and Paul VI, see Georg Denzler, *Das Papsttum und der Amtszölibat*, 2 vols. (Stuttgart: Anton Hiersemann, 1973–1976), 2:325–370. More broadly, see William Bassett and Peter Huizing, eds., *Celibacy in the Church*, Concilium 78 (New York: Herder and Herder, 1972).

61. See Carlen, *Encyclicals*, 5:203–221, at 210.

62. AS VI/4, 550–551, 551–554.

63. AS IV/5, 34.

64. AS IV/4, 686–688, and 688–689.

65. See Prignon, *Journal conciliaire*, pp. 128, 136.

66. See Velati, "Completing the Conciliar Agenda," in Alberigo/Komonchak, *History*, 5.211–221.

67. AS IV/5, 560–563.

68. See Burigana, *Bibbia nel concilio*, pp. 395–396. Jared Wicks called my attention to this change.

69. See the extensive treatment of this complicated story in Christophe Théobald, "The Church under the Word of God," in Alberigo/Komonchak, *History*, 5:275–358; and Burigana, *Bibbia nel concilio*, pp. 363–434.

70. See the commentary by a *peritus* deeply involved in the development of the text, Umberto Betti, *La Rivelazione divina nella Chiesa: La trasmissione della rivelazione nel capitolo II della costituzione dommatica Dei Verbum* (Rome: Città Nuova Editrice, 1970).

71. AS V/3, 352–354, at 354: "Una maggiore esplicita chiarezza si desidera nel porre prima ed al di sopra di tutti gli altri mezzi ermenenutici la Tradizione el il Magistero della Chiesa."

72. AS V/3, 377: ". . . si dica più chiaramente e più esplicitamente della natura costitutiva della Tradizione, quale Fonte della Rivelazione."

73. See Jan Grootaers, "Le crayon rouge de Paul VI: Les interventions du pape dans le travail des commisions conciliaires," in Lamberigts, *Commissions conciliaires*, pp. 316–351, at 340–342.

74. AS V/3, 409–410.

75. AS V/3, 459–461.

76. These two documents are unpublished, but Giovanni Caprile quotes extensively from Paul's letter to Frings, a text Caprile received from the pope himself, "Tre emendamenti allo schema sulla rivelazione: Appunti per la storia del testo," *Civiltà Cattolica*, 117/1 (1966), 214–231, at 231. See also Théobald, "Church under Word," in Alberigo/Komonchak, *History*, 5: 330.

77. AS IV/5, 700 and 705: ". . . quo fit ut Ecclesia certitudinem suam de omnibus revelatis non per solam Sacram Scripturam hauriat."

78. AS IV/5, 741.

79. AS IV/6, 292–294.

80. AS IV/6, 317–319, 323–331, 332–335.

81. AS IV/6, 415.

82. See Hünermann, "Final Weeks," in Alberigo/Komonchak, *History,* 5:384.

83. AAS 59 (1967), 5–24.

84. AS IV/6, 689–695.

85. See Prignon, *Journal conciliaire,* pp. 162, 168, 174–175.

86. On John Ford, see Eric Marcelo O. Genilo, *John Cuthbert Ford, S.J.: Moral Theologian at the End of the Manualist Era* (Washington, DC: Georgetown University Press, 2007), especially pp. 47–59. On Colombo's role, see Prignon, *Journal conciliaire,* pp. 222, 225, 248.

87. See Grootaers, *Actes et Acteurs,* pp. 224–250; Turbanti, *Mondo moderno,* pp. 742–759; J. M. Heuschen, "Gaudium et spes: Les modi pontificaux," in Lamberigts, *Commissions conciliaires,* pp. 353–358; and Jan Grootaers and Jan Jans, *La régulation des naissances à Vatican II: Une semaine de crise* (Leuven: Peeters, 2002), which contains an appendix of forty documents related to this crisis. For more general treatment, see Robert McClory, *Turning Point: The Inside Story of the Papal Birth Control Commission, and How Humanae Vitae Changed the Life of Patty Crowley and the Future of the Church* (New York: Crossroad, 1995), especially pp. 77–85. For a concise summary of the history of the Papal Commission by a member of it, see John Marshall, "My Voyage of Discovery," *The Tablet* (November 23, 2002), pp. 8–9.

88. See the vivid and detailed narrative by Prignon, *Journal conciliaire,* pp. 219–260.

89. See Tanner, *Decrees,* 2:1104 (n. 51): ". . . in procreatione regulanda, vias inire non licet, quae a magisterio, in lege divina explicanda, improbantur."

90. For detailed descriptions of these closing ceremonies, see Hünermann, "Final Weeks," in Alberigo/Komonchak, *History,* 5:465–483; and Caprile, *Cronache,* 5:499–526.

91. AS IV/7, 635–640.

92. See AS IV/7, 617.

93. AS IV/7, 643–644.

94. For the official text, see AAS 57 (1965), 952–955.

95. AS IV/7, 654–662.

96. AS IV/7, 868–871.

97. AS IV/7, 874–884.

98. See Claude Soetens, "Les messages finaux du Concile," in Doré, *Volti di fine concilio,* pp. 99–112. See also Prignon, *Journal conciliaire,* p. 264.

99. AS IV/7, 885.

Index

accommodation. *See* adaptation to locality
Action Française, 81
adaptation to locality, 14, 38–39, 140, 268–269, 298
Adenauer, Konrad, 90
Ad Gentes Divinitus, 238–239, 268–269, 287
Adzhubei, Alexis, 165
Aeterni Patris, 41, 62–63. *See also* Aquinas, Thomas (Thomism)
African episcopates, 122
Agagianian, Grégoire-Pierre, 170, 182, 239, 257
aggiornamento, 9, 37–39, 86, 130, 140, 215, 239, 268, 283, 292, 299–300
Alfrink, Bernhard, 117, 138, 144, 145, 155, 235–236, 237, 281; exchange with Ruffini, 179
American (U.S.) episcopate, 121, 197, 213, 217, 241
Ante-Preparatory Commission, 19–20
anti-Semitism. *See Nostra Aetate*
Antonelli, Ferdinando, 129–131
Antoniutti, Ildebrando, 166
Apostolicam Actuositatem, 5, 229–230, 280, 282, 291, 296–297, 305
Apostolica Sollicitudo. See Synod of Bishops
appointment of bishops, 65
Aquinas, Thomas (Thomism), 13, 62–63, 70, 78–79, 146, 240, 259, 270, 296, 310
Arab nations, *Nostra Aetate* and, 220, 225, 250, 275–276
arms race. *See* nuclear weapons

Arriba y Castro, Benjamin, 254, 273
art, modern, in churches, 14, 140, 298; its use restricted, 88
Assumption of the Virgin Mary. *See* Immaculate Conception
Athenagoras, Patriarch, 198, 199–200, 287
Aubert, Roger, 88
auditors, lay, 27, 173, 230
Au milieu, 64

Bacci, Antonio, 179–180, 187
Balthasar, Hans Urs von, 80
Bandeira de Mello, Carlos Saboia, 179
baptism, 133, 186, 230, 295
Barth, Karl, 235, 310
Bäuerlein, Stjepan, 230
Baumgartner, Augustin, 27
Bea, Augustin, 96–97, 114–116, 286, 288; and *Divino Afflante*, 84, 116; and *De Fontibus*, 145–146, 150–151; and *Nostra Aetate*, 195–196, 219, 222–223, 276; and crisis (October 1964), 224–226; and *Dignitatis Humanae*, 255–256, 257; and celibacy, 272
Beauduin, Lambert, 74, 117
Bekkum, Bishop Willem van, 135
Belgians, 121
Benedict XVI, Pope. *See* Ratzinger, Joseph
Benedictines, and Liturgical Movement, 71–73
benefice system, 231, 300
Benigni, Umberto, 68, 71

Beran, Josef, 256
Bettazzi, Luigi, 180
Bible. *See* Scripture
Biblical Commission, Pontifical, 68
Biblicum, 71, 84, 89, 109, 145, 219, 278
Billot, Louis, 77, 156
birth control, 6, 236–238, 265–266, 284–285,
  296, 311–312. *See also Casti Connubii*
Birth Control Commission, Papal, 237, 266,
  284, 285
Bishops, On the Pastoral Office of (decree). *See
  Christus Dominus*
Bishops' Secretariat, 122–123
Bismarck, Otto von, 67, 88, 303
Bombay (Mumbai), Paul VI's visit to, 247–248
Borromeo, St. Charles, 103
Browne, Michael, 110, 182, 190, 207–208, 216,
  228, 230
Buber, Martin, 80, 204
Buddhists/Buddhism, 221, 223, 250, 308
Bugnini, Annibale, 129, 139

Câmara, Bishop Helder Pessôa, 122, 123
Caminada, Costantino, 228–229
canons, as genre, 43–45, 306
Carli, Luigi, 111, 189–190; and Germans on *De
  Fontibus*, 146; and vote (October 1963), 193,
  205; and "Regulations," 209–210, 241; and
  Christus Dominus, 210; and *Dei Verbum*, 249;
  and *Nostra Aetate*, 250–251; and *Gaudium et
  Spes*, 264
Casti Connubii, 81–82, 236, 237, 284, 285. *See
  also* birth control
Catholic Action, 81, 229–230
Catholic Eastern Churches, On the (decree). *See
  Orientalium Ecclesiarum*
Catholic historiography, continuity in, 66
Čekada, Smiljan, 217
CELAM, 122, 123, 178
celibacy, 6, 27, 59, 175, 179–180, 231, 270–272
center-periphery relationship, 9–11, 137, 173–176,
  269, 298, 302–305, 311. *See also* centralization
  in Vatican; collegiality; episcopal conferences
Cento, Fernando, 162, 229, 233, 280
centralization in Vatican, 31–32, 56–57, 65,
  125–126, 302–304. *See also* center-periphery
  relationship; Curia, Roman
Central Preparatory Commission, 20, 117,
  270–271
charism, 11, 50, 85, 186, 296
Charue, André-Marie, 121, 277
Chenu, Marie-Dominique, 36, 75, 79, 87, 120,
  258–259

Christian Democracy, 5, 64, 83–84, 90, 106,
  302
Christus Dominus, 189–193, 210–211, 276, 296,
  304–305
Church, On the (constitution). *See Lumen
  Gentium*
church and state. *See Dignitatis Humanae*
Church in the Modern World, On the (consti-
  tution). *See Gaudium et Spes*
Cicognani, Amleto, 76, 127–128, 129, 139, 284,
  285; and *De Fontibus,* 150; and *De Ecclesiae
  Unitate*, 153; and Coordinating Commission,
  161–164; and crisis with moderators (1963),
  182–183; and *Nostra Aetate*, 220, 225; reproves
  the Group, 251–252
Cicognani, Gaetano, 129
Civiltà Cattolica, 248
Code of Canon Law (1917), 27, 31, 65, 82, 141,
  282
Coderre, Gérard, 235
Coetus Internationalis Patruum. See Group of
  Fathers, International
collegiality, 7, 49, 163, 177, 180–185, 302–305, 311;
  and Melkites, 125; warning memo to Paul VI
  (1964), 202–203; four presentations on (1964),
  208–209. *See also* primacy, papal
Colombo, Carlo, 121, 181, 218, 284
colonialism, end of, 91, 298. *See also* world-
  church
commissions, relationship to assembly, 101–102,
  185, 190, 193–194
Communism, 17, 20, 23, 63, 81, 91, 111, 235, 250,
  256, 260; John XXIII and, 165–166
concelebration, 138, 206
Conception Abbey, Missouri, 72
Conciliarism, 7, 30, 77–78, 303
Conference of Delegates, 123–124, 146
Conference of the Twenty-Two. *See* Conference
  of Delegates
Congar, Yves, 40, 41, 78, 87, 113, 119–120, 250,
  261; on De Smedt, 155–156; on Murray and
  Pavan, 242
Congregation for the Doctrine of the Faith. *See*
  Holy Office, Supreme Congregation of the
Congregations, Vatican. *See* Curia, Roman
Congress of Vienna, 57–58
Connell, Francis, 213
conscience, dignity of and freedom of, 7, 50, 59,
  165, 214, 296, 308. *See also Dignitatis Huma-
  nae; Gaudium et Spes*
conscientious objectors, 266
conservative, as designation, 292
Consilium on liturgy, 139

Index

organization of the council, 127–128, 168–169 (chart), 205. *See also* "Regulations"

Orientalium Ecclesiarum, 232, 241, 245

Ottaviani, Alfredo, 84, 97, 108, 116, 130, 137, 162; and John XXIII, 96, 104; exceeds time-limit, 137–138; and *De Fontibus*, 141–142; and *De Ecclesia*, 153–154; and *Gaudium et Spes*, 162, 233, 264; and *Lumen Gentium*, 164; in conclave (1963), 166, 167; and October vote (1963), 183, 185; clash with Suenens and Frings, 185, 192–193; and Doctrinal Commission, 185, 279, 285; and church-state, 213, 216; and birth control, 285

Pacem in Terris, 165, 196, 214, 235

panegyric. *See* epideictic rhetoric

Parente, Pietro, 75, 137, 208

participants in council, numbers and origins of, 21–23

Pascendi, 41, 69, 228

Paschal Mystery, 131–132, 265, 295

patristic revival, 75–77, 87. *See also* "nouvelle théologie, la"

Paul VI, Pope, 105–108, 166–173, 286, 293–294; reproves Lateran University, 89; interventions, 107–108, 180–185, 201–202, 224–226, 240–245, 271, 278–279, 280, 284–285; and *Sacrosanctum* (as cardinal), 134; and *De Ecclesia* (as cardinal), 158; reform of Curia, 171, 282–283; allocutions, 172, 197–198, 206–207, 245–246, 253–254, 276, 282–283, 287, 288; relationship to assembly, 172–173, 185, 246, 294; in the Holy Land, 198, 199–200; and *Nostra Aetate*, 221, 250, 251; and schema on missions, 239; and *Nota Praevia*, 244–245; in India, 247–248; Mass in Italian, 248; and negative press, 248; and Synod of Bishops, 252–253; at United Nations, 262–264, 275; and indulgences, 281

Pavan, Pietro, 165, 218, 242

Péguy, Charles, 40

Pellegrino, Michele, 261

Penance, Sacrament of, 133

"people of God," 11, 141, 174, 177–178, 203, 207, 253

Perfectae Caritatis, 239, 276, 301

periti, 21, 23, 26, 205

Philips, Gérard, 119, 154, 164, 173, 189, 202, 244

pill, the contraceptive, 83, 236

Pironio, Eduardo, 230

Pius IX, Pope, 59–61

Pius X, Pope, 64–65, 68–71, 72–73, 128, 134, 305

Pius XI, Pope, 17, 38, 80–83, 230. *See also Casti Connubii*; *Mortalium Animos*

Pius XII, Pope, 15, 83–89, 91, 104, 302; considers a council, 17; and liturgy, 20, 85–86; his "silence," 79, 83, 221; and church-state, 254; and indulgences, 280; beatification of, 283

Pizzardo, Giuseppe, 84, 88

Pontifical Biblical Institute. *See* Biblicum

Pontifical Institute of Mediaeval Studies, 20, 78

popes' relationship to councils, 10, 28–33

population explosion, 237, 238

Preliminary Explanatory Note. *See Nota Explicativa Praevia*

Preparatory Commissions, 20–22, 97, 128, 158, 161, 290, 293

Presbyterorum Ordinis, 230–232, 270–274, 287–288, 305

Press Office of the council. *See* media and the council

priesthood of all believers, 186–187, 230, 296

Priests, On the Ministry and Life of (decree). *See Presbyterorum Ordinis*

Priests, On the Training of (decree). *See Optatam Totius*

Prignon, Albert, 121

primacy, papal, 10, 15–17, 61, 302–303. *See also* collegiality

progressive, as designation, 292

Propagation of the Faith, Congregation for the, 124, 238, 269

Providentissimus Deus, 68

Quadragesimo Anno, 81

Quiroga y Palacios, Fernando, 216

Rahner, Karl, 79, 119; and world-church, 13, 298; under suspicion, 87; and *De Fontibus*, 145; and *De Ecclesia*, 154; and *Gaudium et Spes*, 235, 258, 259, 265; and *Dei Verbum*, 278–279

Ratzinger, Joseph, 120, 145, 244; and Cardinal Frings, 76, 120, 192; and *Gaudium et Spes*, 234, 235, 258, 265

"Regulations," 100–102, 137, 151, 170, 180–185, 205, 294

Religious Liberty, On (declaration). *See Dignitatis Humanae*

Renan, Joseph Ernest, 67

Renewal of Religious Life, On the (decree). *See Perfectae Caritatis*

Rerum Novarum, 63–64

ressourcement, 40–43, 75–76, 86, 140, 215, 239, 268, 273, 300–302, 303

Index　🙠